ADAM PENDLETON

ALEC MAPES-FRANCES
ADRIENNE EDWARDS
ANDRÉA PICARD

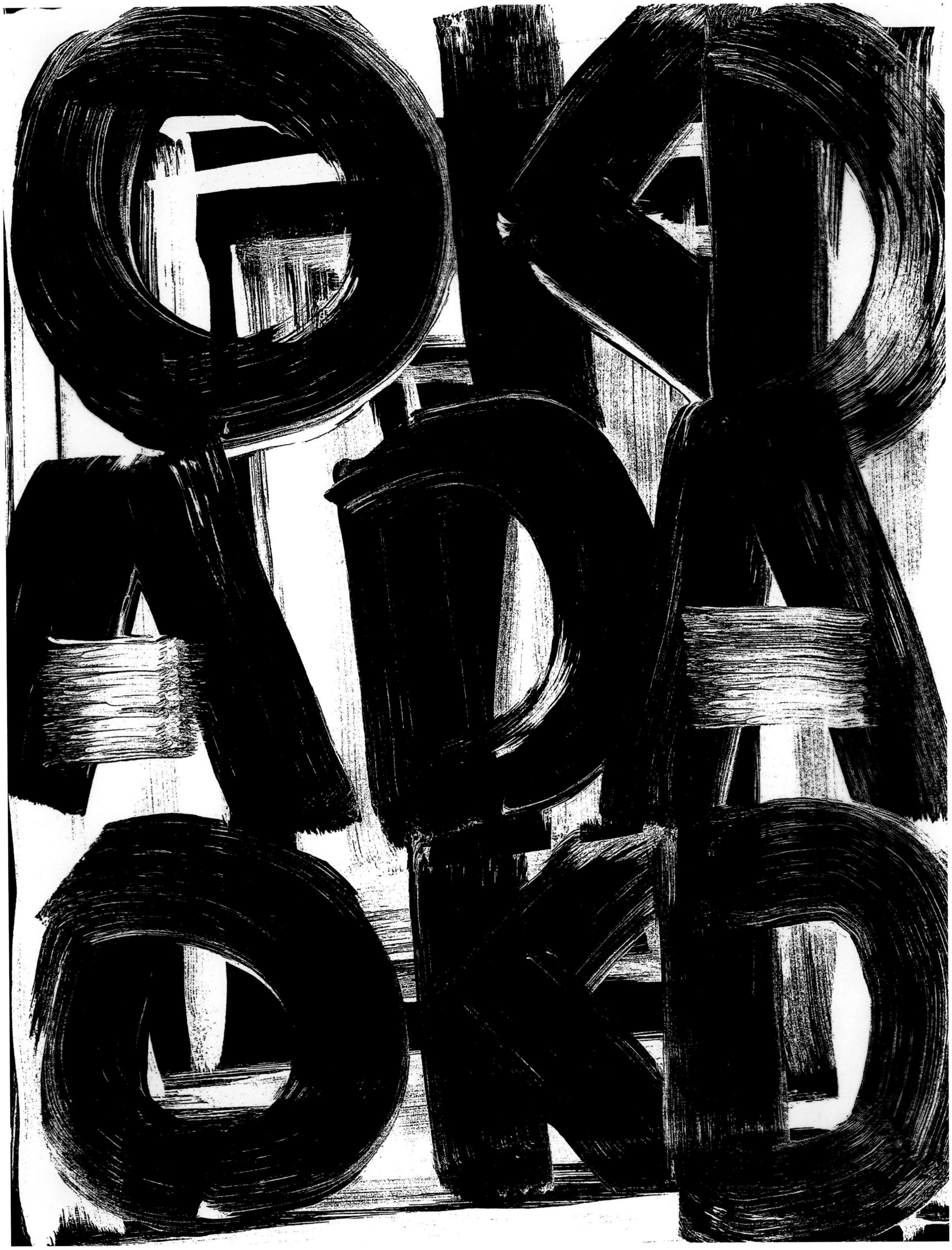

UNTITLED (DETAIL), 2018
SILK-SCREEN INK ON MYLAR
27 PARTS: OVERALL
DIMENSIONS VARIABLE
EACH: 97 X 74 CM

CONTENTS

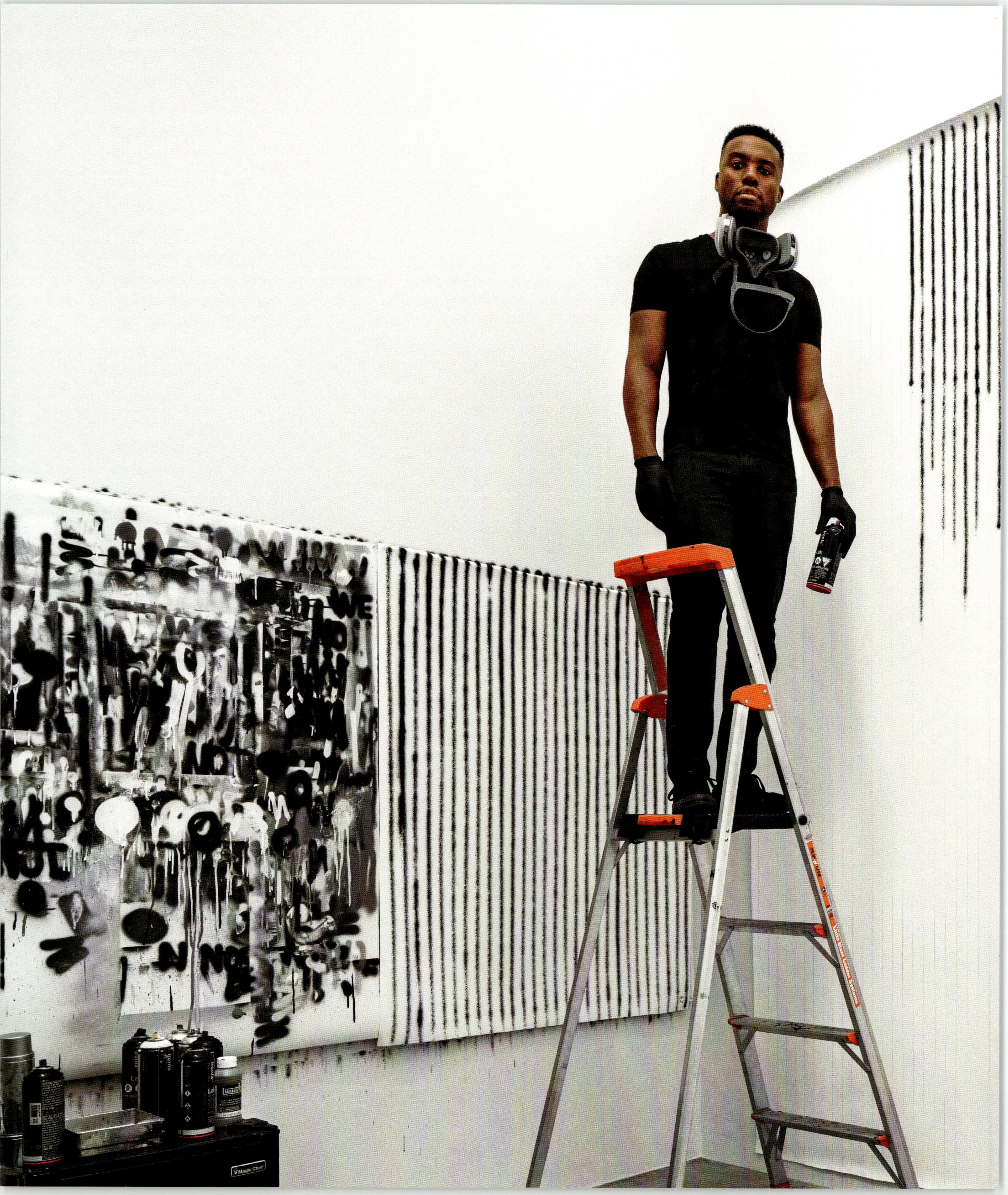

007 INTERVIEW

Alec Mapes-Frances in conversation with Adam Pendleton

ALEC MAPES-FRANCES: *In 2008, you wrote a text called 'Black Dada'. It's sometimes called a manifesto, but it's also poem-like. It has a strong formal structure and is more polyphonic than monologic, sampling several historical manifestos and poetic texts. Were you thinking about the manifesto as a genre when you wrote 'Black Dada'? And how does this piece continue to guide your work?*

ADAM PENDLETON: You'll always notice – and it's probably a kind of productive defect – that I like to say something is something, and then at the same time say, adamantly, that it's not that. In this instance, though, it's due to a series of accidents that 'Black Dada' became known as a manifesto. It is, yes, a kind of declaration of how I want to be and function as an artist. But in order for it to work for me in an effective way, it has to remain open and in flux. I always refer to it as the 'Black Dada' text. Other people began to refer to it as a manifesto. But at the same time, if you open the *Black Dada Reader*, you see that the title of the section that contains the 'Black Dada' text is 'MANIFESTO'. So I create these problems for myself. Maybe it's a way to create conversation, something to talk about, something I have to explain myself out of, or something I'm explaining myself into and out of at the same time.

Is it a manifesto, or isn't it? I think I have a problem with the historical understanding of what a manifesto is, and the 'Black Dada' text seeks to re-litigate that historical understanding. A manifesto is a monolith in a certain way – it's oriented in one direction – whereas the 'Black Dada' text splinters into many different directions, at least in the first sections. But when you get to the last section, which is 128 sentences, then you actually do get these more declarative statements:

Black Dada: we are not naive
Black Dada: we are successive
Black Dada: we are not exclusive
Black Dada: we abhor simpletons and are perfectly capable of an intelligent discussion!

And you get to the heart of the matter in a series of questions – 'Did our conceptual artists join hands with our freedom fighters? / Did they demonstrate in Birmingham? / Did they cover their faces when the hoses were turned on them?' – that problematize the relationship between conceptual art and civil rights, or the avant-garde and black history. But all of those things are too concrete for me, even as I feel compelled to acknowledge and speak to them. It's kind of like, 'Yes, that, but also everything else'. I think that's very much how the 'Black Dada' text functions: it's a space to absorb language, to absorb positions, to absorb material, in the broadest sense. It's formally structured in order to do so, and that's also how it's structured from a theoretical standpoint.

MAPES-FRANCES: *In the modernist lineage, the manifesto takes a position, seeking to manifest as a singularity in history. On the other hand, you're very careful to cultivate a sense of open-endedness here. And yet you're very particular about the boundaries of your archive, your collection of language, positions and material, which is always being revised without getting out of control.*

PENDLETON: Right. I think people misunderstand open-endedness to mean 'any and everything'. I like to leave things open-ended, but I'm also very specific in regards to what I bring into a seemingly capacious space. So 'boundaries' is a good word, and one of the things the 'Black Dada' text does, functionally, is create the boundaries for Black Dada.

It's important to note that the text began its life not as something for people to read, but as something for people to hear. It's a script, really. It's a script for performance. And I was initially very hesitant to publish it in written form. One of the reasons for this was that I thought people would read too much into it. When you're listening to something, it's a very different kind of dynamic. It's about: does this compel me? Does this propel me? Whereas when you're reading something it becomes a very different kind of study, a different kind of work.

previous pages,
ADAM PENDLETON, BROOKLYN, NEW YORK, 2019

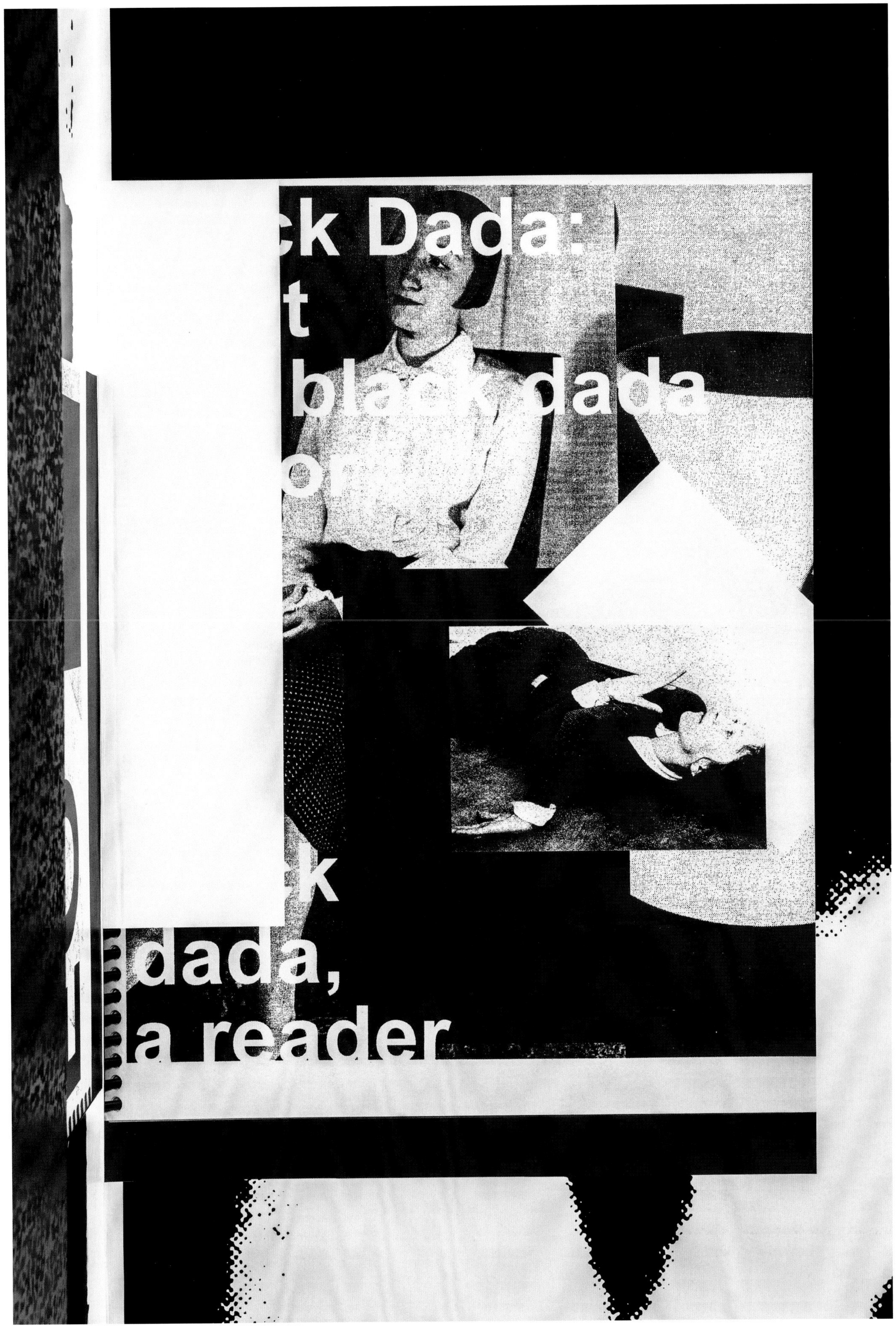

PERSONNE ET LES AUTRES, 2015
EXHIBITION DETAIL

BELGIAN PAVILION AT THE
56TH VENICE BIENNALE, 2015

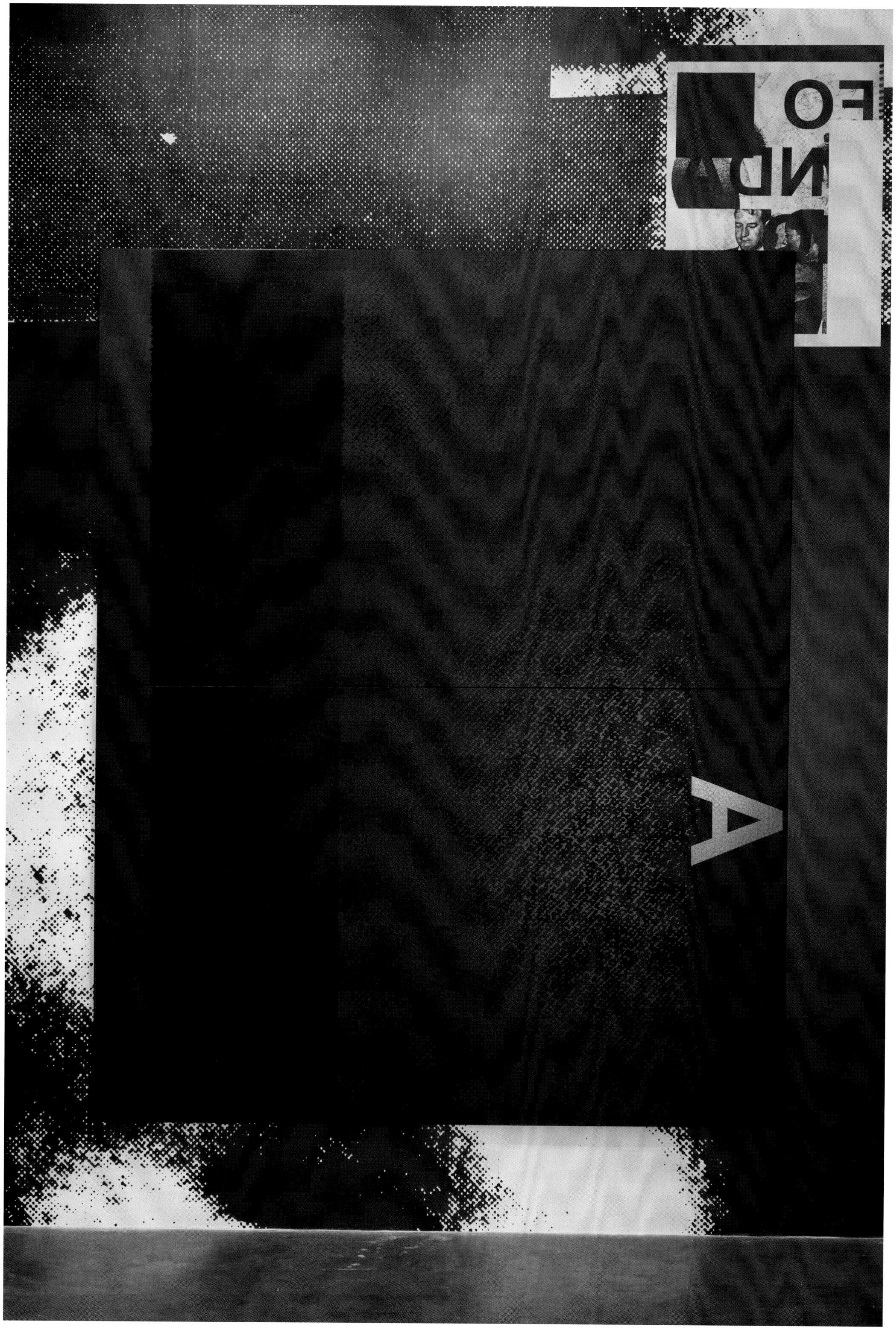

BLACK DADA/COLUMN (A/A),
2015
SILK-SCREEN INK ON CANVAS
2 PANELS: OVERALL 244 X
193 CM
EACH: 122 X 193 CM

INSTALLATION VIEW AT
CONTEMPORARY ARTS CENTER,
NEW ORLEANS, 2016

opposite,
PERSONNE ET LES AUTRES,
2015
EXHIBITION DETAIL

BELGIAN PAVILION AT THE
56TH VENICE BIENNALE, 2015

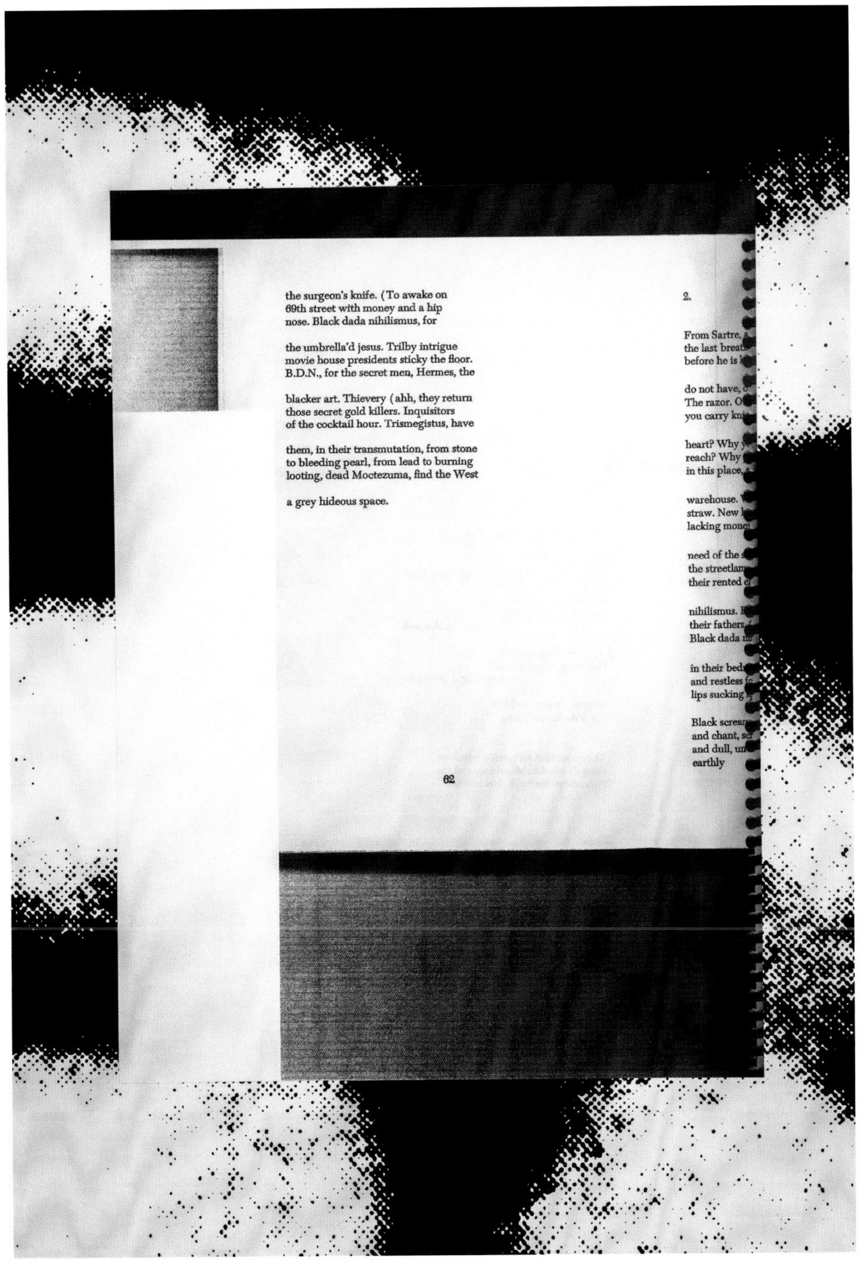

I began writing the piece near Paris in 2008, and I had some books with me. One of the books I had was by Ron Silliman, *The Age of Huts (compleat)*. It's a very procedural text. And I followed Silliman's formal logic: placing sentences next to each other in sequences, and then repeating these sequences while regularly inserting new sentences to create slightly different sequences. A lot of the language is actually pulled directly from *The Age of Huts*. And 'it's a matter of fact', which opens each of the eight sections of the text, was the name of the project curated by Krist Gruijthuijsen, embedded within Manifesta 7, for which 'Black Dada' was commissioned. I was asked to show these static works on the wall and also provide a performance. Hence, the 'Black Dada' text.

So … what was I writing about? It's funny. Was I writing about Black Dada, or was I writing towards Black Dada? I still don't know quite how to answer that. There's a more straightforward question that I can answer: is the text still productive for me? And I would say that it is. And its ability to be open and opaque, to abstract and to represent certain ideas, still makes it a productive thing for me.

MAPES-FRANCES: *I think the unanswerable question – about whether you were writing about or towards Black Dada – actually speaks to how your work makes use of recursive functions: feeding a process back into itself in such a way that the origin of the process and the processed material remains obscure. In other words, it is always difficult to know where or when or in what direction the writing or the imaging is happening. When I look at a line from the text or one of the images you use in your artworks, I wonder: did this come from inside or from outside? Is this stored somewhere in the 'Black Dada' text? Does it precede 'Black Dada' or was it introduced later? Things come out of the text and move onto the walls and then move back into the text.*

PENDLETON: I like this idea: from the wall to the text and back again. Black Dada, one could say, began as a refusal to perform, a desire to go back to the problematic space of the wall, or the gallery. It was a reaction to *The Revival*, my 2007 performance work, which pre-dated 'Black Dada'. The question was: how can ideas that function on the wall or on the page have the same kind of immediacy and weight as the ephemeral gesture that's performed?

There are similarities between how *The Revival* functioned and how 'Black Dada', and eventually the book *Black Dada Reader*, function. They both became places to create relationships between different positions (textual, historical, theoretical). They were archives, really, born from an impulse to collect, to re-document and revise that which has already been documented or inscribed.

MAPES-FRANCES: *Both of these collections –* The Revival *and* Black Dada Reader *– are built using pre-defined formats or modes of address as their containers. For* The Revival, *the format is the church service; for the* Reader, *it's the scholarly reader or course reader. Both of these are pedagogical formats, formats for edification, and your appropriation of them seems to encourage and/or perform a different kind of study.*

PENDLETON: A kind of deep study is the work. It can be visual study, or study bearing out a revisionist impulse, and the idea of creating a temporary canon instead of a permanent canon – something that's only assembled in order to disassemble – is central. In that way, it's both form and counter-form. That's the labour of the artwork, and the labour that I do as an artist, but it's also an expectation that I have for the viewer. I think you can create a 'classroom' in different ways: in the space of the reader, or in the space of the painting. There are different ways to build the temple.

There are many other examples of this. One that comes to me is Adrian Piper's two-volume book *Out of Order, Out of Sight*. Of course, in that instance it's primarily her own critical writing, but it's the same impulse to revise and to create a kind of canon and body of knowledge around the work that you do. I see that as maybe a necessary step for any artist, but certainly as a necessary step for myself.

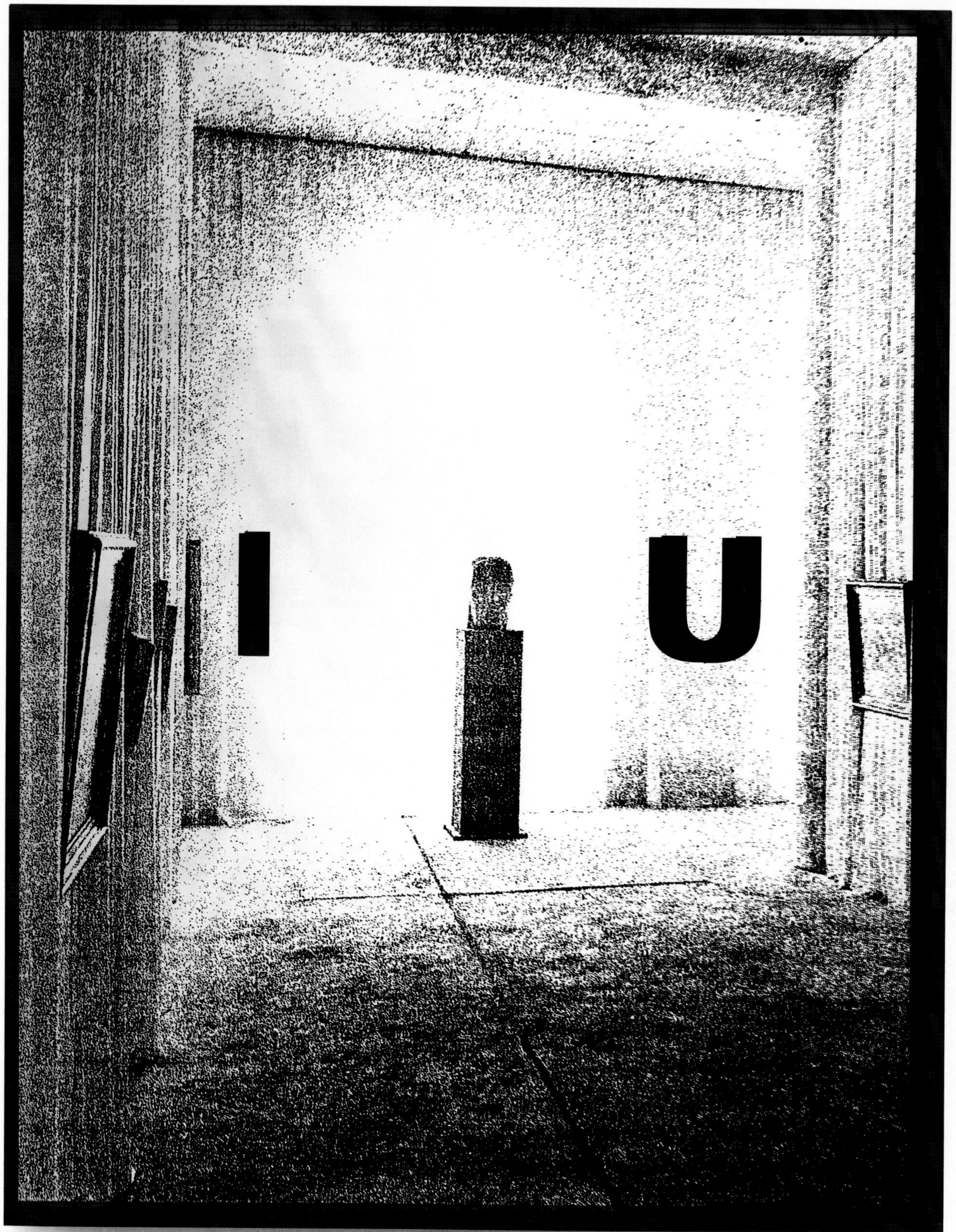

SYSTEM OF DISPLAY, IU (WITHOUT/DOCUMENTA I, KUNSTHALLE FRIDERICIANUM, 1955), 2010
SILK-SCREEN INK ON PLEXIGLASS AND MIRROR
162 X 124 X 8 CM

opposite, from top,
SYSTEM OF DISPLAY, D (AROUND/JEAN-MARIE STRAUB, NOT RECONCILED, OR ONLY VIOLENCE HELPS WHERE VIOLENCE RULES, 1965), 2011
SILK-SCREEN INK ON PLEXIGLASS AND MIRROR
25 X 25 X 8 CM

SYSTEM OF DISPLAY, X (EXTENDED/JEAN-LUC GODARD, LE GRAND ESCROC, EPISODE FROM LES PLUS BELLES ESCROQUERIES DU MONDE, 1964), 2011
SILK-SCREEN INK ON PLEXIGLASS AND MIRROR
25 X 25 X 8 CM

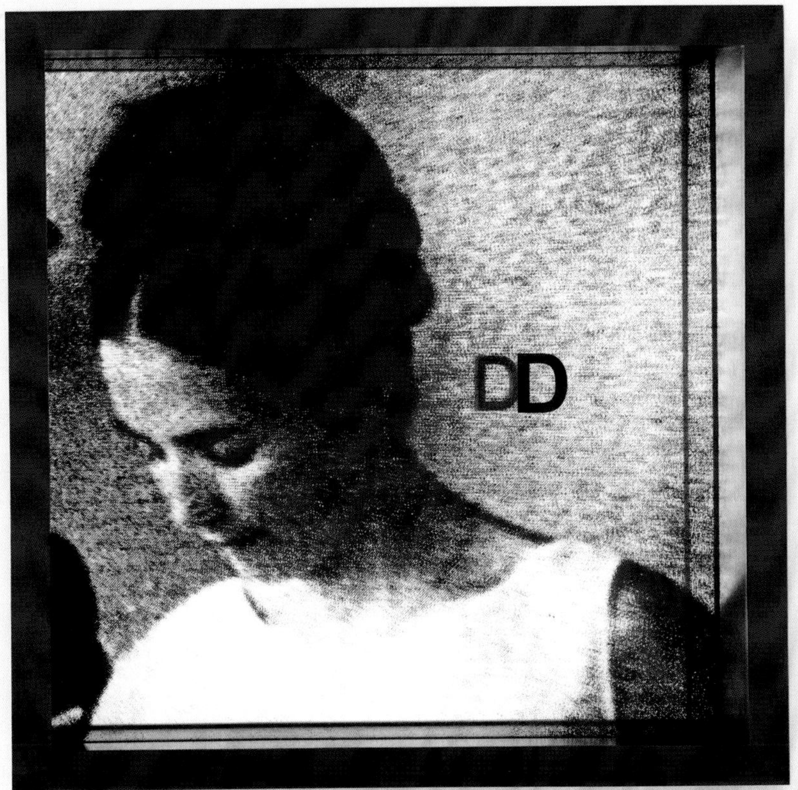

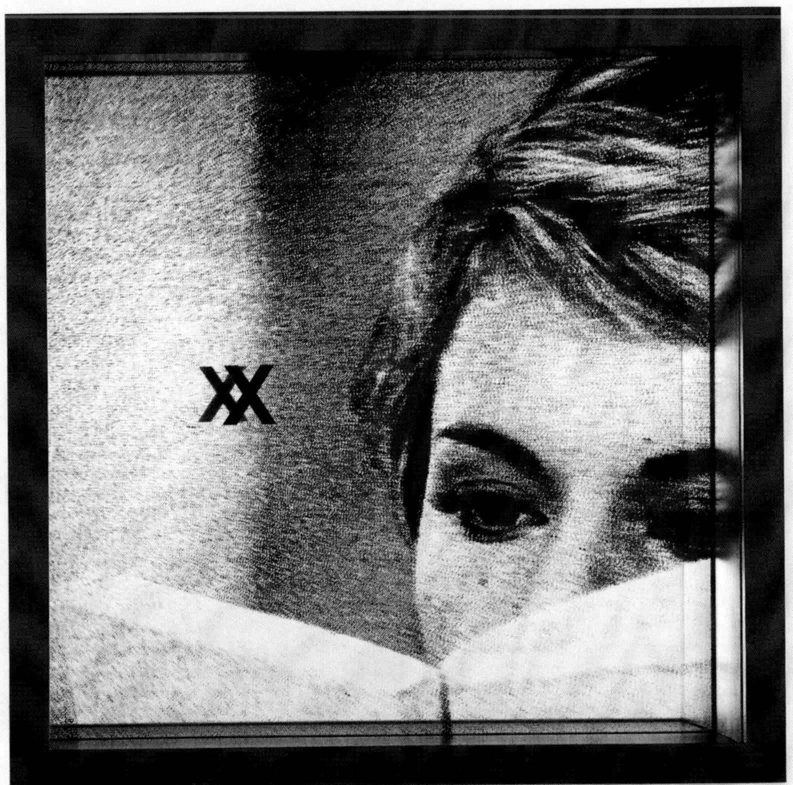

MAPES-FRANCES: *There's also a playful didacticism in the* Black Dada *paintings and the* System of Display, *which both use standardized typographic forms to label and point and indicate, as in a vitrine, a diagram or an atlas. But, of course, these works provide very little in the way of information. So much has been subtracted.*

PENDLETON: It becomes this conundrum. Either they function very well, or very poorly! And it becomes hard to determine which it is. In any instance, it's about what Hal Foster calls the 'scene of representation', and the problems inherent in that specific site of engagement. These works – *Black Dada* and *System of Display* – put into question the object and the viewer, and the status and position of each. In a way they're teachers: they seek to re-educate us, and to look again at the terms under which we engage with information. They're informative, but it's a situation of information gone awry. There's an absurdity here. And this is one of the things I've always enjoyed about the poets whose writing often informs my work – poets like Ron Silliman, Joan Retallack and Hannah Weiner: the absurdist impulse gets us closer to the truth.

MAPES-FRANCES: *This would be the absurdity of highly rational, authoritative systems functioning irrationally, like Weiner's* Code Poems, *or Broodthaers's museum displays, or Borges's encyclopedia.*

PENDLETON: From certain vantage points, the procedures are rational, but result in profound absurdities. I'm thinking of a poem like Retallack's 'A I D /I/ S A P P E A R A N C E', in which letters are incrementally subtracted from a source text. The text is seven lines long and the subtraction or erasure occurs in seven stages, beginning with the letters A I D S, and metastasizing through the adjacent letters in the alphabet (B H J C E R T, then F G K Q U, and so on). The text quickly mutates into illegibility or a-signification – lines like 'lm no onny plly pp no on o' – and continues until nothing is left.

I always wonder: what are the stakes involved, and how do you mark out the territory that's being explored? Retallack's poem was written for Stefan Fitterman, who died of AIDS in 1993, and so in this case the incoherence is tied to the incoherence of a historical moment of loss and death. Does absurdity always signify historically? Or does it always need to be a self-conscious absurdity? And – to take the Borges example – are there things that just come to us as absurd because they're different or other? And when does that difference matter?

The hard part of a project like Black Dada is: what happens to it the longer you work on it? How do you continue to destabilize it and draw it into question? I actually don't want things to perform authority; I want things to *be* authoritative. I want the *System of Display* to *be* authoritative. They're authors of their own truths. It's just that encounters with them – their manifestations – are other. But still deserving of time and space and creating conditions for time and space.

MAPES-FRANCES: *Maybe one could think of the project as scenographical: a catalogue of scenes of representation, which is to say a catalogue of formats, laying them on top of one another and looking for where the patterns align and diverge.*

PENDLETON: We come back to this notion of a pre-existing format, and I think in the instance of writing like Retallack's or Silliman's, the pre-existing format is natural language, on the most basic level, the alphabet, and steps above that, words, sentences and literature. And in each instance you also have to identify what you're working against. That's the refusal work. I like that term: the refusal work, the work of refusing. And it's also to defuse, to take the heat out of or to take the lustre off that which is already functionally known. You have to get to the origin of something: like, what are the origins of Black Dada and what kind of space did it originate in or from? I've recently been asking myself – and maybe this is a pointless exercise – whether this is a patriarchal or a matriarchal space. What kind of space does it nurture, and what kind of space was it born from? But maybe if I tether it to either/or, I'll end up with a child I don't want.

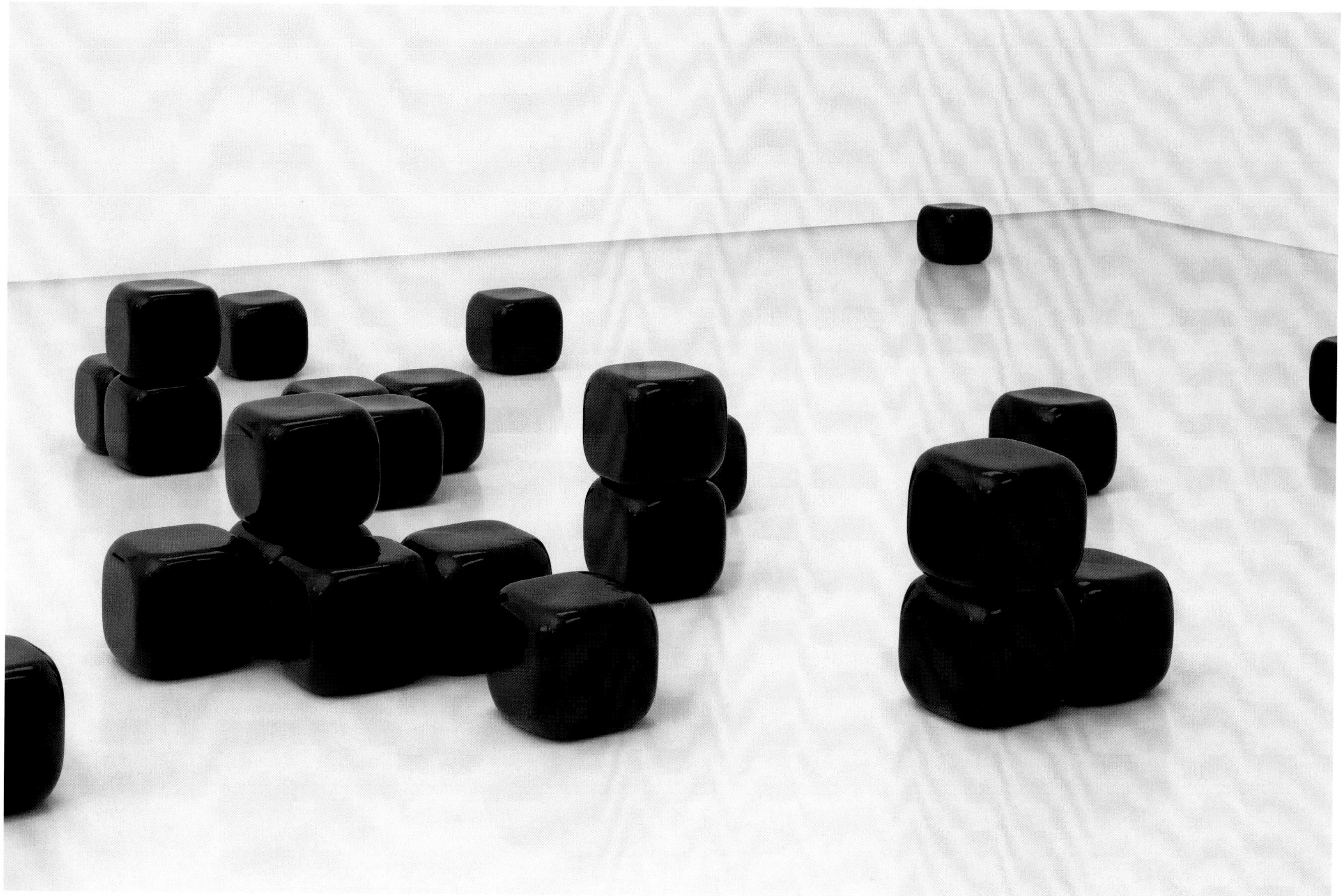

But I do ask, what does this come out of, and what edifice does this position deconstruct and reimagine? For me, that's also what poetry does – sometimes, not always. Language becomes destabilized, becomes other, becomes a tool that has temporarily lost its utility. We realise that language has the potential to dismantle itself even within the grammars that sanction it, the grammars with which we're most familiar. This poetics has a residual quality, leaves us with the fragment. The fragment can function as something that's whole and complete, but articulates a position that's functionally incomplete.

MAPES-FRANCES: *Of course, this paradox of incompleteness becomes very concrete in your work. In the* Black Dada *paintings, you're using incomplete photocopies of Sol LeWitt's* Incomplete Open Cubes *(1974), which is itself a complete set of the 122 ways of not making a complete cube, and adding your own analogically incomplete text.*

PENDLETON: It's interesting to think about how the *Black Dada* paintings exist as paintings, and I was recently thinking about them in relation to performance, and in relation to exhaustion, and in relation to that which is combinatorial in its outlook and approach. I don't know if that kind of discussion often happens in relation to a painterly space. I'm always thinking about the status of these objects, and the desire or drive to look at the paintings. Or do I perform for these paintings? Do I perform in relationship to these paintings? That's where this idea of performance and exhaustion comes into play: how does my body of work exist according to the limits that these paintings outline? Again, it's a notion of boundaries, in this abstract black space.

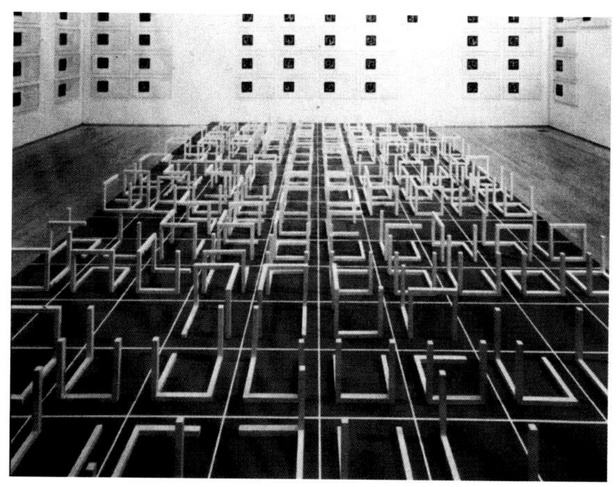

SOL LEWITT
INCOMPLETE OPEN CUBES, 1974
122 WOOD SCULPTURES, WHITE PAINT
EACH: 20 X 20 X 20 CM

BLACK DADA (A/A), 2019
SILK-SCREEN INK ON CANVAS
2 PANELS. OVERALL 244 X 193 CM
EACH: 122 X 193 CM

opposite,
(UNTITLED) SMALL BLACK CUBES, 2007
GLAZED CERAMIC
DIMENSIONS VARIABLE
EACH: 15 X 15 X 15 CM

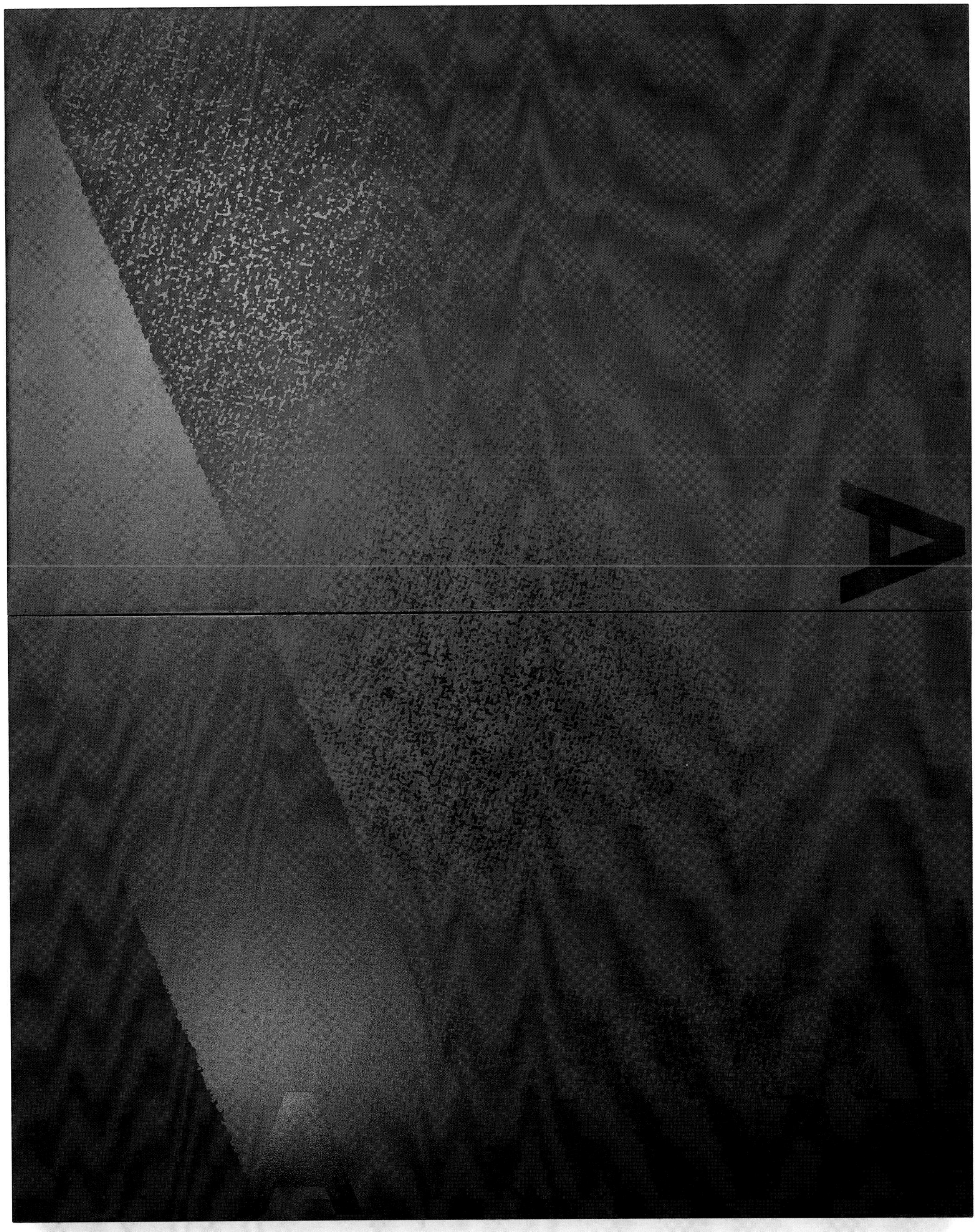

BLACK DADA DRAWING (A),
2018
SILK-SCREEN INK ON PAPER
66 X 53 CM

BLACK DADA DRAWING (B),
2018–19
SILK-SCREEN INK ON PAPER
66 X 53 CM

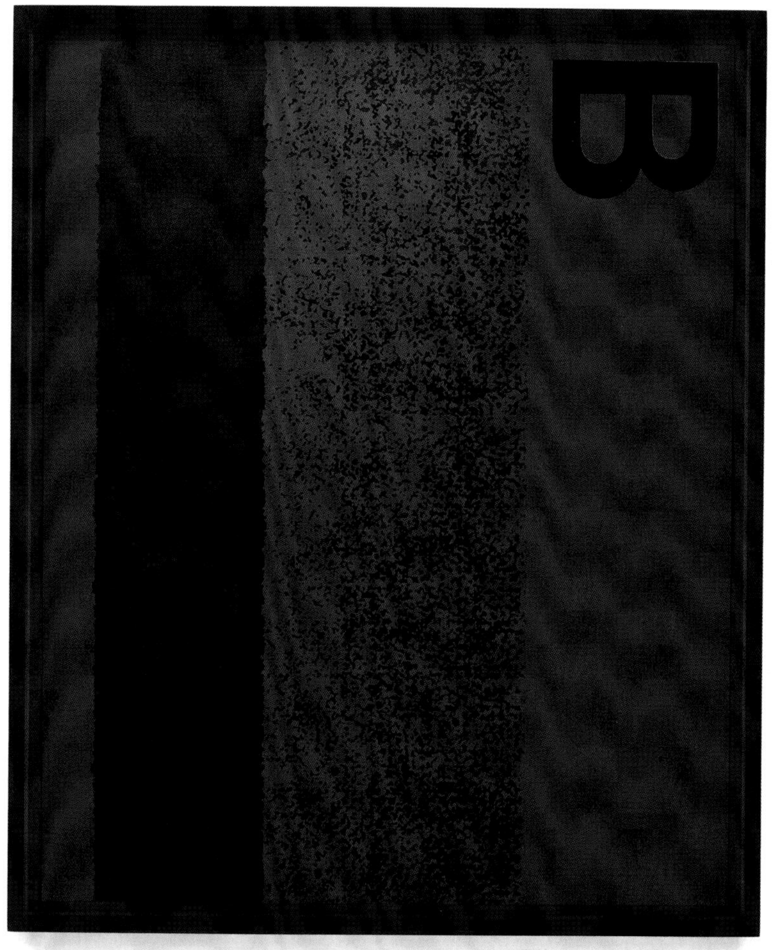

BLACK DADA DRAWING (C),
2018–19
SILK-SCREEN INK ON PAPER
66 X 53 CM

BLACK DADA DRAWING (D/D),
2018
SILK-SCREEN INK ON PAPER
66 X 53 CM

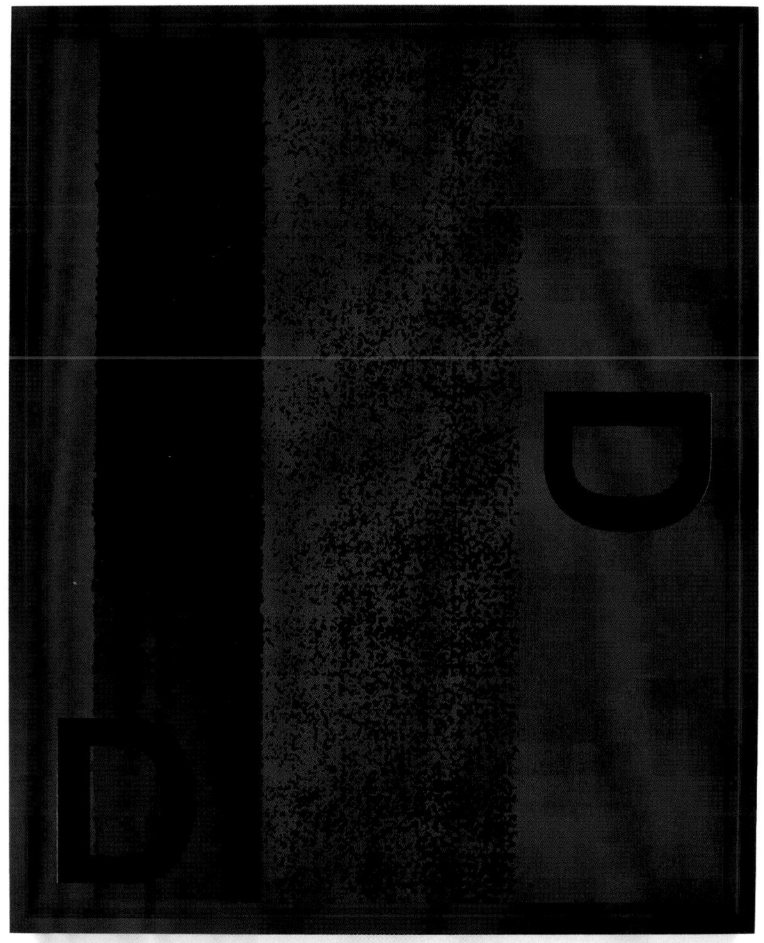

But I can also describe them in very simple terms: 96 x 76. Diptych. Pulling apart, fragmenting the phrase 'BLACK DADA', enlarging, cropping *Incomplete Open Cubes*. I think about one of the turning points in the work of Rudolf Stingel, which was when he created an instruction book that dictated how to make his paintings. I think about that gesture, and then I also think about Robert Ryman and how there was always something instructional about how he made a painting. He sort of drove people's attention to the most banal aspects of paintings – the support, the surface, the pigment, these kind of basic elements – in order to show how full they were. And the *Black Dada* paintings do something very similar. I can tell you what they are – there's almost an ingredient list – but the actual encounter is still very strange. I like that. It turns out that the painting isn't what I say it is. Somebody recently asked me, 'How does racism in America figure into your work?' And my response was, 'We're not what they say we are'. And I think that's also the character of the final painting: it's not what I say it is. The language, the parameters, are inadequate for the encounter.

MAPES-FRANCES: *There's also some indeterminacy within the image-making process itself – within the photocopying and printing that you do – that resists parameterization.*

PENDLETON: It's a question of the algorithmic in relation to process, to a kind of poetics, to performance, to form. There are acts or moments of translation that dictate the character of the work and allow it to create confusion, interference, noise.

MAPES-FRANCES: *And this noisiness stands out against a controlled ground. Many of the newer paintings, beginning with the* Untitled (A Victim of American Democracy) *paintings, use a series of lines as the ground, and even though they're very different from the* Black Dada *series, there are lines in both that divide space in a regulated way, beneath the noisy interference patterns that the image processing adds on top. Do you see a connection there?*

PENDLETON: When you mention these lines, I think about Julius Eastman's language: 'That person or thing which is fundamental'. It appears in a fascinating statement, the introduction to his 1980 Northwestern concert. He talks about this 'basicness'. If you think about these bodies of work, the paintings that came after the *Black Dada* paintings, the *Untitled (A Victim of American Democracy)* paintings started with the basic gesture of making quick, linear spray-painted marks across the surface of the canvas, and it was only later that I realized that what I was in fact trying to do was make a line. I kind of simplified that process, and started lining the canvases and then spraying on the line. There's a direct correlation there, for me, between the *Black Dada* paintings and these lines, in that the *Black Dada* paintings are black – that's what's basic about them, they're just colour – and the *Untitled* paintings have parallel lines. It's almost as if I have to have these basic elements and then create confusion around them, which is where their status changes. This confusion is how they broadcast, how they announce themselves. That's what registers.

So you've created this basicness, this fundamental ground – what do you do with it? Often my reaction is to disturb what might be misrecognized as its purity – to queer this ground, to do something with language on top of it. I add a stamp: the last part of making the *Black Dada* paintings is marking them with these letters, and in the *Untitled* paintings there's the same stamping, putting this language on top of the lines. There are these layers that create the effect of distance that allows for interpretation.

MAPES-FRANCES: *What does the 'basic' become for you once you apply these operations?*

PENDLETON: It reveals itself as always having been false. I would never accept anything as basic. I mean, Eastman's explanation is absurd. It doesn't make any sense. It's like a pot with no soup in it. He's using this word that's so fraught, so full of everything, and he's saying 'It's very basic'. And he's saying you can't have anything without it.

UNTITLED (A VICTIM OF AMERICAN DEMOCRACY), 2017
SILK-SCREEN INK AND SPRAY PAINT ON CANVAS
213 X 152 CM

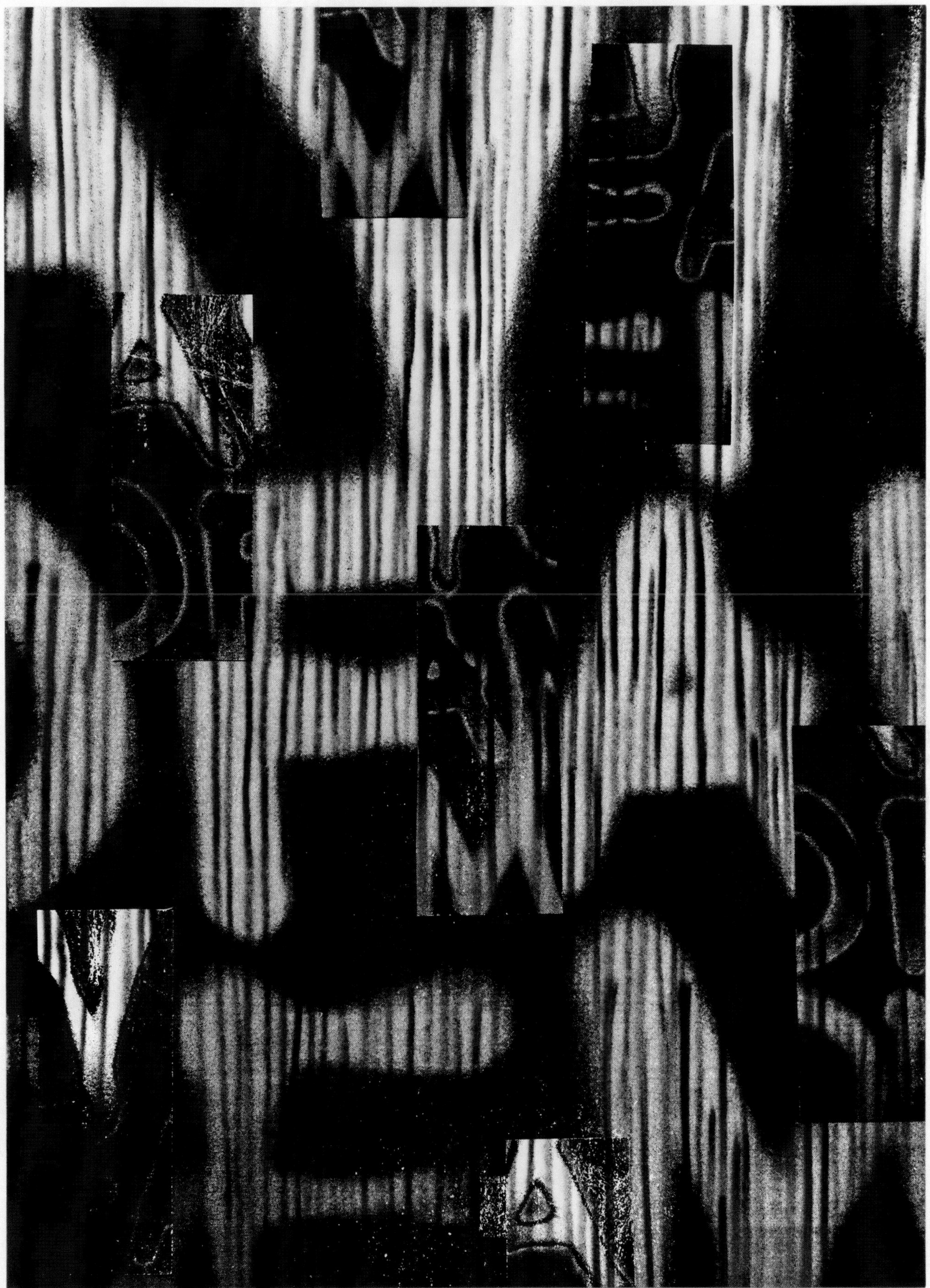

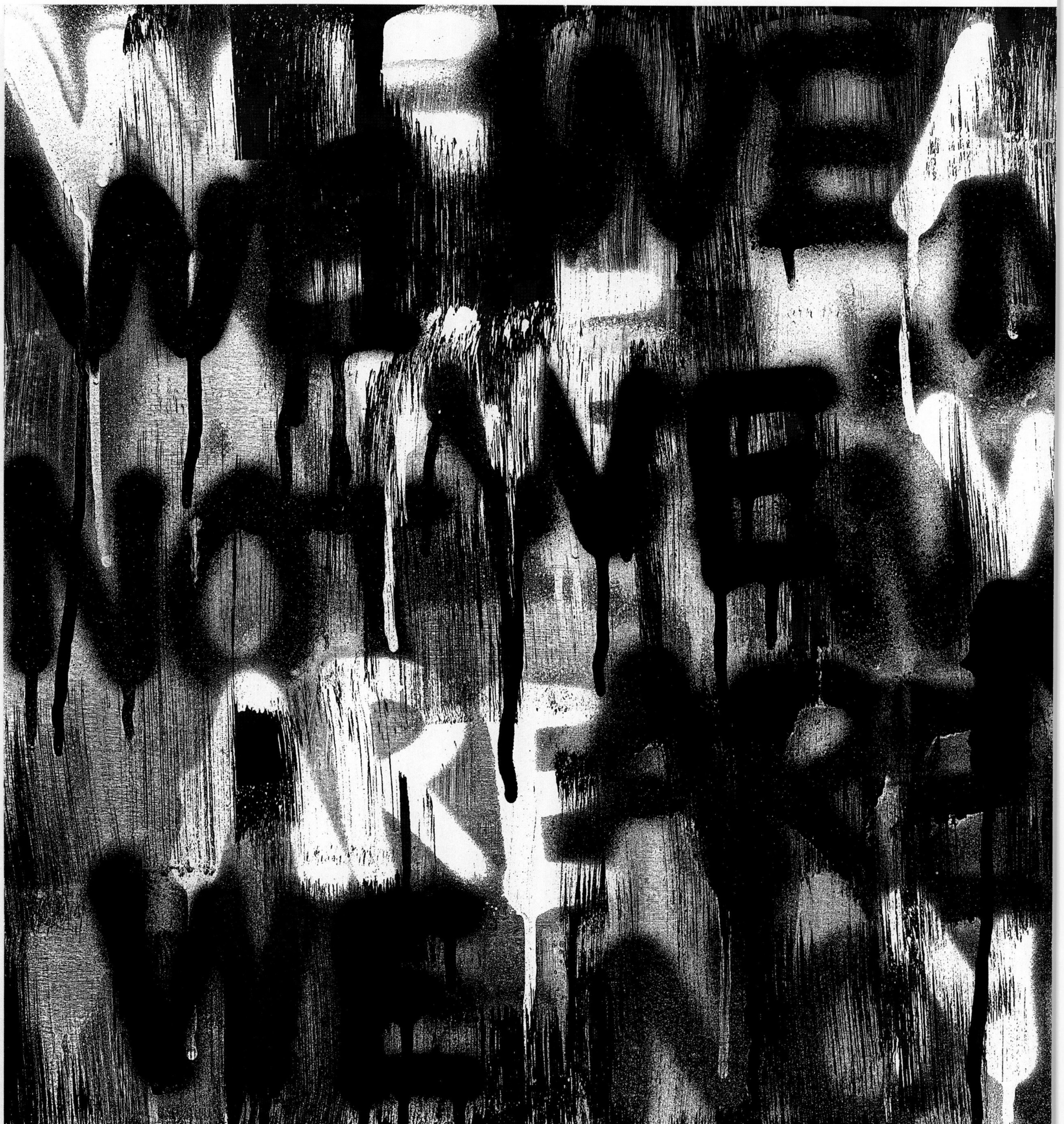

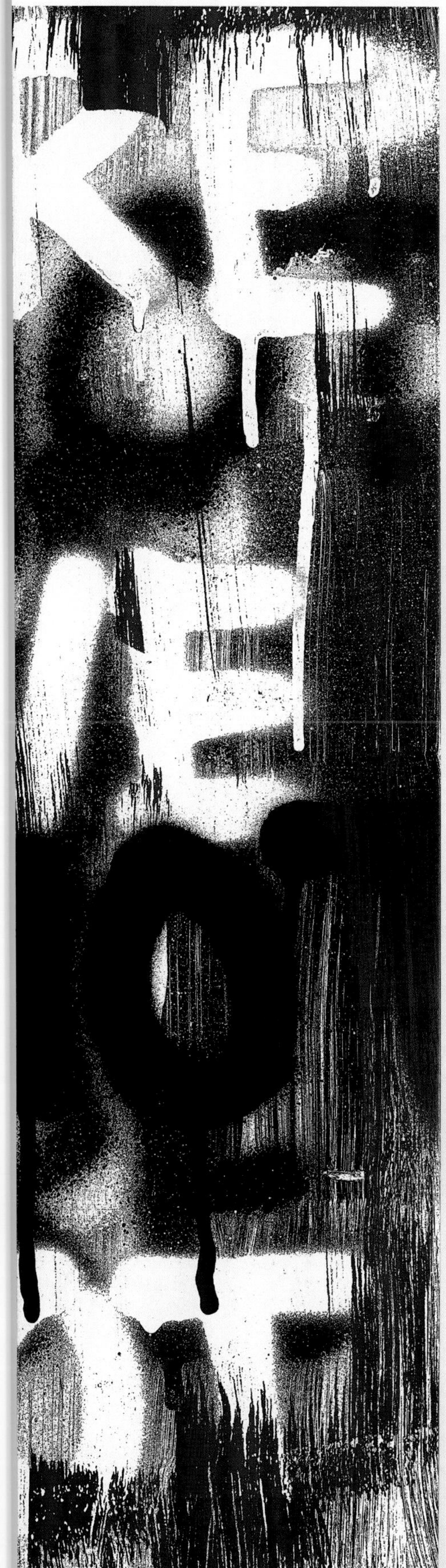

UNTITLED (WE ARE NOT), 2019
SILK-SCREEN INK ON CANVAS
244 X 305 CM

MAPES-FRANCES: *In that introduction, he's also placing it in the context of political economy: he's describing chattel slavery as 'basic', as primitive accumulation.*

PENDLETON: I'm using 'basic' as a formal analogy, but of course Eastman is using it to name this historical situation, too. He's accepting it as a given. That's what everything comes out of. Everything comes out of this corrupted, corroded thing. And since everything comes out of that, it's basic. In a way, he's saying, 'When you look at me, that's what we're talking about, so let's just acknowledge it'.

I always wonder if it's a kind of 'moving right along'. I always think about that: are we moving along? Or does this stop you in your tracks? Are the *Black Dada* paintings, or the *Untitled* paintings, or my use of this word 'Black' – which has an Eastman-like basicness – a way of moving along? To say 'Black Dada' – is it a way to move right along, to push through? I think about these different bodies of work, especially the *Untitled (WE ARE NOT)* paintings, which are specifically a reaction to Eastman's language, but also refer back to the 'Black Dada' text ('we are not naive / we are successive / we are not exclusive / we abhor simpletons and are perfectly capable of an intelligent discussion! / thus saith the lord'), and wonder if it's about trying to be the most black, the most abstract, as a kind of strategic interpellation, as a way of moving on.

MAPES-FRANCES: *Maybe this is European Dada's posture as well – conceiving of practice and identity as a diversion?*

PENDLETON: Yes, and moving on from the horrors of World War I. That's the core of the Dadaist impulse – 'We can't ignore these horrors, but let's move on anyway'.

A lot of this is about distraction, and playing with distraction and focus. That's often the role that language plays in my work. Because it distracts you, it forces you to focus. And I think that's similar to this Eastman title, 'Gay Guerrilla'. You listen to the music and you're like, 'What does this have to do with it?' I think it was a kind of distraction, a way of changing the terms of engagement. That's what I mean by 'move on' – once you're distracted, maybe you're able to focus in a more autonomous way. I'd say that someone like Gilles Deleuze – who's been an influence – writes to distract, or writes distractedly, if you think about how the ideas refract and oscillate and collect. They fall apart and are brought back together. He picks things up and drops them and picks them up again.

MAPES-FRANCES: *It's maybe about reading things 'poorly', improvisationally, or in an ad hoc way, rejecting the usual modes of scholarly reverence.*

PENDLETON: It's almost like you're talking about my work! It's about poor readings. That's the only kind of reading you can have. Poor images, things scanned and copied quickly.

But I refuse to prop myself up with this European framework. For instance, I think of the masks that I use. These are values that I use as someone who's borrowing. I use these Dan masks, and what I think the masks do is distract. They transform, they create a vibrational space and a distance, in relation to a certain performance of identity, in relation to a performance of self. That's a very different way of thinking about forms, or images, or cultural spaces that are driven towards or driven by a kind of distraction. And driven by the impulse to transform, to transfigure, to become something else. And that's also at the heart of Black Dada. It's a kind of filter that takes things that exist – images, texts – and it distracts and filters and makes the familiar strange and the strange familiar. It masks things; it puts masks on texts and images. That's a consistent thrust behind a lot of the visual projects that I take on: this filtering or masking of familiar or basic elements.

MAPES-FRANCES: *I'm wondering how you think about this masking within your moving-image pieces, which you call video portraits, and which are concerned with kinds of performance. Are there similarities and differences between your approaches to these media?*

next pages,
CRAZY NIGGER (AFTER JULIUS EASTMAN, NUMBER 2), 2018–19
LATEX INK ON ADHESIVE VINYL
DIMENSIONS VARIABLE

UNTITLED (MASKS), 2019
SILK-SCREEN INK ON MYLAR
4 PARTS: OVERALL DIMENSIONS VARIABLE
EACH: 131 X 100 CM

INSTALLATION VIEW AT GALERIE MAX HETZLER, BERLIN, 2019

UNTITLED (MASKS) (DETAIL), 2019
SILK-SCREEN INK ON MYLAR
4 PARTS: OVERALL DIMENSIONS VARIABLE
EACH: 131 X 100 CM

PENDLETON: The difference between media matters the most when it comes to voice, and how the voice becomes animated and displayed. And, of course, the question of authorship: who is the author?

Those video portraits really started when I was thinking about Gertrude Stein's text portraits and their debt to Cubism. She was thinking about Cubism in the pictorial sense and applying it to her writing. That fascinates me, because that tension is what I'm often engaging with. There's something in how all of my images are scanned, quickly, using the copy machine, and how, across media, I'm interested in this kind of stuttering, this inability to articulate. For instance, in the video portrait of Lorraine O'Grady, there are moments when she's almost unable to speak. In a way, I'm putting memories in her mouth; I'm putting images in her mouth; I'm putting history in her mouth. And she does something with it; she does something to it, by the very act of enacting or speaking the words, the script. And that feeling – and I would say it's a feeling – between director and actor, or author and subject, really becomes provisional. It becomes a provisional space in all of these portraits. In other words, who is what? Who is functioning as director or actor? These relationships become muddled. But they're all about speaking and listening and being heard. I think that's how these distinctions between media and between bodies of work become indistinct.

MAPES-FRANCES: *There's a feeling of directness, in that sense, that almost becomes paradoxical because of the degree of manipulation that's evident.*

PENDLETON: I hope the work is full of these excited multiplicities where positions are scattered and lost, where we kind of lose our positions. That's a necessary place to be. Without a position. But there's also this understanding, within my body of work, that you're always without and within any position at any given moment. I'd ask myself the question: are these things functionally distinct?

I always think about, in relation to the video works, the title of my 2016 exhibition *Becoming Imperceptible*. I love that title. Andrea Andersson, who curated the exhibition, came up with it. It was during our first or second studio visit, when we began working on that show together, that she said she wanted to call the show this. And I think what drove her to that title were these questions around how I become legible within the space of the work. It's funny how I'm more willing to talk about 'we' than 'I', in the language in 'Black Dada', for instance. Or at least when I talk about 'I', it's positioned very differently. Recently, I've been making these statements in the Mylar works – 'But now I am' – which of course leads to the question, 'What?' 'Now you are what?' But when I talk about 'we' in the *WE ARE NOT* paintings, it's like this declaration, but it's also incomplete. But it's still 'we are not'; it's somehow more assertive in the negative. And I think the portraits go even further in questioning how or if I become legible within the space of the work.

MAPES-FRANCES: *And there's also a question of the legibility of the subject. Does the subject come with you into imperceptibility? Do you abscond with the subject?*

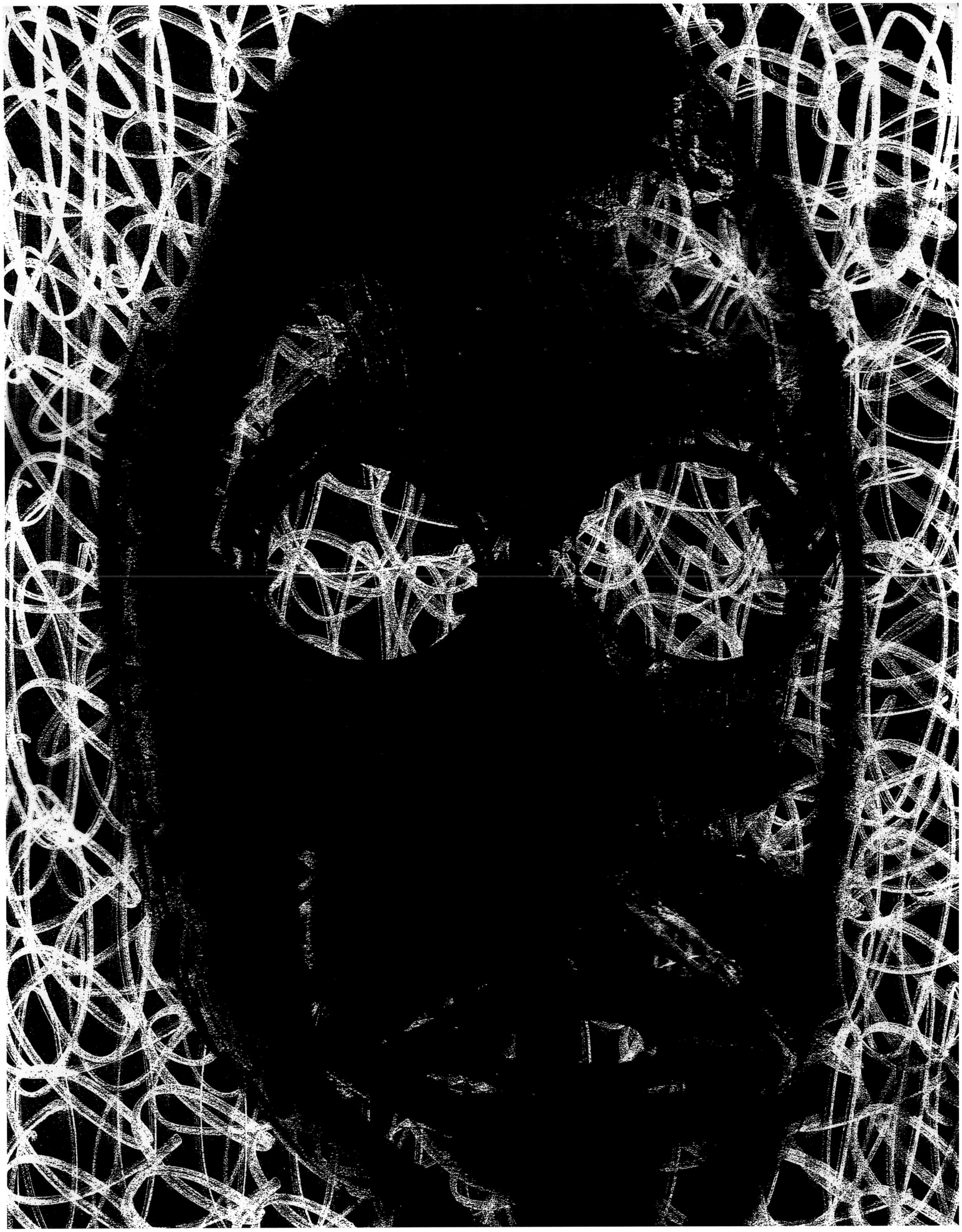

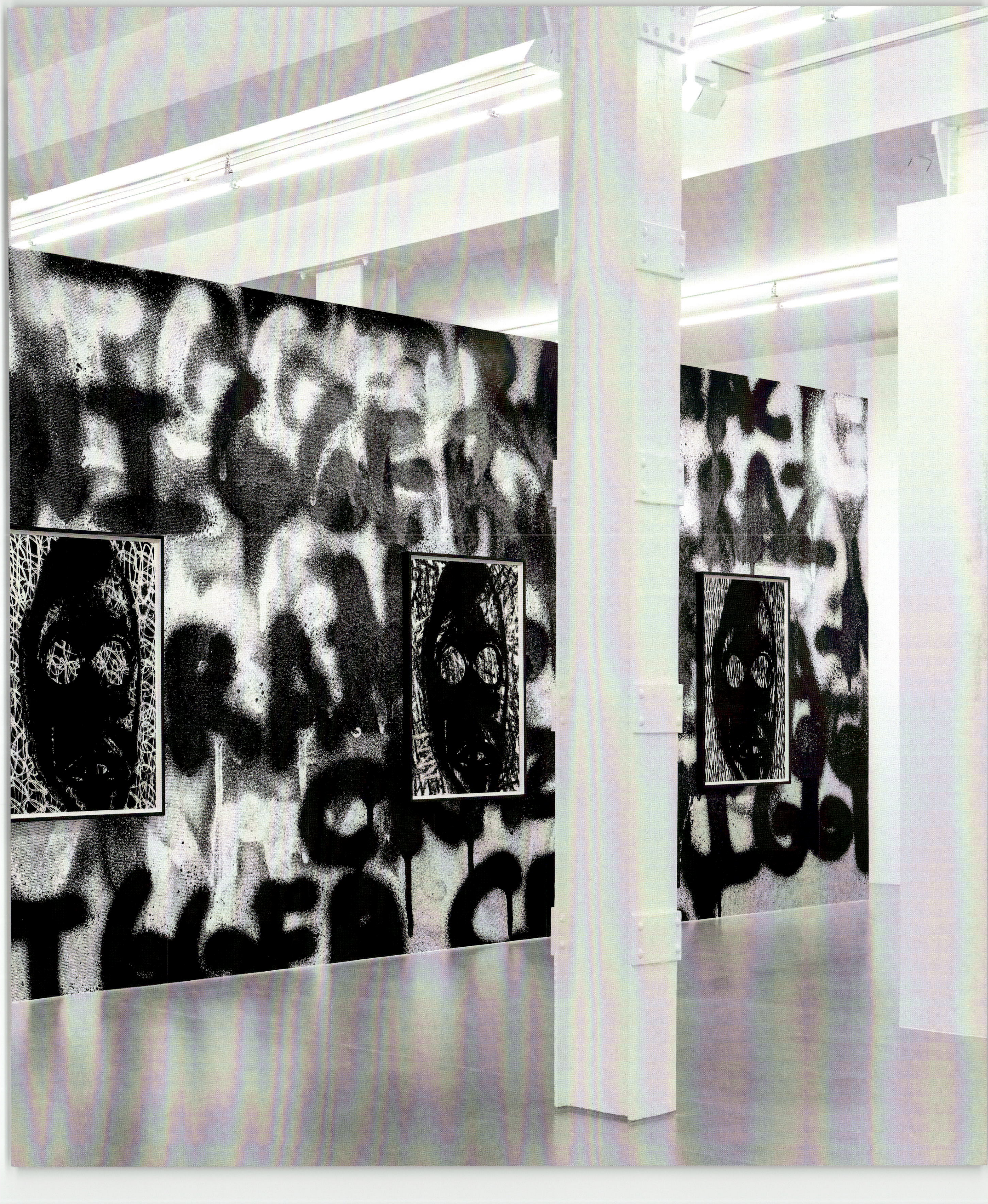

BUT
NOW
I AM

BUT NOW I AM (DETAIL), 2018
SILK-SCREEN INK ON MYLAR
4 PARTS: OVERALL
DIMENSIONS VARIABLE
EACH: 131 X 100 CM

previous pages,
CRAZY NIGGER (AFTER JULIUS EASTMAN), 2018
LATEX INK ON ADHESIVE VINYL
DIMENSIONS VARIABLE

from left,
BUT NOW I AM, 2018
SILK-SCREEN INK ON MYLAR
4 PARTS: OVERALL
DIMENSIONS VARIABLE
EACH: 131 X 100 CM

UNTITLED, 2018
SILK-SCREEN INK ON MYLAR
131 X 100 CM

INSTALLATION VIEW AT
GALERIE EVA PRESENHUBER,
NEW YORK, 2018

PENDLETON: It's also related to scale and scope. Those are terms that I think are pertinent to Black Dada: what's the scale and scope of this idea? And in a different but similar way, this relates to the video portraits, in that the video portraits each create a 'world'. In *Ishmael in the Garden: A Portrait of Ishmael Houston-Jones*, for instance, there's this cinematic feeling: that I'm creating a world that Ishmael exists within. What's the scale and scope of this world? I think the video portraits pose these questions to the viewer, but also to the subject. What is the scale of this? How big is this? I've spoken about this a lot, and you can even raise it to the level of the query 'What does art do?' In layman's terms, how big is art, as an idea, as a tool? What can it do? And that's where ethical questions begin to leak in, not so much having to do with purpose but with potential, and with intent. Why do you do this? The what and the why.

Fred Moten is always saying 'come prepared'. I wonder if a part of the work of the person who's creating the thing, and part of the work of the person who's encountering the thing, is to be prepared. To be prepared for the encounter. And I think these portraits really develop this expectation.

MAPES-FRANCES: *I'm also interested in your use of moving images and cinema prior to actually producing moving-image works yourself. I thought of* System of Display, *which collects film stills – many from Godard or Straub-Huillet films – and indexes them.*

PENDLETON: I'm glad this word 'index' finally came up, because there's this indexical aspect or drive to the work. Particularly, of course, with the *System of Display* works, which I might also describe as tone poems, especially if you think about the letters, which have recently become single letters, but which were, in the earlier works, as many as four letters. They're like utterances; they speak in non-signifying phonemes, like 'R' or 'A A'. And together they create a network of utterances.

I did use film stills. I think a film still precludes unfolding: it's a moving image that's been halted, that won't resolve, much in the same way as a text that refuses to be read. But the *System of Display* put these images back into motion. And I would add that some of the images are actually not film stills, but rather still photographs taken on set. I'm not sure if that's an important distinction.

MAPES-FRANCES: *It might be. Those are already at least second-order images, excluded from the authored cinematic 'work' while remaining as marginal descriptions of that work.*

PENDLETON: It's as though the photograph is the skeleton of production, of how this thing is produced, which is for me of the same species as the script, the skeletal frame, in a similar way.

MAPES-FRANCES: *And the script is, of course, very important to you. Anything can be used as a script for something else, for generating another process.*

PENDLETON: These are the modes and methods – the script enables certain modes and methods of production, works as a mechanism for making the art, for creating the conversation. I've probably never said this, but I feel like so much of my work is saying, 'I want to have a conversation with you'. Even the format of the *Reader*, even the modes and methods of abstraction are intended to create a conversational space. Looking at the 'Black Dada' text, you can see how it's broadcasting that. It keeps posing these questions to a 'you':

can you feel it?
does it hurt?
is this too soft?
do you like it?
do you like this?
is this how you like it?

is it alright?
is he here?
is he breathing?
is it him?
is it hard?
is it cold?
does it weigh much?
is it heavy?
do you have to carry it far?

It's conversational, and invitational. But if we have a conversation, is it important to know what we're talking about?

MAPES-FRANCES: *Or is it more important for there to be things that give us the sense that we can talk?*

PENDLETON: Or is committing to the conversation enough? Is being here, within the space of the work enough? But, really, it's what you just said – knowing that we can talk.

MAPES-FRANCES: *And without the necessity of mastery.*

PENDLETON: It's hard to even pretend you're going to master the subject. I think that's something that's fleshed out in the portraits. If you think about Lorraine O'Grady or Ishmael Houston-Jones or Yvonne Rainer, it's impossible to master the subject.

MAPES-FRANCES: *And impossible for the subjects to master themselves. I think of the moment in* Just Back from Los Angeles: A Portrait of Yvonne Rainer *when Yvonne Rainer reads an excerpt from her own memoir without even knowing what it is. At least not at first.*

PENDLETON: Much of this is about memory, about resuscitating memories, and the texture of things from the past. I like thinking about it that way – the texture of things from the past. How it feels, and how you touch it. That's also something that I perpetually confront. How do you resuscitate and touch things from the past today, and what's the purpose of that?

MAPES-FRANCES: *There's always a balance that one has to maintain between preserving a historical texture or historical sense and the expediency of abstracting or extracting things. What can be pulled out of its historicist container, and at what points should one do so?*

PENDLETON: Right. I like thinking about containers. The gridded Mylar works are containers for different marks, gestures and departures: visual departures, textual departures, incomplete utterances, visual and otherwise, some of them historical. And they're also efficient. In these more provisional spaces, like the Mylars, there's an efficiency to how they're made. They borrow from and re-interpret each other. There's an efficiency to this recombination. And I always think about efficiency in relation to urgency. There's a different kind of urgency that I've taken on in this kind of project. Black Dada, and the question of what Black Dada looks like, has become more urgent for me, and the Mylar body of work, in particular, addresses this as a series of drafts.

There are these three moments in the 'Black Dada' text:

In 1969 a young June Jordan dedicated her poem 'Who Look at Me' to her son Christopher:

We come from otherwhere

In part we grew by looking back at you

BLACK DADA.

UNTITLED, 2018
SILK-SCREEN INK ON MYLAR
131 X 100 CM

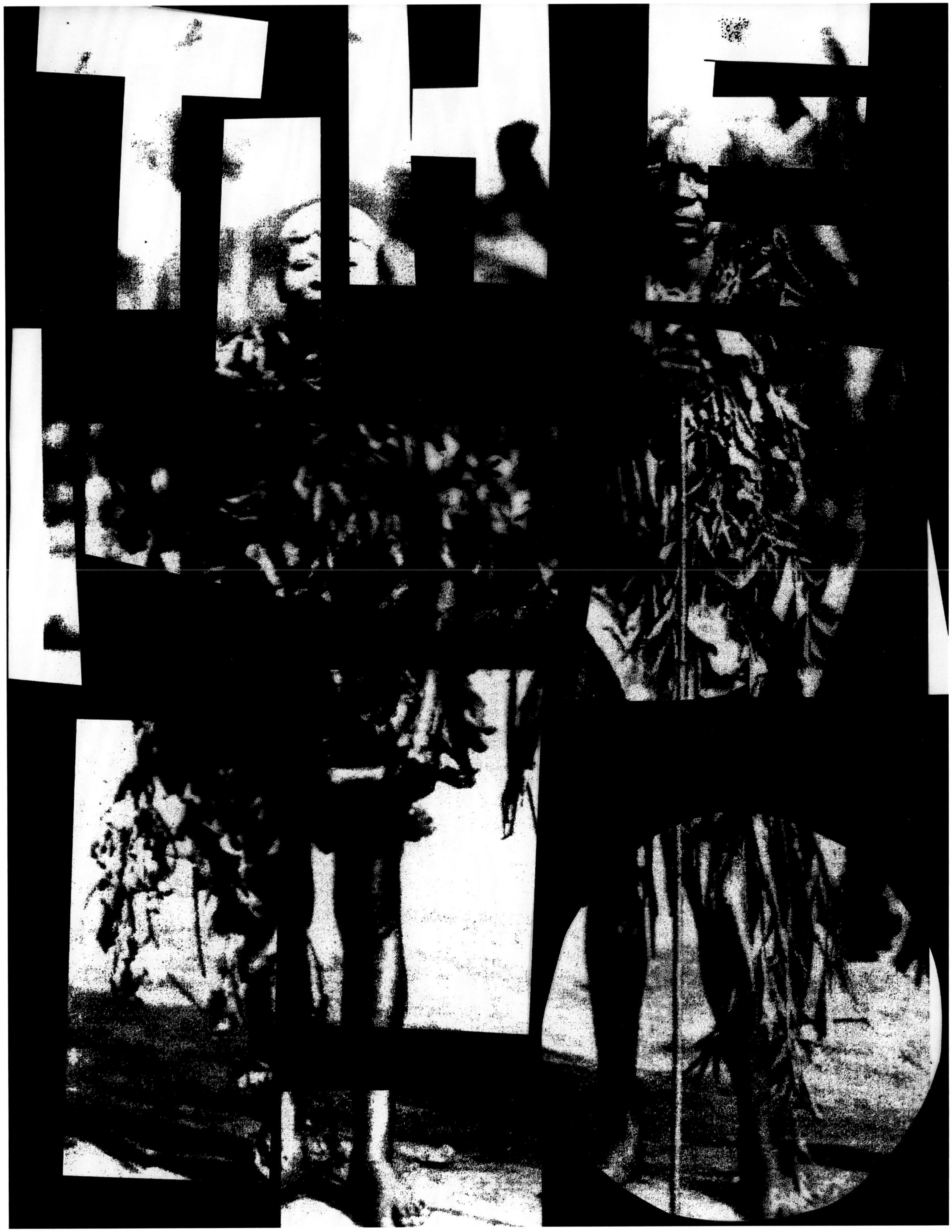

That's a way of saying something very concrete about Black Dada – 'In part we grew by looking back at you' – and about how this act of 'looking back', about how we resuscitate, how we sustain ourselves by looking back. And it's about looking back at multiple things at once, many of them sort of simultaneous. Following that, we have: 'In 1952 John Cage composed his famous silent work *4'33''*'. You think about the time and place in which that's dreamt up, sitting in a room and saying, 'Let's see: four minutes and 33 seconds, a work of art'. And then you think about these other things: 'Do you still notice the 1960s?' And there's this tension: 'Malcolm X arrived in Harlem in the early 1950s', which is clearly of historical importance. It's like, 'meanwhile, across town…'.

But I'm trying not to place values on these things myself. I'm just trying to look at them in relation to each other. It becomes a question of burden. Do you want this to be burdensome? What do you want to do with it? I don't mean to be Rousseauesque or laissez-faire about it – like, a 'Let the children teach themselves' kind of attitude – but it does always come down to 'What do you want to do with it?' I think I'm asking myself that question, but also asking you. And I think the idea is for the canonical avant-garde to come out wounded, yet worthy.

MAPES-FRANCES: *There could be a lot to say about the placing of responsibility on these teachers and students. We keep coming back to these pedagogical terms, and with the figures of the teacher and the student there are these intractable problems of attributing moral responsibility – of displacing and distributing, as you put it, 'burdens'.*

PENDLETON: I can't help but think that teachers are often nothing but representations of the problems of the past. The student is always off-course. These gestures are, maybe, a series of corrections.

In the newest portrait, with Kyle Abraham [*What Is Your Name? Kyle Abraham, A Portrait*, 2018–19], there's a very different relationship between us. It's the first portrait in which the subject is close to me in age. With everyone else, there's a kind of teacher-student relationship. But I think that's one of the more generous and generative elements of the work: what is there to gather from that which was, and how does that which was exist today? How can it compel us forward?

WHAT IS YOUR NAME? KYLE ABRAHAM, A PORTRAIT,
2018–19
SINGLE-CHANNEL COLOUR VIDEO
19 MIN. 39 SEC.
DIMENSIONS VARIABLE

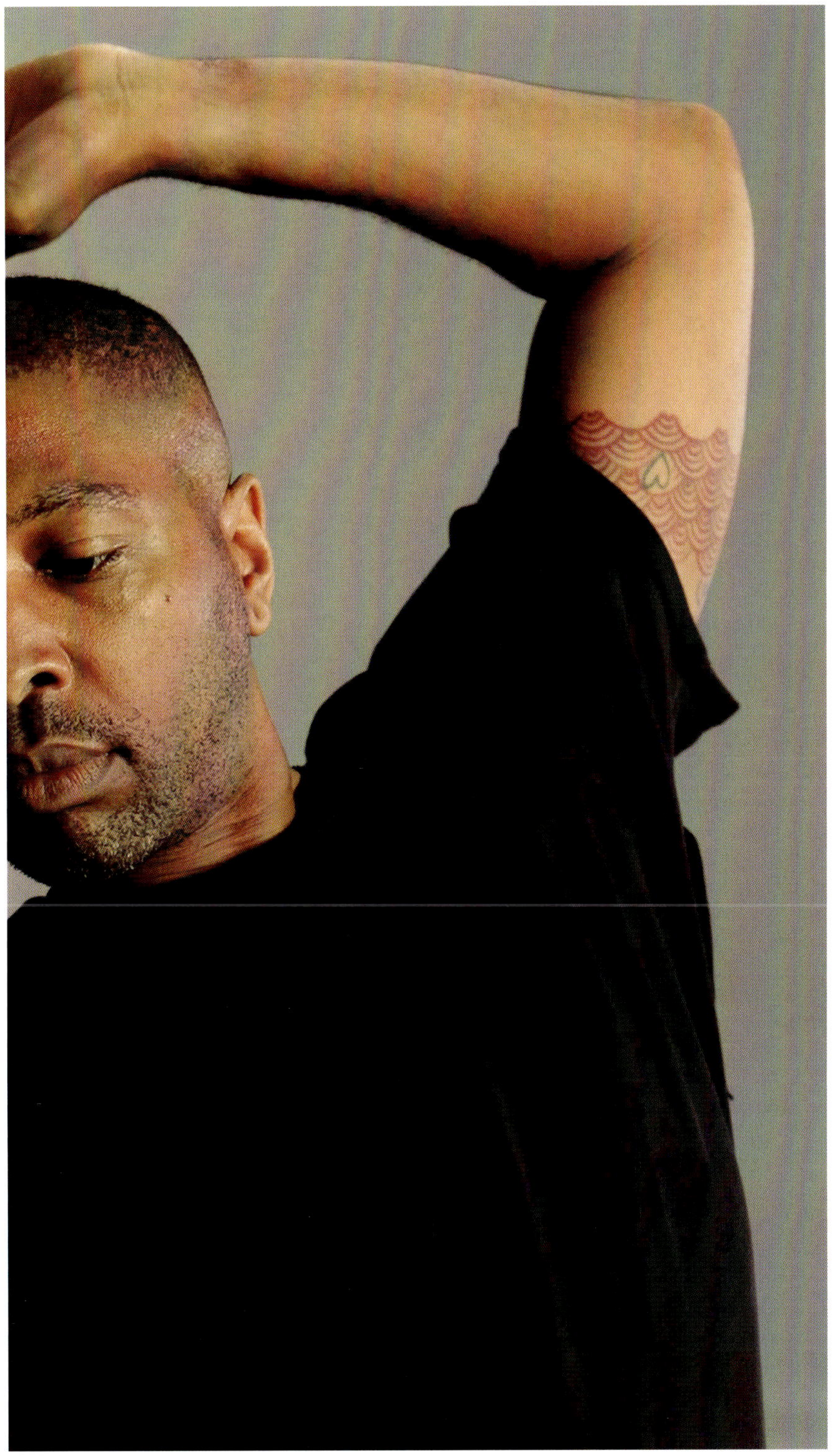

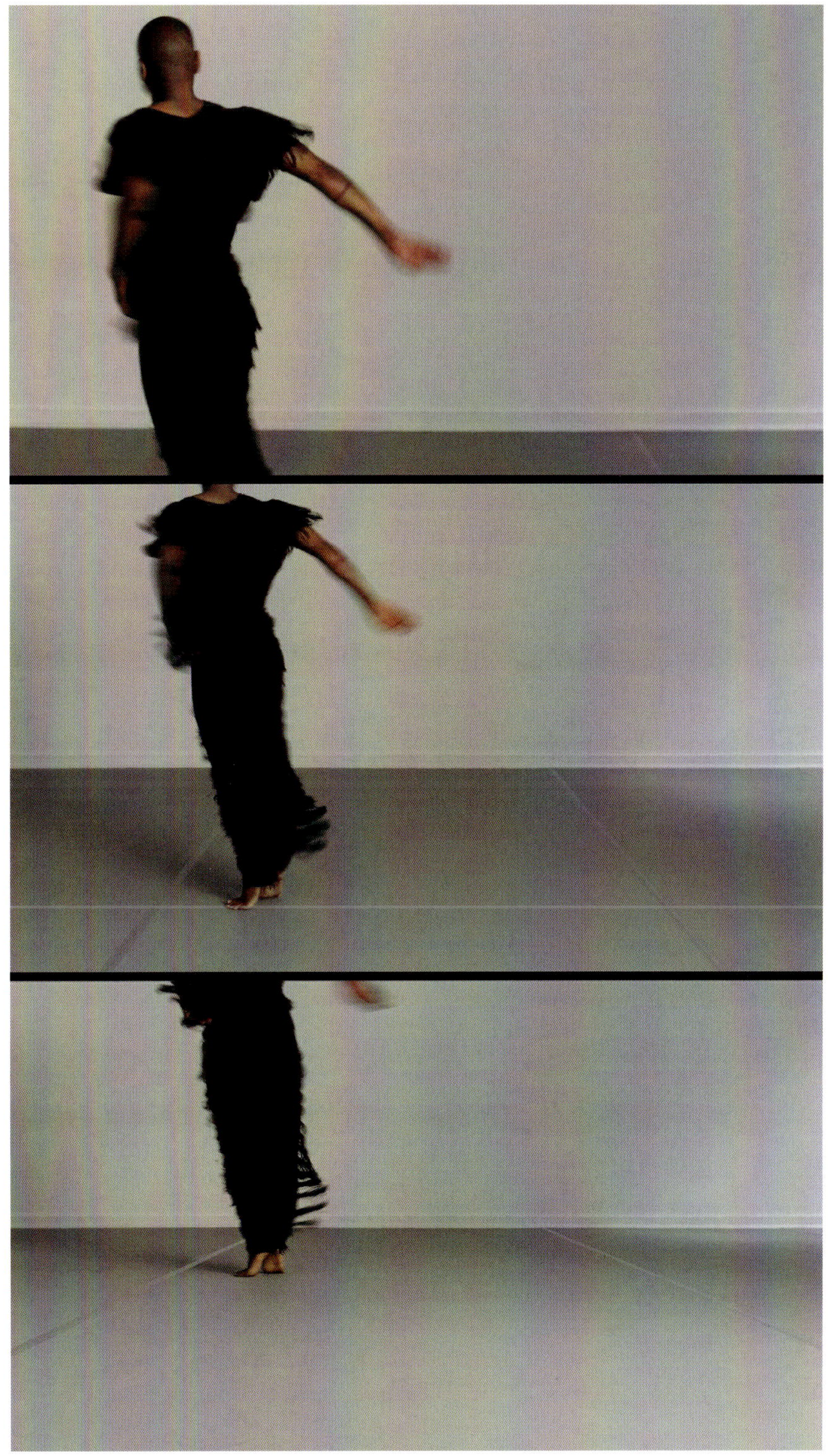

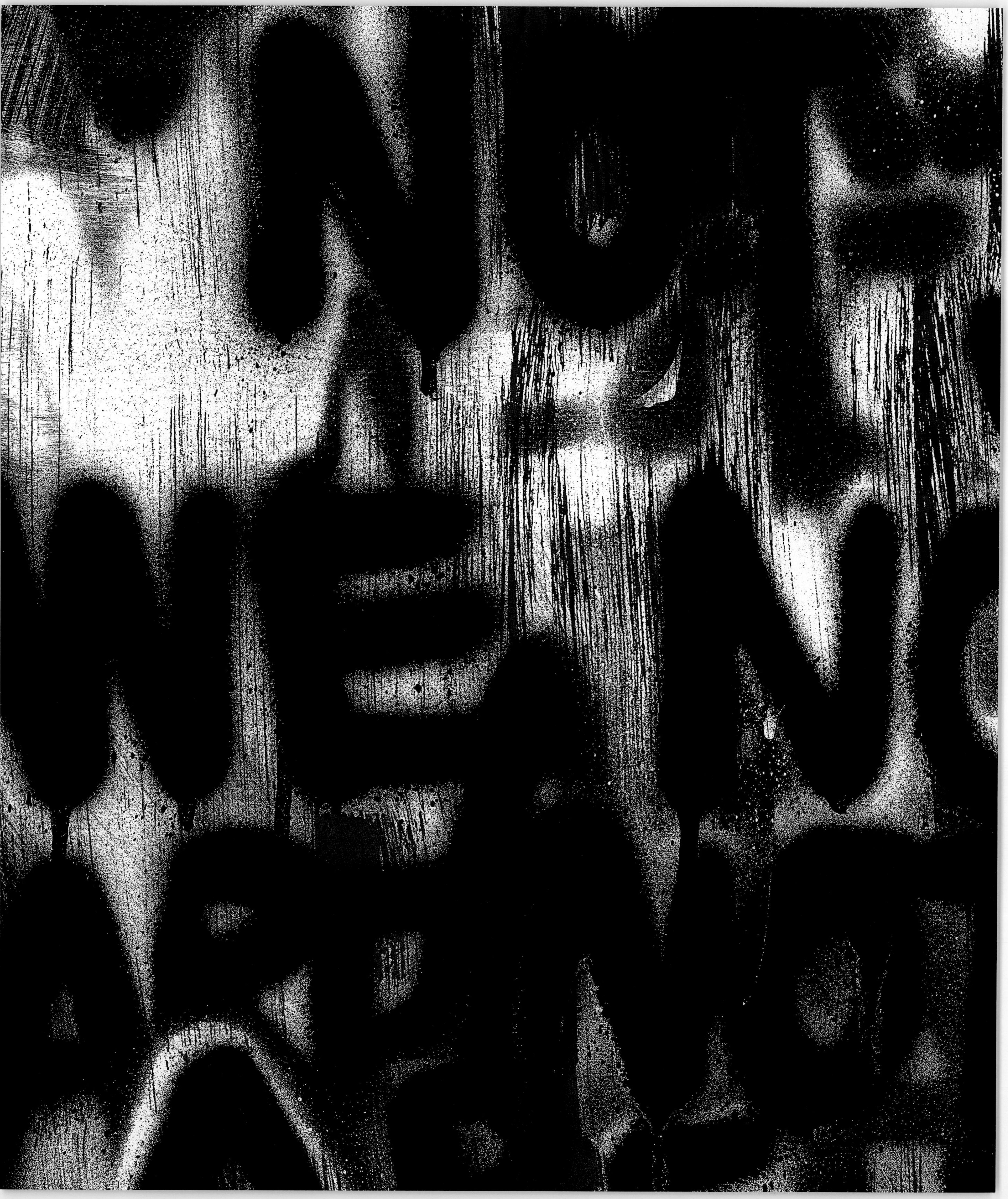

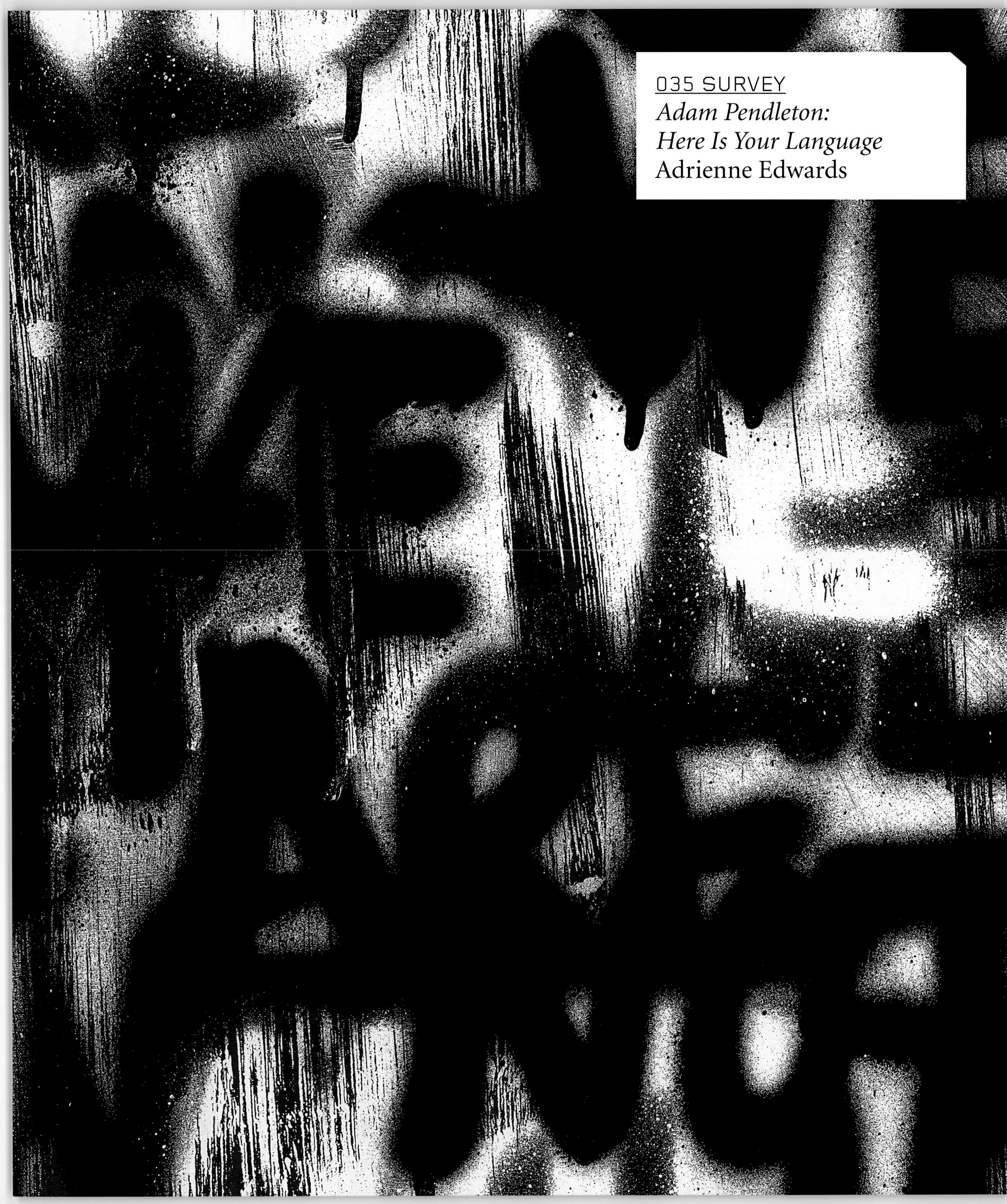

035 SURVEY

Adam Pendleton:
Here Is Your Language

Adrienne Edwards

1

Adam Pendleton's art is an acknowledgement of and a response to history, understood as a series of patterns and structures through which it manifests and makes itself known. His work can be seen as a form of semiotics that takes the personal, the affective, the historical and the quotidian as raw material in the composing of poetic, abstract and often constrained forms. For Pendleton, abstraction is algebraic, a capacious and multivalent experimentation with the limits of a special system of notation, manipulation and variation. Within this system, language plays a key role – as material, technique, form, style, concept and machine. Whether appearing in the form of installation, painting, performance, sculpture or the moving image, language – often appropriated and repeated – performs as a systematic architecture in his works.

Pendleton's interest often lies in collecting and recombining sentences, fragments and words. The presentation of this material has varied, but the underlying drive to collect and assemble has largely remained the same. In *Untitled (WE ARE NOT)*, for instance, a series of paintings begun in 2019, spray-painted text is repeatedly layered on top of itself, and across the painting's surface. The phrase 'WE ARE NOT' breaks down into a field of various combinations: 'WE NOT NOT WE ARE… WE NOT ARE NOT WE ARE…'

Some of the principal influences on Pendleton's procedural and combinatorial approach to textual material lie in twentieth-century American poetry and poetics, and, in particular, the work of authors like Susan Howe, Ron Silliman, Lyn Hejinian and Leslie Scalapino. Associated with Language poetry, these authors emerged in the 1960s and 70s in the United States, and Pendleton occasionally refers to them directly. Although their individual projects varied widely, the Language poets tended to employ methods of juxtaposition, using strikingly dissimilar images, words or fragments without a clear sense of connection or voice. Scholars Lee Bartlett and Jerome J. McGann have conceived of Language poetry as 'an alternative to established forms of realism and idealism, significant for its capacity to disrupt and deconstruct those forms of order'.[1] Poet Joan Retallack, who collaborated with Pendleton on 'The Supposium', an event presented in 2014 at the Museum of Modern Art in New York, views the Language poets as providing 'a powerful and much needed antidote to the ubiquity of the bland and innocuous in so-called mainstream literature'.[2] If a general understanding of Language poetry is to be had, it can be seen as 'the repressed "other" of a dominant "workshop" poetics, theoretically sophisticated where it is naïve, philosophically skeptical where it is idealistic, and politically oppositional where it is accommodating'.

We can situate Language poetry's importance to Pendleton's work through poet Jena Osman's description of the genre as an alternative in which 'poetry can reflect actualities, the ways in which poetry can have a socio-political existence'.[4] In thinking of the capacities of Language poetry against an 'Aristotelian/dramatic model', Osman explains three vital points: '1) turning the reader/spectator into a critical observer, 2) the work of art should force the reader/spectator to make decisions, and 3) social being determines thought rather than vice versa'.[5] Language poetry tends to complicate our typical use of language, resisting easy legibility, mainstream formal structures and a reliance upon meaning. As Osman has it, 'the result was a blast of poetry where language was made material in numerous ways. Rather than the poem leading the reader by the hand toward a safe and predetermined conclusion … the poem presented the reader with language to observe and make decisions about'.[6]

The act of materializing language as a socio-political experience is always already a collective endeavour. That is to say that the act of appending a plurality and diversity of individual, distinct sources to make a 'new' composition thickens the constellation of relations. Any 'new' work engaged in the language-making methodology of this mode of poetry has to a greater or lesser degree negated the overdetermined aims of originality, which for its practitioners is never the point. Rather, the aim is to build unattributed assemblages, such that the seeming anonymity enables a recognition of the whole rather than the one. In so doing, the proposition of language is that it is not '*about* the world but is *in* the world itself', as Andrew Ross has it in *Marxism and the Interpretation of Culture*.[7]

While Pendleton frequently cites the Language poets and their techniques, he does not do so without simultaneously complicating them. His work places such modes of language-making within broader or alternative canons, correlating them to texts, movements, and histories beyond their disciplinary or institutional boundaries. This way of working would become known as Black Dada, a paradigm that Pendleton first named in 2008. Pendleton has described Black Dada simply as 'a way to talk about the future while talking about the past. It is our present moment'.[8]

An important precursor to Black Dada was Pendleton's 2007 cross-boundary performance *The Revival*, which reveals how language would come to operate in his work as a mode of image-making. In addition to writing the score, he also designed the set and seating, and collaborated with Jason Moran and Alicia Hall Moran on the musical direction. *The Revival* took the format of a religious service. A twenty-eight-person choir, clad in black robes, enters the capacious Stephan Weiss Studio and takes its position on two-part, multi-tiered plywood platforms, in total darkness, except for a music stand, lit from above. We hear

previous pages,
UNTITLED (WE ARE NOT)
(DETAIL), 2019–20
SILK-SCREEN INK ON CANVAS
244 X 305 CM

THE REVIVAL, 2007
PERFORMANCE

PERFORMA 07, NEW YORK, 2007

below,
UNTITLED, 2009
PERFORMANCE

ARTISTS SPACE, NEW YORK,
2009

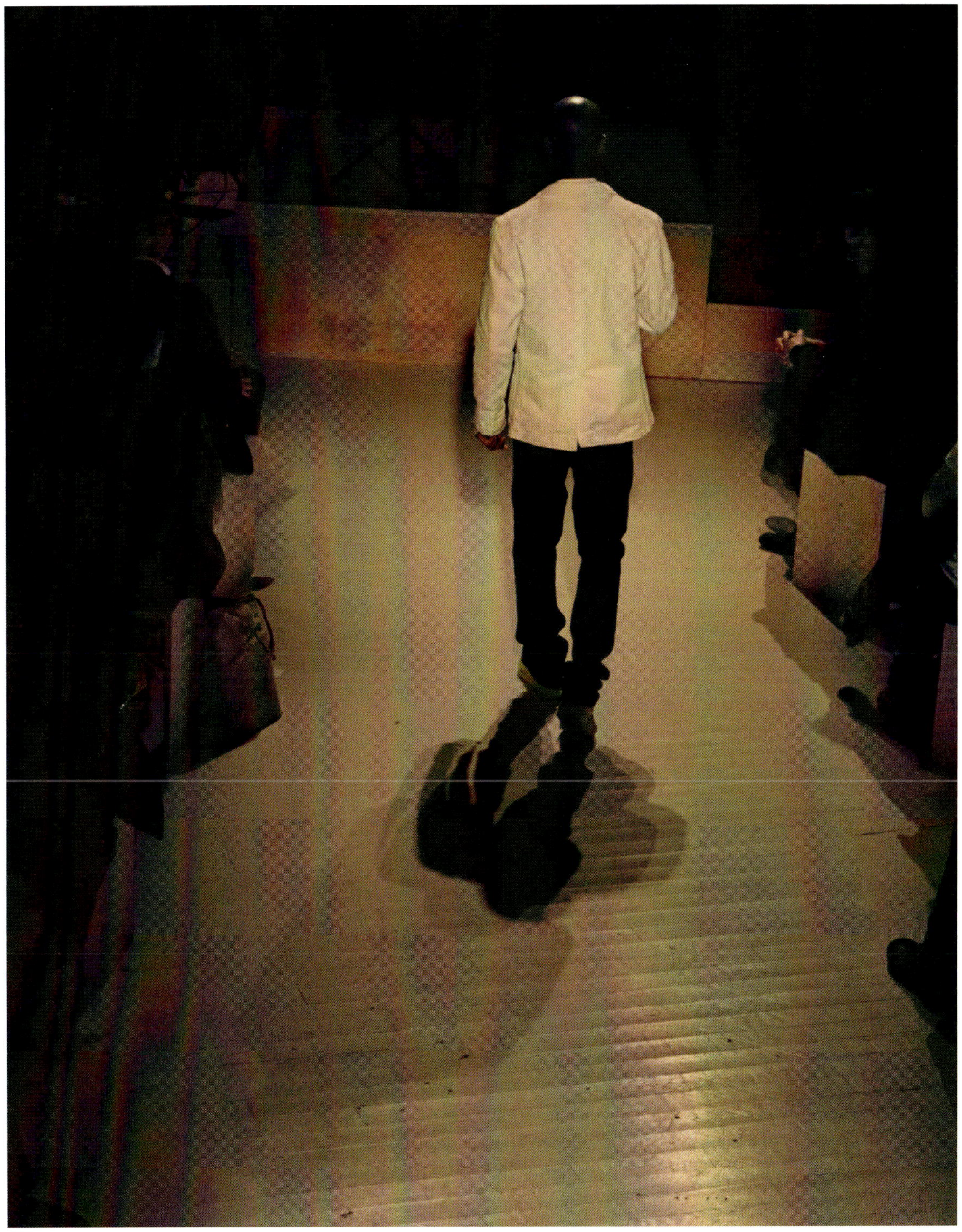

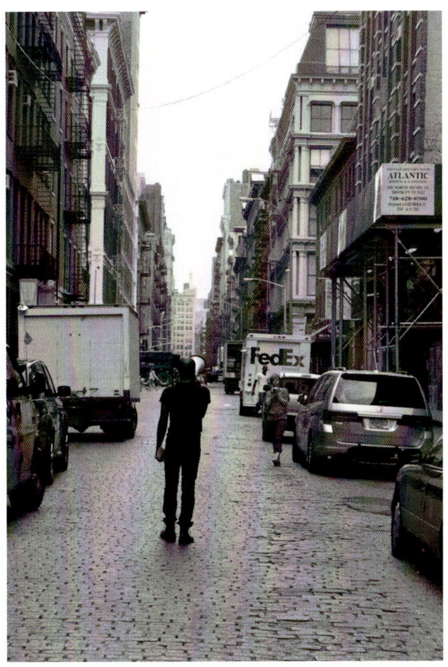

Pendleton reciting text that he has composed in a measured, methodical cadence, meandering through repetitions of phrases about ethical and political values. The space is gradually illuminated as Pendleton spits out what he calls 'symbols' – vernacular, hate-filled speech acts common to the Dozens, a game of spoken words between two contestants played out in black communities in the United States, whose aim is to insult with the greatest flair. Then he emerges, austerely dressed in a white jacket and oxford shirt, gleaming black pants and fluorescent yellow sneakers, walking into the centre of the space to ascend a square, raised platform as interdisciplinary artist Jason Moran plays the piano. Pendleton repeats the phrase he first uttered at the start of the performance: 'We lived on a small island stone nation, love'.

Ten minutes into the piece, the choir's music swells with the sonic beauty of a hymn. As the artist articulates words such as 'fat chance' and 'erotic', the choir responds *a cappella*: 'Glory'. The incongruence of these verbal offerings creates a tension that is the result of the profane or the mundane being placed in direct relation to the sacred. In Pendleton's sacrilegious sermon, he tells us: 'The experience of language is not isolated. It is an act taking place in the world like all else. It is not the act, separate, describing the world. It is, it occurs, in real time'.[9]

THE REVIVAL

(The stage and seating-cubes form an empty presence, pristine and aesthetically lit. The audience take their seats. Once this process is complete the CHOIR come out and take their positions. Lights go black. The aisle is lit in a soft line of light. SOLOIST walks down the aisle singing 'i like the sunrise.' As the SOLOIST finishes her song-cycle she joins the CHOIR. Aisle light remains on as ADAM'S voice is heard. The rest of the stage is dim. ADAM eventually will come into view, walk down the aisle and step onto his platform.)

ADAM:

we lived on a small island stone nation.

we lived on a small island stone nation, love.

without sound. without color. without stone. without garlic.

steel
bell
drops
wave
glory

Here is your language.

On the gay marriage initiatives alone

1.1 million against us
1.2 million against us
2.2 million against us
2.6 million against us
3.2 million against us

60 million people whom we live and work with every day think we are immoral. "Moral values" was top of many lists of why people supported George Bush. Not Iraq. Not the economy. Not terrorism, "Moral values." In case you need a translation that means us. It is hard to stand up to so much hate. Which of course is just the way they want it. Please know that a huge portion of the population of the United States hates us. I don't mean dislike. I mean hate. You may not choose to call it hate, but I do.

First there was the bailiff, and we broke the bailiff. And then there was God, and we broke God. And lastly there was cock, an we broke that, too. Freed the ground, freed religion, freed the body. And went up this hill, standing together naked like the old

1

female pack, growing to eat and not to market, friends to cattle who we milked but never slaughtered, joining the strips and dancing in the commons, the three day's labor that we gave to priests, gave instead to the hungry, turned the tithe barn into a hospital and found cunt beautiful that we had hidden and suffered shame for, its lovely shapelessness, its colour all miraculous, what they had done made dirty or worshipped out of ignorance, do we now-

Symbols.

Old faggot.

Fat bitch.

Old hag.

You were my first.

-Monuments are embarrassing to Dutch culture.

I'm looking for a wife.

The body against the world, asshole.

You don't have to look.

Why don't you try on this dress?

I'm looking for a wife.

She was confident earning 98,000 dollars a year.

Bully

Jabber

at

(By 'at' PREACHER will have stepped onto platform. Aisle light off. Spotlight on PREACHER. JASON AND BAND modestly lit…low-key still -like the music).

we lived on a small island stone nation.

we lived on a small island stone nation, love.

2

without sound. without color. without stone. without garlic.

steel
bell
drops
wave
glory

Here is your language.

(JASON AND BAND stop)

why a low exterior regresses

(Pause)

I've tried to offer leadership to the democratic party and the nation.

If in my high moments…I have done some good…offered some service…shed some light…healed some wounds…rekindled some hope…asserted war on apathy and indifference…or anyway along the way helped somebody than this campaign has not been in vain.

(J AND BAND begin 'Abide With Me'. Lights up on CHOIR)

I've tried to offer leadership to the democratic party and the nation.

If in my high moments…I have done some good…offered some service…shed some light…healed some wounds…rekindled some hope…asserted war on apathy and indifference…or anyway along the way helped somebody than this campaign has not been in vain.

He performed my language.

(J AND BAND stop)

why azaleas

The experience of language is not isolated. It is an act taking place in the world. Like all else. It is not the act, function, separate, describing the world. It is. It occurs in real time.

(CHOIR and J AND BAND join in for the 'Glories')

sunsets

3

forest
glory
fat
chance
glory
erotic
glory
wave
associated
castle
blame
studies
glory
bell
drops
bleacher
diameter
glory
fissuring
or
letting
it
going
whole
for
completed
glory
somebody
says
glory
used
described
scripture
open
to
more
or
glory
happens
whatever
stops
arrangement
glory
finite
whole
the

4

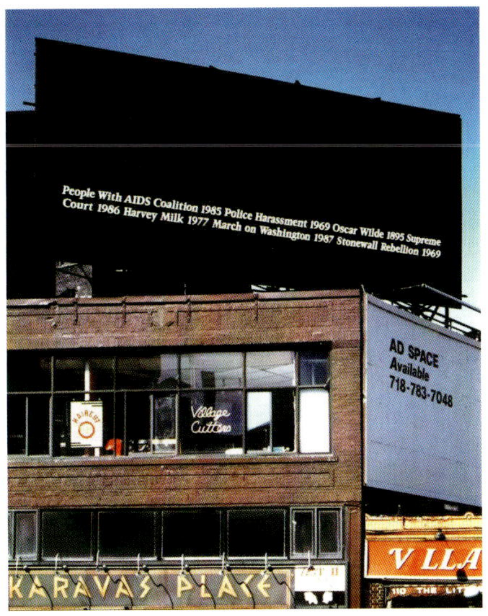

FELIX GONZALEZ-TORRES
'UNTITLED', 1989
BILLBOARD IN SHERIDAN SQUARE,
GREENWICH VILLAGE, NEW YORK

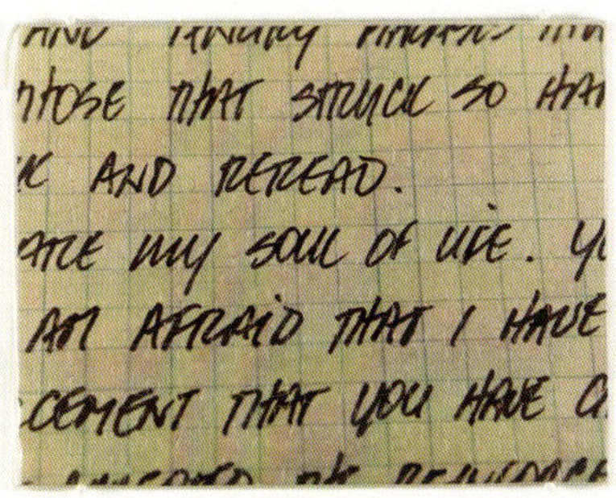

FELIX GONZALEZ-TORRES
'UNTITLED' (MY SOUL OF LIFE), 1991
C-PRINT JIGSAW PUZZLE IN PLASTIC BAG
19 X 24 CM

Pendleton's score for *The Revival* is one early instance in which collage becomes activated as a primary mode in his art. The musical spine of the performance collages jazz composer Duke Ellington's 'I Like the Sunrise', the evening's opening solo; gospel singer Kurt Franklin's 'Brokenhearted' and 'Afterwhile'; and hymns such as 'Abide With Me'. The musical elements are amplified by striking speech acts composed as collaged fragments from an unlikely range of textual sources, which act as counterpoints to Ellington's optimistic big band sound and the guttural, profound crescendos that are a hallmark of the spiritual. To achieve this sense of discord, Pendleton extracted poet Donald Hall's *Without* (1998), where the loss of syntax and punctuation literally materializes the reality of Hall's wife suffering and dying; Paolo Javier's *60 lv bo(e)mbs to lv* (2005); John Ashbery's 'From Estuaries, from Casinos' (1992); a collection of essays on Language poetry by Charles Bernstein, *Content's Dream: Essays 1975–1984* (1986); gay activist and writer Larry Kramer's infamous speech *The Tragedy of Today's Gays* (2005); playwright Howard Barker's *The Castle* (1985); architect Rem Koolhaas's influential tome *S, M, L, XL* (1995); and civil rights activist and politician Jesse Jackson's address before the Democratic National Convention when he ran for the American presidency in 1988, among others.

Throughout the score, Pendleton repeats the phrase: 'Here is your language'. The repetition is poignantly located as a call-and-response or as a simultaneous summoning and deployment of the collective, the plural in relation to the individual. Through the amalgamation here of such varying sources and extracts, the phrase is directed towards the darker, deeper and emotional dimensions of life: a failed bid for power, the death of a spouse, the alienation of queer life and love, contending with solitude and humiliations and so on. In exploring his interest in language, Pendleton is not responding to literature as a writer per se (though he does write scripts for his performances and video portraits), but as a visual artist who happens to work in a range of media. Indeed, he has described *The Revival* as an 'object', because of the importance of its structural framework. The language becomes plastic, almost fungible within this framework. Pendleton's conceptual paradigm also specifically concerns the capacity of speech acts, particularly their affective force, in the sense of Zora Neale Hurston's articulation of blackness in language in her 1934 essay 'The Characteristics of Negro Expression' in which she contends: 'His very words are action words' and 'the Negro thinks in hieroglyphs'.[10]

A related though distinct example of emotional conceptualism is artist Felix Gonzalez-Torres's *'Untitled' (My Soul of Life)* (1991), a jigsaw puzzle that reproduces an excerpt from a handwritten letter placed in a plastic bag. Its language is personal and evocative, yet incomplete in its sentiment, except for the eponymous phrase, which is centred in the work. Gonzalez-Torres's evocation of the fragmented possibility of a collective whole through the jigsaw puzzle can be compared with Pendleton's minimalist set fabricated from modest materials such as plywood. Pendleton's vertical spacing of language in his scores also recalls Gonzalez-Torres's 'dateline' and *Untitled* text works, in which combinations of dates and names of events, people and places are presented in sparse white text on a black background. Gonzalez-Torres's 1989 billboard work to mark the twentieth anniversary of the Stonewall rebellion, for example, reads:

People With AIDS Coalition 1985 Police Harassment 1969
Oscar Wilde 1895 Supreme Court 1986 Harvey Milk 1977
March on Washington 1967 Stone Wall Rebellion 1969

The opening passage of *The Revival* contains the equally economical and equally emotionally resonant:

On the gay marriage initiative alone

1.1 million against us
1.2 million against us
2.2 million against us
2.6 million against us
3.2 million against us

In spatializing language in this way, Pendleton and Gonzalez-Torres illustrate related approaches to sensual conceptualism: both establish a conceptual paradigm that can hold emotionally charged content. Pendleton's culling from books, like Gonzalez-Torres's data sets and personal correspondence works, is a form of portraiture that captures information returned to us in fragments, heightening the relationality between word, date and data as evidence of one's times, and self-reflexively, of one's place in time and among things.

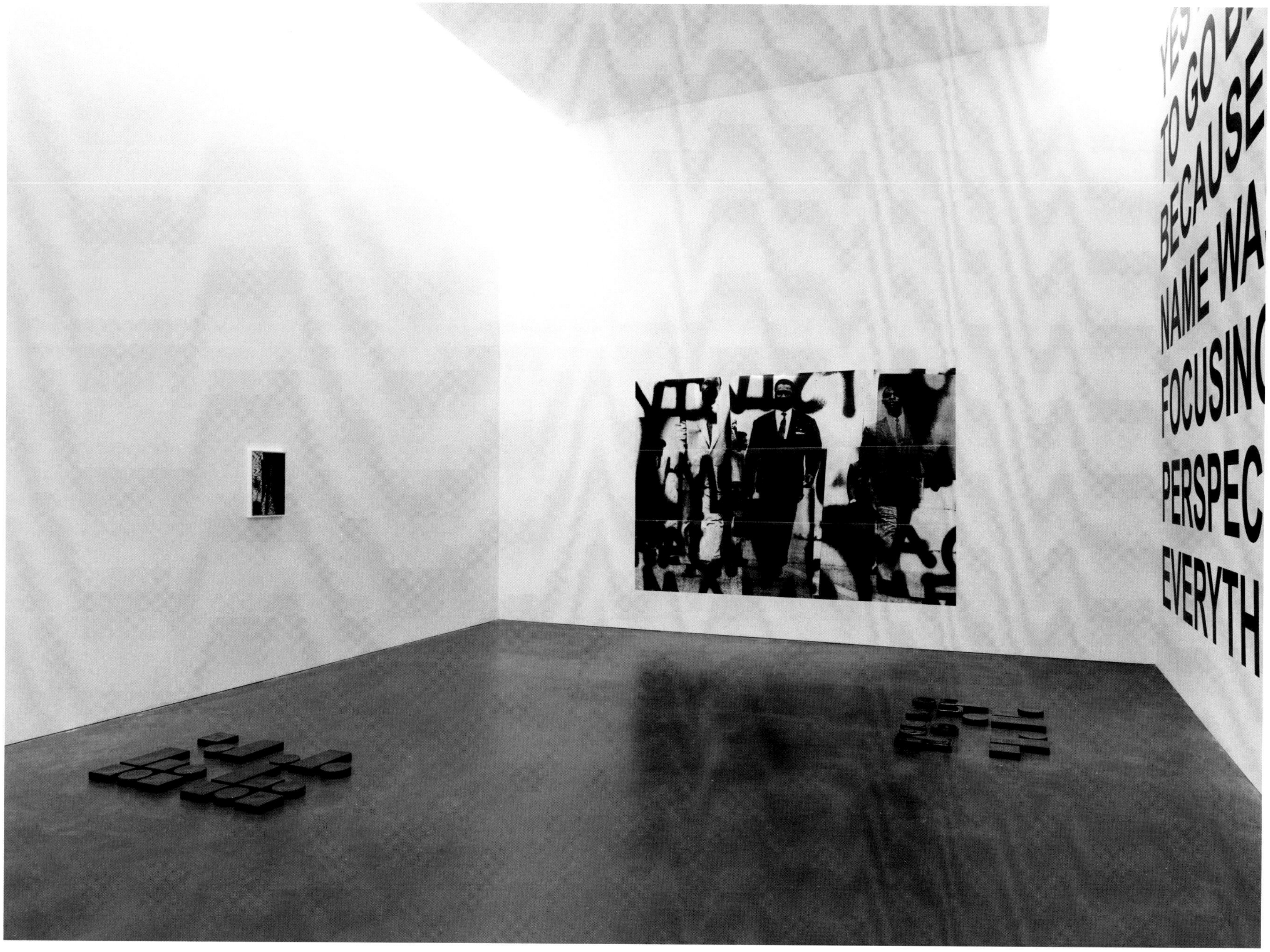

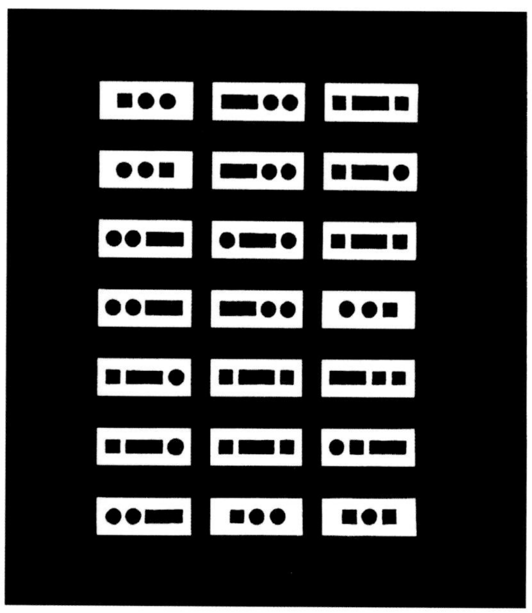

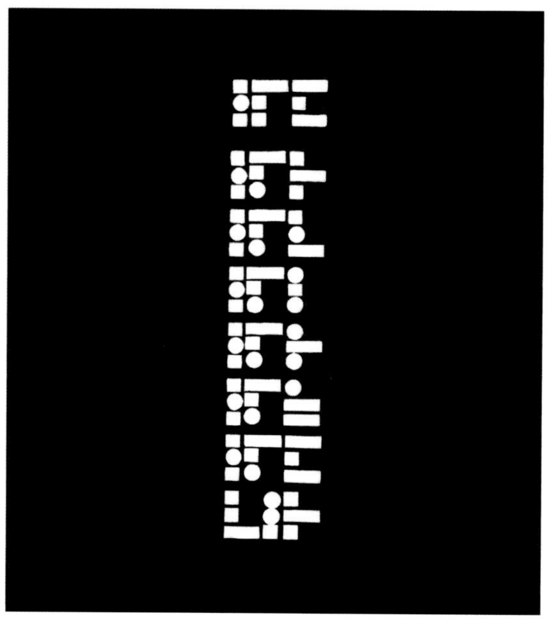

PAGES FROM 'QRD LIGHT' AND 'CHW PIRATES', IN HANNAH WEINER, *CODE POEMS: FROM THE INTERNATIONAL CODE OF SIGNALS FOR THE USE OF ALL NATIONS*, STATION HILL PRESS, BARRYTOWN, NEW YORK, 1982

NOTES ON BLACK DADA NIHILISMUS (PROPER NOUNS), 2009
ACRYLIC PAINT ON WALL
DIMENSIONS VARIABLE

INSTALLATION VIEW AT INSTITUTE OF CONTEMPORARY ARTS, LONDON, 2009

opposite, wall, from left,
UNTITLED (SMALL WATER), 2016
SILK-SCREEN INK ON MIRROR POLISHED STAINLESS STEEL
48 X 33 CM

UNTITLED (1958), 2016
SILK-SCREEN INK ON MYLAR
9 PARTS: OVERALL 221 X 316 CM
EACH: 74 X 105 CM

YES BUT, 2008
ACRYLIC PAINT ON WALL
DIMENSIONS VARIABLE

floor, from left,
UNTITLED (CODE POEM LOS ANGELES BLACK), 2010–2016
GLAZED CERAMIC
4 RECTANGLE, 7 CIRCLE AND 7 SQUARE UNITS: 117 X 81 X 4 CM
OVERALL RECTANGLE: 15 X 30 X 4 CM
CIRCLE: 15 Ø X 4 CM
SQUARE: 15 X 15 X 4 CM

UNTITLED (CODE POEM), 2016
GLAZED CERAMIC
4 RECTANGLE, 6 CIRCLE, AND 5 SQUARE UNITS: 117 X 81 X 4 CM
OVERALL
RECTANGLE: 15 X 30 X 4 CM
CIRCLE: 15 Ø X 4 CM
SQUARE: 15 X 15 X 4 CM

INSTALLATION VIEW AT MUSEUM OF CONTEMPORARY ART, DENVER, 2016

In 2009, Pendleton began a series of *Wall Texts* that bring to mind his performance scripts. Bold, direct and yet also somehow oblique, they use language appropriated from books and recall the work of notable conceptualists such as Renée Green's *Space Poem* banners; Theresa Hak Kyung Cha's black ink works on cloth, paper, or her body; and the typographic texts of Lawrence Weiner and Robert Barry. Showcasing word associations as diaristic accounts, The *Wall Texts* cite *The Future(s) of Film* (2002), a collection of interviews with Jean-Luc Godard, Samuel R. Delany's science fiction novel *Dhalgren* (1975), and 'Black Dada Nihilismus' (1964), a poem by Amiri Baraka (then known as LeRoi Jones).

The influence of Language poet Hannah Weiner's sensibility can be found in Pendleton's *Code Poems*, begun in 2009, a series of sculptures employing methods of interpolation and (re)combination. Based on Weiner's book with the same title, published in 1982, these works are made up of glazed ceramic squares, rectangles, and circles, placed in loosely gridded formations on the floor. Weiner's experimental visual and verbal assemblages employed as their basis the International Code of Signals, a nineteenth-century system for communicating at sea that used finite schemes of Morse code and flag semaphore to encode limited, pre-determined messages. Over time, Pendleton has re-presented Weiner's version of the system, introducing his own arrangements and adding to the controlled and refined cacophony of signs.

A large-scale *Code Poem* was commissioned by Public Art Fund for Pendleton's first outdoor sculpture in 2016 in City Hall Park in Manhattan. It was installed

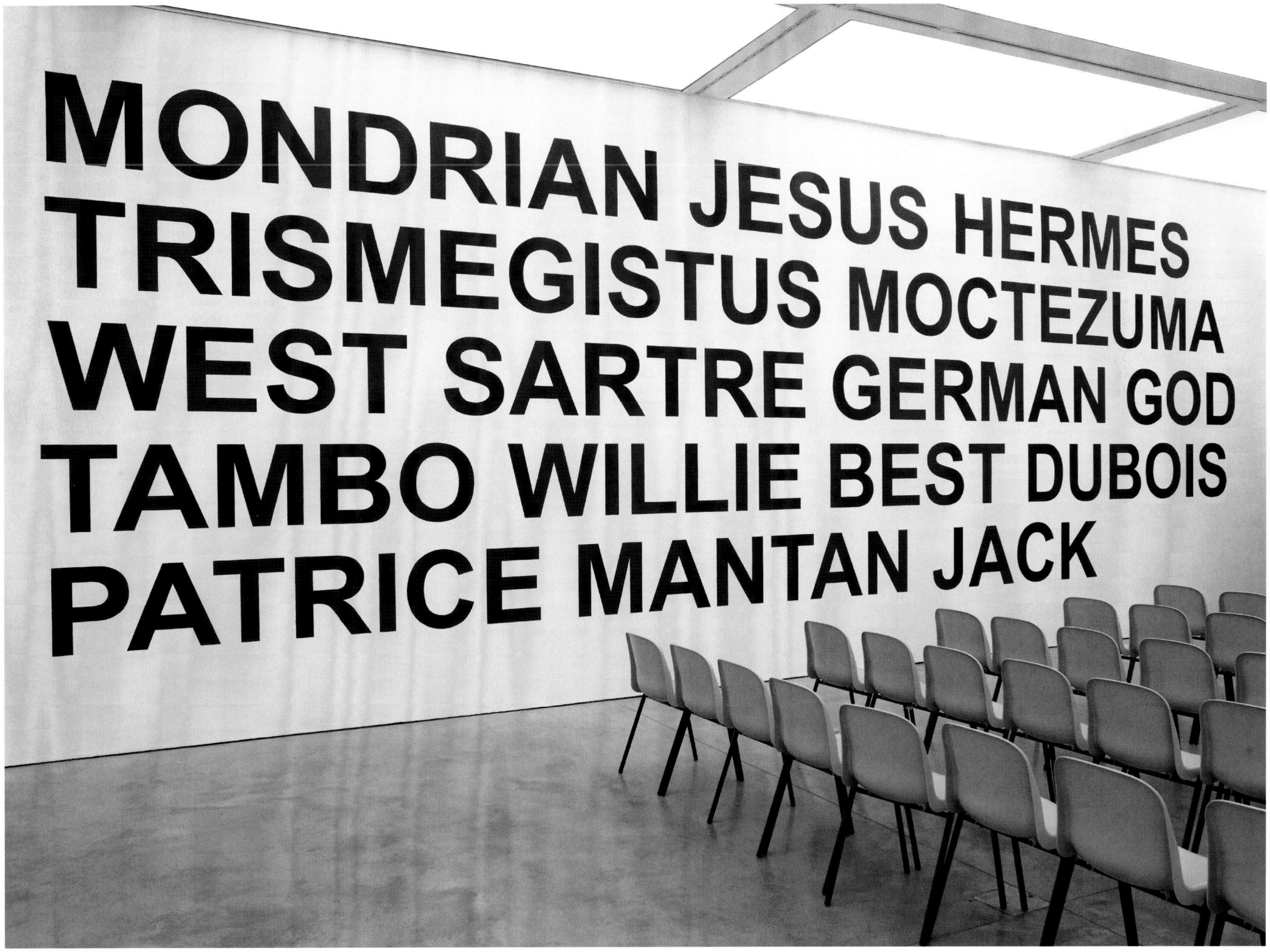

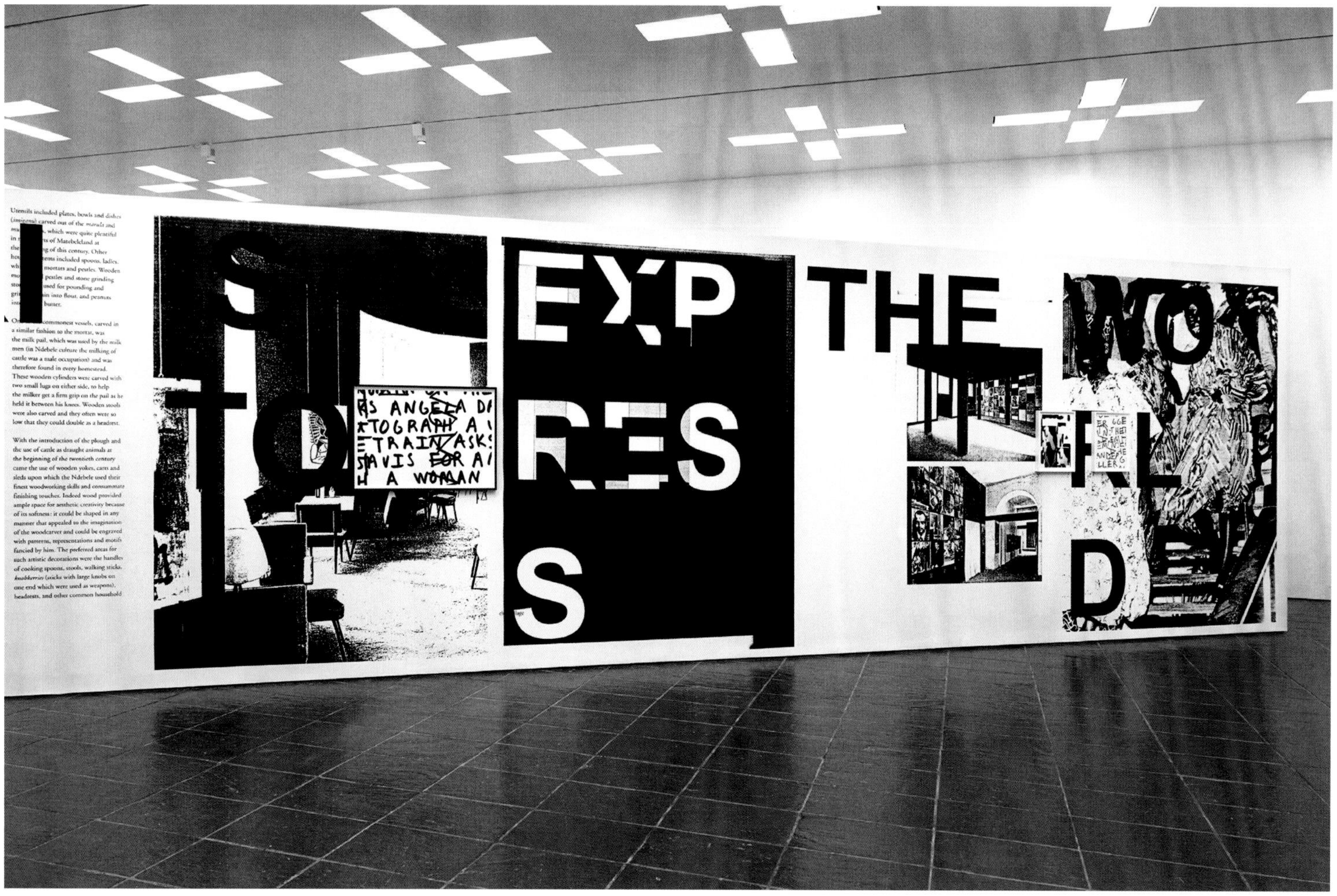
EXP
THE
RES
S

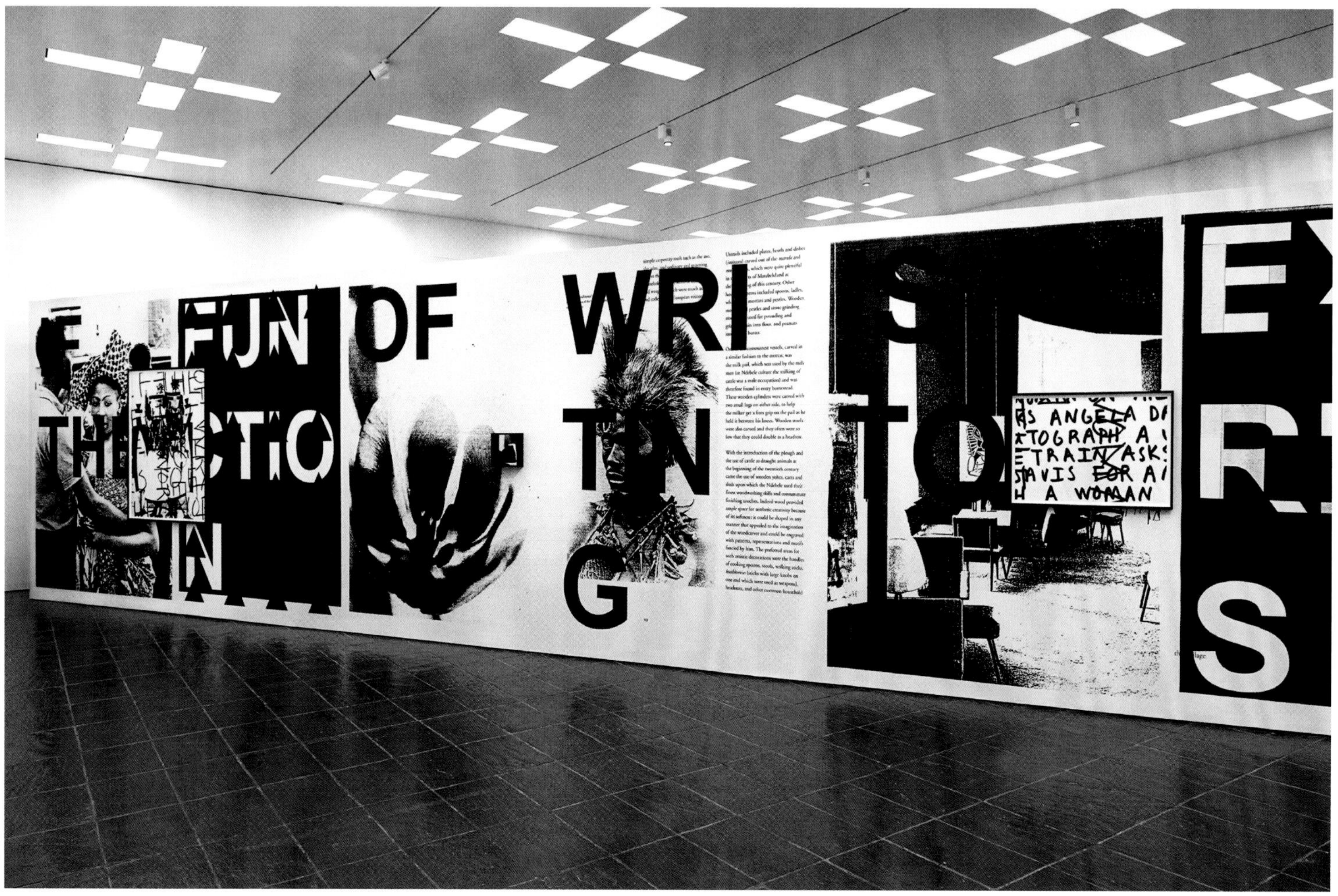
FUN
OF
WRI
G

opposite, above,
IF THE FUNCTION OF WRITING, 2017
LATEX INK ON ADHESIVE VINYL
DIMENSIONS VARIABLE

from left,
A WOMAN ON THE TRAIN ASKS ANGELA DAVIS FOR AN AUTOGRAPH, 2016
SILK-SCREEN INK ON MYLAR
59 X 84 CM

UNTITLED, 2016
COLLAGE ON PAPER
39 X 27 CM

UNTITLED, 2017
COLLAGE ON PAPER
39 X 27 CM

below,
IF THE FUNCTION OF WRITING, 2017
LATEX INK ON ADHESIVE VINYL
DIMENSIONS VARIABLE

from left,
DADA DANCERS (LARGE STUDY), 2017
SILK-SCREEN INK ON MYLAR
131 X 100 CM

SYSTEM OF DISPLAY, U (SUN/ JOSEFA ZIKÁNOVÁ, UNTITLED, EXERCISE FROM THE STATE SCHOOL OF GRAPHIC ART, PRAGUE, 1935), 2016
SILK-SCREEN INK ON PLEXIGLASS AND MIRROR
25 X 25 X 8 CM

A WOMAN ON THE TRAIN ASKS ANGELA DAVIS FOR AN AUTOGRAPH, 2016
SILK-SCREEN INK ON MYLAR
59 X 84 CM

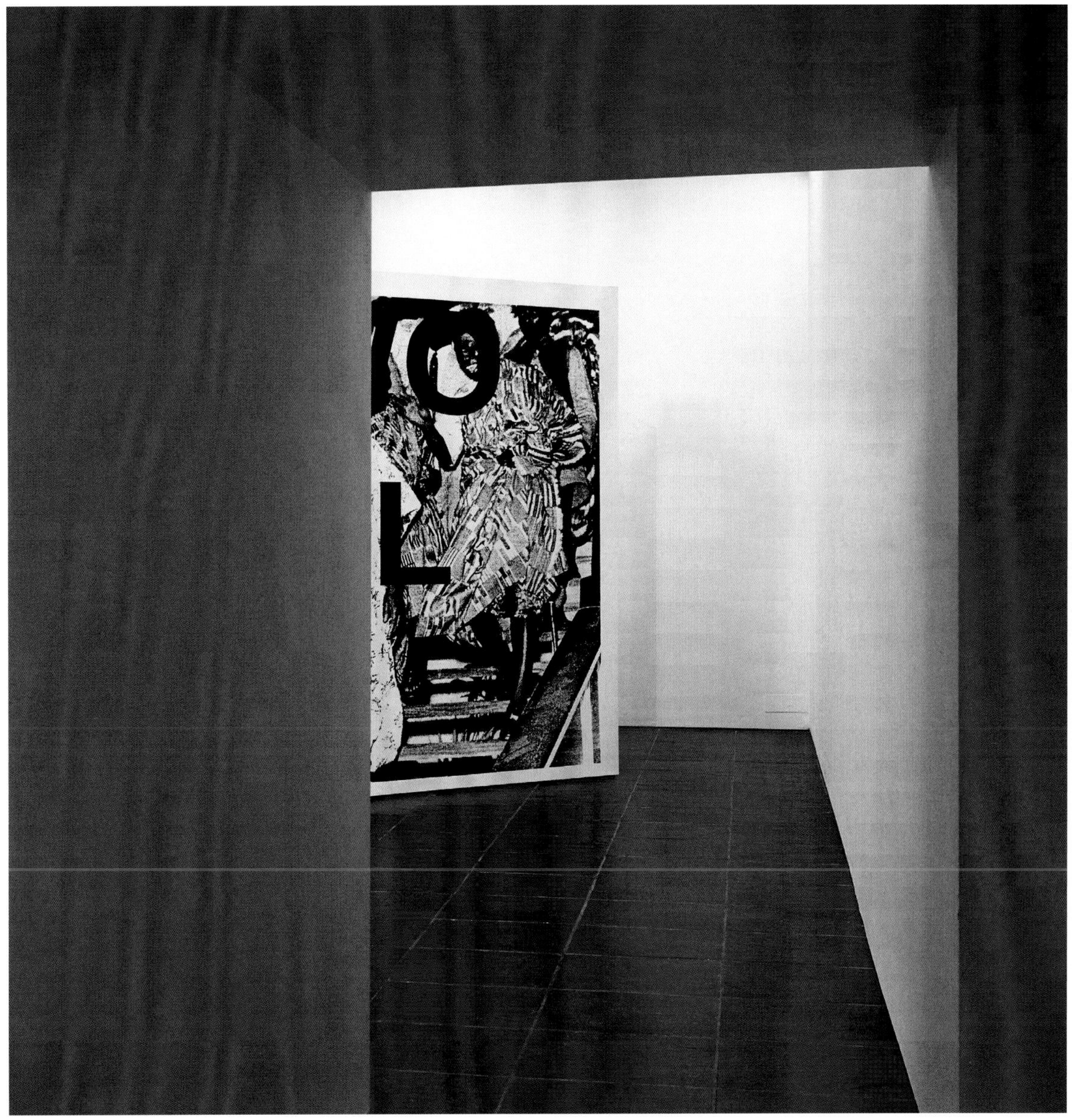

IF THE FUNCTION OF WRITING, 2017
LATEX INK ON ADHESIVE VINYL
DIMENSIONS VARIABLE

INSTALLATION VIEW AT BALTIC CENTRE FOR CONTEMPORARY ART, GATESHEAD, ENGLAND, 2017

at a critical moment in the Black Lives Matter (BLM) campaign, 'an ideological and political intervention' founded by Alicia Garza, Patrisse Cullors and Opal Tometi that erupted following a number of high-profile extra-judicial killings of black people, such as Trayvon Martin, Eric Garner, Michael Brown, Sandra Bland and many others. The New York-based BLM group Millions March NYC and other committed allies took up residence on the sculpture, hosting conversations, meetings and rallies there.

2

From the very beginning, Black Dada was a meta-container that encapsulated the entirety of Pendleton's production and thought. It began as a 'manifesto', meant to be performed live. This text was organized using the techniques of repetition, interpolation and expansion of Language poet Ron Silliman's 'Ketjak', both an overarching name for the entirety of his poetry and the name of the first poem in his book *The Age of Huts* (1986). In its iterating format, Pendleton's manifesto compares with Sol LeWitt's art and resembles both the constrained writing of Oulipo and the 'New Sentence' style pioneered by Silliman. Black Dada also includes the *Black Dada Reader*, in which Pendleton assembles the conceptual foundations that ideologically buttress his practice, as well as a series of black monochrome paintings.

The *Black Dada* painting series expands the permutational methodology of Sol LeWitt's *Incomplete Open Cubes* (1974), in which LeWitt systematically explored the 122 ways of 'not making a cube, all the ways of the cube not being complete'.[11] Pendleton crops, scans and enlarges small fragments of photocopies of LeWitt's white-painted structures, capturing a plane, a corner or an edge. The enlargement is then divided horizontally into halves to form a new whole: a 96 x 76 inch diptych. Superimposed on the image, the words 'Black' and 'Dada' are set in Arial Bold capitals, which Pendleton aligns with the edges of the frame. Letters are subsequently subtracted from each word until only a few remain. Each painting's subtitle reflects the remaining letters. The floating planes cut from LeWitt's cube and applied to fill the composition have an aesthetic affinity with the hard-edge abstractions of artists such as Virginia Jaramillo, Kenneth Noland, Alvin Loving, Frank Stella and James Little. The number of letters and edges varies from painting to painting such that some feature as many as six letters, while others have only one or two, and sometimes only a single edge of the enlarged cube.

Pendleton's visually charged, culturally compounded and conceptually rigorous paintings use the elasticity of the monochrome to amplify the abiding relationship between abstraction and blackness, in its many and varied manifestations. They are information paintings, meaning that they are a vector of aggregated pictorial incidents in which material facts (line, colour, letter) are processed by machines and imprinted upon the divided support that is in actuality a topology of transactions.

The modularity of LeWitt's cubes also influences *Untitled* (2007–16), uniform sets of glazed ceramic cubes, as well as the *System of Display* series, screen-prints on mirror and plexiglass that coincided with the burgeoning Black Dada paintings. *System of Display* presents a way of building an open, networked and incompletable index as a work of art. Pendleton's ideas for the series evolved from and concretized during a residency at the Isabella Stewart Gardner Museum in Boston in the autumn of 2008. He was particularly intrigued by how the museum's collections reflected the proclivities of one individual, resulting in a quirky assemblage of archives and artworks. Living and working in the museum daily, Pendleton aimed to create an object that could respond to the drive to collect, yet forge a critical engagement with such an impulse and with history. He was concerned with important questions of value that play a fundamental role in art museums and was particularly invested in questioning the status of what is collected, archived, preserved and therefore transformed. Such a process of preservation is a process of transformation insofar as the work of art is made to represent social, cultural and economic capital. Thus, the *System of Display* objects needed not only to provide a system of preservation, but to actually fill the system with content (text and image) that could be evaluated and transformed. As a body of work, *System of Display* acts through processes of accumulation and repetition: appropriating language and images drawn from archival resources and presenting them in different configurations and combinations. Pendleton's 'archive' is his personal library of books on literature, art, design, experimental dance, film, history and philosophy. He mines these books – which include *The Short Century: Independence and Liberation Movements in Africa 1945–1994* (the expansive 2001 catalogue for the exhibition curated by Okwui Enwezor) and volumes from the Cinema One and Modern Film Scripts series, specifically those on Jean-Marie Straub and Jean-Luc Godard, to name only a few – for images that he employs throughout the series. Typically, the images are cropped to 9 x 9 inches, but as of 2010 these works have been made, more uncommonly, at the scales of 48 x 48 and 63 x 48 inches. Influenced by artist Joan Jonas's use of mirrors as formal structuring devices that reveal and obscure the viewer's spectatorship, and as tools to fragment and destabilize perception, Pendleton chose to reproduce the cropped images in silk-screen ink on mirrors. Each work also contains one or more superimposed letters, which become enigmatically conflated with the image. As Pendleton describes it, the 'image [is] perhaps functioning as language and the text is perhaps functioning as image'.[12]

As with the *Black Dada* paintings, in encountering the *System of Display* objects, the viewer does not have access to the total system informing, animating and ultimately indexing the work. As in the former black monochromes, the *System of Display* works feature isolated letters from the words referenced in the works' titles. In this case, words and letters are again sourced from Pendleton's library. He often returns to one of his favourite books, Silliman's *The Alphabet*, and pulls a letter/word pair from its first sentence: 'If the function of writing is to express the world…' Other selections are made from lines in the Black Dada manifesto; choreographer, filmmaker and writer Yvonne Rainer's memoir *Feelings Are Facts* (2006); writer and conceptual artist Helen Mirra's *Cloud, the, 3* (2007), which is an index rendered from John Dewey's *Reconstruction in Philosophy* (1920); and a range of twentieth and twenty-first century experimental writers such as Susan Howe.[13] A kind of bibliographic citation, the title of the work includes finally the selected word, the selected letter, and a caption for the selected image.

For example, in *System of Display, A (NATIONAL/ Ian Berry, couple dancing during the Independence celebrations, Congo, 1960)* (2017) the image of the couple has been cropped with only the woman's face remaining, which is silk-screened onto the back-mirrored panel, while the glass veneer has a floating letter A printed on the reverse, drawn from the word NATIONAL and placed in the position it would occupy if the entire word had been printed, from left to right. The result of such an approach that relies upon operating at the subterranean level of the work (its concept) raises the prospect of misreading and failure, but for Pendleton that is precisely the point: illegibility marks and thereby activates the work's poetic potential, which is to say, activates a strategy. The viewer, the third element of this three-way exchange, is implicated in the process. Captured by and reflected in the mirror, we are interpolated into the web of citations and subtractions.

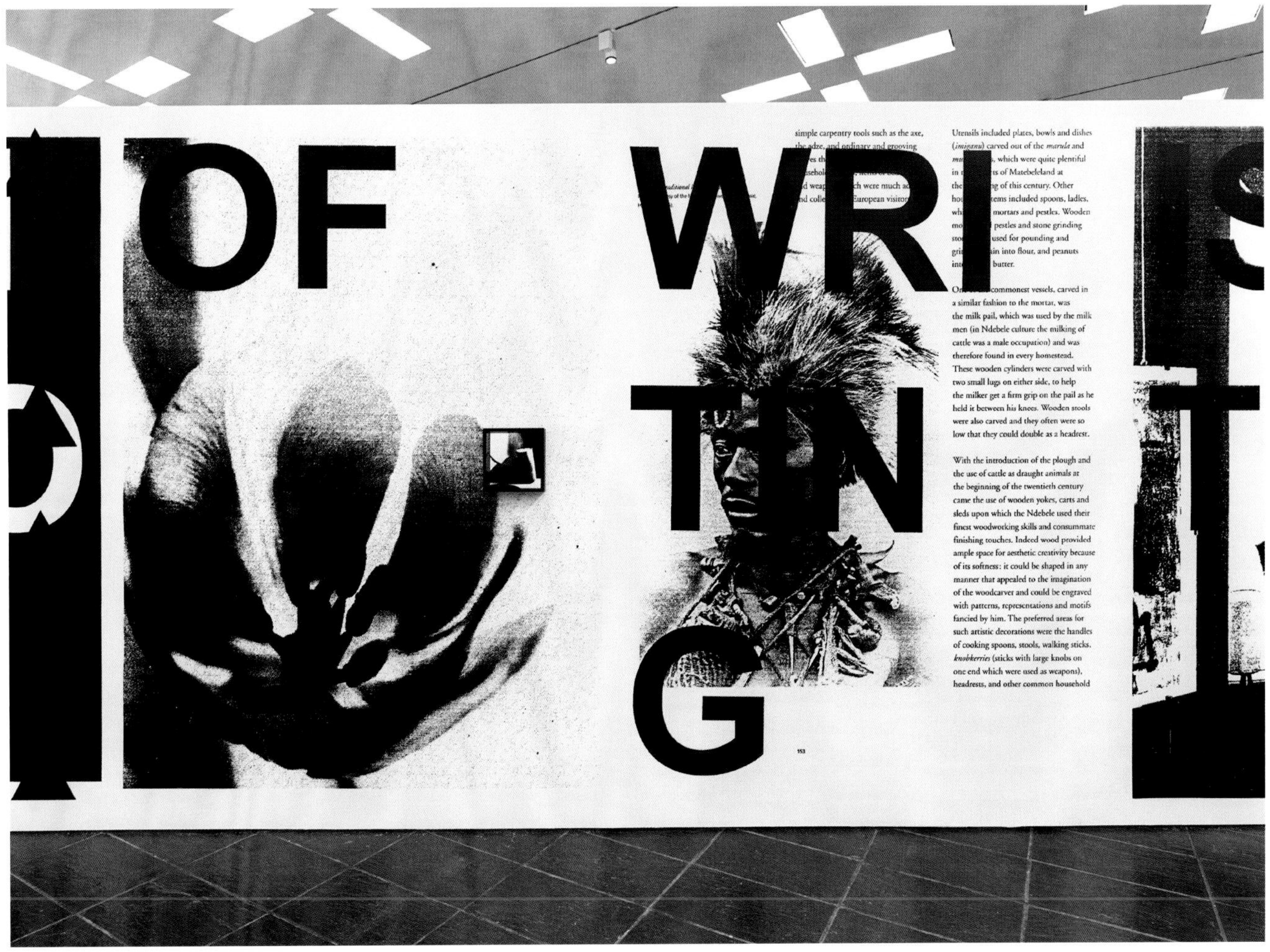

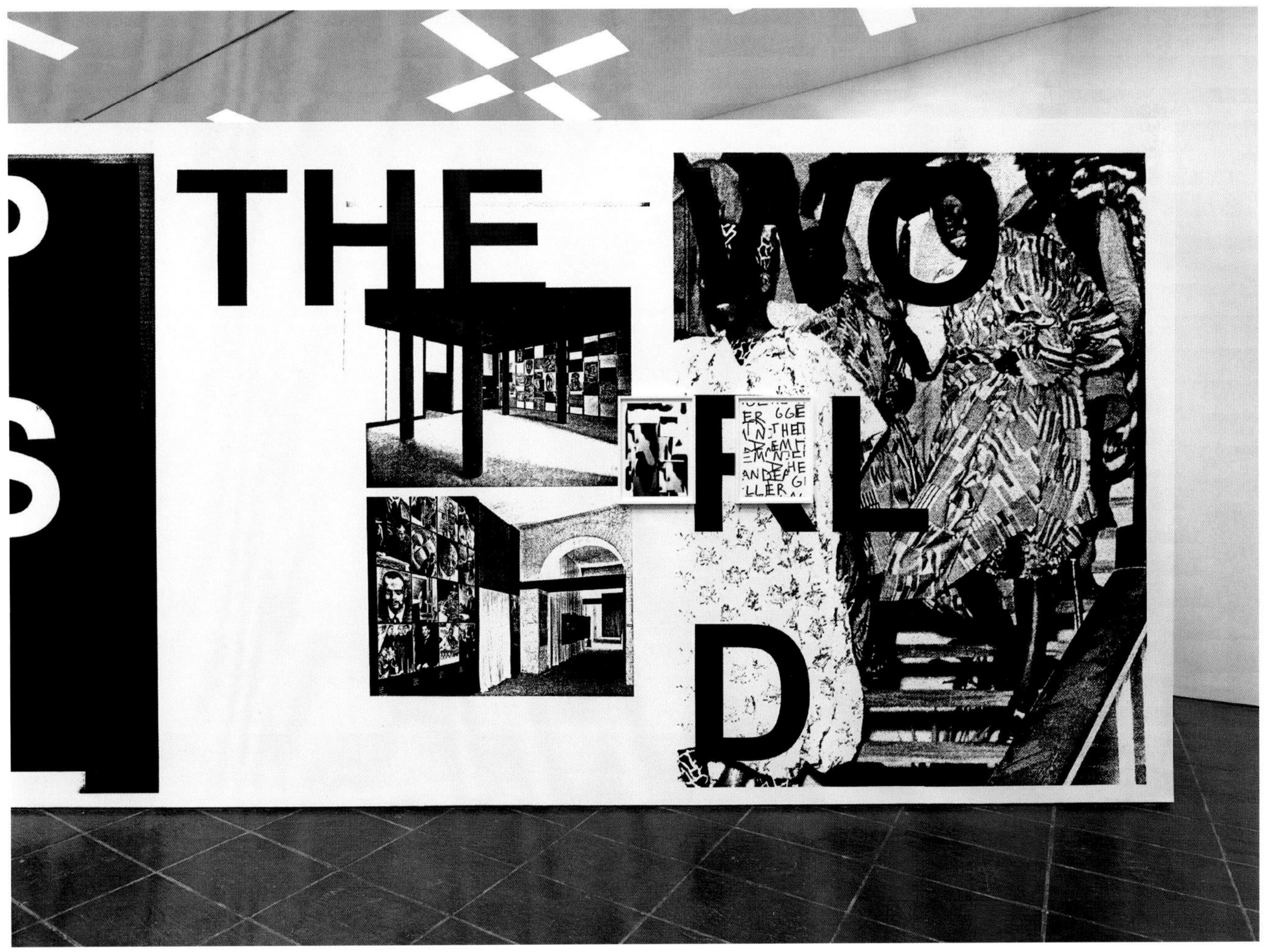

top,
IF THE FUNCTION OF WRITING,
2017
LATEX INK ON ADHESIVE VINYL
DIMENSIONS VARIABLE

SYSTEM OF DISPLAY, U (SUN/ JOSEFA ZIKÁNOVÁ, UNTITLED, EXERCISE FROM THE STATE SCHOOL OF GRAPHIC ART, PRAGUE, 1935), 2016
SILK-SCREEN INK ON PLEXIGLASS AND MIRROR
25 X 25 X 8 CM

bottom,
IF THE FUNCTION OF WRITING,
2017
LATEX INK ON ADHESIVE VINYL
DIMENSIONS VARIABLE

from left,
UNTITLED, 2016
COLLAGE ON PAPER
39 X 27 CM

UNTITLED, 2017
COLLAGE ON PAPER
39 X 27 CM

INSTALLATION VIEW AT BALTIC CENTRE FOR CONTEMPORARY ART, GATESHEAD, ENGLAND, 2017

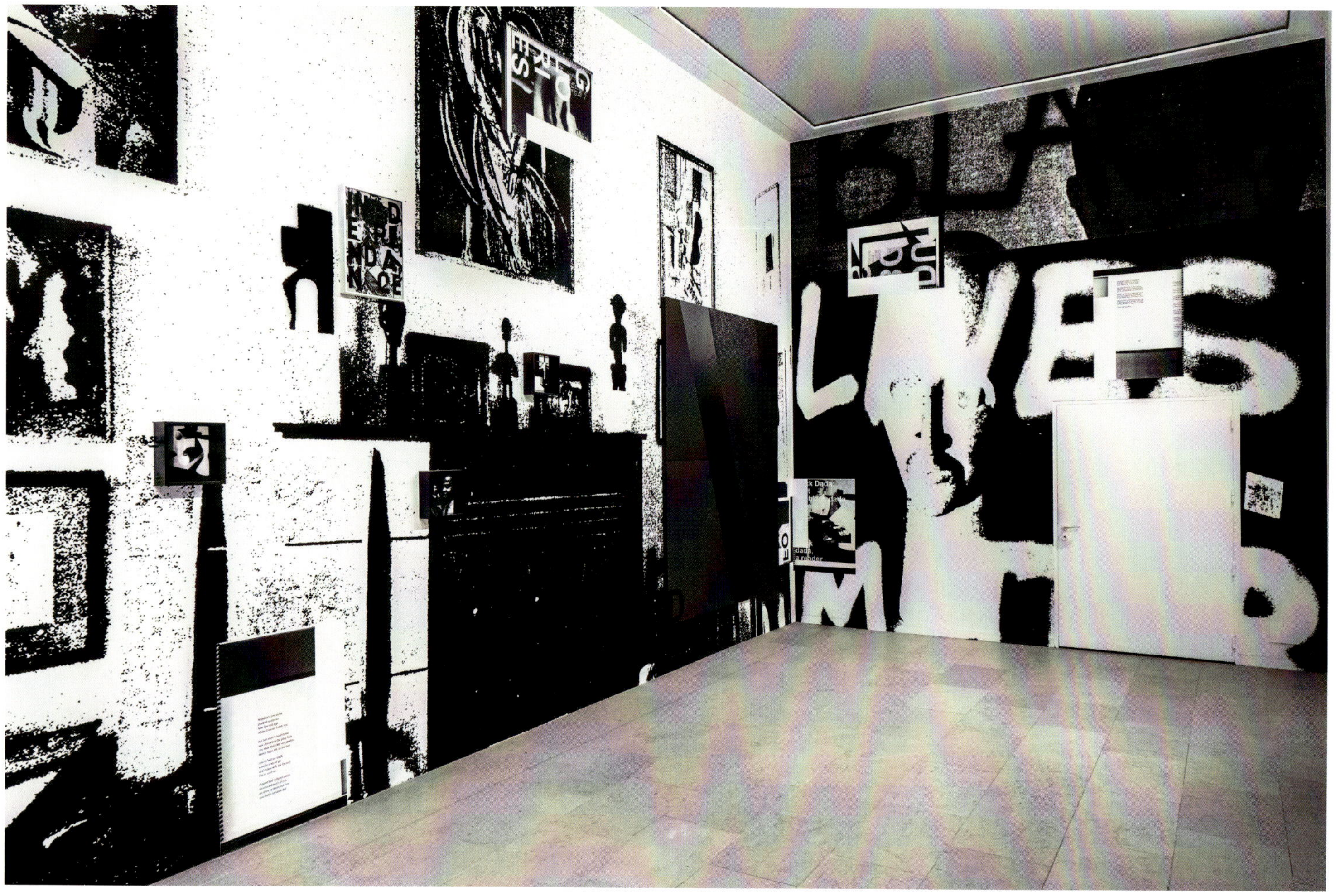

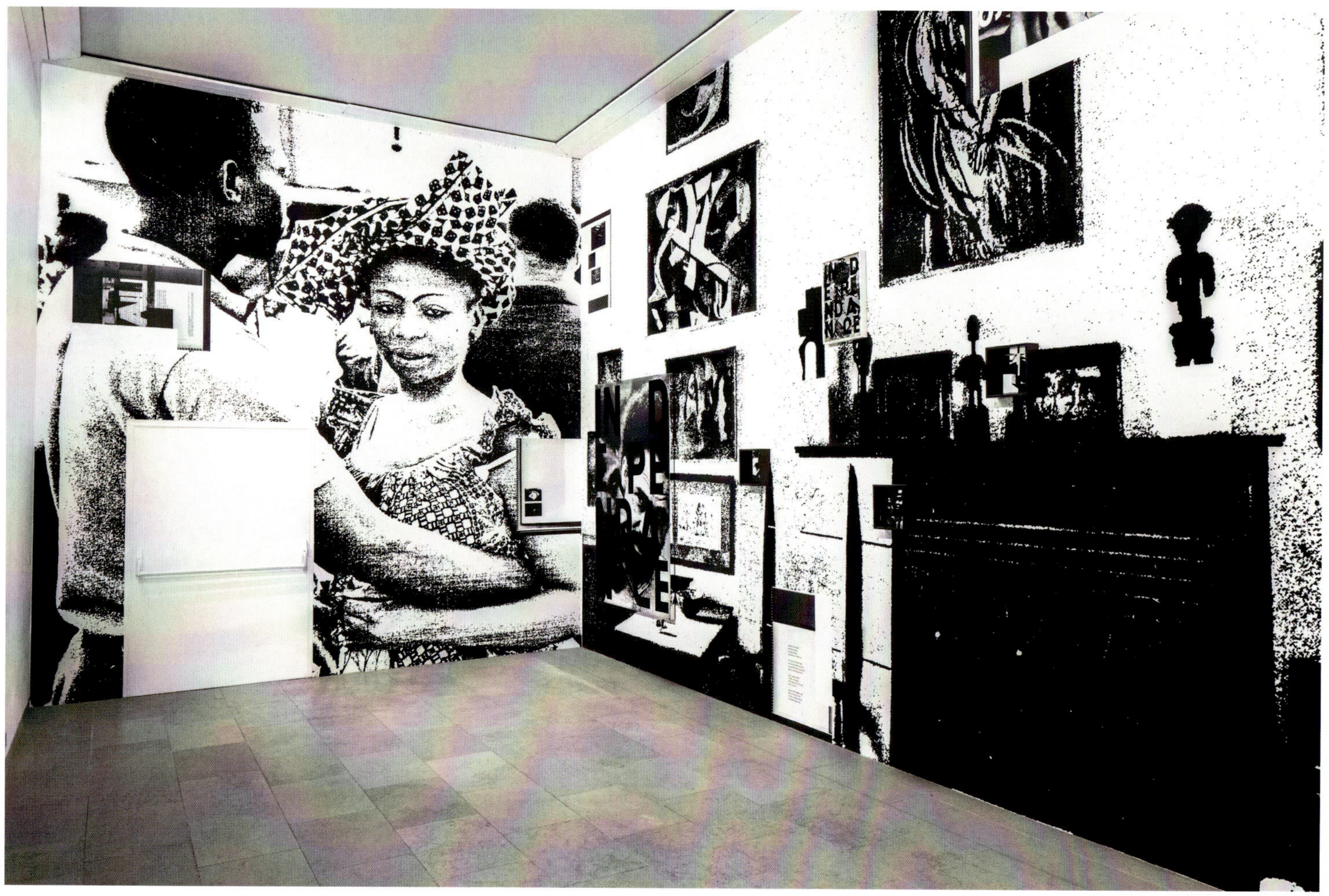

top, back wall,
BLACK LIVES MATTER #1, 2015
LATEX INK ON ADHESIVE VINYL
DIMENSIONS VARIABLE

bottom, back wall,
IAN BERRY, COUPLE DANCING DURING THE INDEPENDENCE CELEBRATIONS, CONGO, 1960 (WALL WORK), 2015
LATEX INK ON ADHESIVE VINYL
DIMENSIONS VARIABLE

next page,
INTERIOR OF LOUISE AND WALTER ARENSBERG APARTMENT, 1919, 2015
LATEX INK ON ADHESIVE VINYL
DIMENSIONS VARIABLE

from left,
INDEPENDANCE (HARVEST: 3,000 YEARS), 2014–15
SILK-SCREEN INK ON MIRROR POLISHED STAINLESS STEEL
193 X 133 CM

SYSTEM OF DISPLAY, E (MEMORIES/HEINZ LOEW, PRIMARY THREE-DIMENSIONAL DESIGN ELEMENTS, 1928), 2012
SILK-SCREEN INK ON PLEXIGLASS AND MIRROR
25 X 25 X 8 CM

MAGICIENNE, 2015
SILK-SCREEN INK ON MIRROR POLISHED STAINLESS STEEL
48 X 33 CM

SYSTEM OF DISPLAY, G (WAITING/IAN BERRY, COUPLE DANCING, GHANA, 1962), 2015
SILK-SCREEN INK ON PLEXIGLASS AND MIRROR
25 X 25 X 8 CM

SYSTEM OF DISPLAY, H (HOUR/PRELIMINARY COURSE OF L. MOHOLY-NAGY, N.D.), 2015
SILK-SCREEN INK ON PLEXIGLASS AND MIRROR
25 X 25 X 8 CM

BLACK DADA (D), 2014
SILK-SCREEN INK ON CANVAS
2 PANELS: OVERALL 244 X 193 CM
EACH: 122 X 193 CM

INSTALLATION VIEW AT BELGIAN PAVILION AT THE 56TH VENICE BIENNALE, 2015

Both the *Black Dada* paintings and the *System of Display* objects employ varying degrees of abstraction. In fact, one is a kind of release valve for the other, an escape route errantly built into the concepts and methods of execution. The meaning of abstraction is multivalent and operates on different scales and different degrees in these works, as well as others. Non-objective art is a capacious space; indeed, Pendleton's concern for abstraction has less to do with its formal distinctions and more to do with what it is that abstraction can do. In this way, abstraction is a set of rules, tools and methods to be exploited in the work both as matter and as concept. Abstraction marks something in order to obliquely and contingently suggest some deeper meaning, context and history. Language receives the extreme treatment, annihilated in a playful rather than violent way. In this sense, Pendleton's sensibility recalls the work of Brazilian Concrete artist Augusto de Campos, whose visual art combined poetic language with geometric and graphic modes of presentation. Distilling the legible is not reductive. Rather, in tending towards opacity, the fragmentation of language (in and as art) is additive, an act of distention, of expanding profusely in a theoretical sense. These works leverage the perceived perfection of the silk-screen and the unruly inconsistency of the hand, the figurative as text fragment and the abstract line as blur.

The *Black Dada Reader*, published in 2017, is a codex for the work created thus far and an indicator of what is to come. It was initially realized as an evolving compilation of photocopied texts across genre, subject matter and time by Silliman, W. E. B. Du Bois, Stokely Carmichael, Adrian Piper, Hugo Ball, Gertrude Stein, LeRoi Jones (Amiri Baraka), Sun Ra, Pope.L, Ad Reinhardt and others. It performs a critical mimicry of institutional form that is also apparent in the floor-to-ceiling *Wall Works*, first realized in 2015 in the Belgian Pavilion at the Venice Biennale.[14] Perhaps more than any other of Pendleton's works, these installations convey the importance of context and display for the artist. Presented on a monumental scale, they are staging grounds in which arrangements of mirrored objects, black monochromes, 'posters' or book pages are theatrically assembled. The wallpaper-like surface is itself a collage of images and text, and text-images.

In Venice, the installation was a room-sized assemblage of the many bodies of work created to date, including material from the *Reader* (which from this time would increasingly find its way into exhibitions). The wall covering was a palimpsest of an ecstatic *System of Display* with levelled and blurred archival images, as well as spray paint (the first use of this material in Pendleton's art), used to incorporate the words 'Black Lives Matter' into the composition.

In addition to the installation inside the Pavilion, Pendleton fabricated a flag for the movement and installed it on top of the building, which was built during the reign of Belgium's King Leopold II and undoubtedly financed by the massive colonial exploitation, resource extraction and human annihilation of the Congo instigated entirely by this one individual. A larger version of the flag was commissioned by the Frieze Art Fair in New York as part of 'Assembly', a special programme showcasing an array of performances and visual icons of protest, ritual and alternative modes of collectivity. The flag was planted on the bank of Randall's Island at Hell Gate, where the East and Harlem Rivers meet between Harlem and the South Bronx, near what is now officially called Scylla Point, though noted on historical maps as 'Negro Point'.

3

Pendleton coalesces assemblages of time and space through what he describes as 'radical juxtapositions', citing Susan Sontag's essay 'Happenings: An Art of Radical Juxtaposition'. These are poignantly explored in his video portraits, where methods of improvisation, montage, and conflation of figure and ground are presented on parallel tracks in order to propose something new. Such a sensibility also operates in the *Independance* works (2013–), in which type from a 1960 Congolese independence banner is printed over other archival images on mirror polished stainless steel. Pendleton would also use this material and fabrication method to create complex figure-ground exchanges in his letter sculptures (2015–), which have a heightened collaged sensibility. To make them, he silk-screened images sourced from his archive onto letters from the phrase 'BLACK DADA' and the word 'WE', a return to the 'WE ARE…' statements in the 'Black Dada' manifesto.

Beginning as posters and maturing as framed transparencies hung in grids, as well as presented in an artist's book titled *Anthology* (2018), Pendleton's Mylar 'drawings' abstract and mask their source images through the machinations of the photocopier and silk-screen, and incorporate the artist's own mark-making. In order to achieve the kind of scale and immensity for which many of his works are known, Pendleton arranges multiple Mylars together, encompassing entire walls. For each Mylar composition, Pendleton returns to his machine of choice, the photocopier, and layers his own cut-out geometric shapes, marks and handwritten text, often combining these with images from books of masks, ceramics and the decolonization of Africa. He then layers and reassembles this motley crew, prints the arrangements in ink on Mylar and situates them in black frames that are typically arranged in a grid. The grid, such a singular structure in modernist abstraction and conceptual art, here contains the complex network of text, images and motifs long circulating and accumulating in Pendleton's art. The historical and material accumulations of modernism, rendered as a typology across genres, styles, epochs and icons, are levelled in and by the colour black.

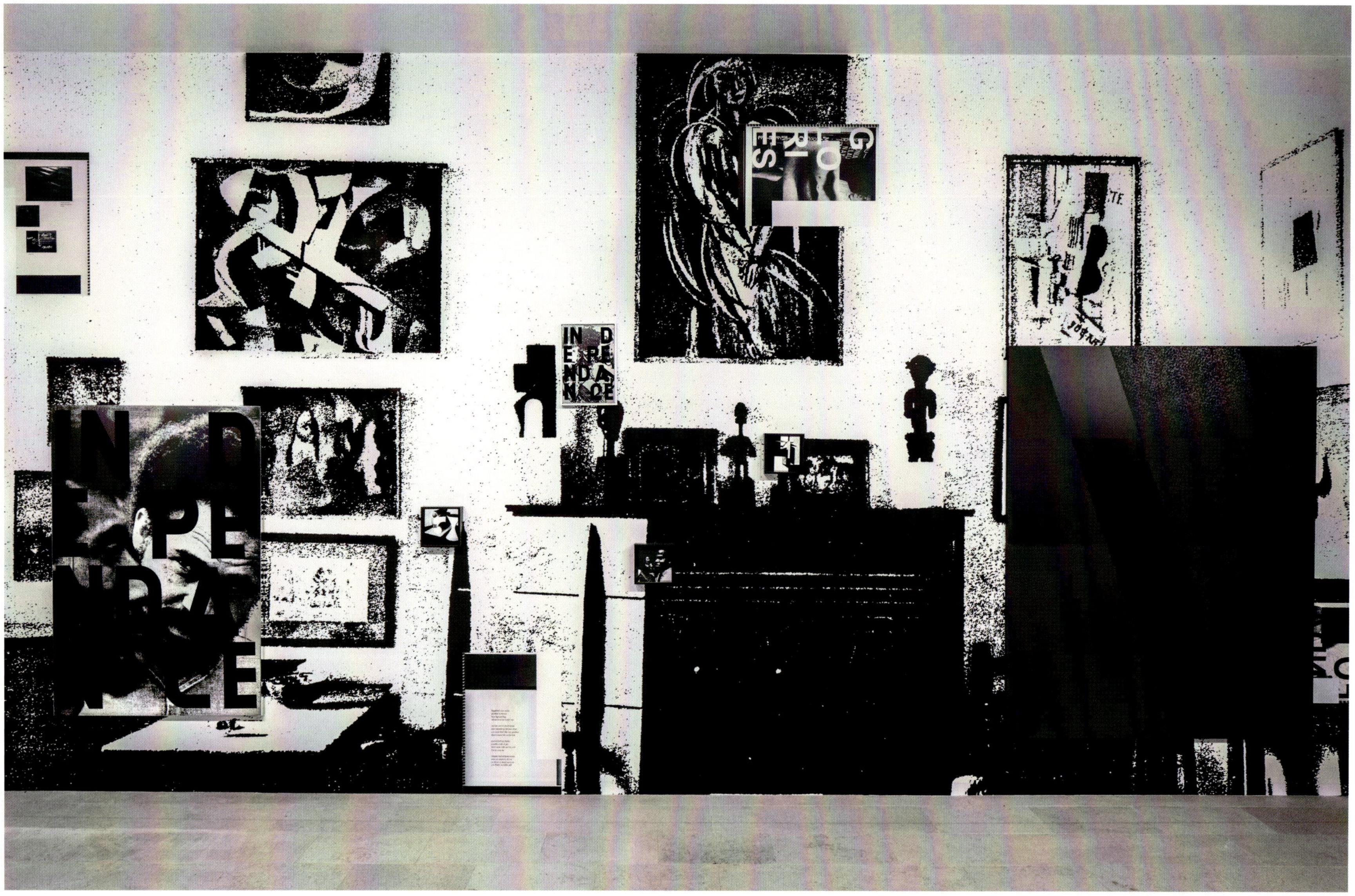

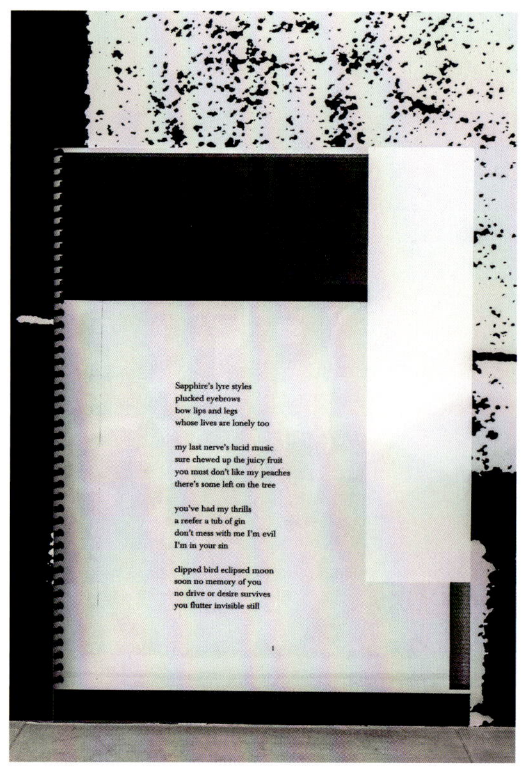
Sapphire's lyre styles
plucked eyebrows
bow lips and legs
whose lives are lonely too

my last nerve's lucid music
sure chewed up the juicy fruit
you must don't like my peaches
there's some left on the tree

you've had my thrills
a reefer a tub of gin
don't mess with me I'm evil
I'm in your sin

clipped bird eclipsed moon
soon no memory of you
no drive or desire survives
you flutter invisible still

PERSONNE ET LES AUTRES, 2015
EXHIBITION DETAILS

BELGIAN PAVILION AT THE
56TH VENICE BIENNALE, 2015

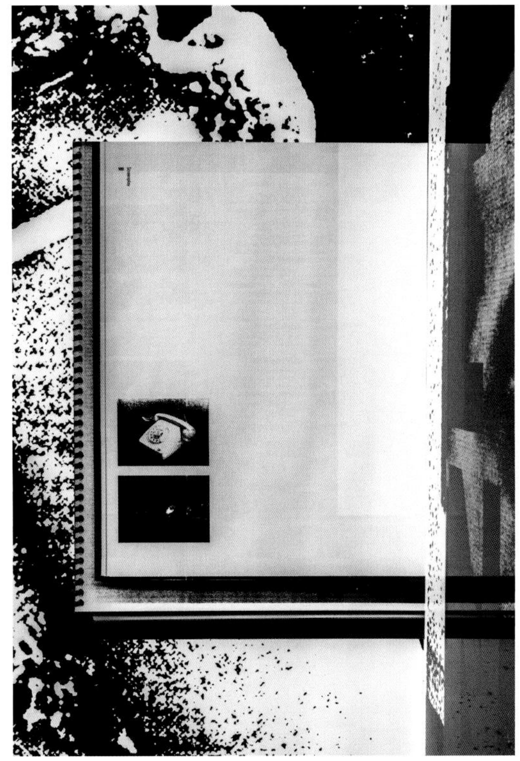

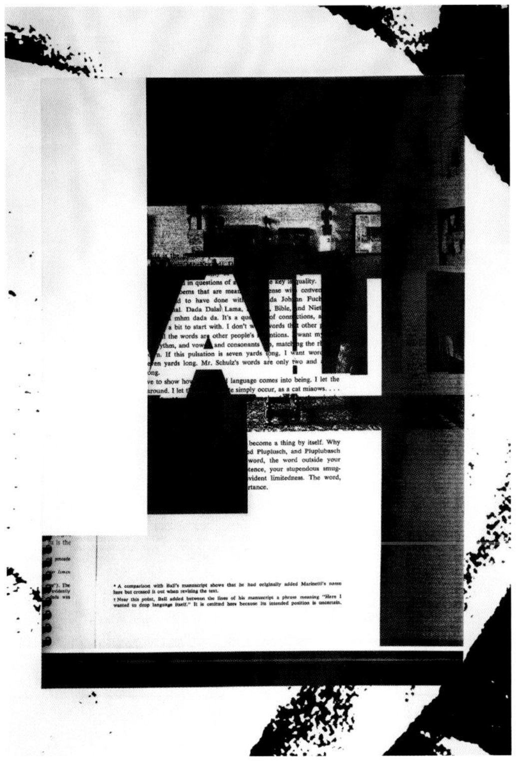

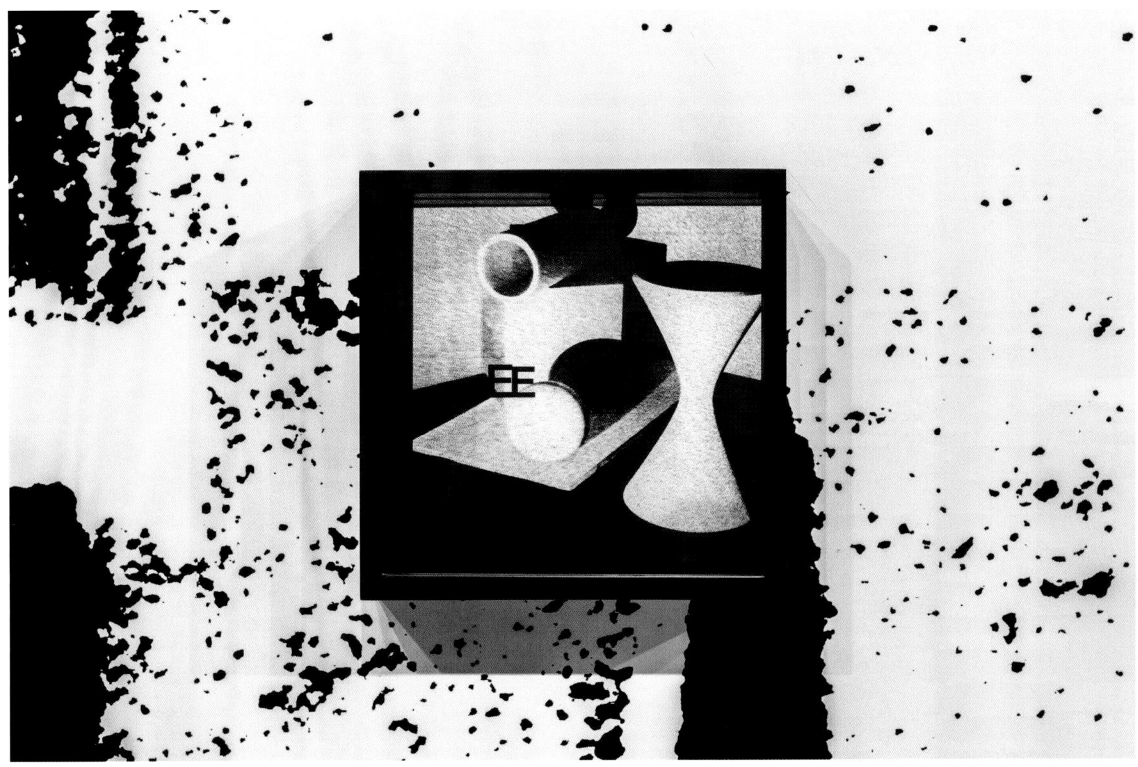

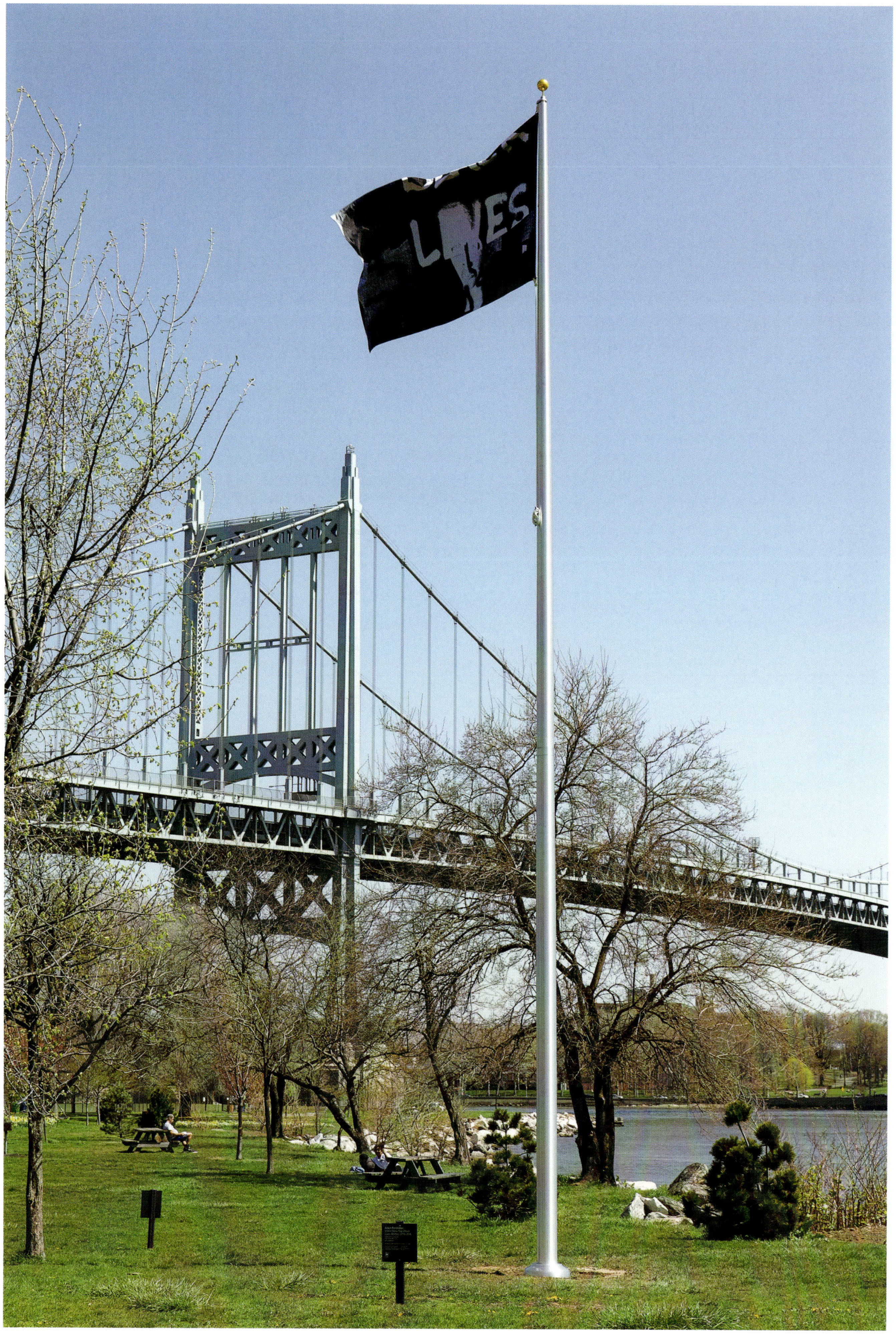

BLACK DADA FLAG (BLACK LIVES MATTER), 2015–18
DIGITAL PRINT ON POLYESTER
183 X 274 CM

INSTALLATION VIEW AT FRIEZE NEW YORK, RANDALL'S ISLAND, 2018

BLACK DADA SCULPTURE #1 (DETAIL), 2015
SILK-SCREEN INK ON MIRROR POLISHED STAINLESS STEEL
3 PARTS: OVERALL DIMENSIONS VARIABLE
LETTER A: 119 X 47 X 2 CM
LETTER D: 119 X 100 X 2 CM
LETTER K: 119 X 105 X 2 CM

next pages,
UNTITLED, 2019
SILK-SCREEN INK ON MYLAR
27 PARTS: OVERALL DIMENSIONS VARIABLE
EACH: 97 X 74 CM

INSTALLATION VIEW AT GALERIE MAX HETZLER, BERLIN, 2019

Recalling Robert Rauschenberg's Combines, the method of recycling silk-screened material in varying configurations in these works would inform Pendleton's first video artwork *BAND* (2009). Opening and closing with the gospel song 'Standing in the Need of Prayer', *BAND*, a twelve-and-a-half minute-long three-channel video, employs live-music performance; draws on Jean-Luc Godard's *Sympathy for the Devil* (1968); documents San Francisco band Deerhoof in the process of creating and recording a new song; and overlays audio from *Teddy*, a 1971 short documentary film about a single day in a black American youth's life whom we hear contemplating his involvement with the Black Panthers.[15] Throughout the piece, images appear as incongruent pulsations that do not corroborate what is heard until the end. For example, the artist interweaves Deerhoof's rehearsals, during which the song lyric 'This is a stick-up! This is a stick-up! / Smash the windows! Smash the windows!' repeats at inconsistent intervals alongside recorded audio of *Teddy* and American soul music. The lyric is actually taken from one of Amiri Baraka's poems, which is also recited in the portion of Godard's film that features black radicals in the junk yard. The only moment in the film when Pendleton does not employ montage is near the end when an extended clip from *Teddy*, captioned 'Black Panthers Headquarters – 1969', shows an abandoned street with police officers carrying rifles and with gunshots audible, alongside Teddy's personal recollection of the day's events, concluding with a resonant 'I judge from experience'. *BAND* would be followed by the video portrait works *Lorraine O'Grady: A Portrait* (2012), *My Education: A Portrait of David Hilliard* (2011–14), *Just Back from Los Angeles: A Portrait of Yvonne Rainer* (2016–17) and *Ishmael in the Garden: A Portrait of Ishmael Houston-Jones* (2018).

Lorraine O'Grady: A Portrait indexes the work of the important conceptual artist and cultural critic. The camera is painfully yet generously close to its subject, at times cropping out most of her mane of hair, fixated on her face. The work conveys a sense of chaos, imperfection and chance, facilitated at the start, when, in the process of setting up the camera and correcting sound levels, there is an ease and charming banter between Pendleton and O'Grady. Pendleton has O'Grady read from a prepared script, a document that conflates Lyn Hejinian's long, highly structured rule-based prose poem *My Life* (1980)[16] with Jena Osman's poem 'Hydra Village' (1995)[17] and the titles of artworks O'Grady has created over the decades.[18] A montage of short takes of O'Grady describing how conservative and marginalized black artists were in 1980 recalls the impetus for her Mademoiselle Bourgeois Noire persona and her guerrilla performances at Just Above Midtown Gallery and the New Museum. She recalls her romantic relationships, her life as a rock critic for *Rolling Stone* and *The Village Voice*, her time as a teacher at the School of Visual Arts, her writing and interest in language, her inspiration for creating *Art Is…*, a collective performance as street procession presented in Harlem

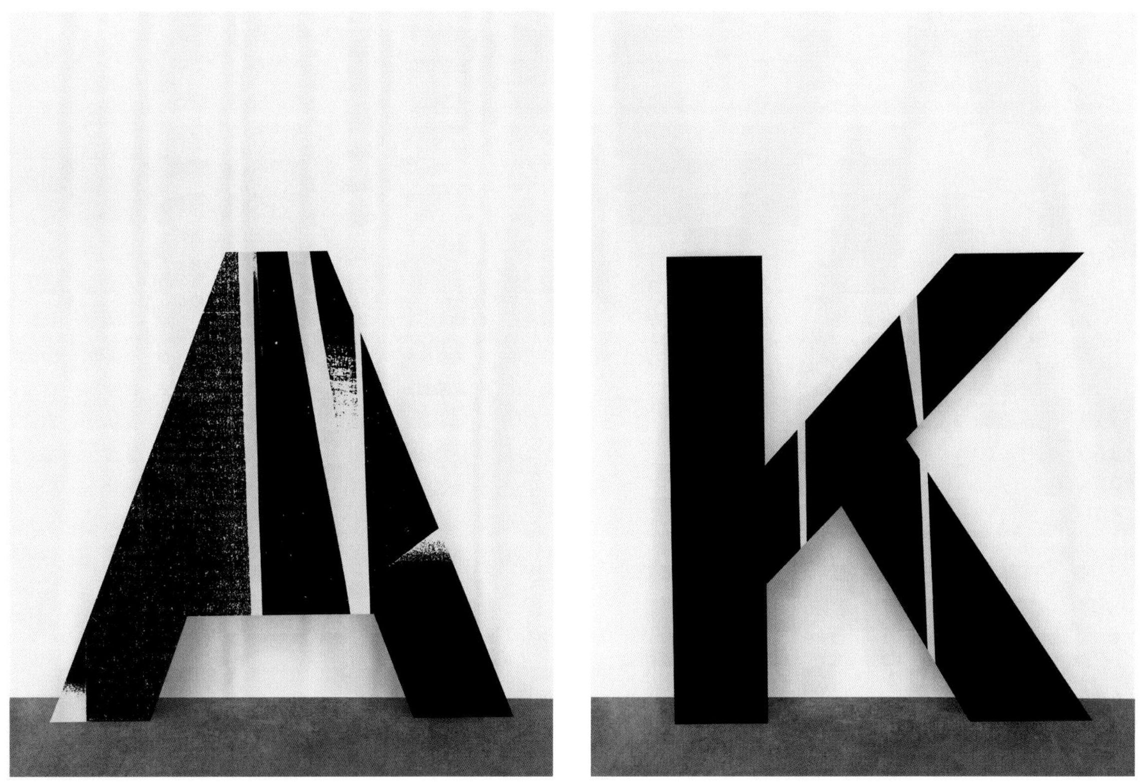

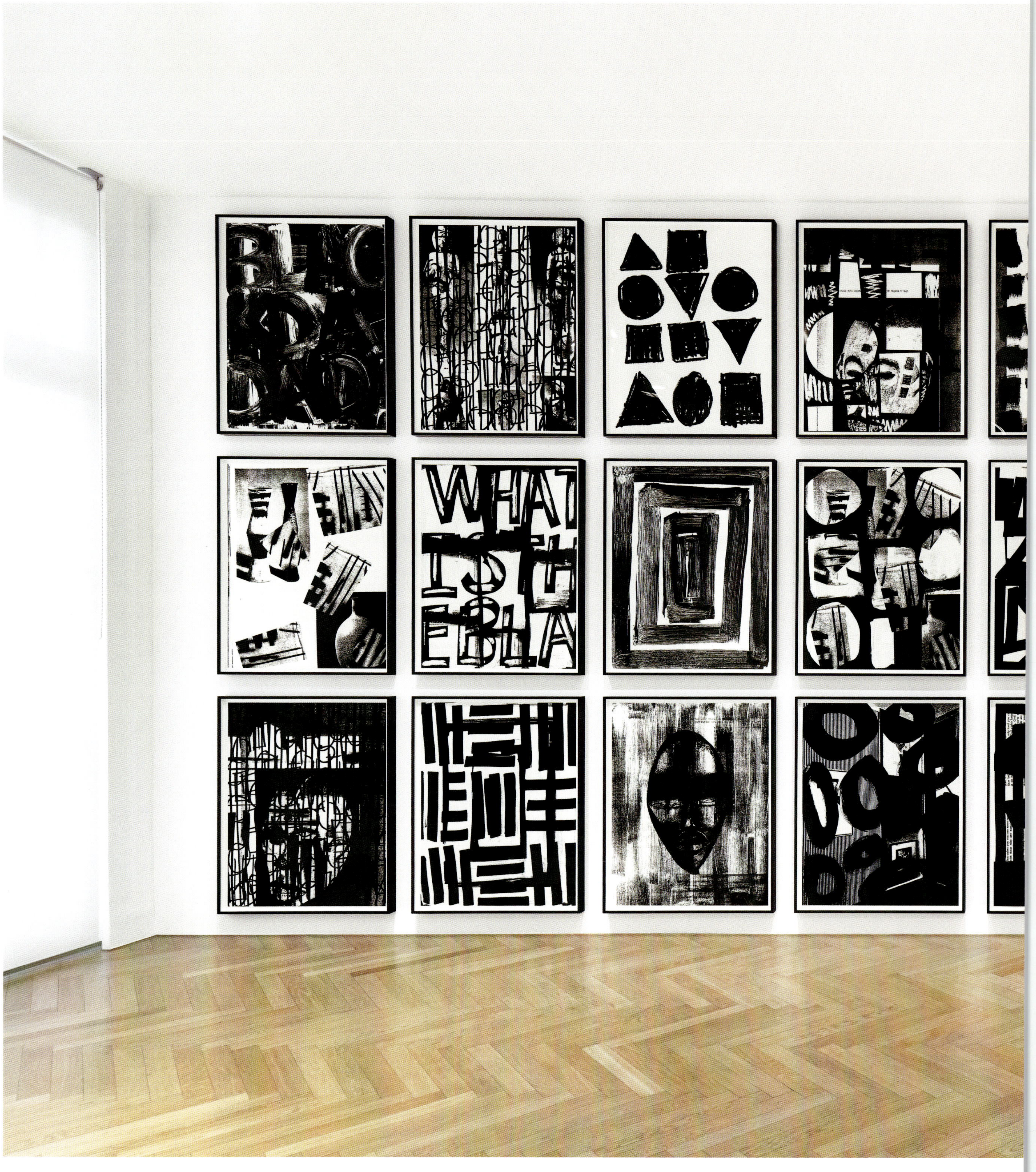
WHAT

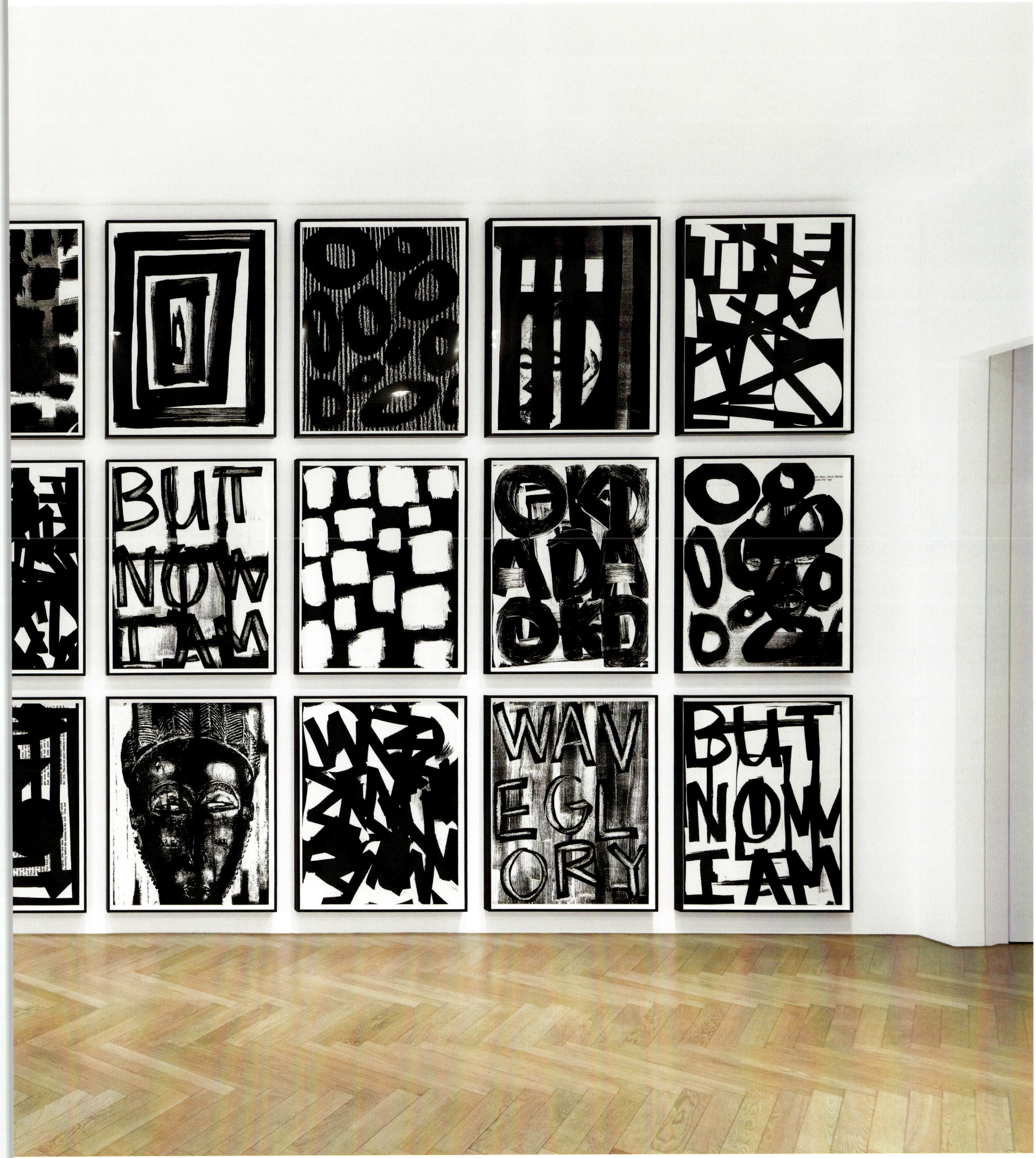
BUT
NOW
I AM
WAV
EGL
ORY
BUT
NOW
I AM

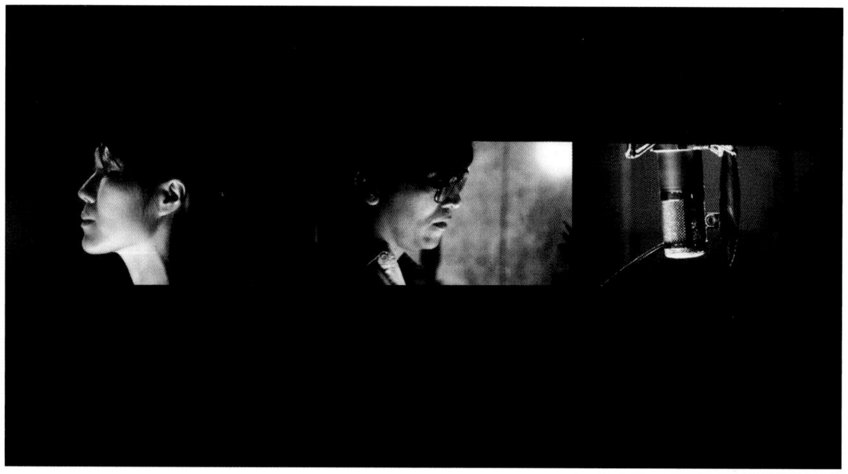

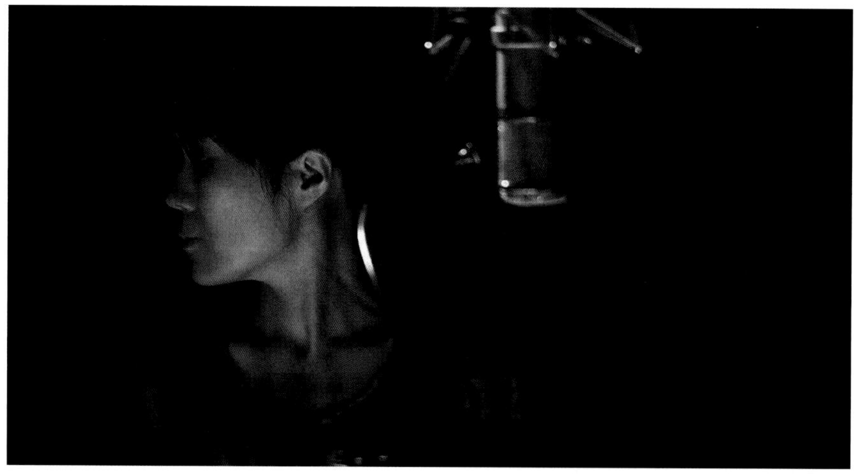

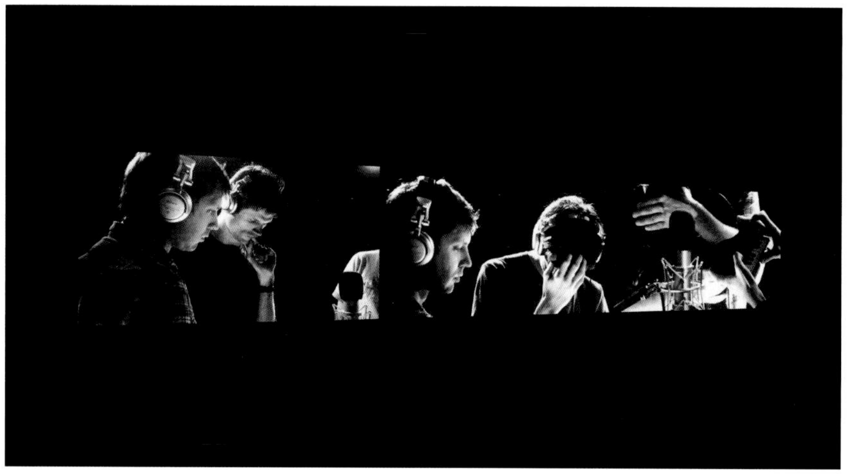

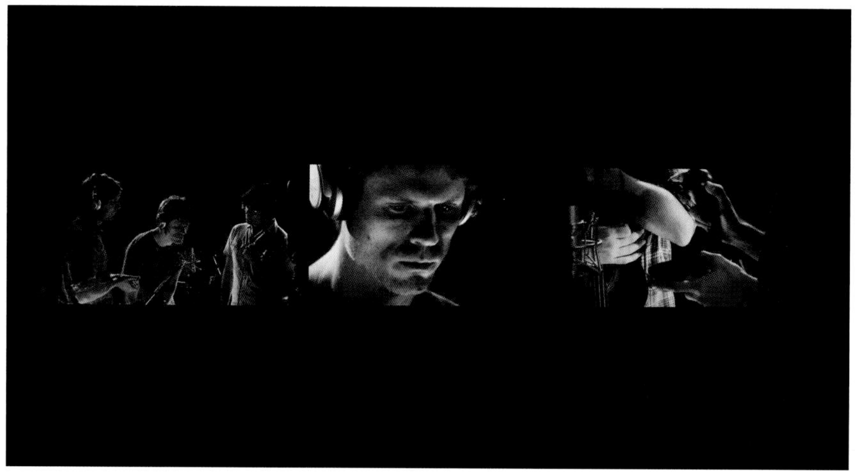

in 1983 during the African-American Day Parade. Pendleton includes the performance images from the parade – essentially a portrait of a community before the crack epidemic and conservative policies of the Reagan administration have taken their toll. The script, drawn from language not wholly O'Grady's own at this point in the film, is ambiguous yet emotional in register as she reminisces about her father and her sister and their deaths, punctuated throughout with the word 'rest'.

In *My Education: A Portrait of David Hilliard*, Pendleton investigates the systems in which blackness is reified through the historical particulars of Black Panther Party founding member David Hilliard. The video was shown for the first time at Pace Gallery in New York in 2014 alongside *Untitled (water)* works (2014), silk-screen-on-mirror paintings that borrow from photographs of water surfaces taken by Josef Albers in 1929 as experiments in order and chaos, and as meditations on memory and movement. Pendleton offers the three-screen, double-sided video as a kind of counterpart to his all-black *Black Dada* paintings, as if to reactivate that which was foreclosed by his material choices. Here, the autobiographical aspects of a concept of racial blackness are presented.

The approximately nine-minute video comprises documentary footage that Pendleton and a film crew captured in 2011 as they drove with Hilliard through a series of neighbourhoods in Oakland, California, the prime loci of the Black Panther organization. They go from empty lots, streets, houses and storefronts, where the Panthers operated programmes for the black working poor, to the site of the 6 April 1968 shoot-out in which Bobby Hutton, Black Panther treasurer, was fatally wounded by police (two days after the assassination of Martin Luther King Jr.). In the video, Hilliard, a lecturer, educator and former Black Panther chief of staff, recalls the shoot-out and the series of events that led to Hutton's death.

opposite,
BAND, 2009
THREE-CHANNEL BLACK-AND-WHITE VIDEO
12 MIN. 29 SEC.
DIMENSIONS VARIABLE

below, from left,
UNTITLED (WATER), 2014
SILK-SCREEN INK ON MIRROR POLISHED STAINLESS STEEL
305 X 152 CM

UNTITLED (WATER), 2014
SILK-SCREEN INK ON MIRROR POLISHED STAINLESS STEEL
305 X 152 CM

INSTALLATION VIEW AT PACE GALLERY, NEW YORK, 2014

Filmed in black-and-white with a meditative, introspective timbre, the video employs multiple camera angles that are montaged to foreground the conflict between Hilliard's recollections and the official state and federal records, as well as to highlight the dissonance between the various interpretations of the Black Panthers in American history. Interspersed throughout are close-ups of architecture, such as expanses of craggy, rocklike grey plaster (a surface typical of homes in California), that act as visual pauses. When an eruption of plaster appears in the midst of Hilliard's cadenced account of the shooting, the insistence of his voice in combination with the abstracted images reminds us that even when the subject is not visible and the scene of the crime has been disinfected long ago, the subject is continuously and insistently called upon again and again.

With *My Education: A Portrait of David Hilliard*, Pendleton slices and sculpts sections of reality that link the moment of then to the moment of now. The portrait inserts a new historical record into the collective archive. It reorients our attention to film's ability not only to observe a life or to materialize a concept but to examine larger social and cultural events in order to reconsider them entirely. Pendleton joins past and present, suspends time and space, much as Hilliard's contemplations enrapture and carry us along.

Considerations of the complexities of personal recollection are also a through line in *Just Back from Los Angeles: A Portrait of Yvonne Rainer*, made with the choreographer, dancer and filmmaker Yvonne Rainer. The pairing of the two artists illuminated a myriad of intriguing intersections and points of departure shared in their art: a love of language, as well as deconstructed and fragmented forms that mine everyday dimensions of life for artistic material, frequently deployed with a sense of irony and a preference for minimalist expression. They are both invested in art's revolutionary possibilities for social change. For Rainer, such a sensibility is evinced in her anti-war protest dances in the 1970s and the feminist dimensions of her radical choreographic style and films. For Pendleton, the socio-political imperative is most recently manifest in artworks such as his Black Lives Matter flag, *Untitled (A Victim of American Democracy)* paintings and wall works.

Pendleton began this work, in his typical fashion, by constructing a script, a pastiche that commences with excerpts from Rainer's own memoir, *Feelings Are Facts: A Life* (2006), including the manuscript 'A list of shameful conditions and occurrences', and a letter from dancer Barbara Dilley, in which nearly every sentence selected begins with the phrase 'I remember…'. These autobiographical sections are interspersed with writings foundational to Pendleton's work, including the Black Power addresses with which he was consumed at the time, Stokely Carmichael's 'The Pitfalls of Liberalism' (1969) and Malcolm X's 'The Ballot or the Bullet' (1964), as well as Keeanga-Yamahtta Taylor's *From Black Lives*

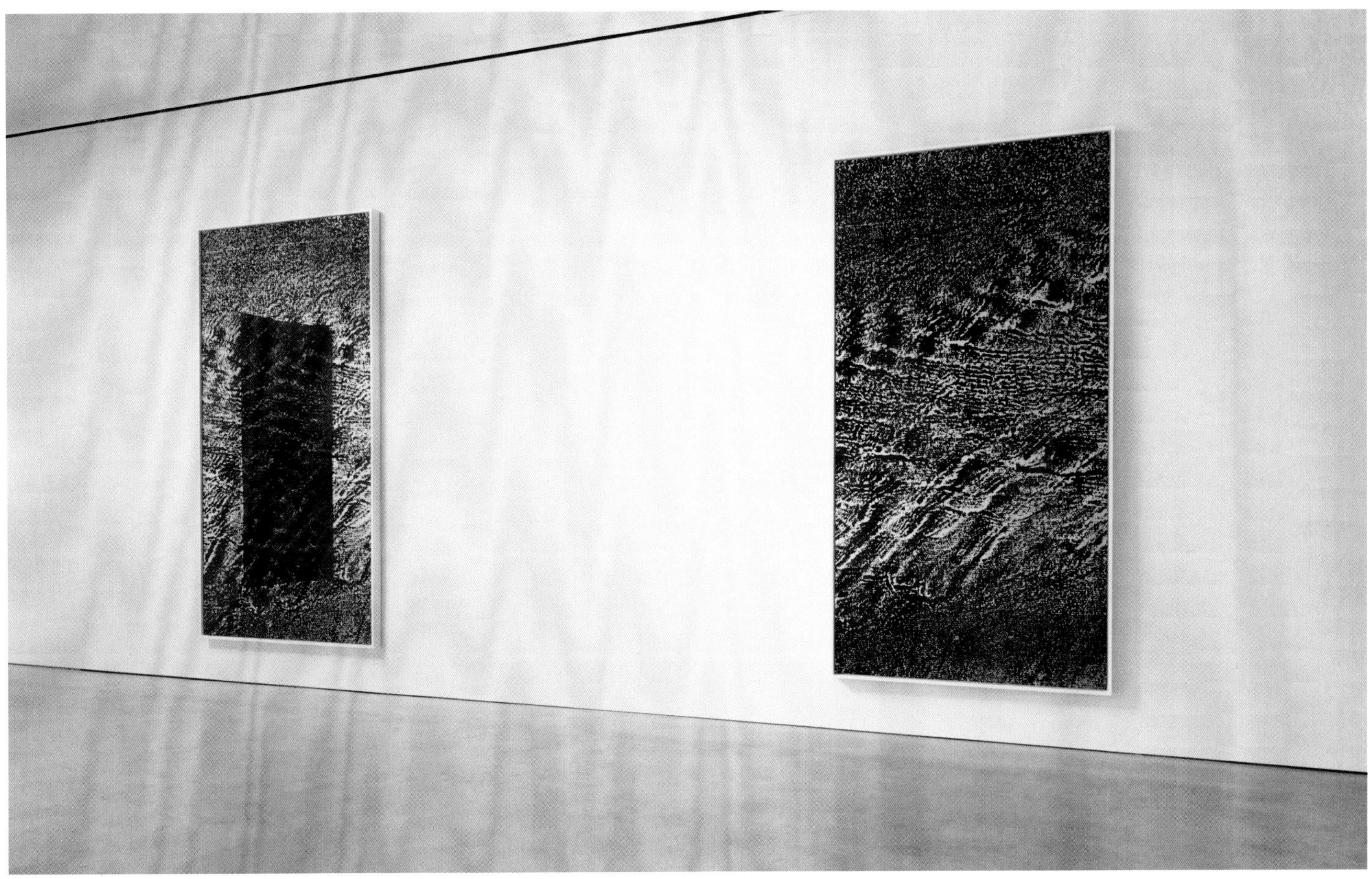

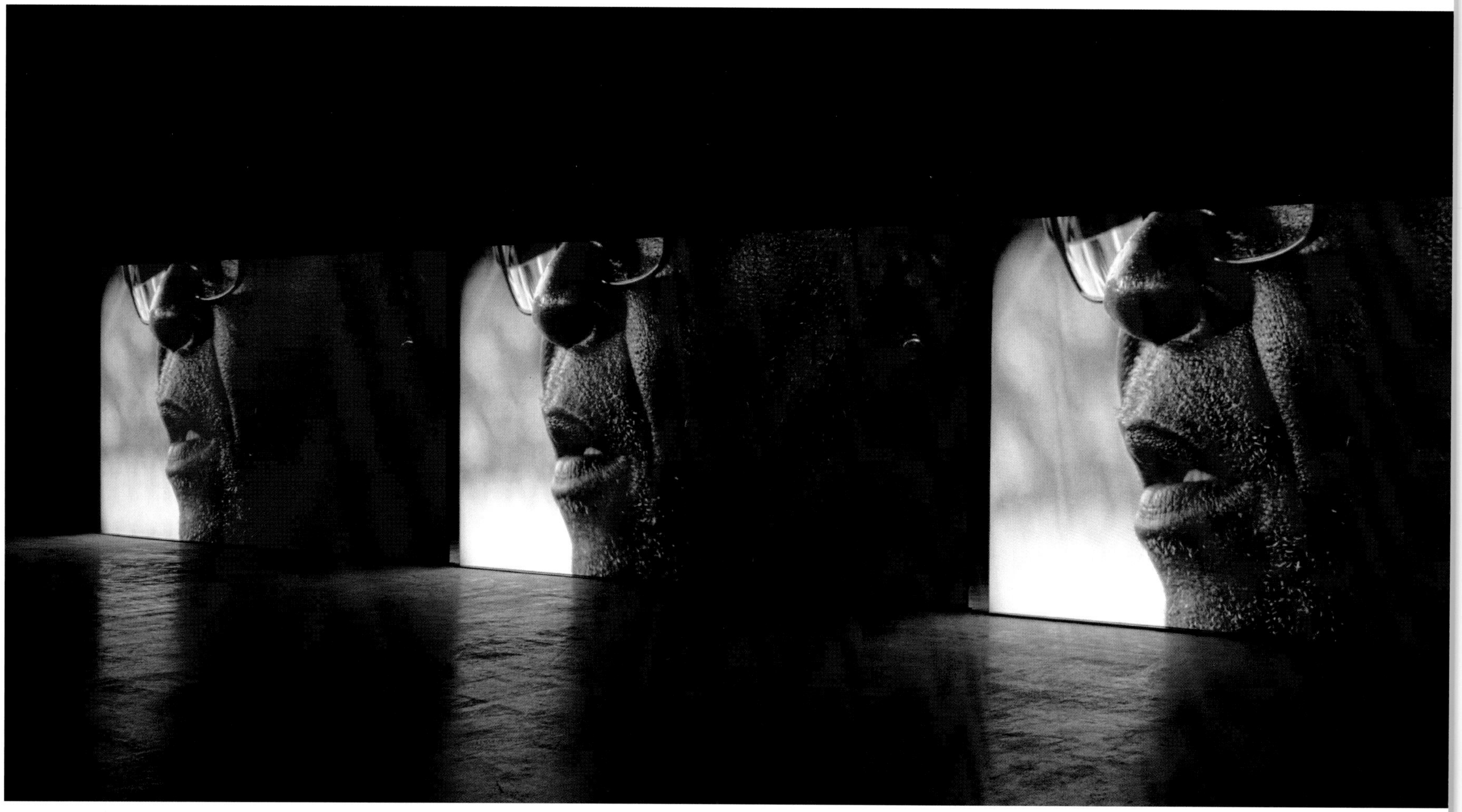

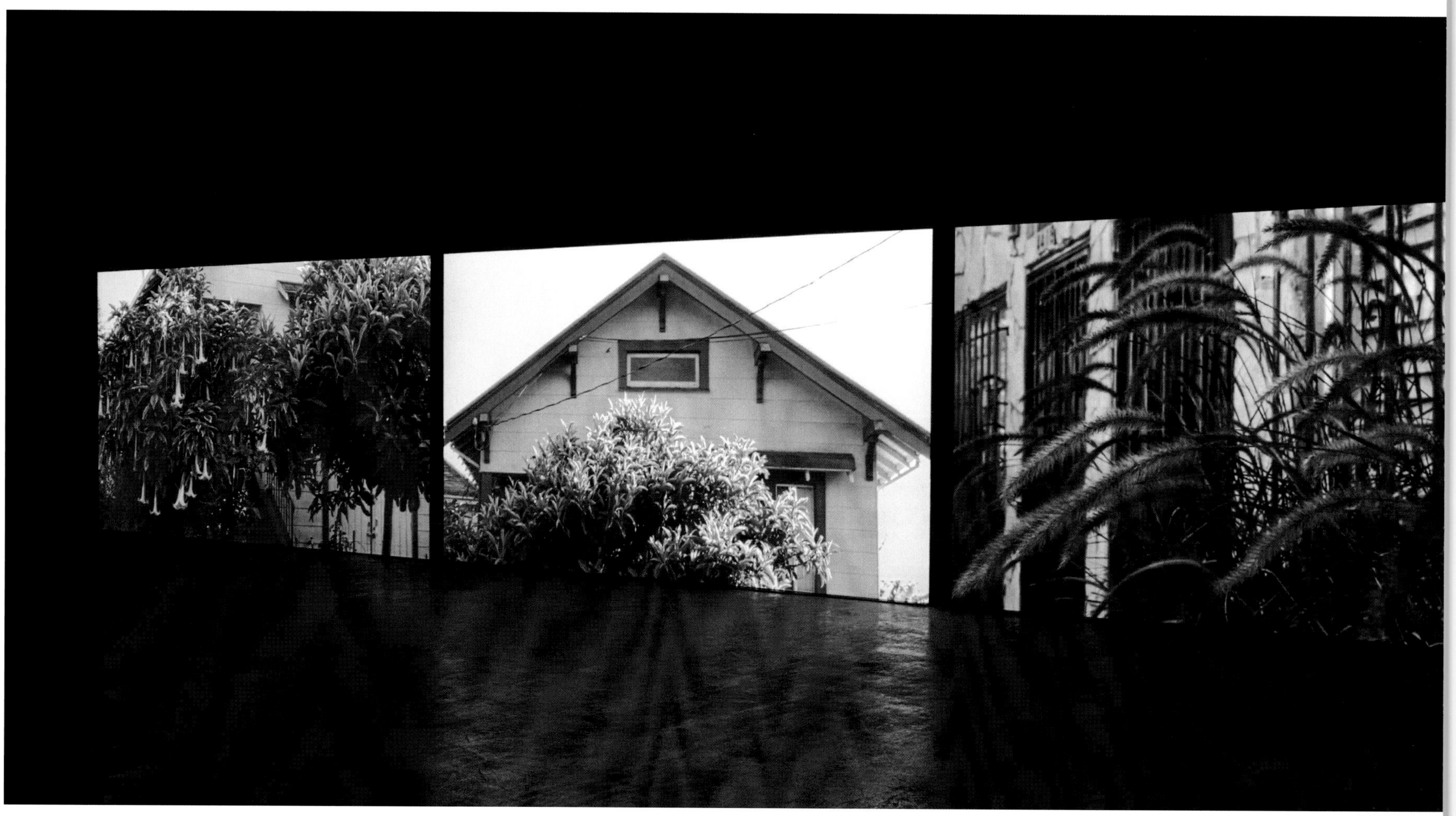

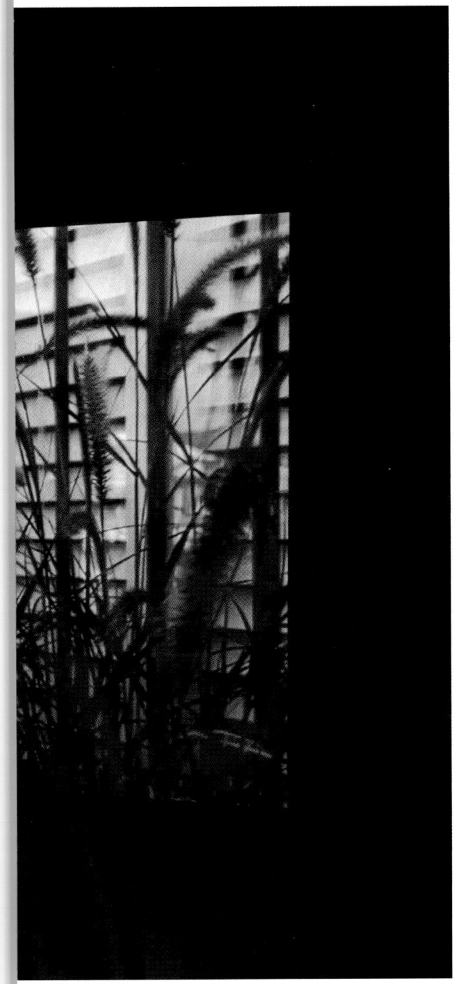

MY EDUCATION: A PORTRAIT OF DAVID HILLIARD, 2011–14
THREE-CHANNEL BLACK-AND-WHITE VIDEO
9 MIN. 19 SEC.
DIMENSIONS VARIABLE

INSTALLATION VIEW AT PACE GALLERY, NEW YORK, 2014

Matter to Black Liberation (2016) and Pendleton's poetry standard, Silliman's 'Albany'.

Filmed at the Ridgeway Diner in Chelsea, one of Rainer's 'offices from home', the approximately fourteen-minute film, a stylistic framing encompassing the façade of the diner and the bustle of afternoon pedestrians on Sixth Avenue to the tune of 'La Mer'. The conceit continues with the pair awkwardly sitting across from one another, ordering the mundane fare typical of an American diner. Pendleton counterposes the obvious stiffness between them with the most intimate of camera angles: close-up and eye level. The result hones our field of vision to the vital movements of Rainer's hands and warm certainty of her face. Rainer explains that she has just returned from Los Angeles where she performed with her contemporaries Steve Paxton and Simone Forti, thus the title of the film, and she describes the choreography and structures of her canonical *Trio A*, first performed in 1966 at Judson Memorial Church. She speaks poignantly about the United States today, about 'disaffection' and 'the illusion of democracy in this country'. We then see her reading a portion of Pendleton's script, quoting Stokely Carmichael talking about liberal white society and the problematic self-appointed role they play as mediators between the races. She teaches Pendleton the 'arm drop', a forceful movement in its profound subtlety and simplicity, and an expression of and experiment in trust and care. From here, Rainer reads texts about the killings of Michael Brown, Ezell Ford, John Crawford III, Tanisha Anderson and Tamir Rice at the hands of law enforcement. Afterwards, the 'I remember…' section of the document and 'arm drop' duet repeat. The film ends with documentation of *Trio A*, over which Pendleton has dubbed the gospel song 'I'm Saved', sung by the Silver Harps.[19]

from left,
BLACK DADA READER (WALL WORK #1) (DETAIL), 2016
LATEX INK ON ADHESIVE VINYL
DIMENSIONS VARIABLE

SYSTEM OF DISPLAY, W (WHEN/IAN BERRY, COUPLE DANCING, GHANA, 1962), 2016
SILK-SCREEN INK ON PLEXIGLASS AND MIRROR
25 X 25 X 8 CM

SYSTEM OF DISPLAY, F (AFFORD/PORO SECRET SOCIETY MASK, MANO, LIBERIA), 2016
SILK-SCREEN INK ON PLEXIGLASS AND MIRROR
25 X 25 X 8 CM

A VICTIM OF AMERICAN DEMOCRACY II, 2015
LATEX INK ON ADHESIVE VINYL
DIMENSIONS VARIABLE

UNTITLED, 2016
COLLAGE ON PAPER
39 X 27 CM

INSTALLATION VIEW AT GALERIE EVA PRESENHUBER, ZURICH, 2016

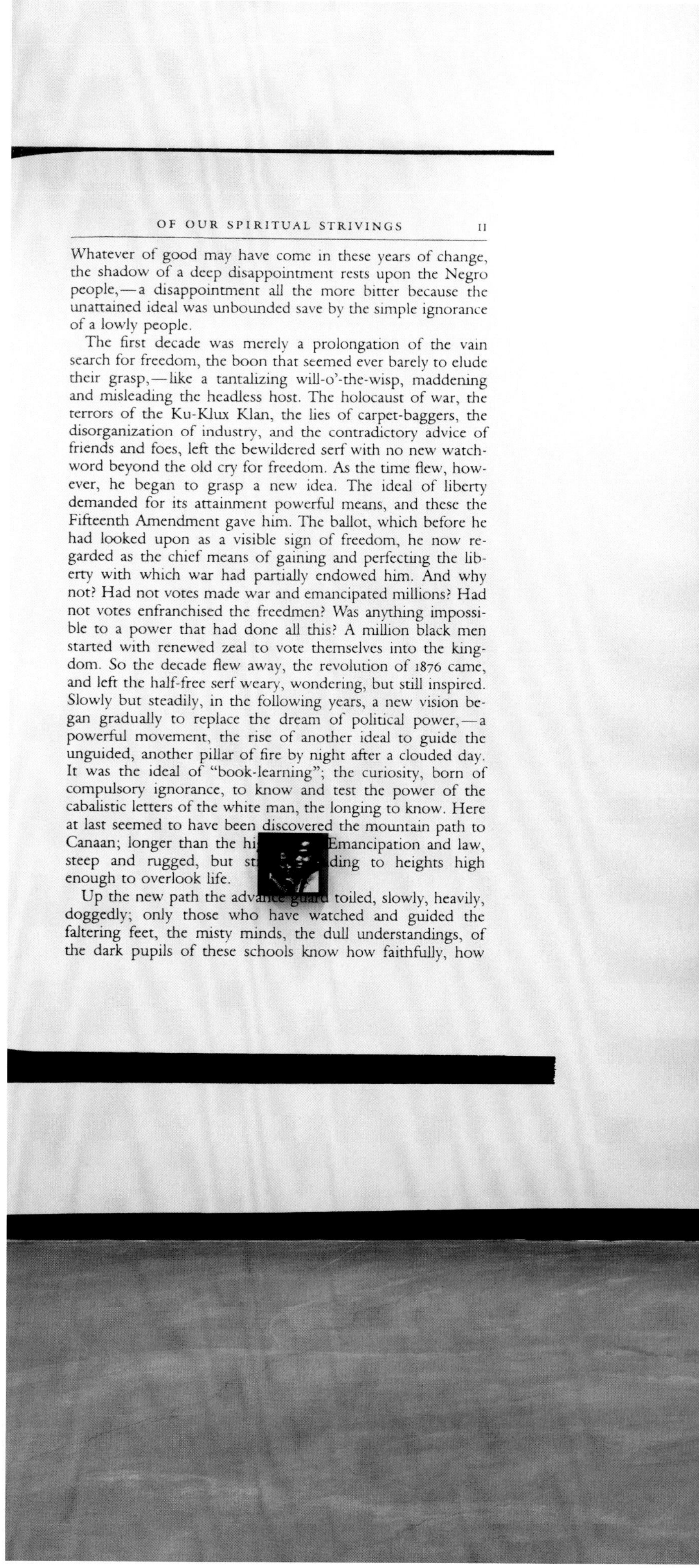

By overlaying black spirituals onto Rainer's movements, Pendleton puts a fine point on these diverse and dissonant modes of experimentation, one perceived to be inordinately expressive in its operations of repetition to entice swells of emotions, and the other renowned for its restraint. And yet, they are both incubated in religious institutions though serving different gods and conditioned to the possibilities of chance, or what we call improvisation. Pendleton knowingly stretches our comprehension of movement, encompassing and collapsing the uneven edges of its range of meanings, the expansiveness inherent to exactly what movement is and can be, and all that is implied in these two distinct traditions: freedom, necessity, divergence, flight, compassion.

Pendleton's dance turn continues with *Ishmael in the Garden* (2018), a portrait of the choreographer and dancer Ishmael Houston-Jones, lush in colour, intimacy and language. Houston-Jones is captured in a garden in his East Village neighbourhood, telling the story of his life and contemplating death. As he recalls the final days spent with Fred Holland, his dance partner for many years, as Holland lay dying in hospice, the camera lingers on Houston-Jones's hands that elegantly shift from being open to fisted to interlaced to tapping, divulging discomfort, acquiescence and anxiety. Houston-Jones reads his vivid writings, providing visceral recollections of queer life in downtown New York, while he strolls through his neighbourhood. We then see him preparing to dance in the sanctuary of St Mark's Church, the home of Danspace Project, where he has made and presented his work and today curates performances. In voice-over, he recalls a series of memories; as with Rainer, each sentence begins with 'I remember…'. Eventually he begins to move in his indelible way – muscular, fluidly strident, vulnerably raw. At one point, the dancer, seated in front of a jewel-hued stained-glass window in the church, recites the portion of the script that extracts a text he wrote recalling a lover's body – the shapes and scents of his orifices and genitals, and their sexual encounters – in terrific detail. Occasionally, a white light flashes across the screen, obliterating the image. Houston-Jones sits in silence, his visage riveting with emotion. After a series of film

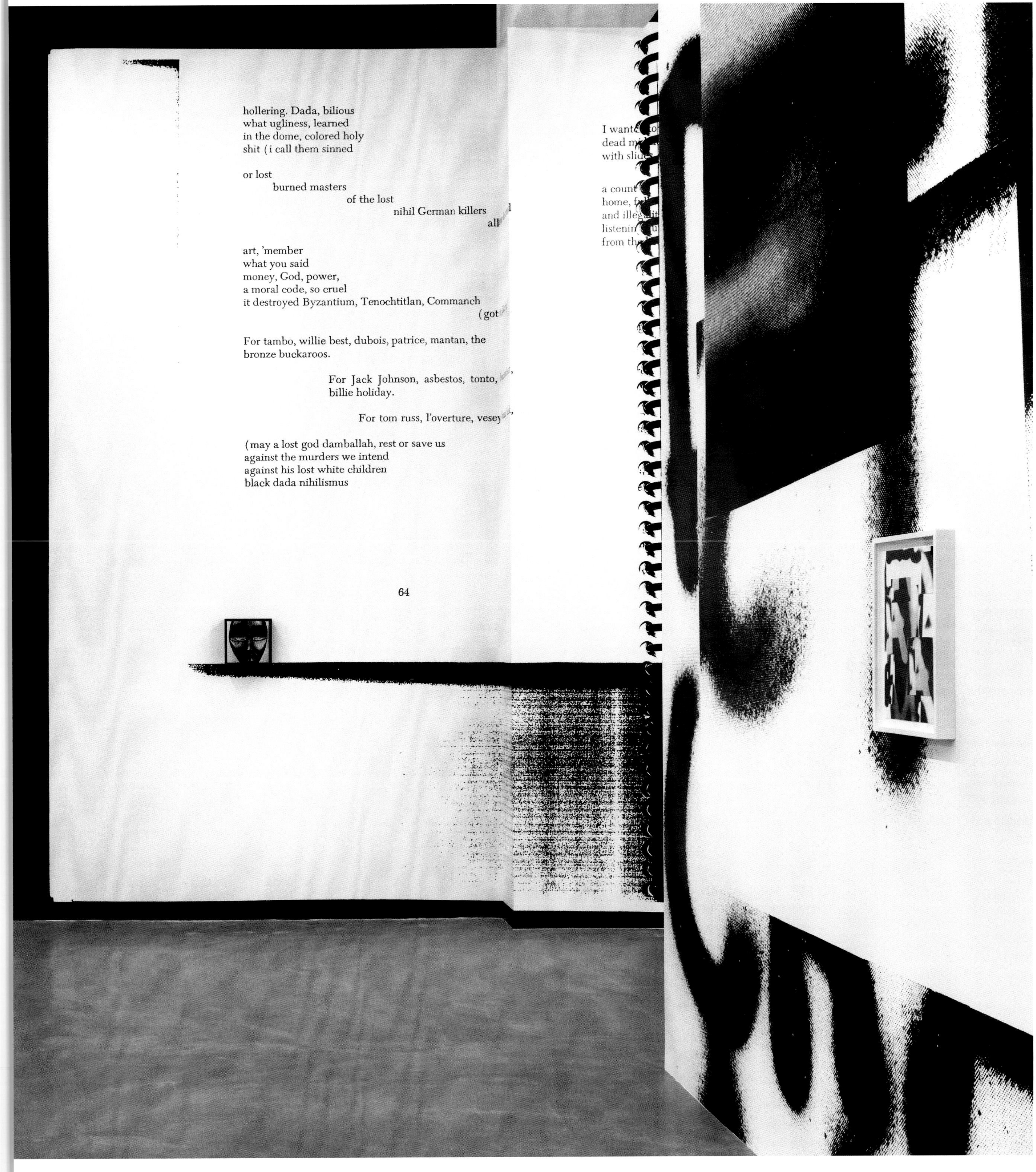
hollering. Dada, bilious
what ugliness, learned
in the dome, colored holy
shit (i call them sinned
or lost
burned masters
of the lost
nihil German killers
art, 'member
what you said
money, God, power,
a moral code, so cruel
it destroyed Byzantium, Tenochtitlan, Commanch
For tambo, willie best, dubois, patrice, mantan, the
bronze buckaroos.
For Jack Johnson, asbestos, tonto,
billie holiday.
For tom russ, l'overture,
(may a lost god damballah, rest or save us
against the murders we intend
against his lost white children
black dada nihilismus
64

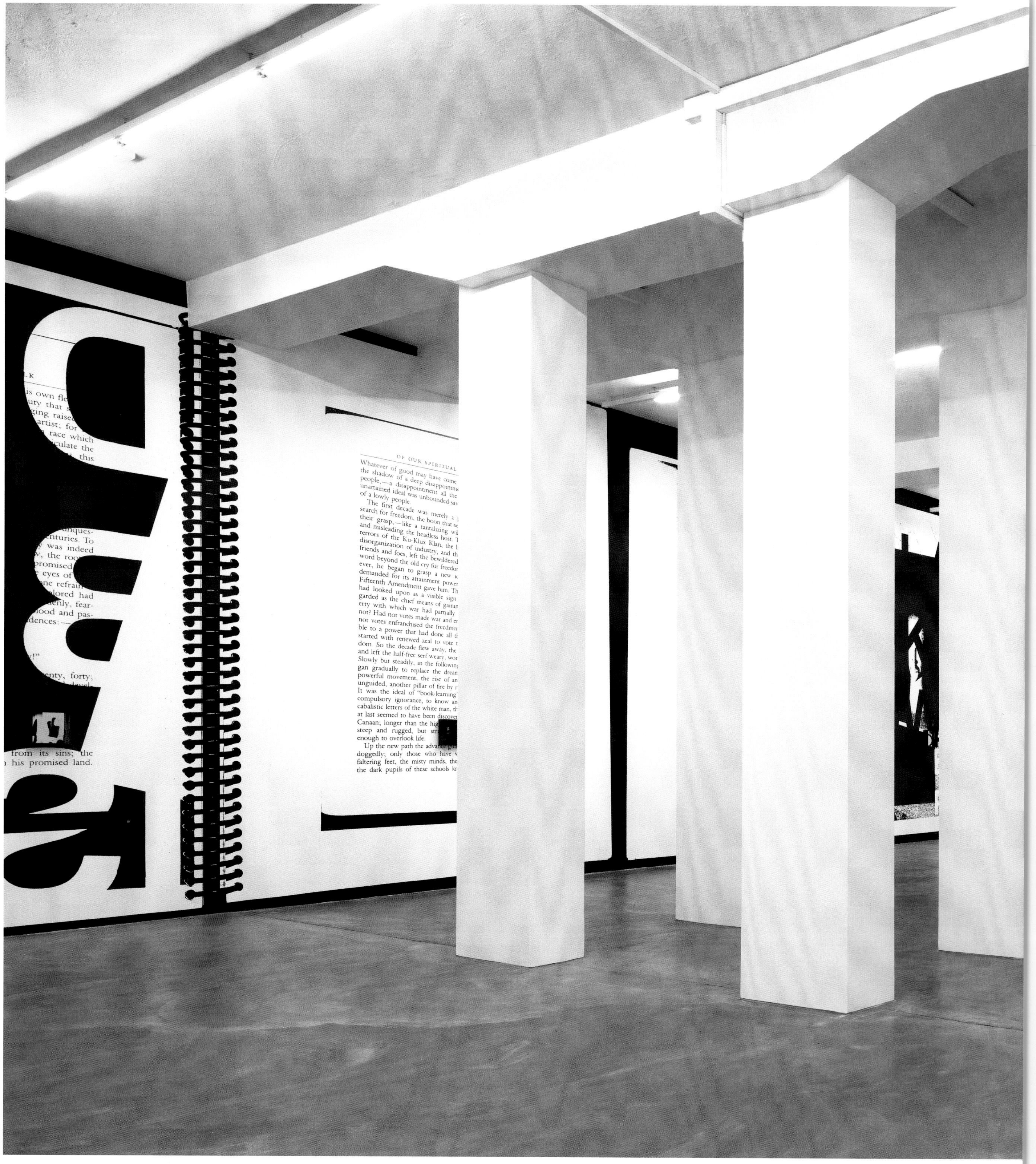
OF OUR SPIRITUAL

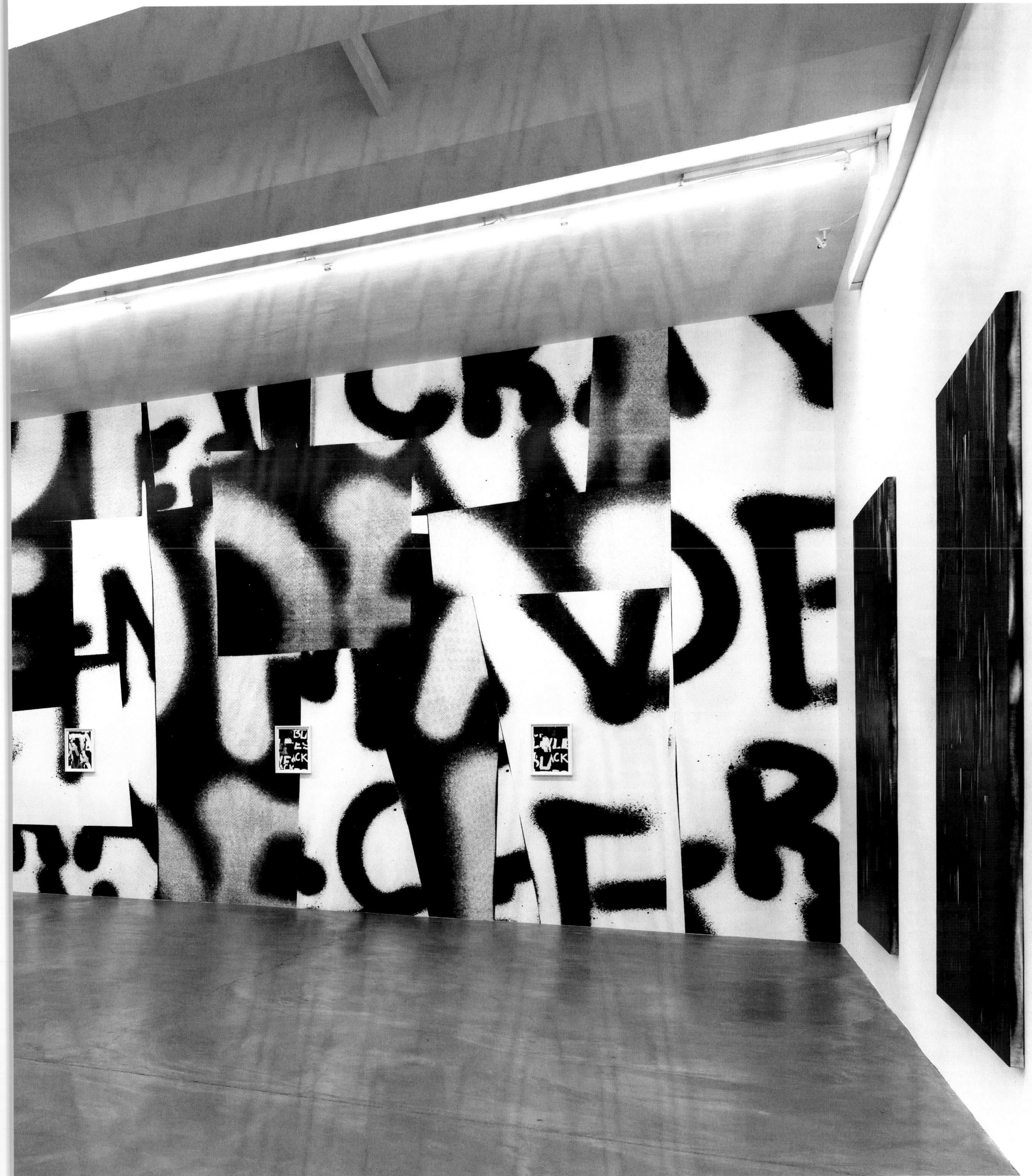

stills of Houston-Jones in St Mark's, we see him dancing in total darkness, except for a solitary spotlight, as he performs an adaptation of *DEAD* (1981), a tally of grave losses in which the performer names his family, friends and those who have influenced his life over the years.

That a portrait is both a representation (capturing a likeness) and a presentation (offering an interpretation) offers a useful parallelism that illuminates the hallmarks of Pendleton's work. As a system of communication, language oscillates in these works between affinity, as in a desire to convey a shared relationship, and alienation, as in the function of dissonance in the use of fragmentation, montage and collage. Such a wager generates uncertainty, ambiguity and indeterminacy as sheer delight in a project in which the only necessity is the production of reading and reading as a mode of production. Pendleton's thought happenings pivot on the innate complexities and given contexts of language, genres and ideas – its openness, implicit and explicit, is its ethical imperative. The artwork's visual, kinetic and conceptual language is optimized as icons in the truest sense, intersecting, transforming, undermining, reinforcing, contradicting and redirecting our attention to the representations of the world (as surface and space, as letter and stutter, as movement and a desire to be moved) from which it draws and in which it takes form.

4

For *Untitled (A Victim of American Democracy)* (2016) Pendleton made collages of the spray-painted words 'A Victim of American Democracy', a quote from Malcolm X's 1964 speech 'The Ballot or the Bullet'. These works have the same all-over style as the black monochrome paintings, but with striations that give them a sense of spatial depth. In the first variants, the ground of the canvas was enveloped with short, linear, black spray-painted marks before being silk-screened. Later variants used straight lines of spray paint at more regular intervals. In any case, the overall affect is vibrational and spectral; mists appear to emerge from behind, between and within the abstract letter forms and broken and unbroken lines. The paintings are expressive and gestural. For Pendleton, there is:

> something democratizing about spray paint – anyone can pick it up. You use it, you make a sign, there's an immediacy, it's functional. There's an inherent value of the street and its aesthetic. I'm just blackening it. I make a black ground. It becomes the ground of the painting in a traditional sense. The figure is the textual collage that uses the language, which is pulled apart and abstracted. There's a tension that pulls at the burden of representation. The figure is abstracted, deconstructed language. I'm interested in how it functions – the shift from total meaning – I can read it – to fragment.[20]

This desire for fragmentation, which Pendleton situates in the formal logics of painting techniques, insists upon far more than the figure-ground spatial relation of the medium. Rather, he is positing the potential of painting through a repeated layering of the self – literally as a victim of American democracy – represented in this instance through the mode of communication by which something we call the self is expressed in the world: language. Its resistance to legibility, its deference to an existence in a different register, tone and level, results in a poetic observation that wavers in the streaks of marks imprinted by Pendleton's hand on the work and in the blabbering, stuttering, disappearing words that question how abstraction functions and how the fragment acts upon the whole.

Such a gestural mannerism brings to mind mid-twentieth-century Action Painting, as much as urban graffiti of the 1960s, 70s and 80s. Perhaps the most notable relation, however, is with French painter Martin Barré (1924–1993), who like Pendleton approached painting conceptually, which is to say, as a construct, an assemblage of artistic, cultural and historical reifying tendencies. Barré began using spray paint in 1963 for his serial striped and *Zebra* paintings, which with their all-over, evenly spaced lines, foreclose the perception of spatial depth, radically withholding a certain legibility essential in interpretations of modernist painting. Another artist whose paintings share a resonance with Pendleton's is the American Christopher Wool, whose layered, rolled and stamped paintings create a misaligned optical cacophony similar to Pendleton's tagged works. The visual (and verbal) dissonance of Wool's 'word pictures', with their measured (if not banal) black-and-white palette of fractured words that disperse letters as figures without limits, is made indiscernible in the quotidian paint flourishes that underlie Pendleton's screenprinted text. There exists, though, a distinction in timbre between these works and Wool's industrial spray-gun paintings that goes beyond a shared mechanism to disperse chroma. It delivers the stark reminder that, depending upon who you are in the world, the urban scenes from which this material is extracted for 'fine art' have entirely different stakes. Their reasoning is fundamentally different: Pendleton, via Malcolm X, reminds us that the streets are sites without recourse, sites of social death and necessarily locations for radical action, too.

The coincidences with Barré and Wool are namely stylistic, but there is also an uncanny affinity between Pendleton's spray-painted text-images and New York School abstract expressionist Norman Lewis's (1909–1979) early black paintings, especially those of the 1950s, though he created black works from 1946 to 1977. While Pendleton employs glossy black silk-screen ink to imbue his works with a bit of shine, Lewis achieves this visceral luminosity differently but with a surprisingly similar effect. While Pendleton's paintings reference and are informed by a range of concepts, including race, other

UNTITLED (A VICTIM OF AMERICAN DEMOCRACY), 2016
SILK-SCREEN INK AND SPRAY PAINT ON CANVAS
272 X 150 CM

previous pages, central wall,
A VICTIM OF AMERICAN DEMOCRACY II, 2015
LATEX INK ON ADHESIVE VINYL
DIMENSIONS VARIABLE

from left,
UNTITLED, 2016
COLLAGE ON PAPER
39 X 27 CM

UNTITLED, 2016
COLLAGE ON PAPER
39 X 27 CM

UNTITLED, 2016
COLLAGE ON PAPER
39 X 27 CM

INSTALLATION VIEW AT GALERIE EVA PRESENHUBER, ZURICH, 2016

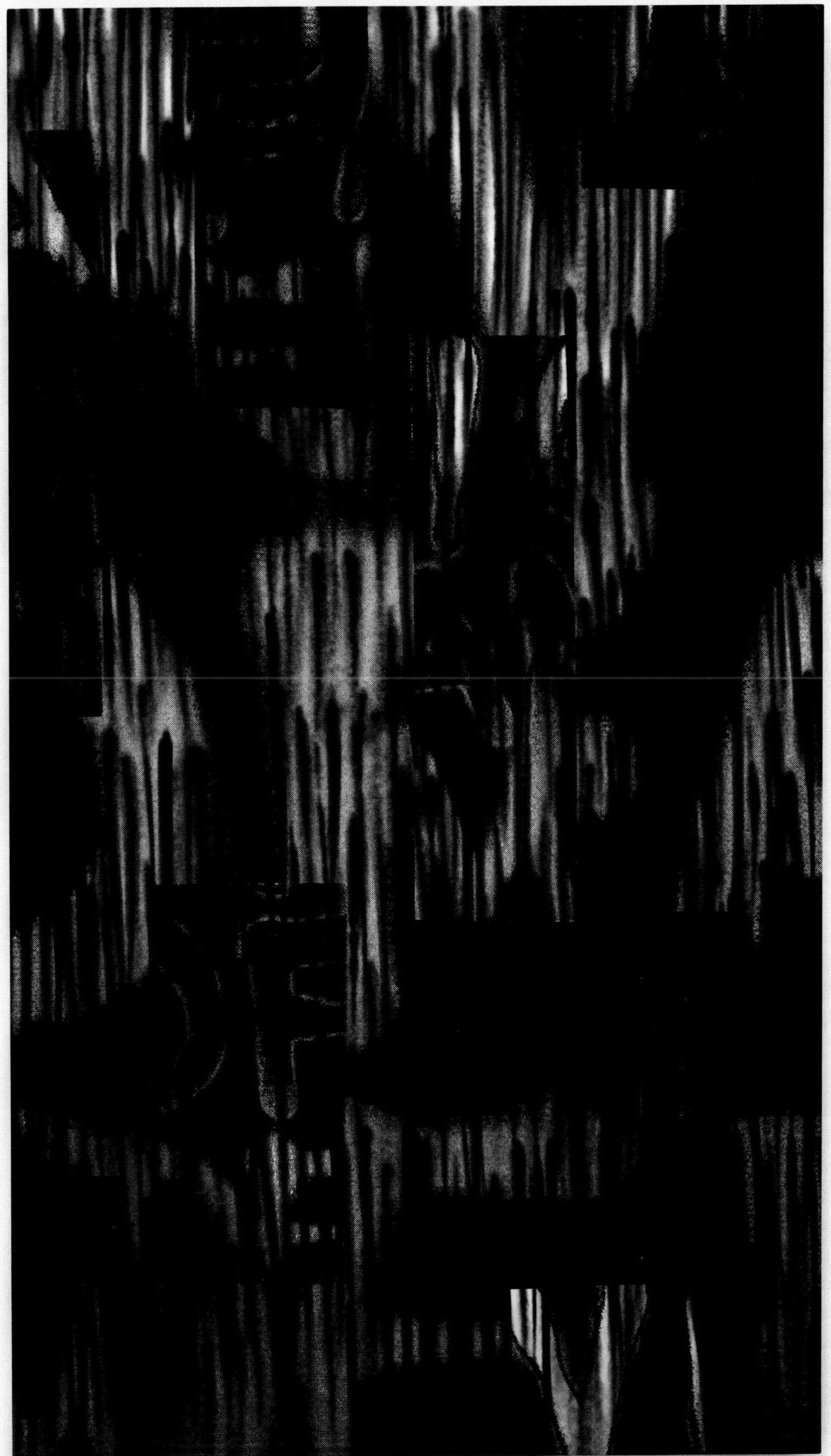

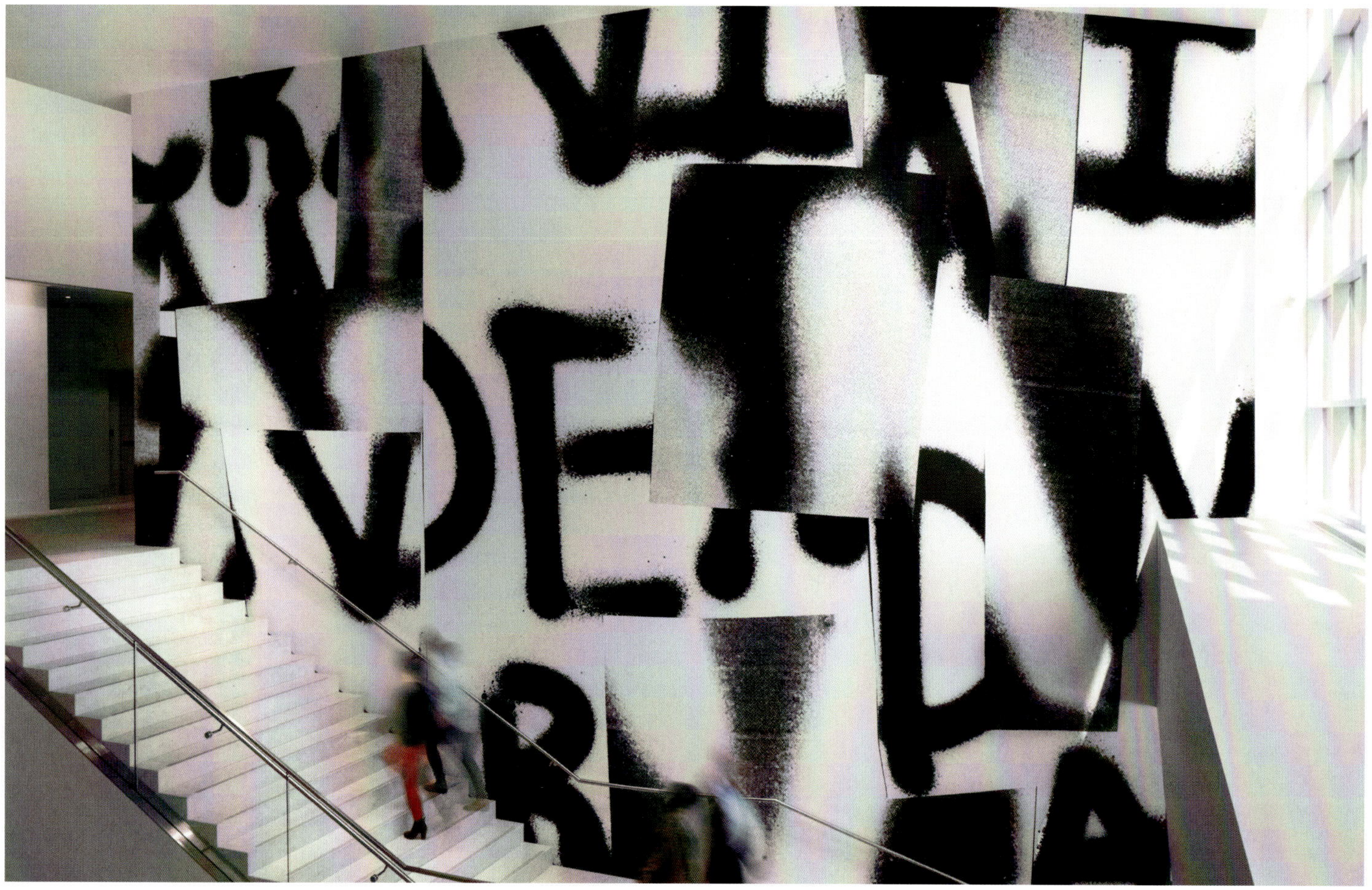

A VICTIM OF AMERICAN DEMOCRACY II, 2015
LATEX INK ON ADHESIVE VINYL
DIMENSIONS VARIABLE

INSTALLATION VIEW AT BALTIMORE MUSEUM OF ART, 2017

registers of identity and a wellspring of social, political and historical realities, Lewis asserted that his interest in the colour black was entirely formal. In remarking upon *Blending* (1951), one of the paintings that resembles most directly Pendleton's gestures in the *Untitled (A Victim of American Democracy)* series, he explains, 'The picture… is a black picture. It has no social connotation to me. I wanted to see if I could get out of black the suggestion of other nuances of color, using it in such a way as to arouse other colors … This was my becoming … using color in such a way that it could become other things.'[21] Lewis, a good friend of Ad Reinhardt, was keenly aware of the pressure put upon his work for a kind of 'authentic' visual representation of blackness as a distinct and identifiable 'African Idiom' or 'Negro Idiom', foreshadowing a debate that continues today, and which ironically instigated a turn to black monochromatic paintings by artists working fifty years after Lewis began his suite of dark works.[22] Nevertheless, Lewis's journals did list some intriguing associations for the colour black, including 'formless', 'void', 'time', 'the dark of absolute freedom', 'inner', 'subterranean', 'absence of color', 'darkness' and so on.[23] For him, as for Pendleton, 'there was a world in blackness'.[24]

The qualities of pluralism, polyphony and all-over-ness of the *Untitled (A Victim of American Democracy)* paintings are expanded in a group of three subsequent bodies of work, beginning with *OK DADA OK BLACK DADA OK* (2017–), a series of 84 x 60 inch works composed of spray paint and silk-screen ink on canvas. Here, Pendleton extends his mattering of language through words, lines and geometric characters, at times more or less densely entangled on the picture plane such that the linguistic phrases, through the process of repeatedly inscribing and overwriting, are indecipherable. 'If' is a recurring word across all of the paintings in this series; the remainder of the marks are distributed in swerving variations. As if a counterpoint to the militant subtraction of language in the *Black Dada* paintings, these exploit a maximalist sensibility, verging on anarchy, to the point of obfuscation that is absolutely irreducible to any one visual element.

Like *Untitled (A Victim of American Democracy)*, the *Untitled (Who We Are)* (2018–) paintings also features spray-painted black lines as the paintings' 'grounds', which are overlaid with the abstracted phrase 'CRAZY NIGGER'. Pendleton takes the provocative phrase from the title of one of the works in 20th-century composer Julius Eastman's 'Nigger Series' (1978–79), whose own investment in that word's 'fundamentalness' recalls how prevalent its use has been in American culture, whether wielded by white supremacists, or by black comedians Richard Pryor and Dave Chappelle, to name just two, or hip-hop musicians today. Its absurdity is inextricably linked to its roots in American racism, a verbal tool to dehumanize, aiming to abstract black subjectivity

from left,
OK DADA OK BLACK DADA OK (BLACK DADA WE), 2018
SILK-SCREEN INK AND SPRAY PAINT ON CANVAS
213 X 152 CM

OK DADA OK BLACK DADA OK (O.K.), 2018
SILK-SCREEN INK AND SPRAY PAINT ON CANVAS
213 X 152 CM

OK DADA OK BLACK DADA OK (DADA O.K.), 2018
SILK-SCREEN INK AND SPRAY PAINT ON CANVAS
213 X 152 CM

INSTALLATION VIEW AT GALERIA PEDRO CERA, LISBON, 2018

to the point of annihilation, and its seemingly endless circulation and ease of deployment in everyday communication. Pendleton's iterative use of the phrase as both 'ground' (underpainting) and 'figure' (image-making) reinterprets Eastman's uncompromising work and thought as a visual field.

In the *Untitled (WE ARE NOT)* (2019–) paintings, Pendleton returns to his 2008 'Black Dada' manifesto, specifically, to the lines: 'Black Dada: we are not naive / Black Dada: we are successive / Black Dada: we are not exclusive…' Here, he refers back to Tristan Tzara's satirical 'Manifesto of Monsieur Antipyrine', delivered at the first public Dada soirée in Zurich in 1916 ('We are not naive / We are successive / We are exclusive'), recasting Tzara's declarations with the insertion of 'Black Dada'. Abridged, echoed and inscribed, 'we are not' … 'we are not' … 'we are not' splutters across the canvas with typical opacity in order to instrumentalize, and therefore undo, varying structural logics of abstraction, the vital heart of all of Pendleton's endeavours.

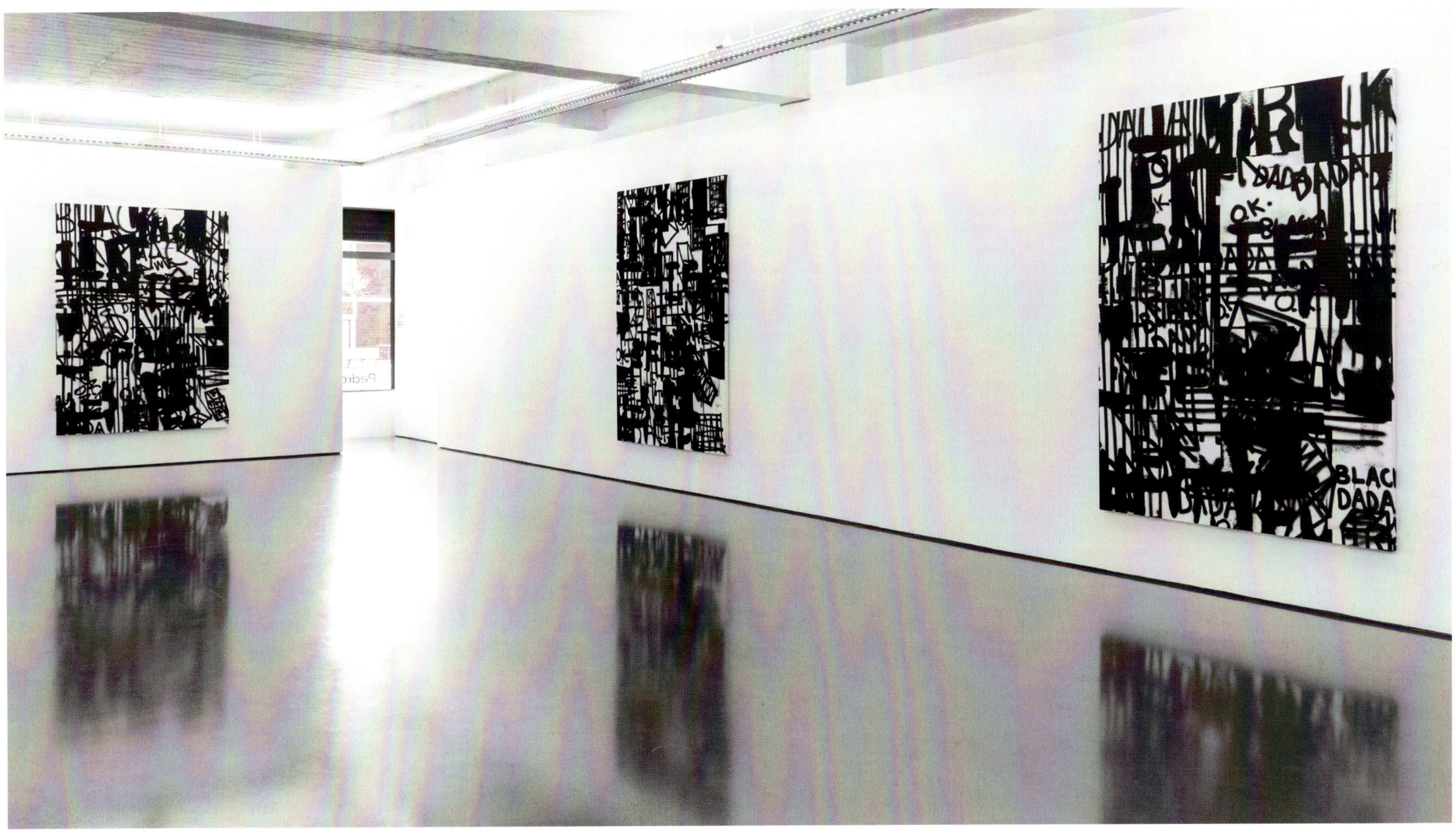

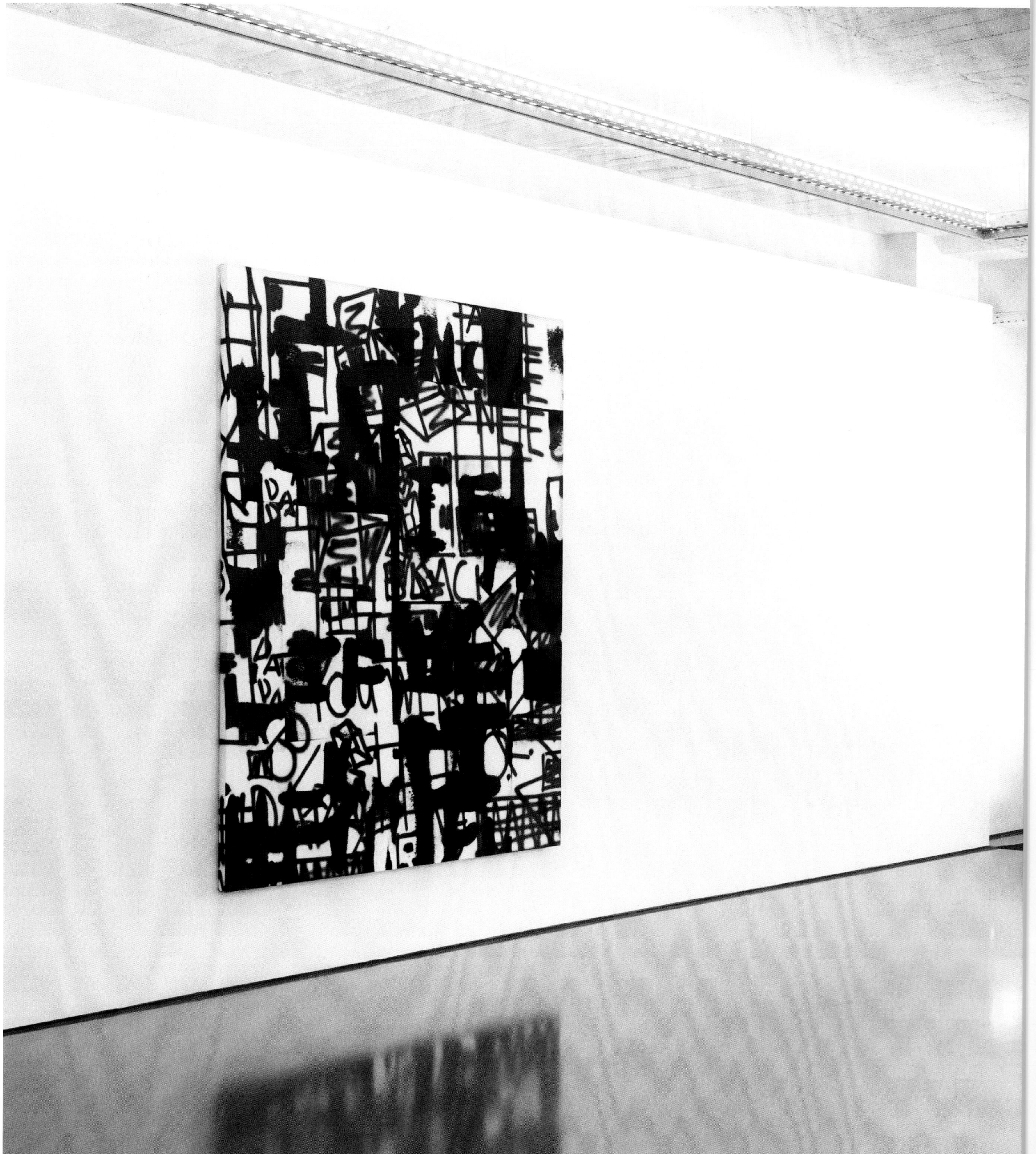

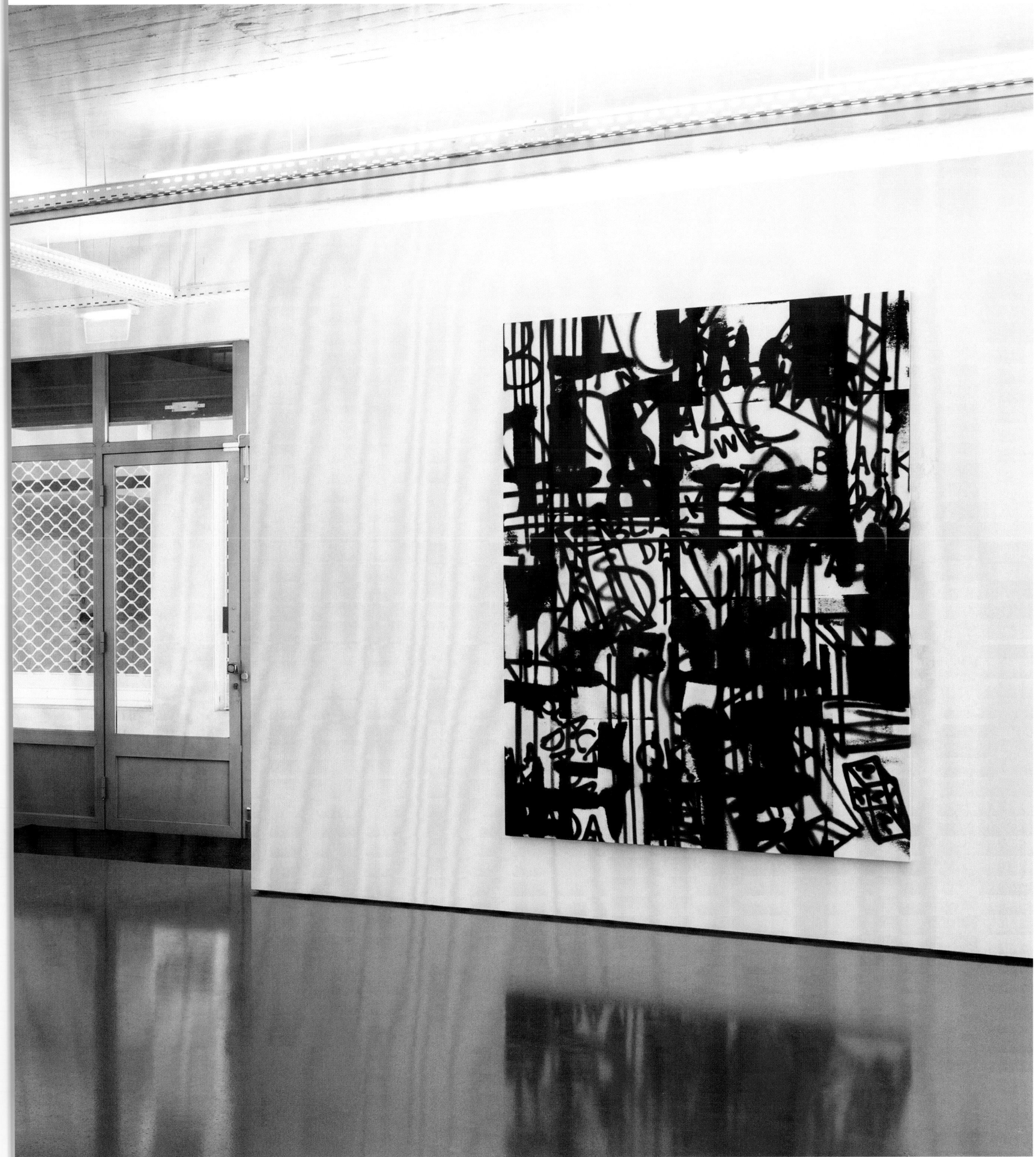

UNTITLED (WE ARE NOT),
2019–20
SILK-SCREEN INK ON CANVAS
244 X 305 CM

previous pages, from left,
OK DADA OK BLACK DADA OK (DA), 2018
SILK-SCREEN INK AND SPRAY PAINT ON CANVAS
213 X 152 CM

OK DADA OK BLACK DADA OK (BLACK DADA WE), 2018
SILK-SCREEN INK AND SPRAY PAINT ON CANVAS
213 X 152 CM

INSTALLATION VIEW AT GALERIA PEDRO CERA, LISBON, 2018

following pages, from left,
UNTITLED (WHO WE ARE), 2019
SILK-SCREEN INK AND SPRAY PAINT ON CANVAS
244 X 175 CM

UNTITLED (WE ARE NOT), 2019
SILK-SCREEN INK AND SPRAY PAINT ON CANVAS
91 X 71 CM

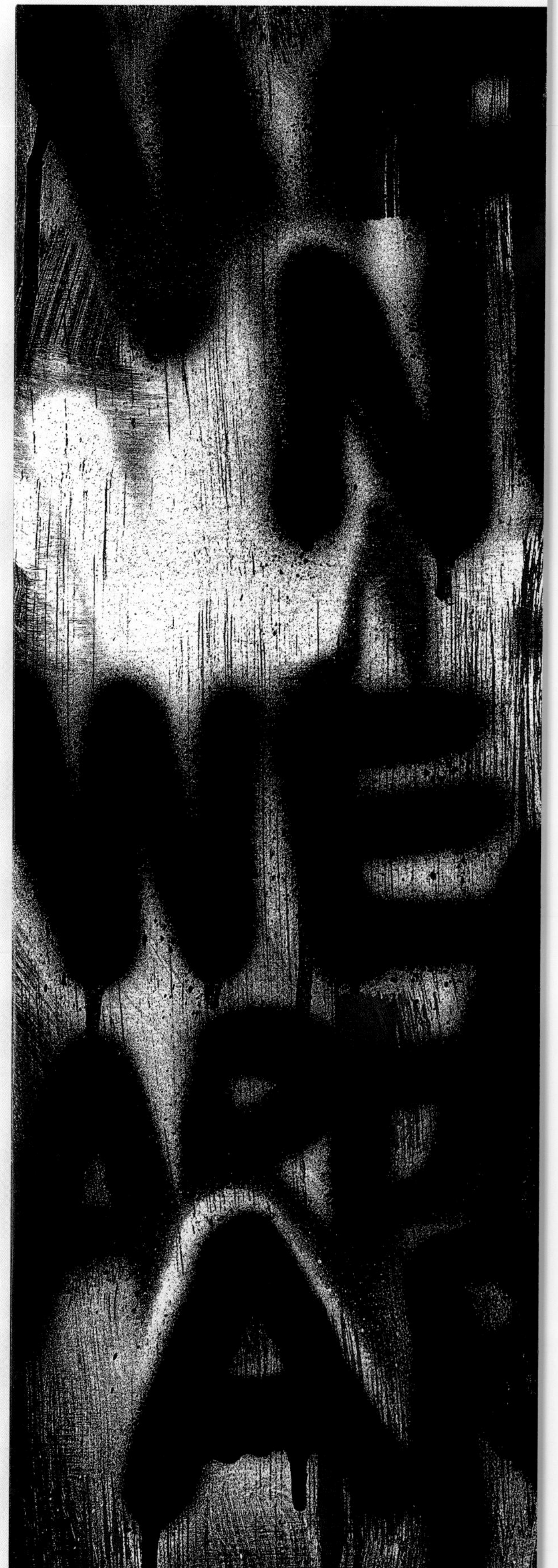

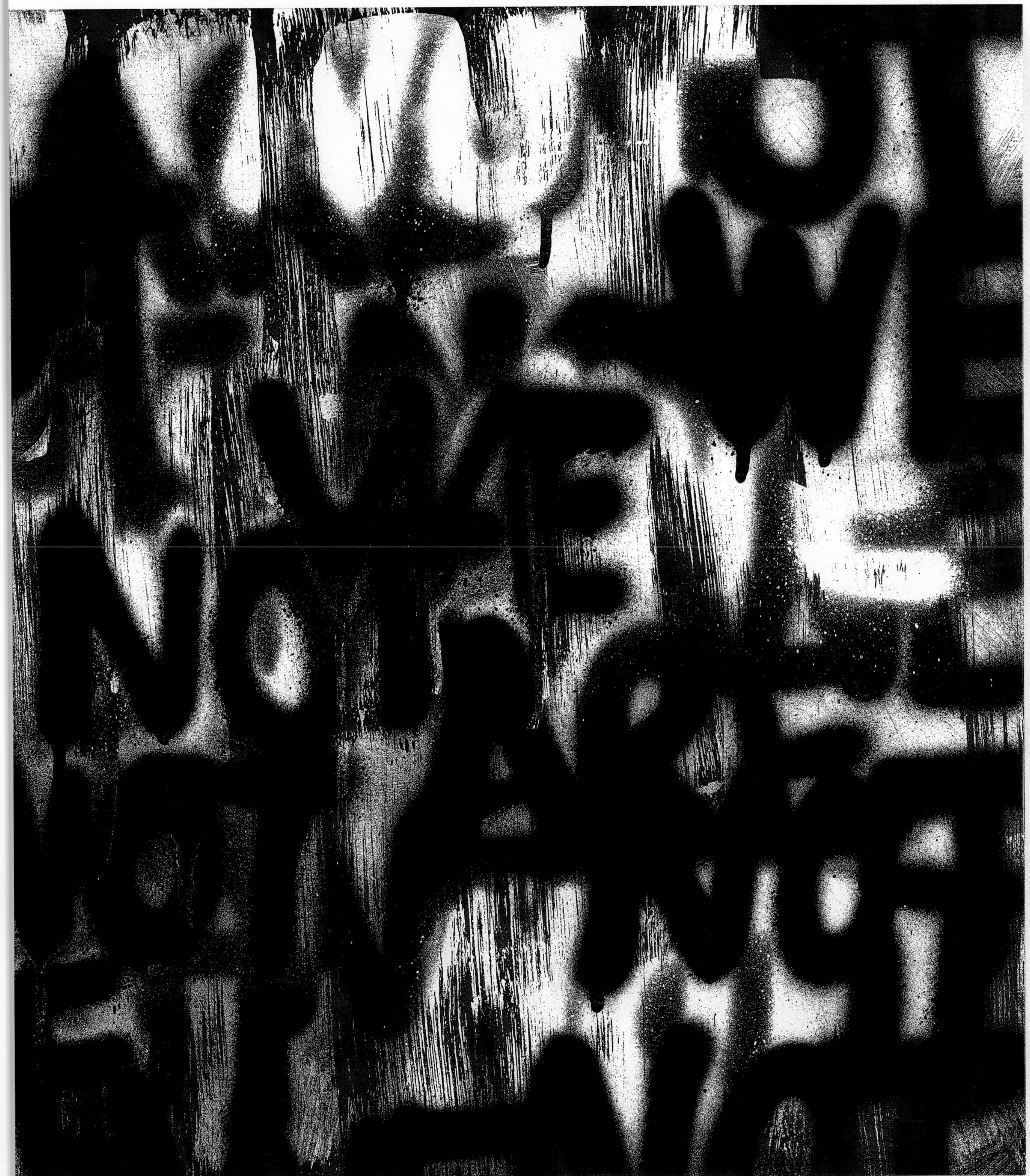

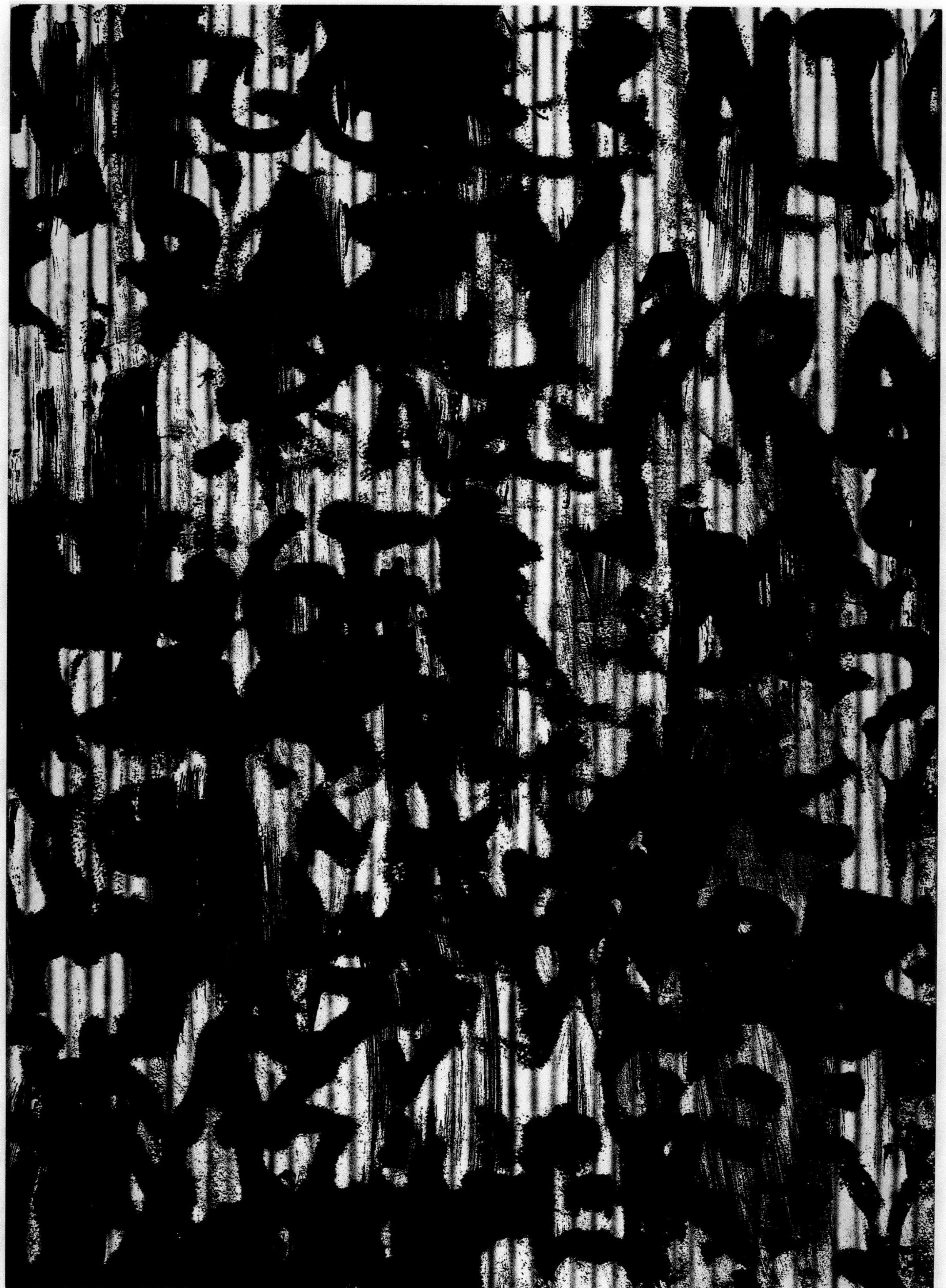

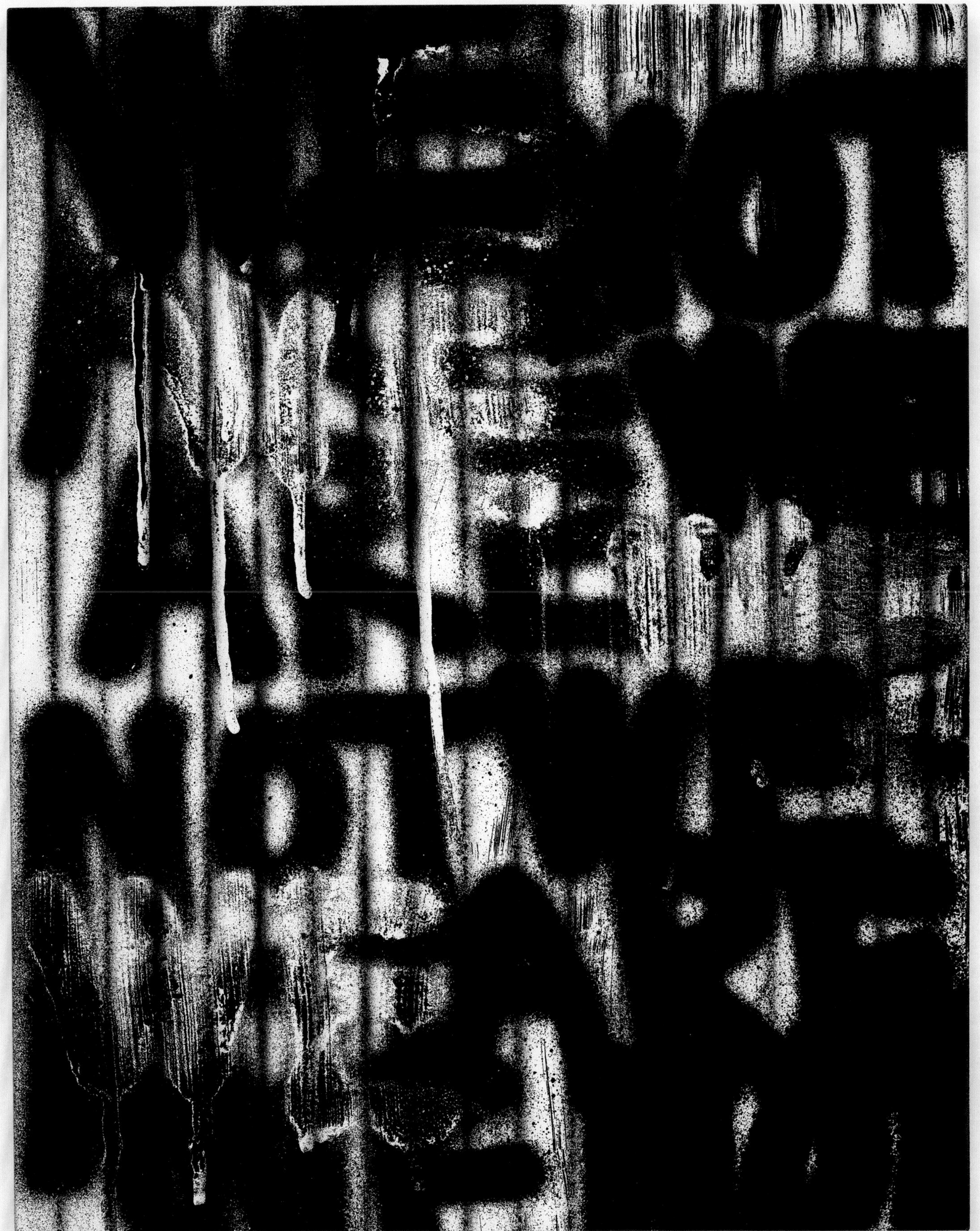

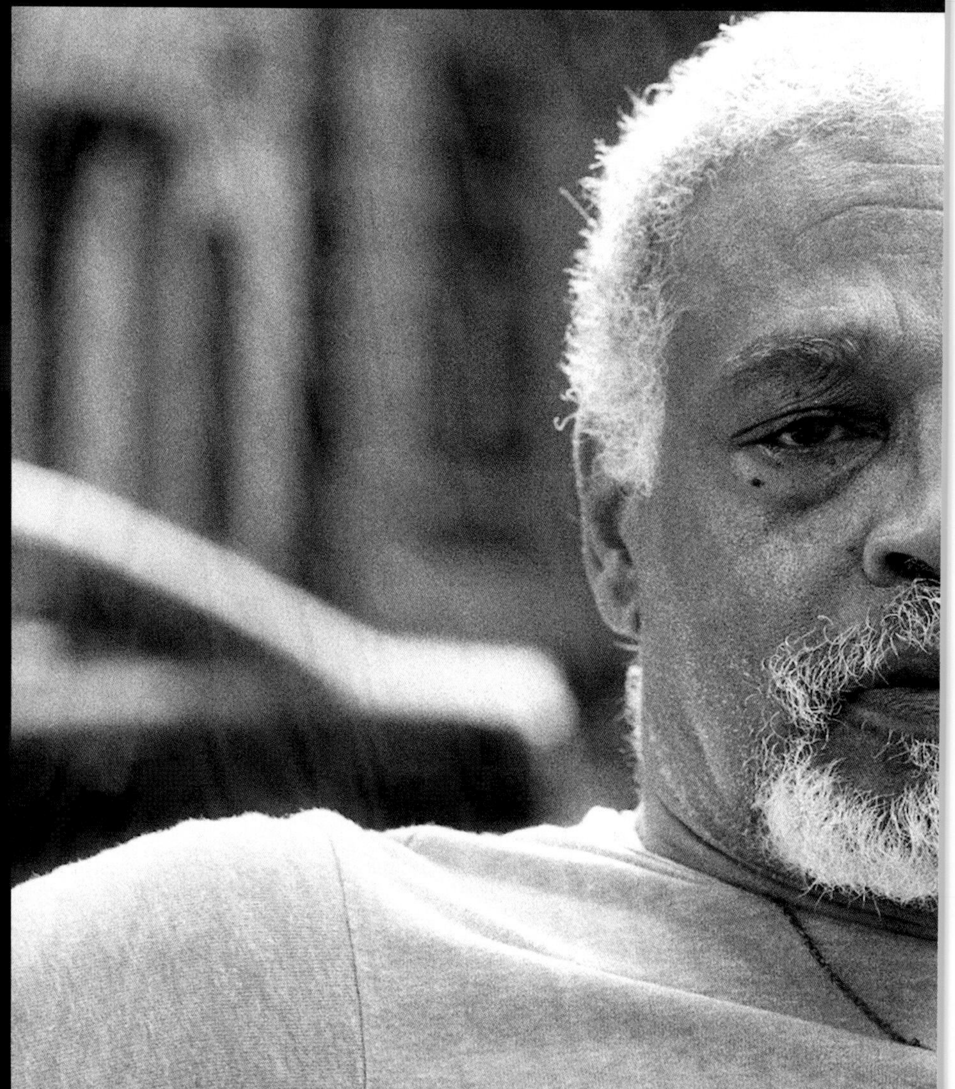

073 FOCUS

'The Cool of the Heat': Adam Pendleton's Video Portraits

Andréa Picard

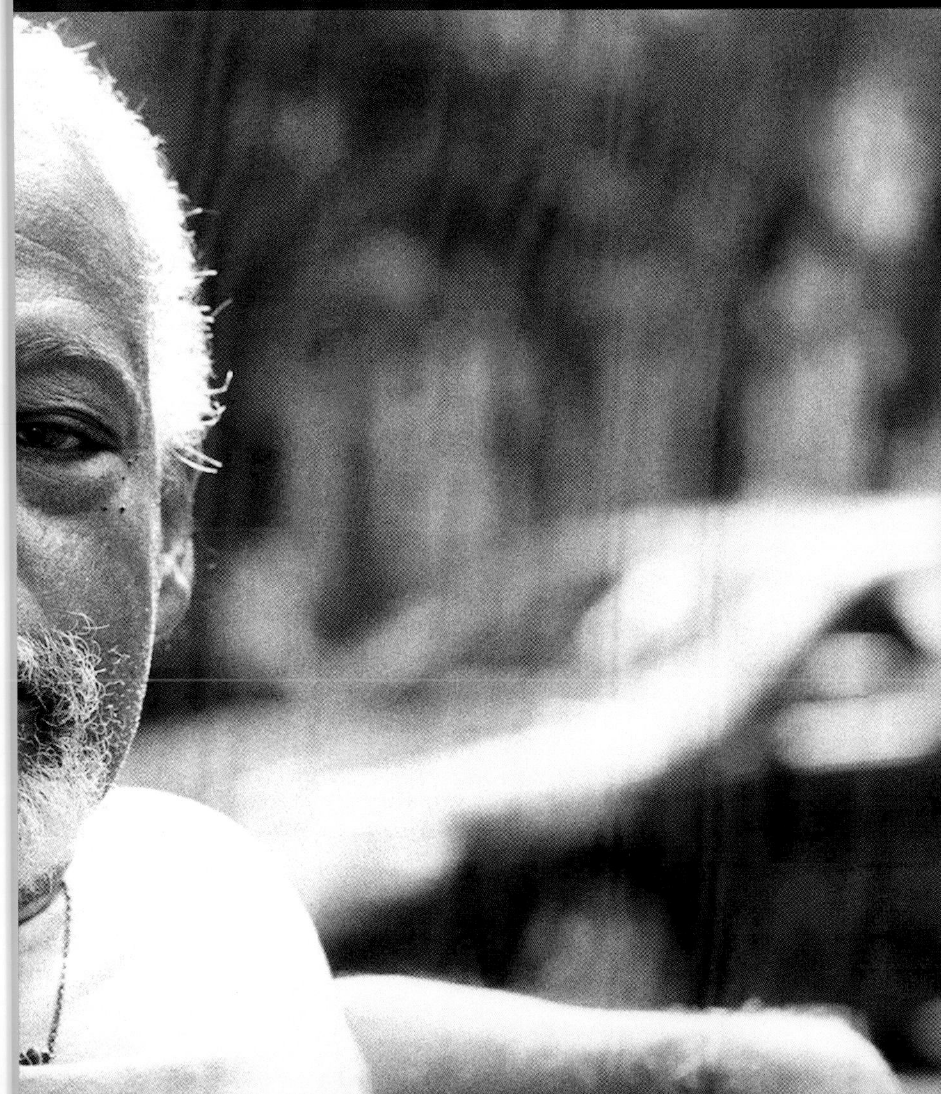

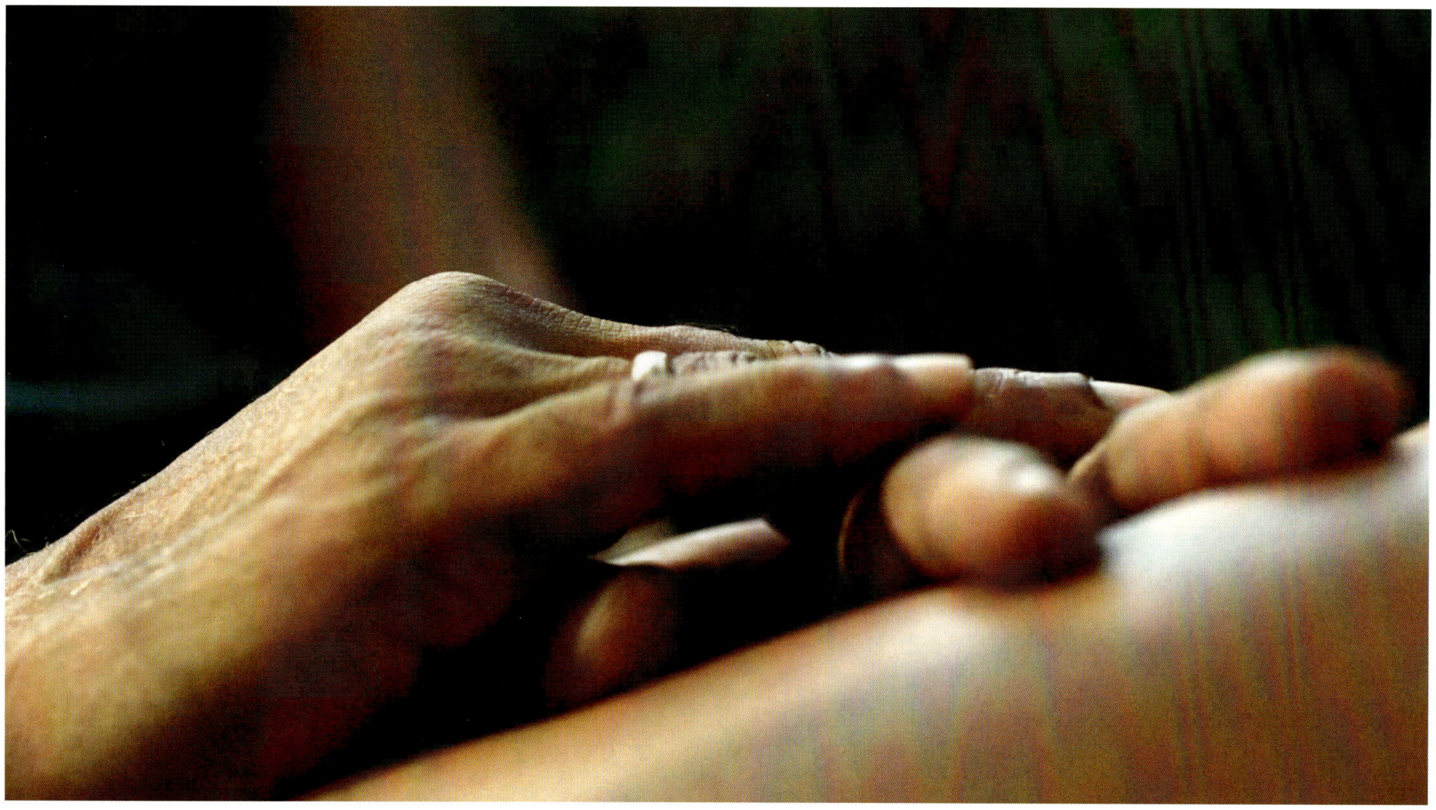

ISHMAEL IN THE GARDEN: A PORTRAIT OF ISHMAEL HOUSTON-JONES, 2018
BLACK-AND-WHITE AND COLOUR VIDEO
24 MIN. 15 SEC.
DIMENSIONS VARIABLE

previous pages,
ISHMAEL IN THE GARDEN: A PORTRAIT OF ISHMAEL HOUSTON-JONES, 2018
BLACK-AND-WHITE AND COLOUR VIDEO
24 MIN. 15 SEC.
DIMENSIONS VARIABLE

INSTALLATION VIEW AT GALERIE MAX HETZLER, BERLIN, 2019

Towards the end of Adam Pendleton's film Ishmael in the Garden: A Portrait of Ishmael Houston-Jones (2018), the titular choreographer and dancer says something disarmingly poetic: that he has always been interested in the 'cool of the heat', 'the dispassion of the passion'. These observations could just as well be applied to Pendleton's own work and process: his wide-ranging, multi-disciplinary practice, which encompasses painting, publishing, collage and more, is consistently fuelled by the heat of risk-taking artists and activists who have campaigned for social justice while simultaneously adopting the cool containers offered by the modernist avant-gardes.

Much has already been said about Pendleton's Dadaist take on the archive, his encyclopaedic exhumations of the social, political and art histories of the twentieth and twenty-first centuries, his penchant for research and citation (even uncredited borrowing), his remixing, reinterpretation and reflection upon fragments, vocabularies and aesthetic discourse in order to transform their meaning for an inscrutable and often disturbing contemporary moment. He both revives and re-contextualizes radical ideas, while establishing kinships and asserting his priorities as a black artist in America. Pendleton's videos bring his formal and thematic concerns into focus. They leverage the abstract possibilities of language, collapsing time across defined lineages of political and artistic expression.

from top,
LORRAINE O'GRADY: A PORTRAIT, 2012
SINGLE-CHANNEL COLOUR VIDEO
22 MIN. 50 SEC.
DIMENSIONS VARIABLE

JUST BACK FROM LOS ANGELES: A PORTRAIT OF YVONNE RAINER, 2016–17
SINGLE-CHANNEL BLACK-AND-WHITE VIDEO
13 MIN. 51 SEC.
DIMENSIONS VARIABLE

Ishmael in the Garden: A Portrait of Ishmael Houston-Jones is the third in a loose trilogy of single-channel moving-image portraits that began with Lorraine O'Grady: A Portrait (2012) and continued with Just Back from Los Angeles: A Portrait of Yvonne Rainer (2016–17). They are intimate encounters between Pendleton and three formidable figures – conceptual artist and critic Lorraine O'Grady, legendary choreographer-dancer-filmmaker Yvonne Rainer, and choreographer, author, performer, teacher and curator Ishmael Houston-Jones. While all three are senior American artists – at least one generation older than Pendleton – the itinerary of each is unique.

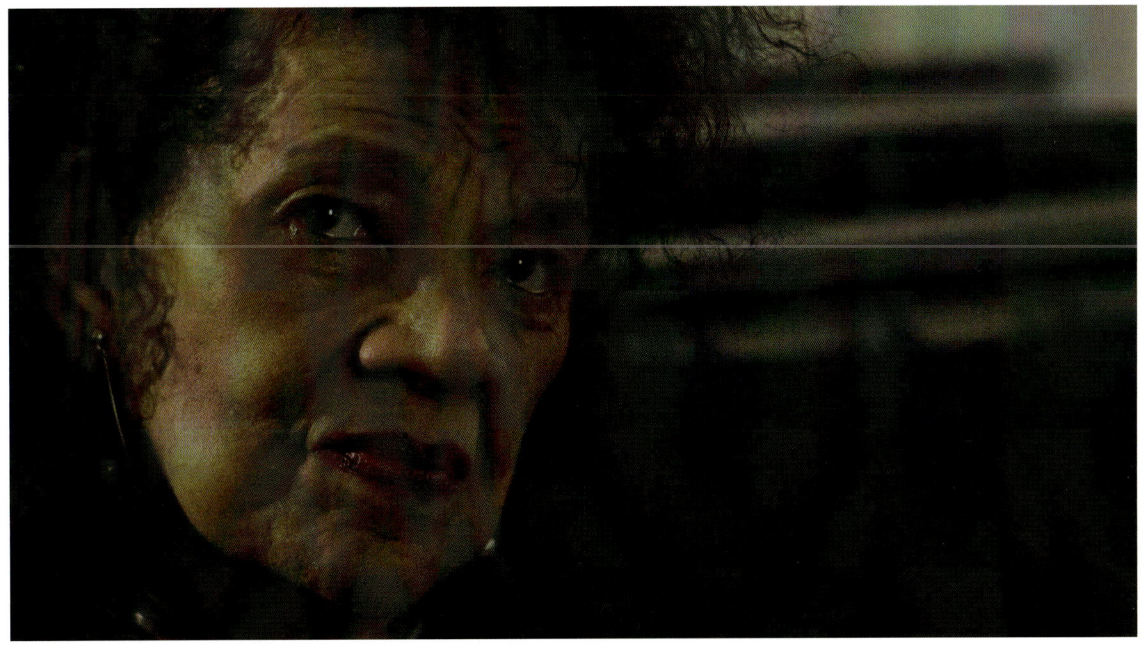

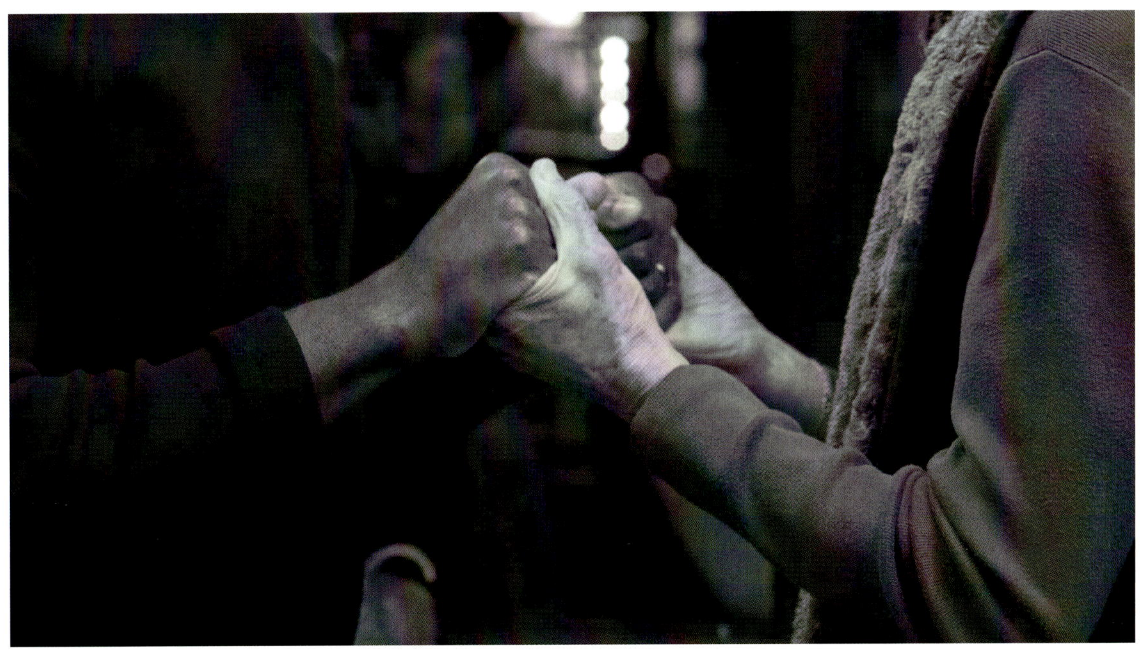

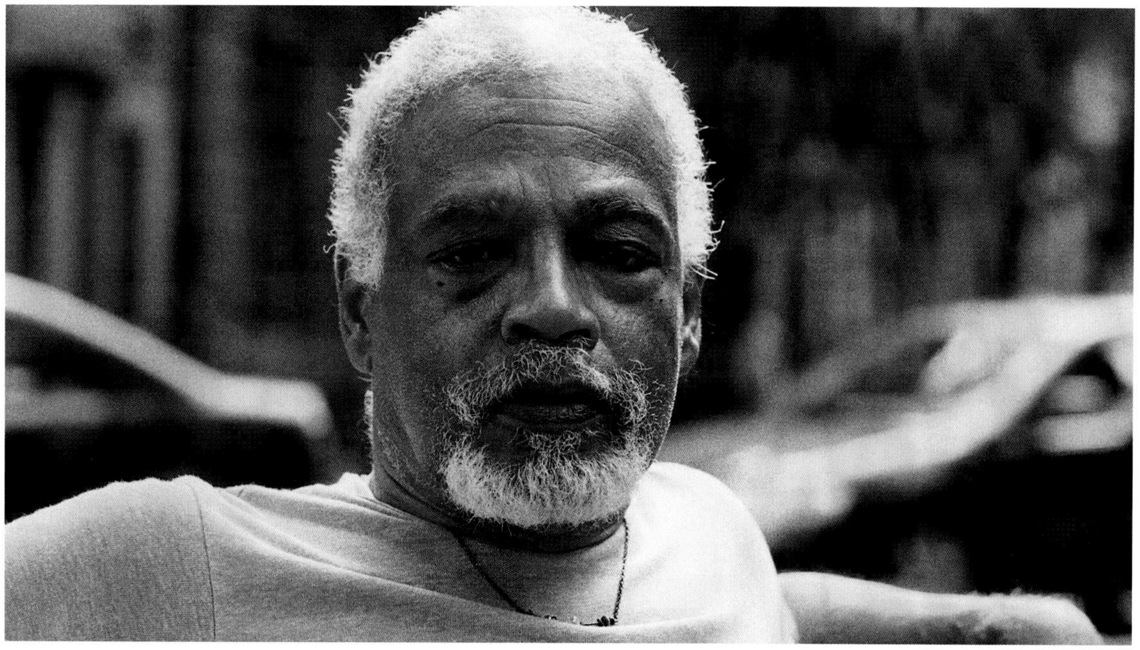

ISHMAEL IN THE GARDEN: A PORTRAIT OF ISHMAEL HOUSTON-JONES, 2018
BLACK-AND-WHITE AND COLOUR VIDEO
24 MIN. 15 SEC.
DIMENSIONS VARIABLE

Lorraine O'Grady began her career in 1980, developing a conceptual practice that addressed patriarchy and anti-black racism in art and culture, often through guerrilla performances. Yvonne Rainer is known for her choreography, beginning with Judson Dance Theater in the 1960s and Grand Union in the 1970s, as well as for her filmmaking, both of which are characterized by a spirit of 'radical juxtaposition'. Ishmael Houston-Jones, also a dancer and improviser, lived in Philadelphia in the 1970s and in Manhattan's East Village in the 1980s, where his frequently collaborative work was shaped by the punk scene and later by the AIDS epidemic.

Pendleton's video portraits are not conventional oral histories; they do not seek to relate their subjects' extraordinary lives as unbroken narratives. Nor are they non-narrative moving-image portraits, like Andy Warhol's screen tests. Rather, Pendleton's portraits generate temporal ellipses, personal recollections and extemporaneous encounters by way of a montage in which alternate blocks of language are assembled and re-assembled. As in the word-portraits of Gertrude Stein, the result is never a comprehensive or authoritative representation of a person, but a composition of movement and insistence that may actually dissolve, rather than clarify, the edges of the subject.

Pendleton produces these portraits with the help of pre-written scripts, which he hands to his subjects to read from on the spot. The scripts are collages of textual material that sometimes include Pendleton's own writing. In each portrait, self-conscious acts of recitation and reading

LORRAINE O'GRADY: A PORTRAIT, 2012
SINGLE-CHANNEL COLOUR VIDEO
22 MIN. 50 SEC.
DIMENSIONS VARIABLE

produce weighted gestures of pronouncement, usurpations of normative dialogue, as well as conduits for beautiful, spontaneous emotion and recall. Pendleton is very much a director here, carefully conducting the action via the camera (whose traces, such as jump cuts, a visible clapper or lens flare, are often self-reflexively embedded in the works) and constructing a cinematic style and rhythm from his editing of shots and sequences. These are not straightforward documentary talking heads; the videos rest in a hybrid zone between documentary and art film. Their deceptively simple and surprisingly moving passages transmit a comingling of personal and public information, all the while creating space for directed dislocation, private longing and performance.

In Lorraine O'Grady: A Portrait, Pendleton uses a cropped close-up as the first image: his subject's face positioned on the far left side of the frame. The artist reads out, as if from memory, a list of her own exhibitions to date. The camera re-frames her and reveals a splash of colour, maybe a floral backdrop, and a mirror behind her. O'Grady is sitting on a sofa in the loft where she has lived for thirty-seven years, poised (naturally glamorous as Pendleton points out) but also slightly destabilized by the camera's constant repositioning and Pendleton's audible directions, which are incorporated into the video as refracted mise-en-abyme. There is an unmistakable playful complicity between subject and artist, and her gaze upon him is tender and open. One can sense mutual respect and admiration.

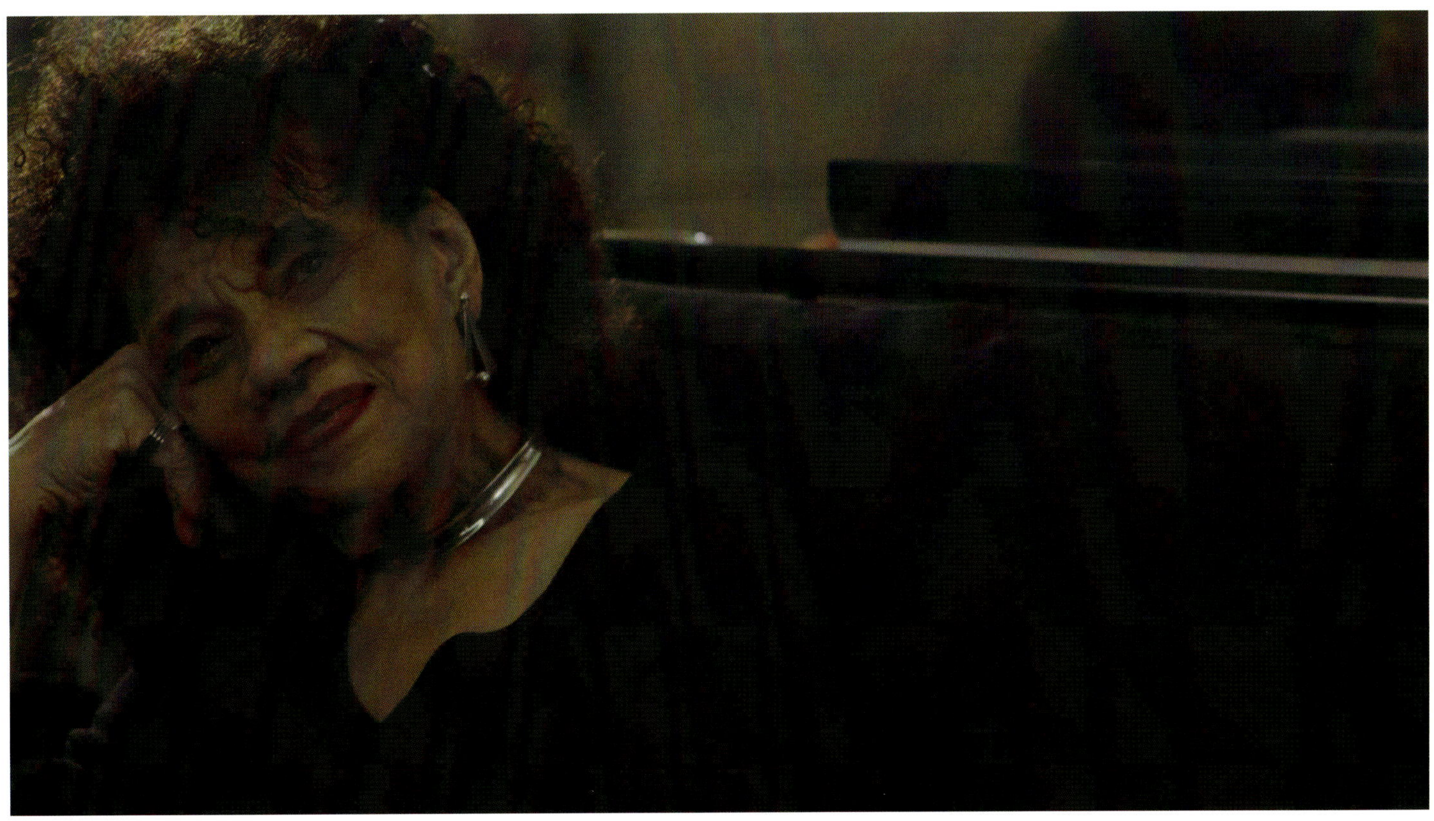

Prompting anecdotes from O'Grady through questions about her personal and professional life, Pendleton toys with chronology, synchronicity and authorship in the video. He makes good use of the jump cut – a <u>Nouvelle Vague</u> and Godardian staple from the 1960s – the staccato rhythms used not only to create multiple Cubist takes on a framed composition, but also to emphasize, cut up and repeat certain phrases that O'Grady speaks: 'Not well made', becomes 'well made' and back again until new meaning is formed. As in many of his other works, Pendleton employs parataxis here as a means to probe the plasticity of language itself. O'Grady, following Pendleton's cues, but also asserting herself beyond his direction, confides thoughts and feelings about a past lover, her family, her impetus and efforts as a black female artist and critic to upend the conservative

<u>LORRAINE O'GRADY: A PORTRAIT</u>, 2012
SINGLE-CHANNEL COLOUR VIDEO
22 MIN. 50 SEC.
DIMENSIONS VARIABLE

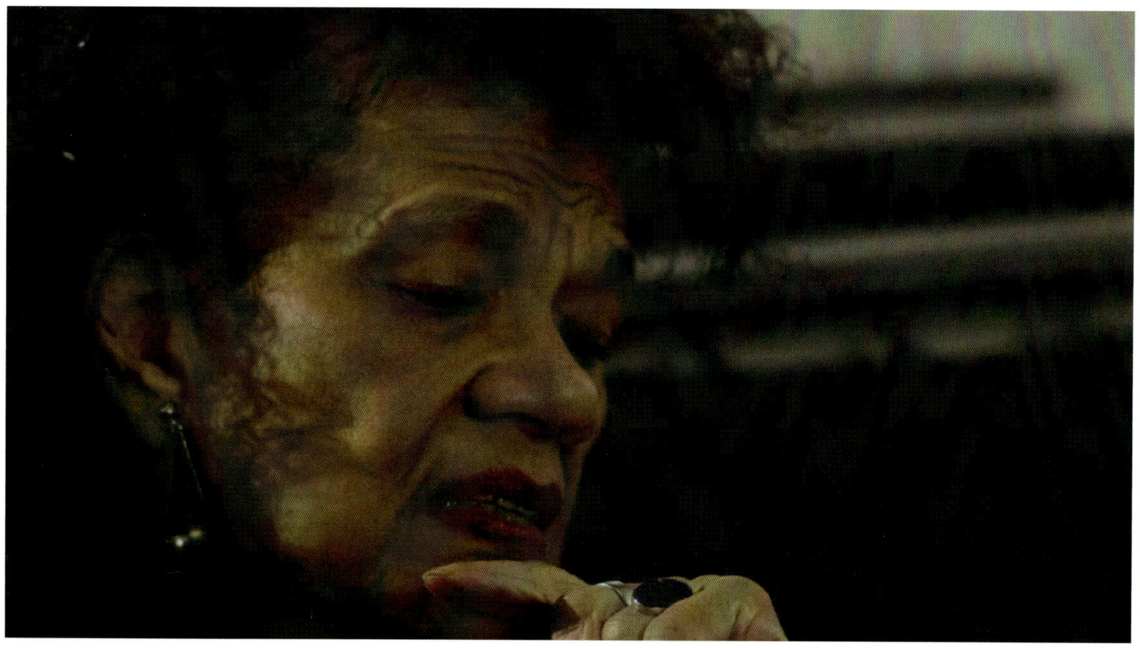

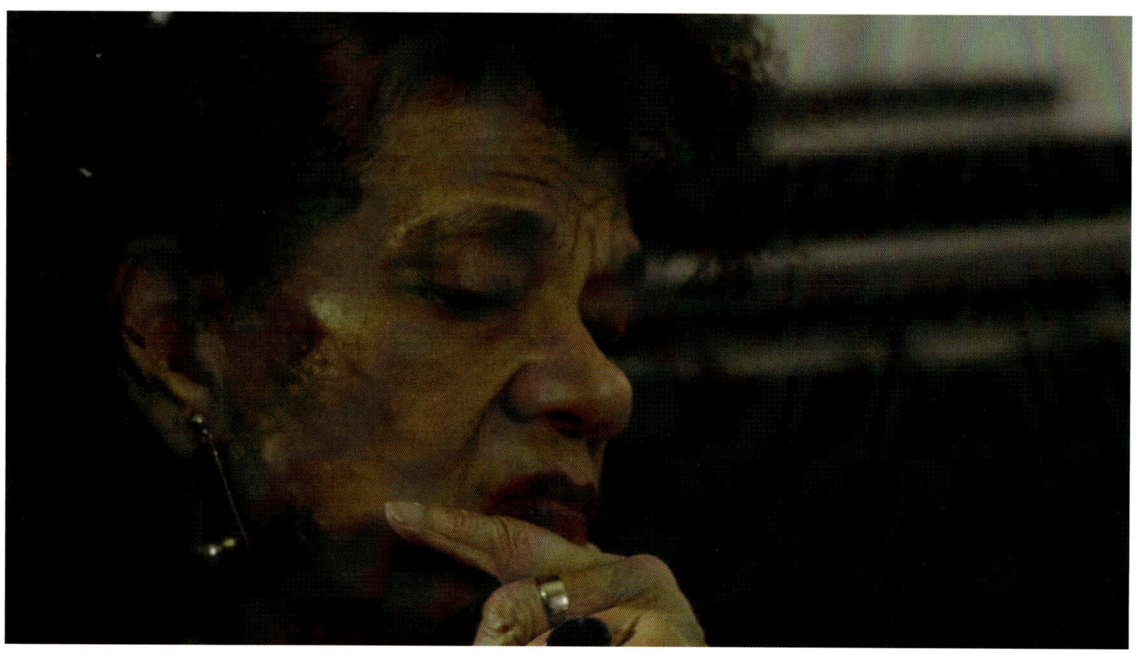

LORRAINE O'GRADY
ART IS..., 1983
PERFORMANCE
AFRICAN-AMERICAN DAY
PARADE, HARLEM, NEW YORK,
SEPTEMBER 1983

conventions of the cultural elite, to break down the barriers between black art and white art. Her autobiographical account, sliced and rearranged, is framed with recitations from Pendleton's script, including passages from American poet Lyn Hejinian's book-length prose poem My Life, itself a fragmented autobiography. The conflation of Hejinian's experimental life-writing with O'Grady's own reflections results in an unexpected slippage of the subject between the two discourses.

Pendleton edits in photographs from one of O'Grady's best-known works, the street performance Art Is... at Harlem's African-American Day Parade in September 1983, in which the artist and a troupe of fifteen performers used large, antique-style gold frames to recast marchers as art. Speaking poignantly about the significance of the street, the freedom of the parade versus the focus of the demonstration, O'Grady challenges the assumption that 'avant-garde art doesn't have anything to do with black people' in a way that resonates strongly with Pendleton's own work.

As Joan Armatrading's 'Woncha Come on Home' plays, a soft flood of Proustian emotion validates what had been quietly building: that we are watching a remarkable woman looking back at her life, at her achievements, the obstacles and hardship left to dangle in pregnant silence. O'Grady's strength and determination are unquestionably a source of inspiration; both she and Pendleton refuse to accept the art-historical relegation of black artists to realist or expressionist positions, instead melding notions of blackness with a conceptualist cool. 'The reading is as important as the understanding', offers O'Grady, and indeed both she and Pendleton, with their predilection for the experimental and non-linear, partake in a world of possibility and a shared ethos that fuses subjectivity with formalism.

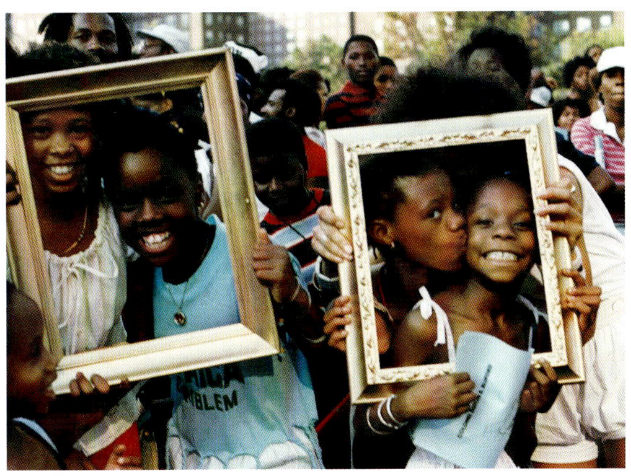

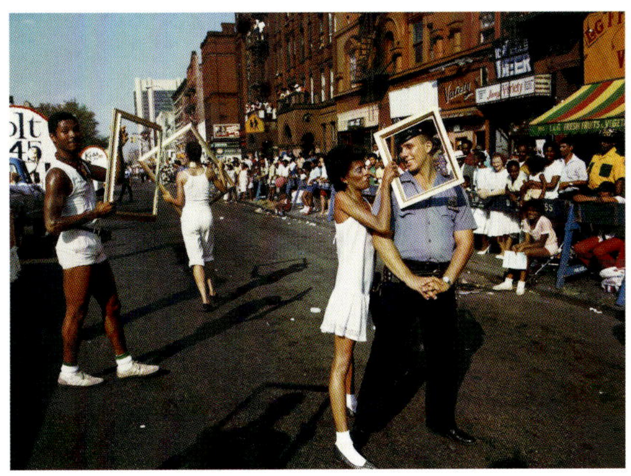

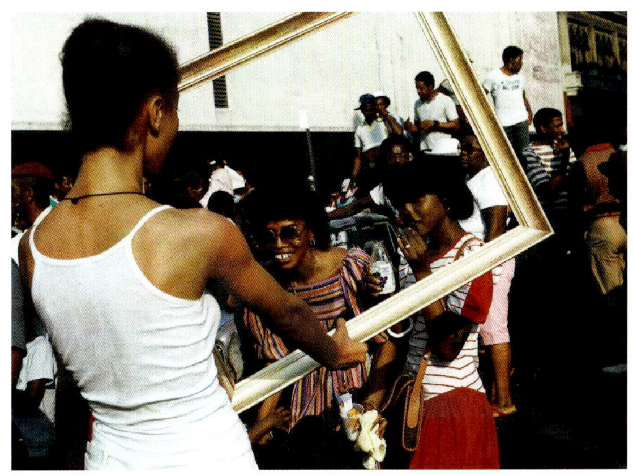

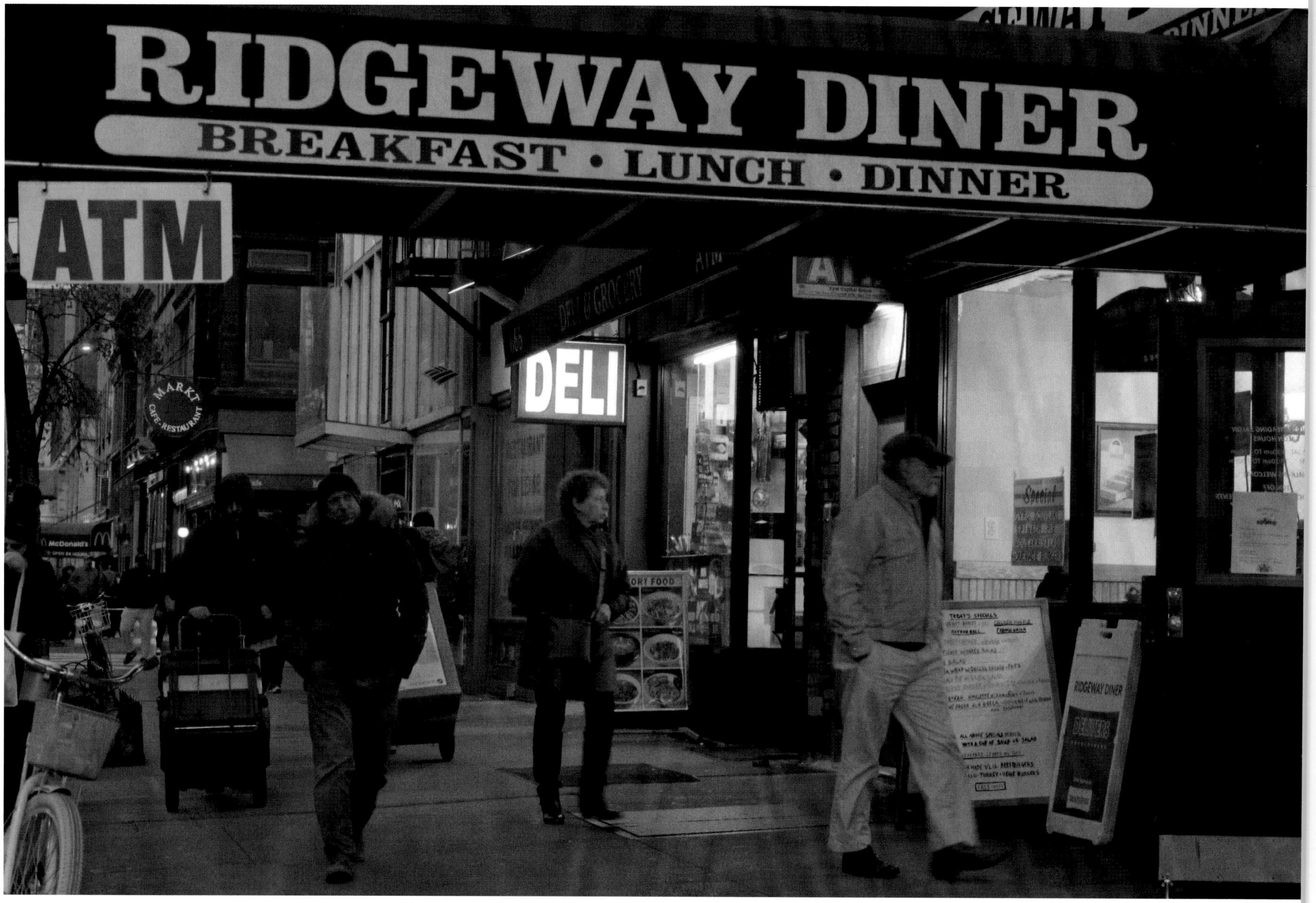

While the portrait of Lorraine O'Grady is shot in colour, and has a stripped down, nervy aesthetic, *Just Back from Los Angeles* begins like an auteurist art-house film shot in winsome black-and-white. As a constant flow of people walk past the diner in two establishing shots, Charles Trenet's classic *chanson* 'La Mer' accompanies them, with a lyrical postcard effect. (Pendleton chose the song after seeing it mentioned in Rainer's 2006 memoir, *Feelings Are Facts*.) Once the camera moves inside the restaurant, the view of Rainer's face is semi-obscured by the arm of the server taking their order: a turkey burger on whole-wheat toast with fries for Rainer, while Pendleton, seated across from her at the table on the right side of the frame, orders a spanakopita and a Greek salad. Banal details, salient details, details fascinating in their ordinariness. We can't help but notice the symmetrical set-up of the composition, with a small painting on the wall perfectly marking the middle of the table.

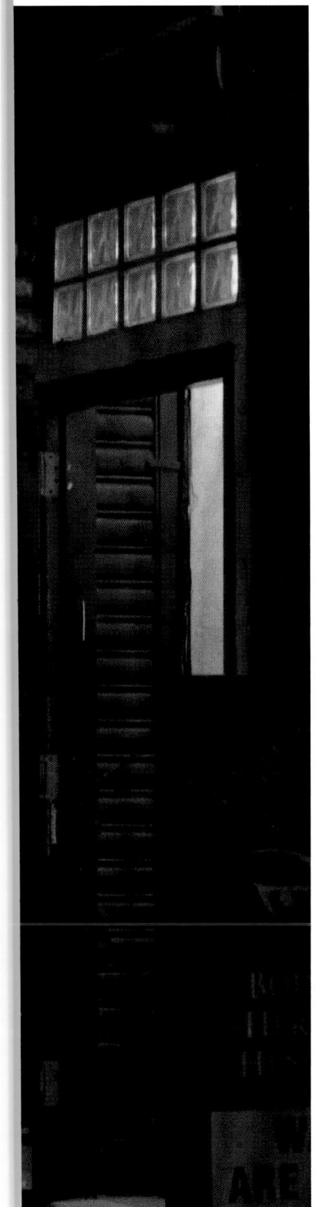

JUST BACK FROM LOS ANGELES: A PORTRAIT OF YVONNE RAINER, 2016–17
SINGLE-CHANNEL BLACK-AND-WHITE VIDEO
13 MIN. 51 SEC.
DIMENSIONS VARIABLE

Rainer is impressed by the numerous facts that Pendleton knows about her. As 'La Mer' continues in the background, a shot through a mirror shows Rainer anticipating Pendleton's questions. 'We're rolling. We're going', he says. Without missing a beat, in her characteristic deadpan manner, she asks 'Where?' It is clear from their slightly stilted exchange that the two do not know each other well. With Rainer turning eighty-two and Pendleton thirty-two, there is a fifty-year gap between them, a significant marker of time.

The title of the film derives from a story that Rainer tells about having just returned from Los Angeles, where she had performed, after a long hiatus, with two of her contemporaries, Simone Forti and Steve Paxton. As she discusses having taught Forti movements from her famous dance piece Trio A, the camera lingers on her gesticulating hands, moving from the table to above her head. A voice-over recording of Rainer reading some of her aphoristic writing accompanies the images. A cut to outside captures a traffic jam before we are back in the diner with Rainer holding a piece of paper – the script Pendleton has prepared and asked her to read. The text is a compilation of language from various unattributed authors; it begins with an extended discussion of racial oppression and the complicity of white liberals. Outside again, a voyeuristic camera watches Rainer teach Pendleton her 'arm drop' move as we hear a cacophony of car horns. The intercutting is sly, and back inside, as Rainer continues to read, objects become the focal point: the painting on the wall, the clock by the coffee machine (the awareness of time ticking forward in a choreography of its own), the stack of glasses, the other diners.

JUST BACK FROM LOS ANGELES: A PORTRAIT OF YVONNE RAINER, 2016–17
SINGLE-CHANNEL BLACK-AND-WHITE VIDEO
13 MIN. 51 SEC.
DIMENSIONS VARIABLE

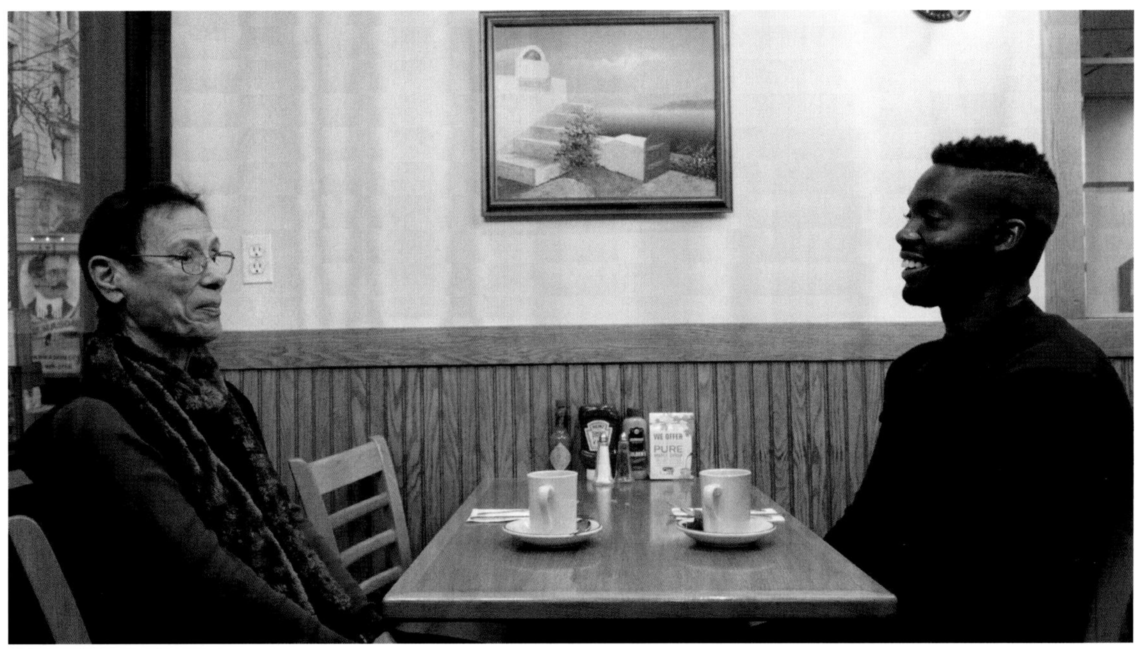

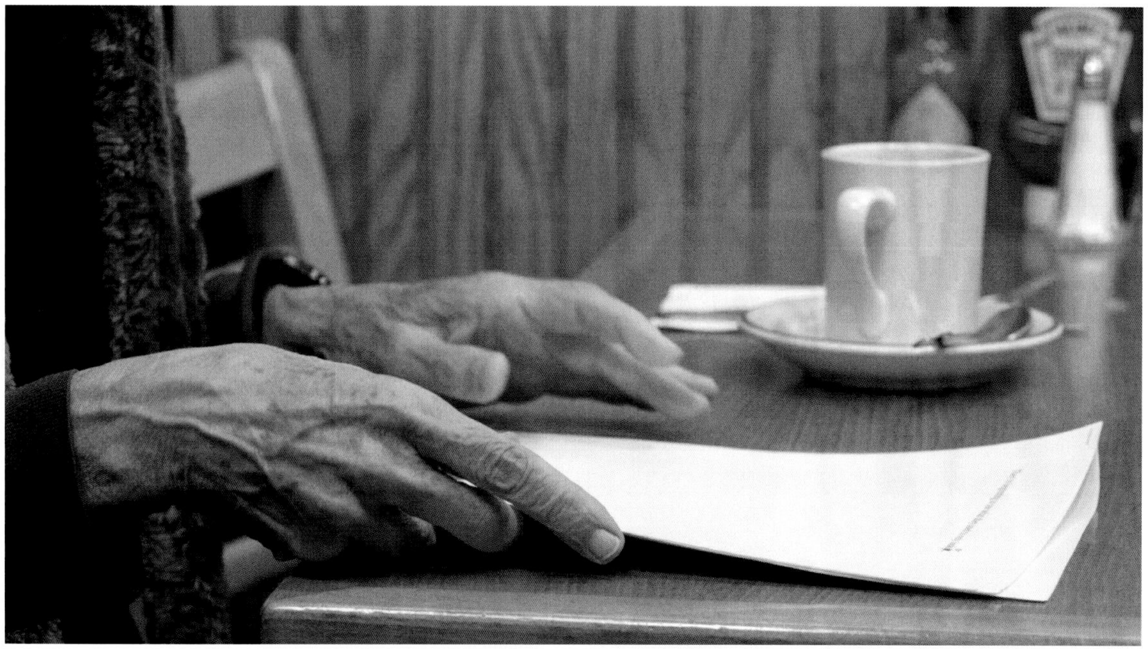

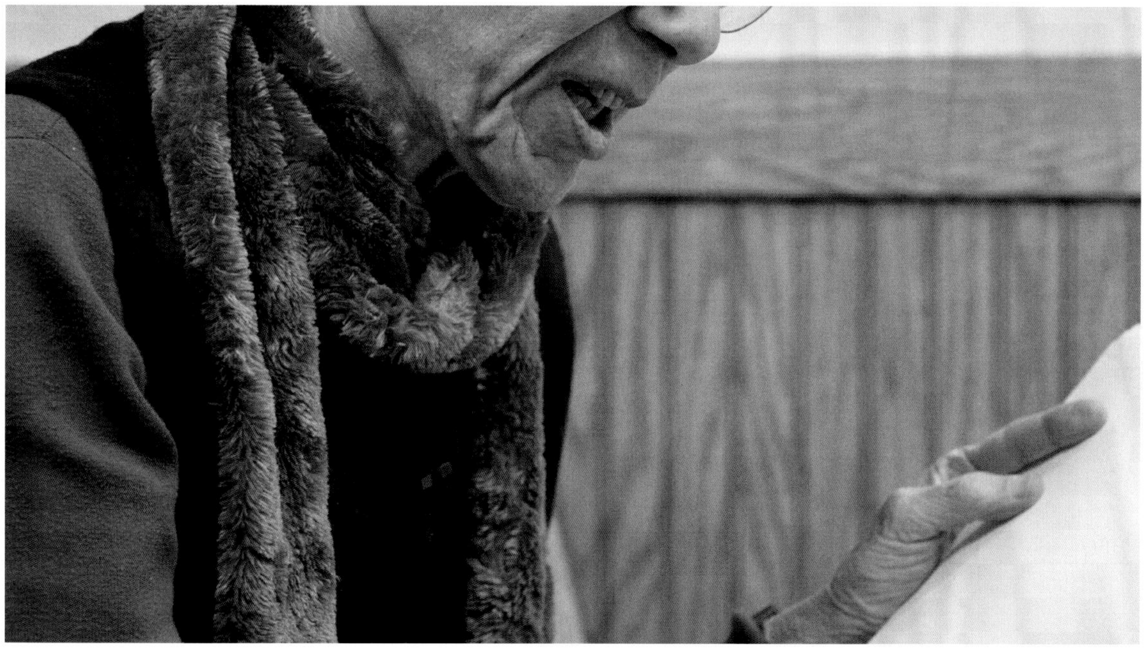

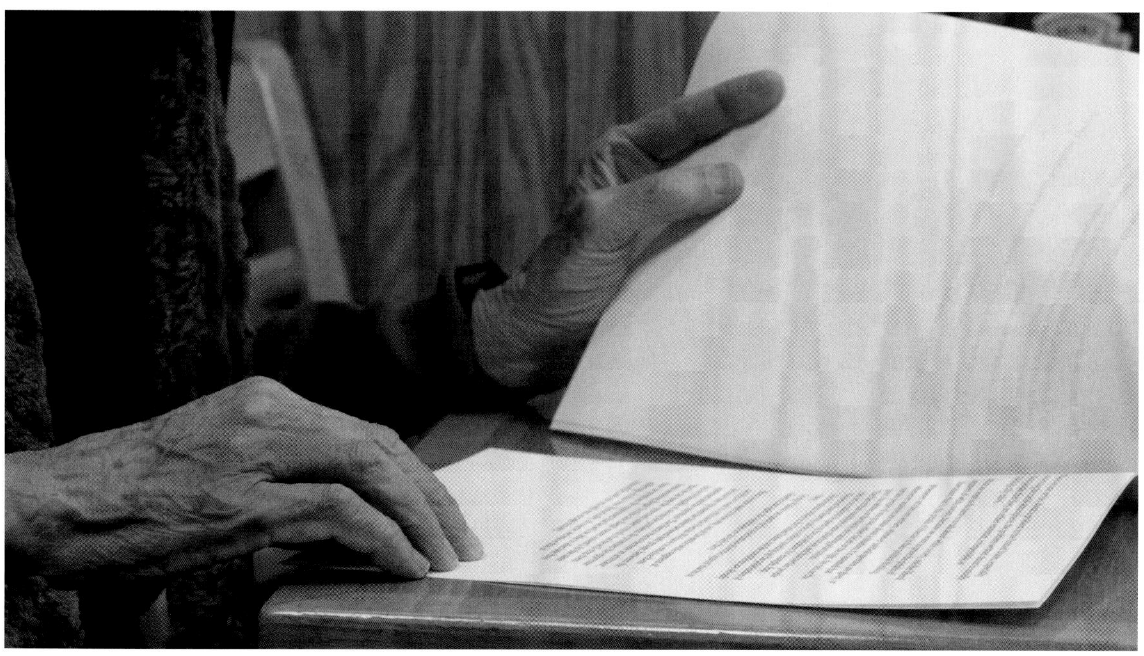

JUST BACK FROM LOS ANGELES: A PORTRAIT OF YVONNE RAINER, 2016–17
SINGLE-CHANNEL BLACK-AND-WHITE VIDEO
13 MIN. 51 SEC.
DIMENSIONS VARIABLE

next pages,
JUST BACK FROM LOS ANGELES: A PORTRAIT OF YVONNE RAINER, 2016–17
SINGLE-CHANNEL BLACK-AND-WHITE VIDEO
13 MIN. 51 SEC.
DIMENSIONS VARIABLE

INSTALLATION VIEW AT PACE GALLERY, LONDON, 2018

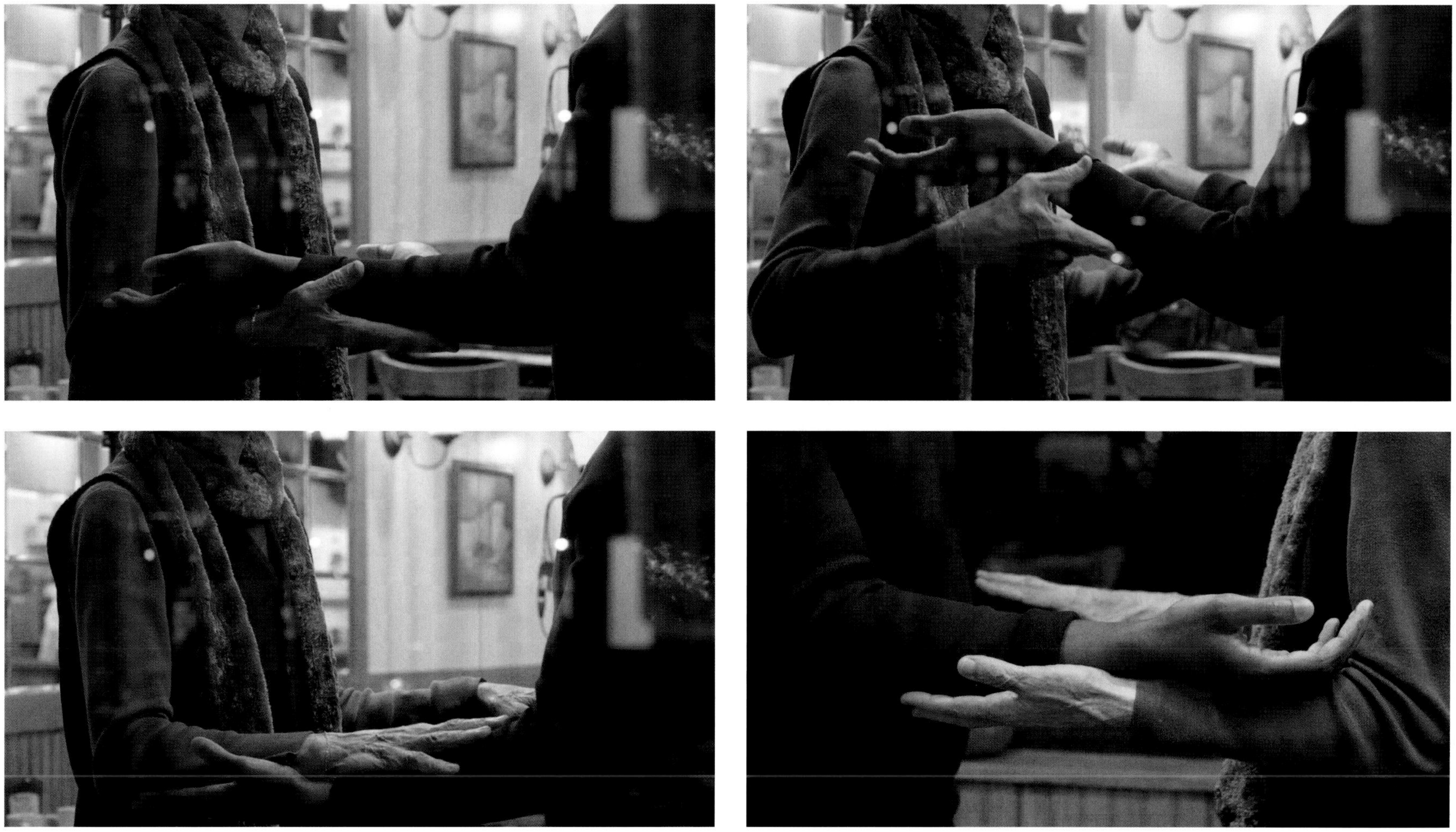

Finally there is silence, as Rainer and Pendleton place their hands on each other's forearms, their controlled, choreographed gestures bouncing lightly with a sense of consoling, comfort and connection. It's a gentle, moving moment, made all the more so by the fact that the earlier discussion of racism, read aloud by Rainer, and her own observation that a large disaffected segment of the population can no longer be denied, still linger from the previous scene. They are landing, as it were.

Rainer then reads a devastating list of black men, women and children murdered by the police in 2014. This passage is interposed between sentences from Rainer's memoir – specifically, sentences from an undated letter written to her by a colleague, Barbara Dilley, reflecting on the experience of performing Rainer's Continuous Project – Altered Daily in Kansas City in 1969. Each sentence begins with the phrase 'I remember'. Rainer is visibly overcome by the juxtapositions, the memories, the ongoing tragedies. 'A line is the distance between', she reads from Ron Silliman's poem 'Albany'. One can comprehend its meaning for a dancer-choreographer, as for an artist-filmmaker, or for any breathing being who has distance to bridge every day and for a lifetime. Footage of Rainer performing Trio A in 1978 concludes the film, as the Silver Harps' gospel song 'I'm Saved' plays, and we are left to contemplate the textures, gestures and sounds of another era like a salvation both offered and denied.

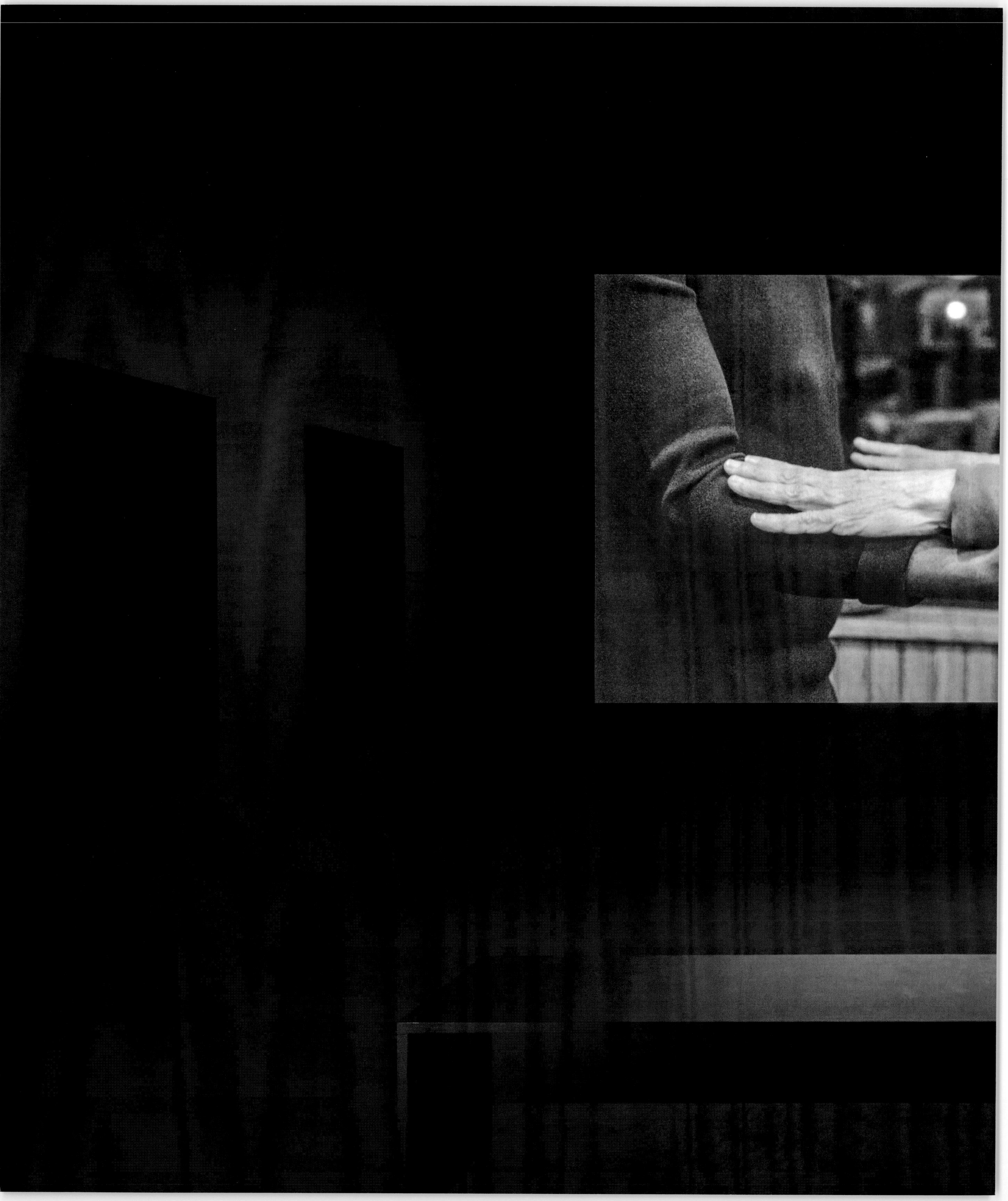

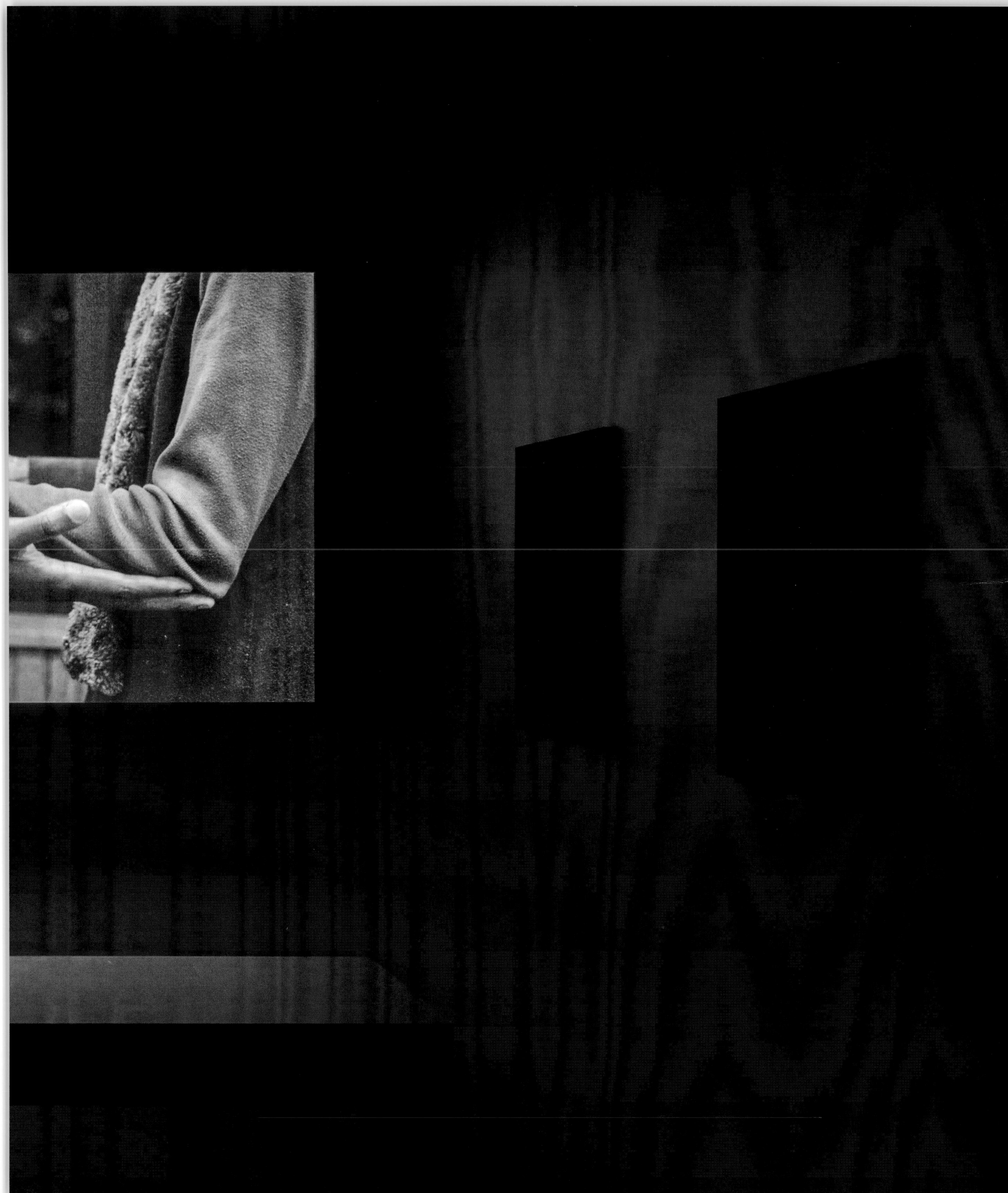

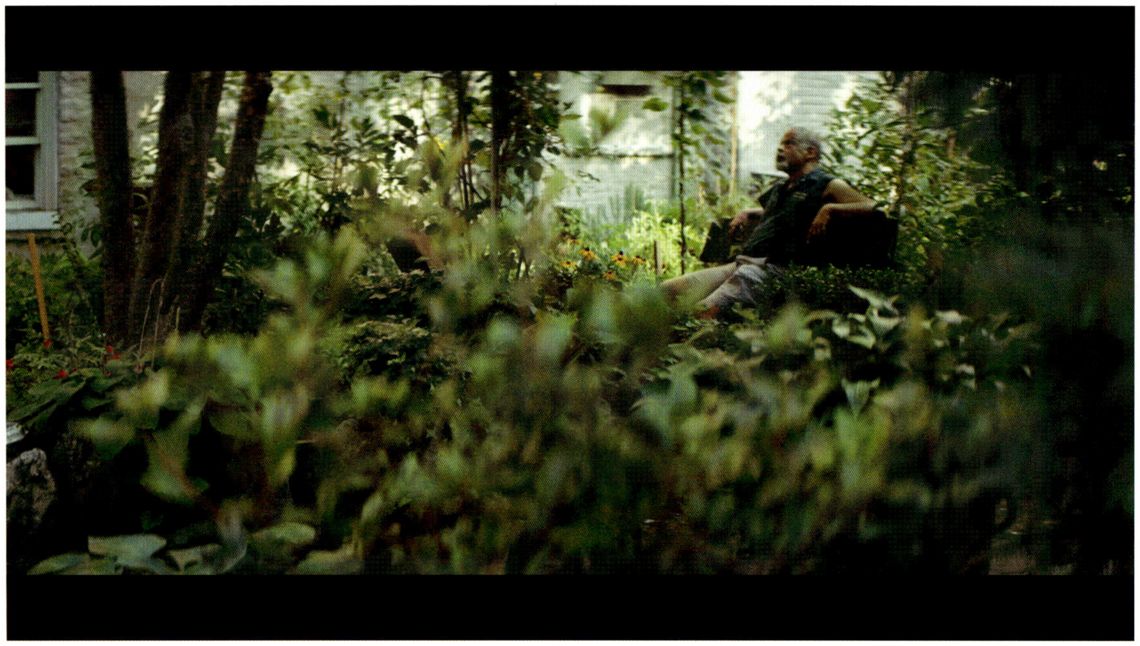

ISHMAEL IN THE GARDEN: A PORTRAIT OF ISHMAEL HOUSTON-JONES, 2018
BLACK-AND-WHITE AND COLOUR VIDEO
24 MIN. 15 SEC.
DIMENSIONS VARIABLE

Pendleton followed up Just Back from Los Angeles with another film about a choreographer, expanding his filmic repertoire to include passages of live dance. Ishmael in the Garden employs a variety of techniques and formats (black-and-white, colour, digital, celluloid, widescreen masking) as it portrays Houston-Jones in the lush greenery of a cloistered garden, and, later, as he dances in St Mark's Church in-the-Bowery in the East Village, the neighborhood where he has lived for the past thirty years.

Internationally recognized for his improvisational dance and language-based work, Houston-Jones has an extraordinary personal and professional trajectory, whose details emerge in the film mysteriously like shards of memory. Recounting intimate details from his biography, his confessional is halting at first. Whether shy or emotional, there is a slight quiver in his voice, which we experience diegetically and as recorded voice-over as Pendleton's camera searches Houston-Jones's sympathetic and solemn face. Themes of fatigue, aging, isolation, death and sex quickly come to the fore, as he recounts his experiences as a performer in queer, punk and dance communities in New York at the height of the AIDS epidemic. The film coaxes catharsis through movement and words.

Electronic music producer Mura Masa's 'give me The ground' opens the work with melancholic sensuality, and the entire film imparts the sensation of floating in a disembodied space as the camera pans from sky to skin. A particularly stirring sequence is composed of close-ups of Houston-Jones's hands, elegantly and precisely moving (a dancer's nervous fidget?) upon his lap as he recounts the painful, visceral memories of watching his friend and collaborator Fred Holland die in a hospice, of massaging his weakened body.

The second movement of the film is shot in black-and-white, the camera hovering over Houston-Jones as he lies on the floor stretching out his body in preparation for rehearsal. The voice-over is a series of recollections read like a poem, each line beginning – as with the lines in the Rainer film – with 'I remember…': 'seeing my father in his coffin … watching a sow give birth … teaching soldiers how to dance in Nicaragua' – all of the indelible details, large and small, that add up to an existence. As he dances the 'Ish Solo' from his famous and controversial piece THEM (1986), a collaboration with Chris Cochrane and Dennis Cooper, his eyes covered with a bandanna, his movements seem to be those of someone swatting away ghosts, of keeping death – and visions of death – at bay. The dancing is hypnotic, intense and gripping.

More protagonist than subject, Houston-Jones is then placed in a static medium shot, positioned before a glorious stained-glass window, shot in widescreen colour, as he directly faces the camera and reads from his erotic fiction. His diction is careful and deliberate, but also charmingly self-deprecating, as he details, with anatomical precision, a sexual encounter with a man. At a remove, he is enacting the cool of the heat.

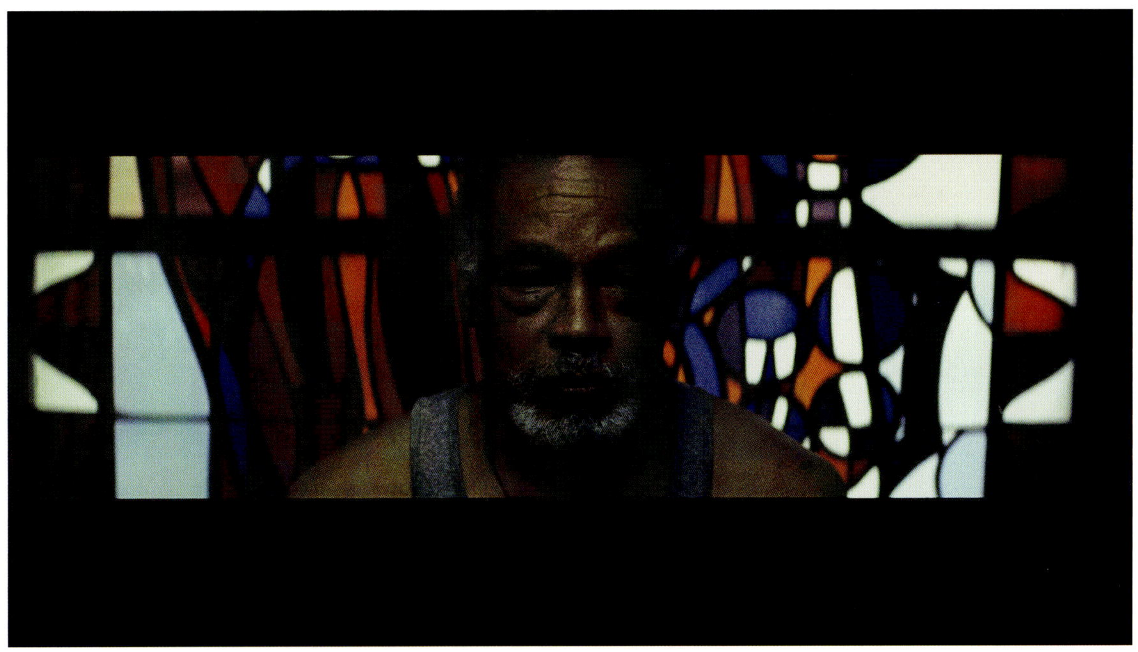

ISHMAEL IN THE GARDEN: A PORTRAIT OF ISHMAEL HOUSTON-JONES, 2018
BLACK-AND-WHITE AND COLOUR VIDEO
24 MIN. 15 SEC.
DIMENSIONS VARIABLE

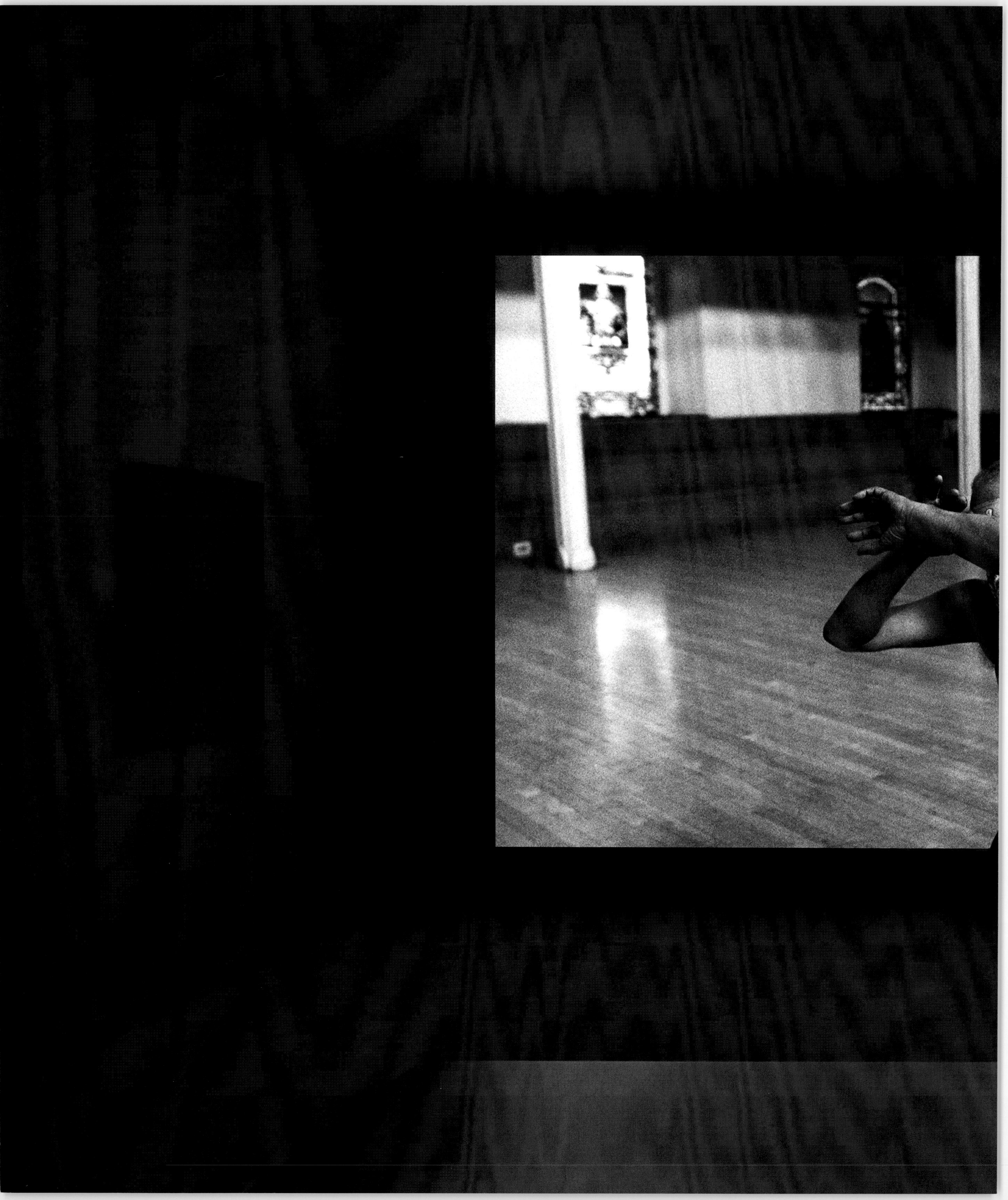

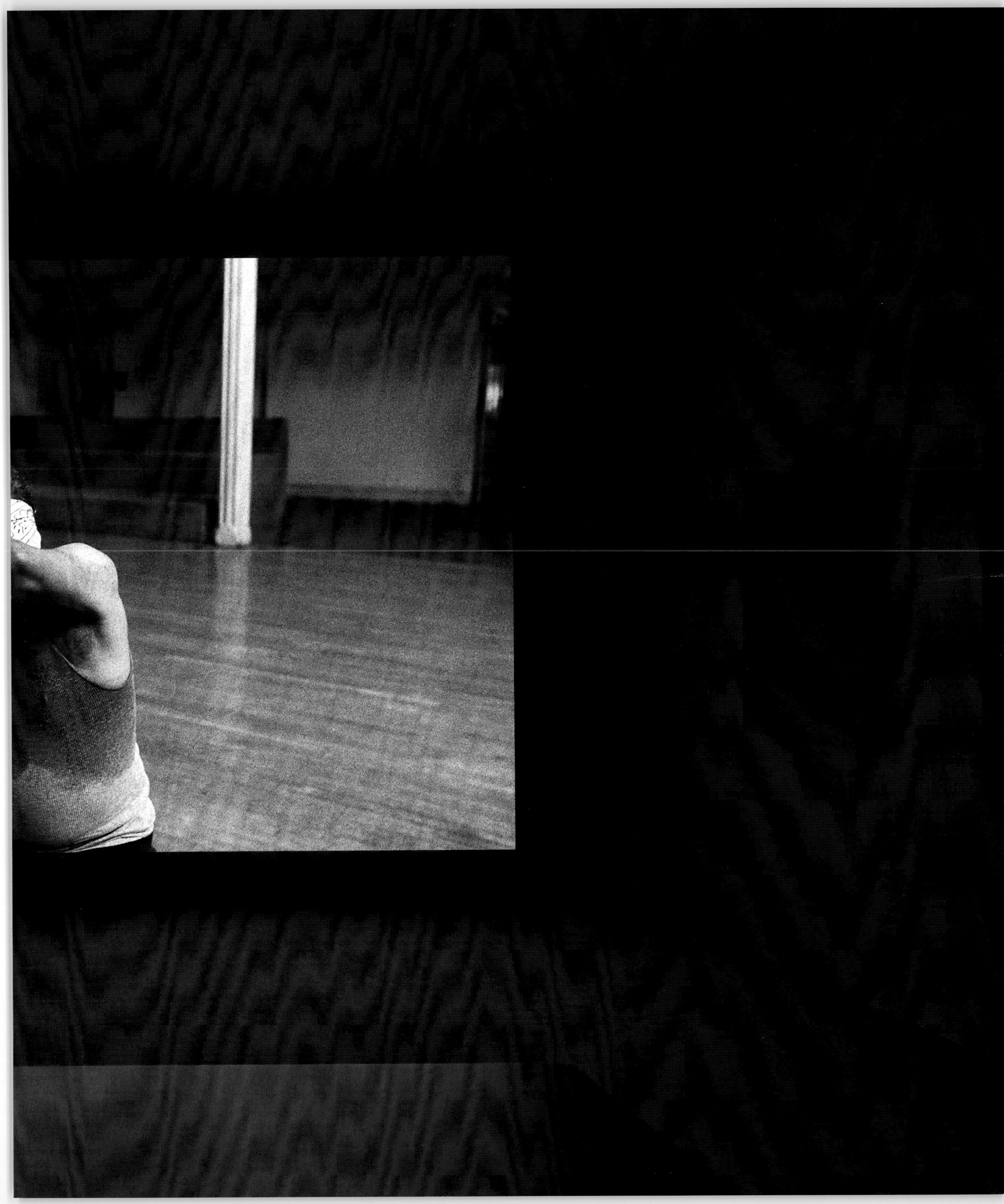

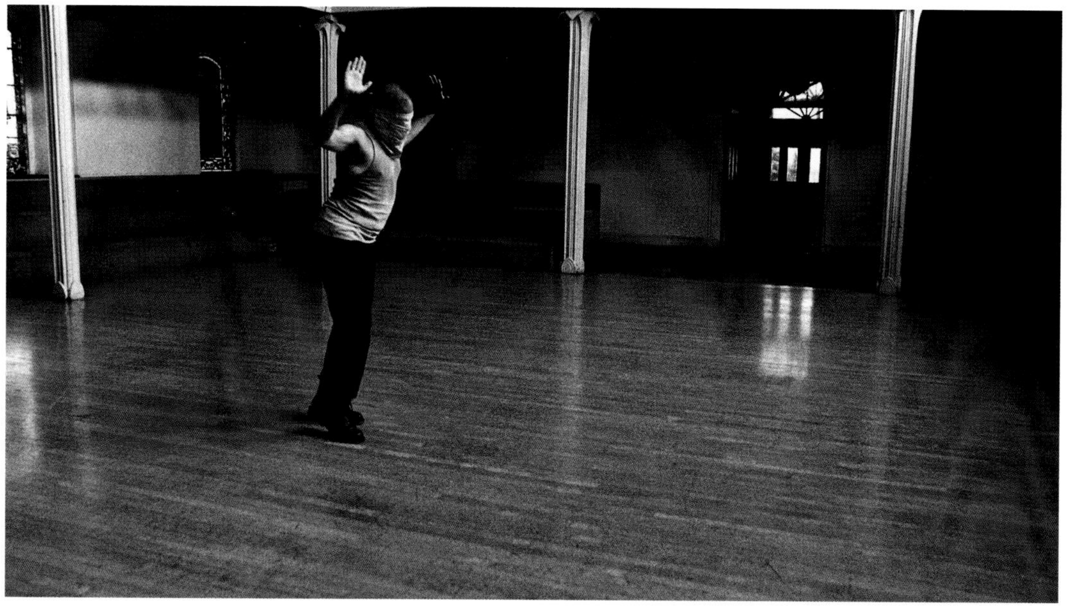

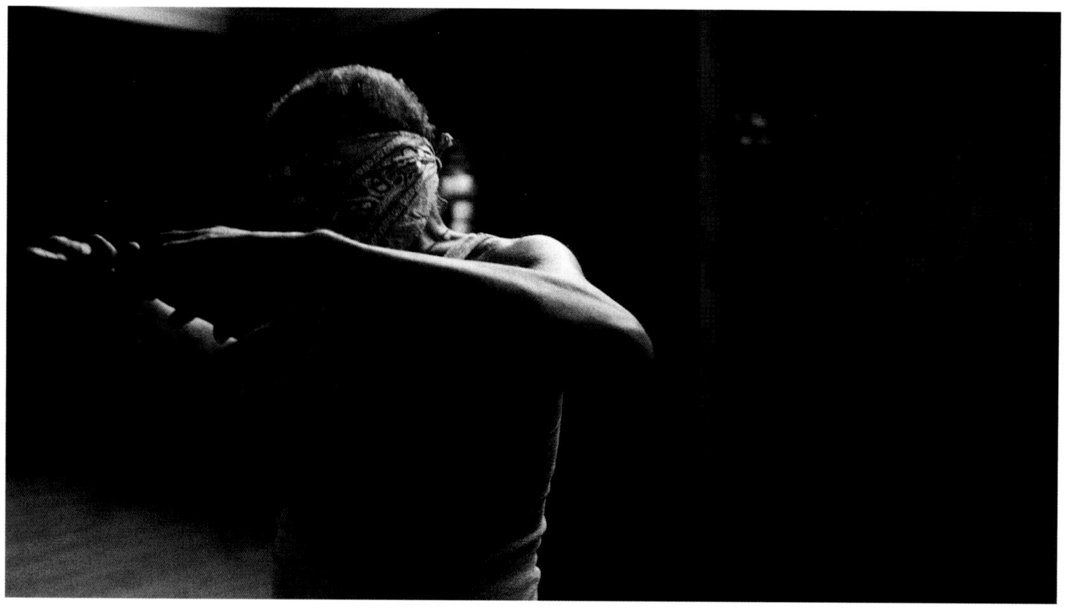

ISHMAEL IN THE GARDEN: A PORTRAIT OF ISHMAEL HOUSTON-JONES, 2018
BLACK-AND-WHITE AND COLOUR VIDEO
24 MIN. 15 SEC.
DIMENSIONS VARIABLE

previous pages,
ISHMAEL IN THE GARDEN: A PORTRAIT OF ISHMAEL HOUSTON-JONES, 2018
BLACK-AND-WHITE AND COLOUR VIDEO
24 MIN. 15 SEC.
DIMENSIONS VARIABLE

INSTALLATION VIEW AT GALERIE MAX HETZLER, BERLIN, 2019

The film switches tone (and format) yet again as we watch Houston-Jones perform an adaptation of his solo performance piece DEAD (1981). He dances in a roving spotlight as his voice lists the names of those who have marked his life and died in the past thirty years.[1] Along with contemporaries like Trisha Brown, past presidents and First Ladies, and every cat he has ever owned, Houston-Jones includes Trayvon Martin and Tamir Rice, whose deaths were a catalyst for the Black Lives Matter movement. The piece, like much of the portrait in which it appears, is a work of performance as remembrance, and remembrance as performance.

These three video portraits explore key moments in American history and art and render them on a human scale. They are affecting as well as intellectually stirring, interrogating gaps, fissures, incompleteness, the poetic and political nature of language, and the spaces between abstraction and historical testimony. The focus is on listening and learning, the vicissitudes of language, and on the ways in which creative gestures and manipulations exist alongside political ones. In this way, Pendleton turns past documents into living ones, reframing the material of memory.

History is literally handed down in these works, and Pendleton is a genuine receiver. But he is also constructing a conceptual framework that takes part in a certain tradition of portraiture – albeit often in order to problematize the limits of representation. He enacts an openness to interpretation, intervening in order to suggest that much spills out beyond the frame. His use of radical visual vocabularies and his fostering of interaction among documents confirm that the past is never dormant, and that our contemporary moment is one that must continue to mine history for future possibilities. With Lorraine O'Grady, Yvonne Rainer, and Ishmael Houston-Jones, Pendleton enlists allies, while also rendering homage. 'A line is the distance between' can be the distance between people, between gestures, between what has occurred and has yet to come, but also that mysterious space between cuts. There is a generosity in these works that emanates hope and resistance, and calls upon human vulnerability and connection as catalysts for change rather than elegiac resignation.

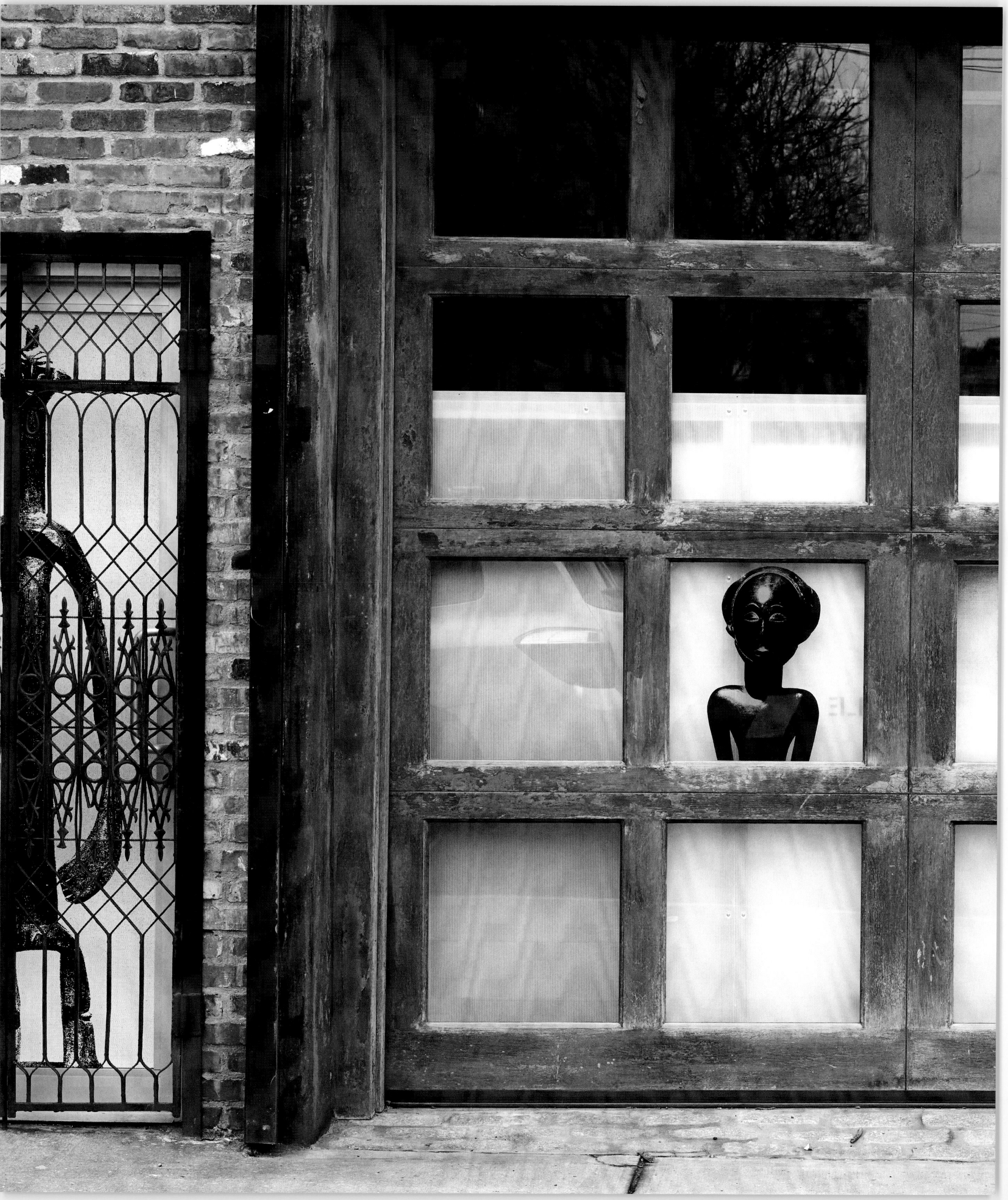

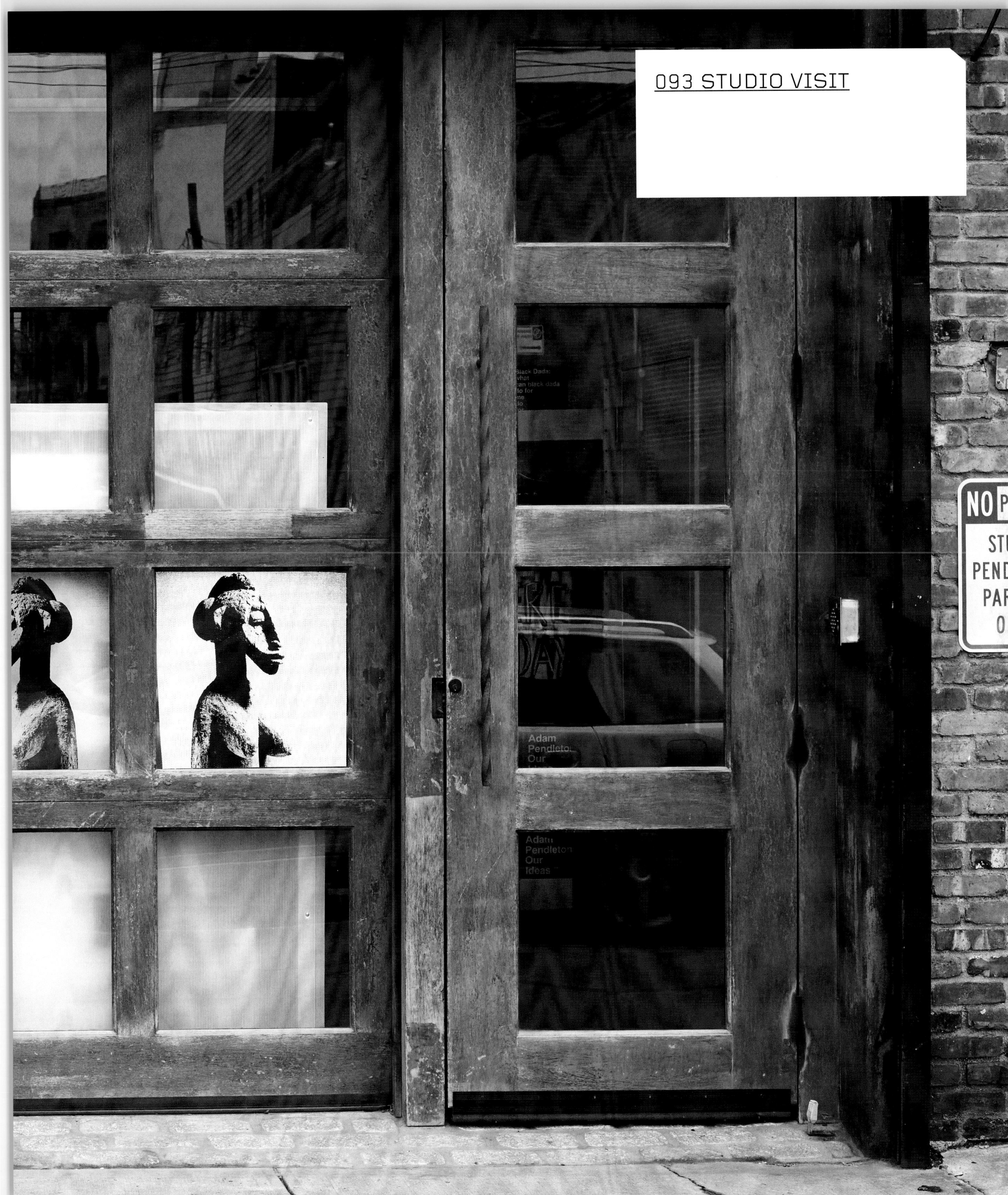
Adam
Pendleton
Our
Ideas

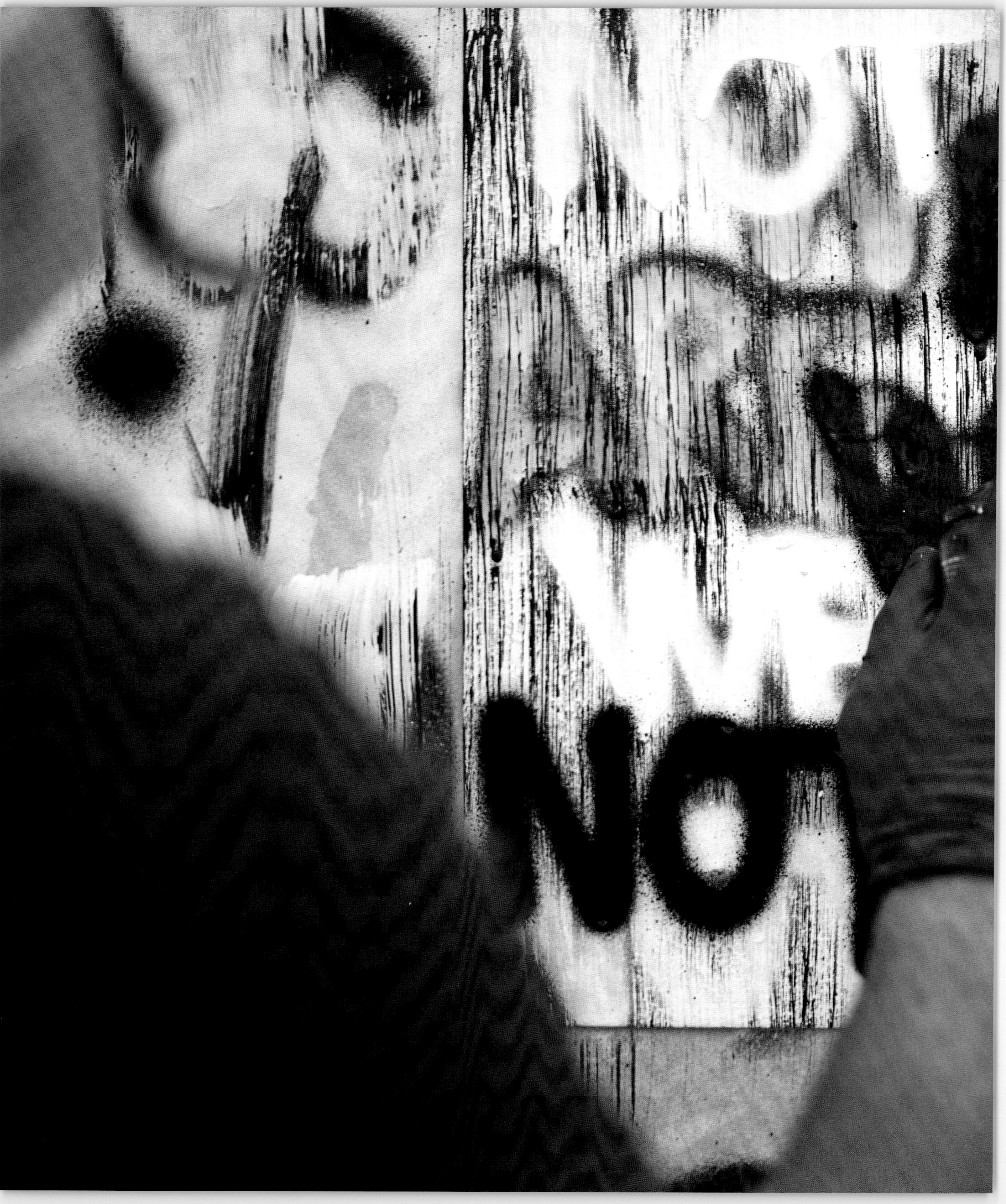

NO
NO

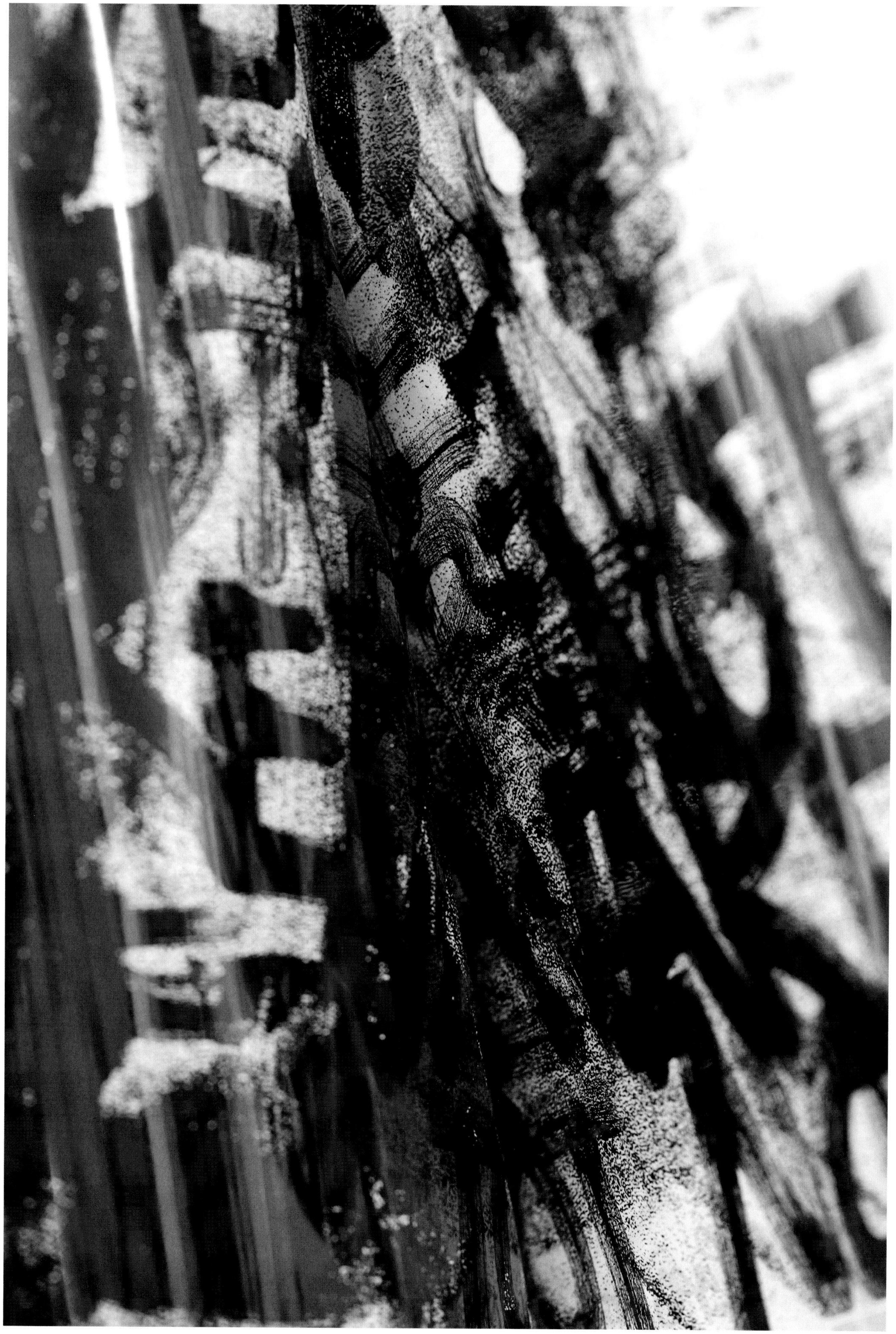

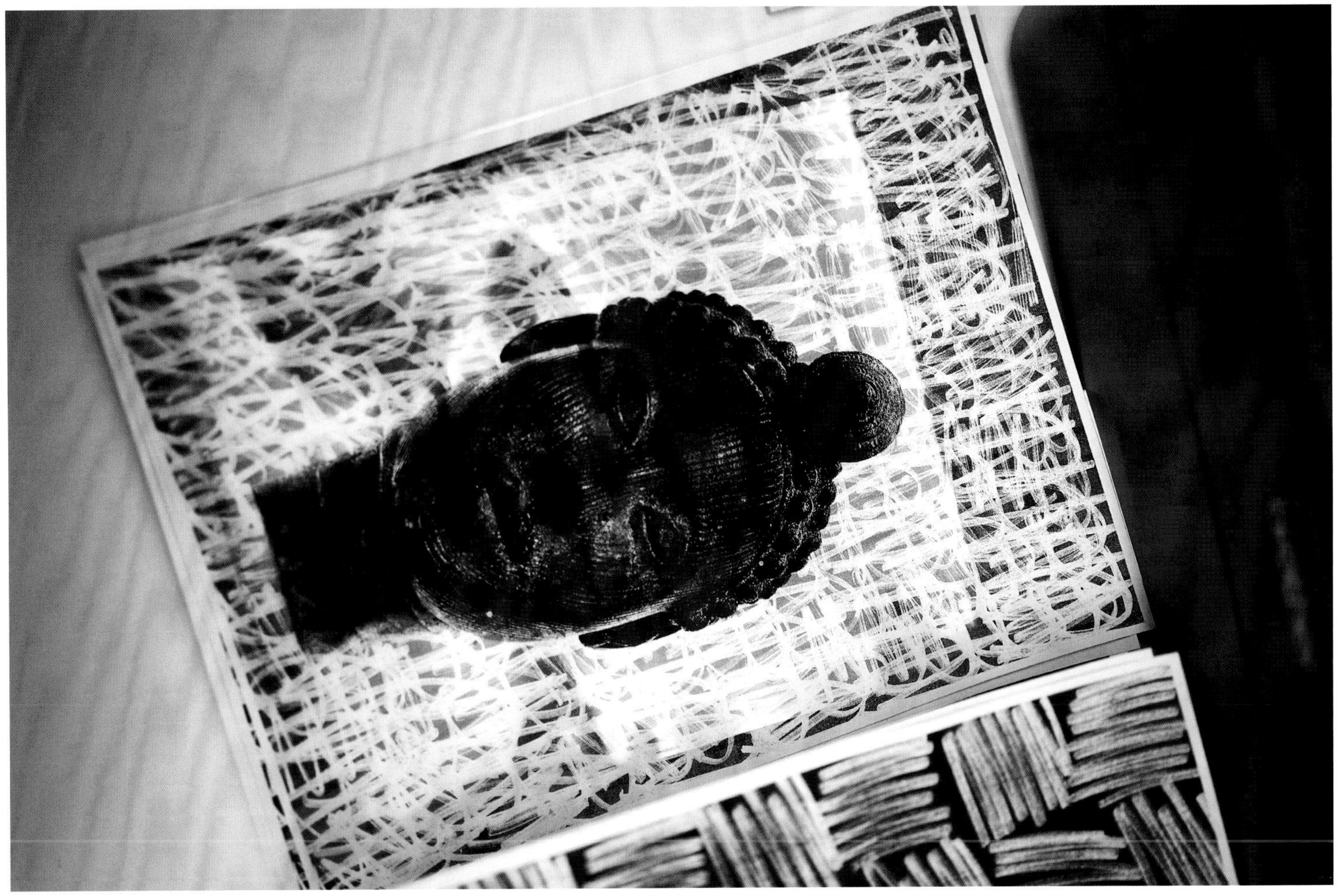

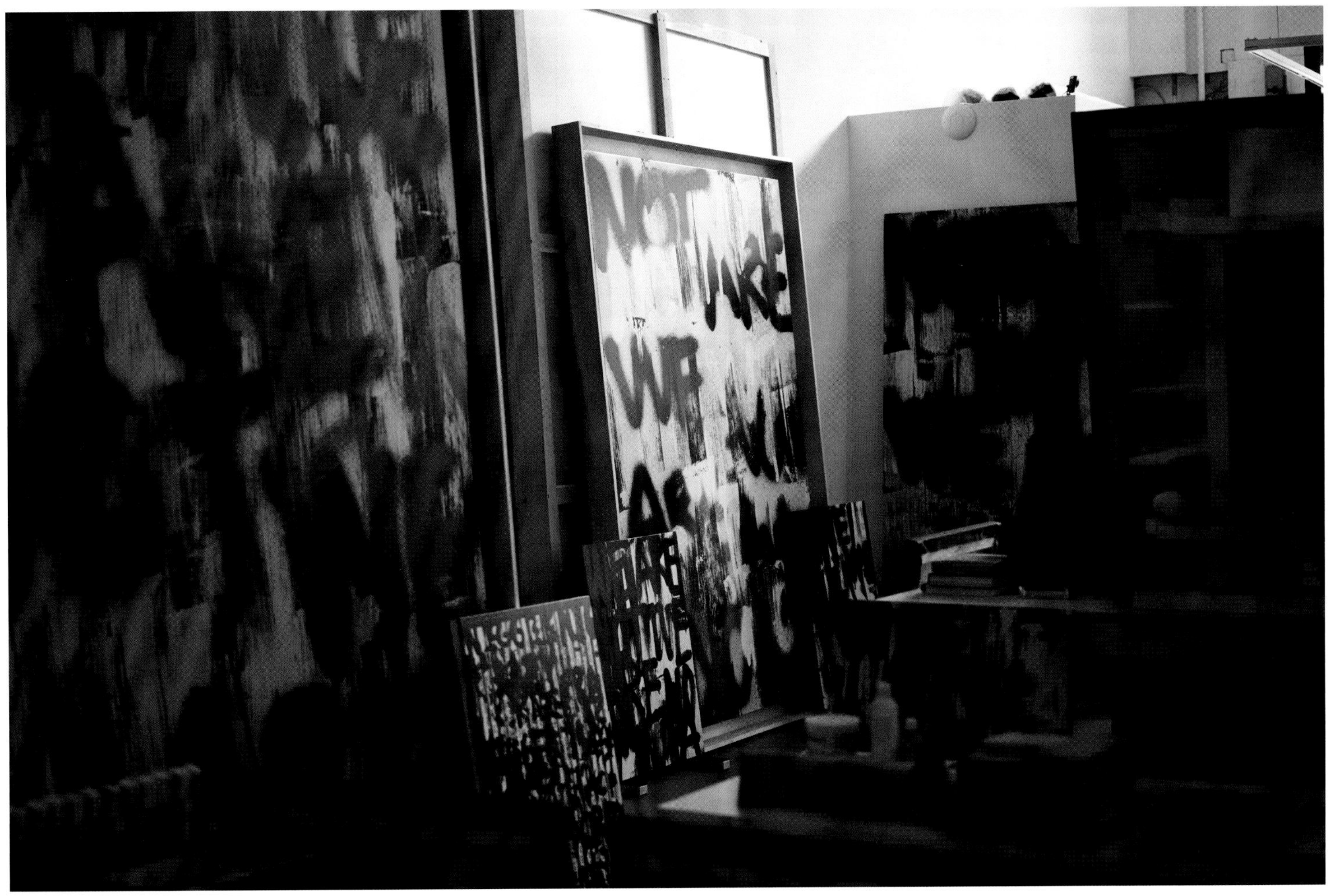

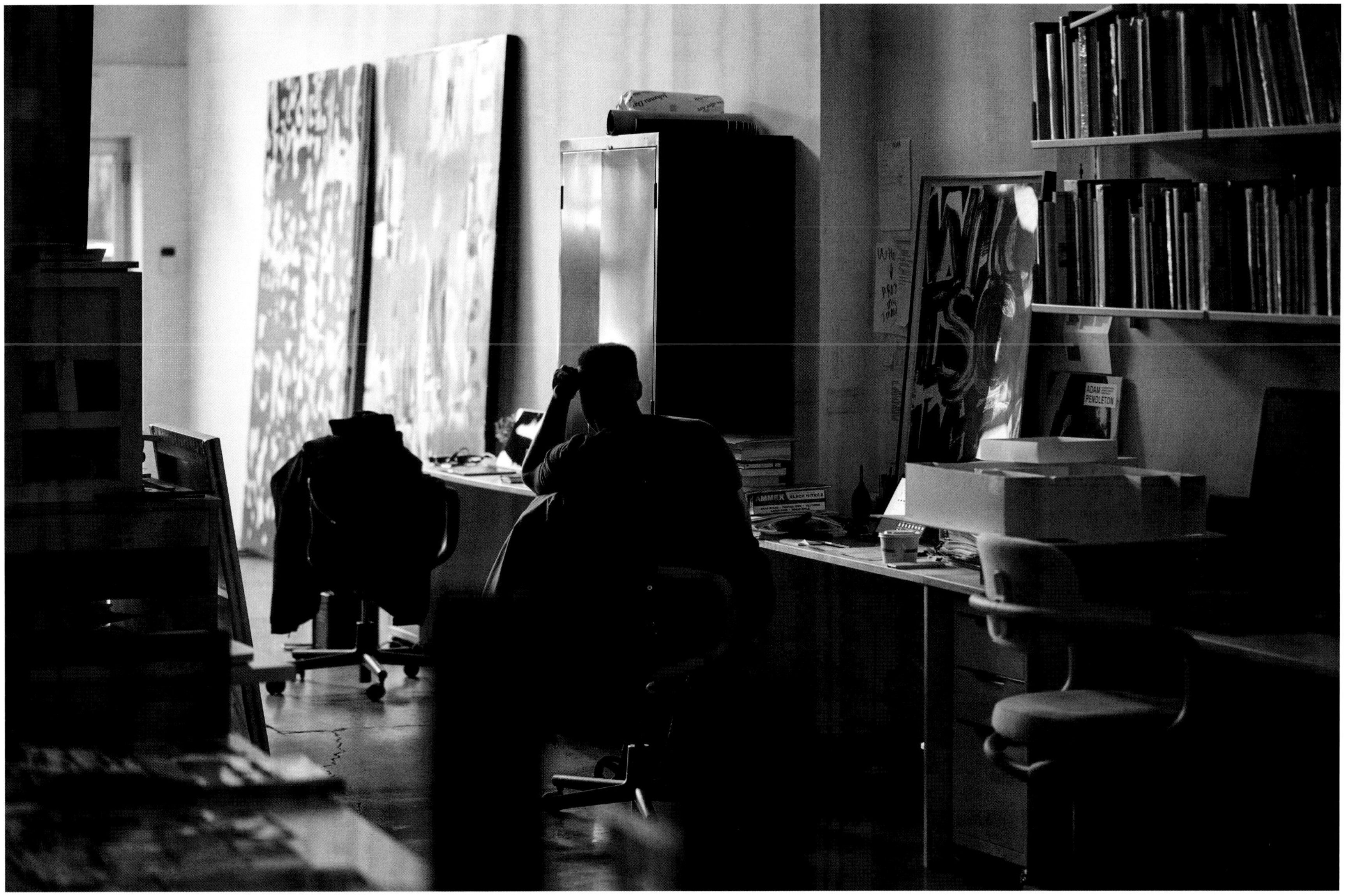
ADAM
PENDLETON

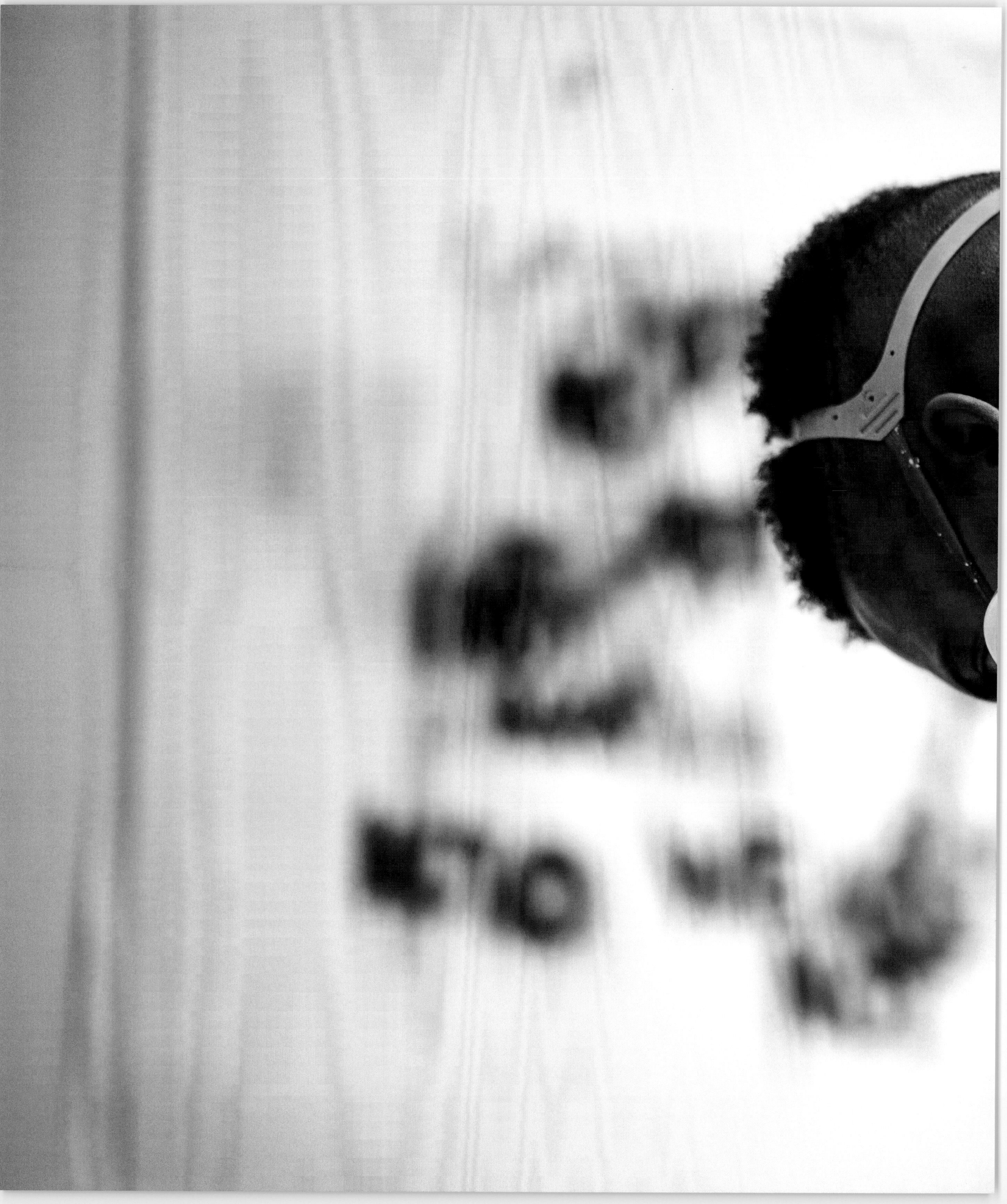

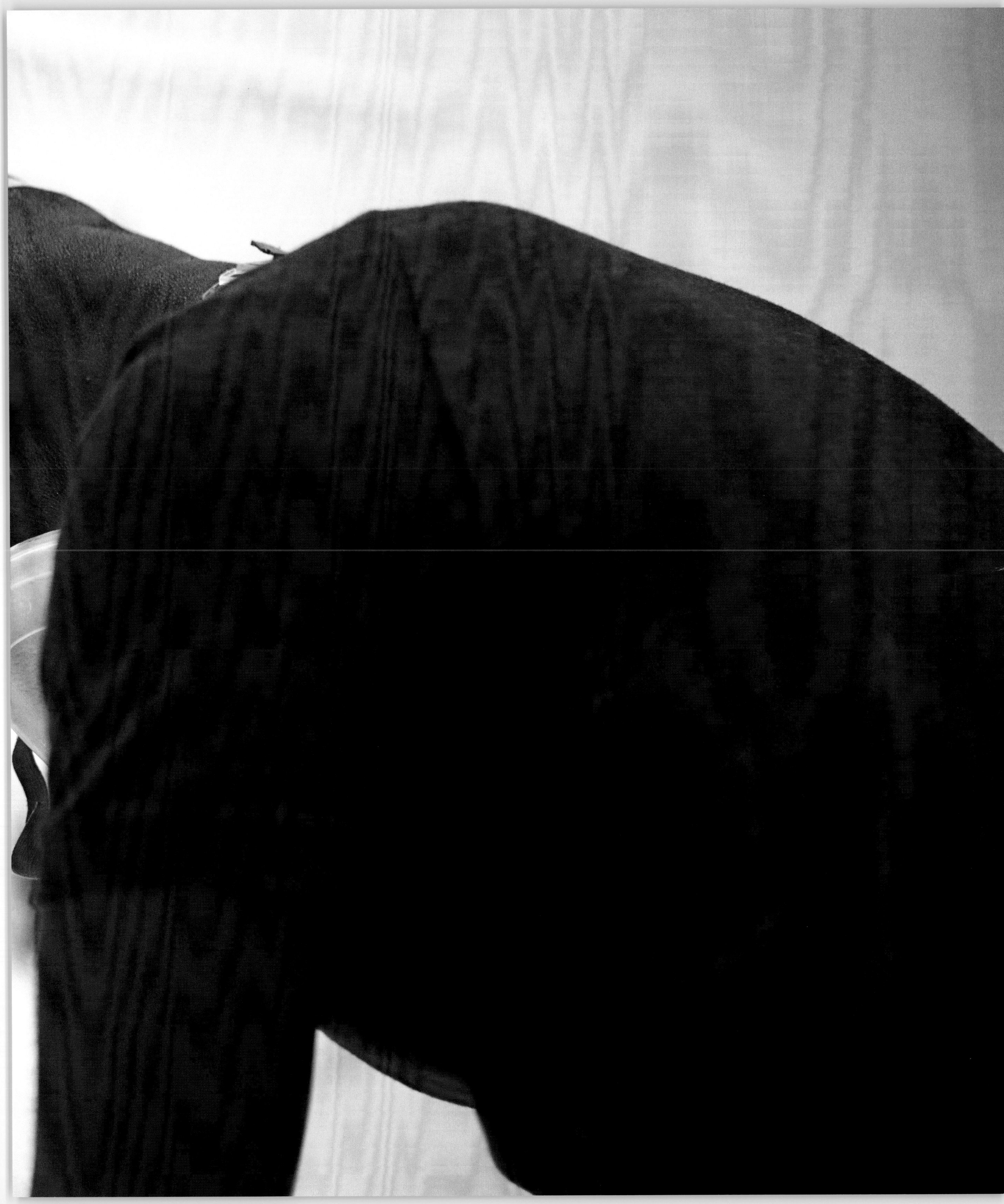

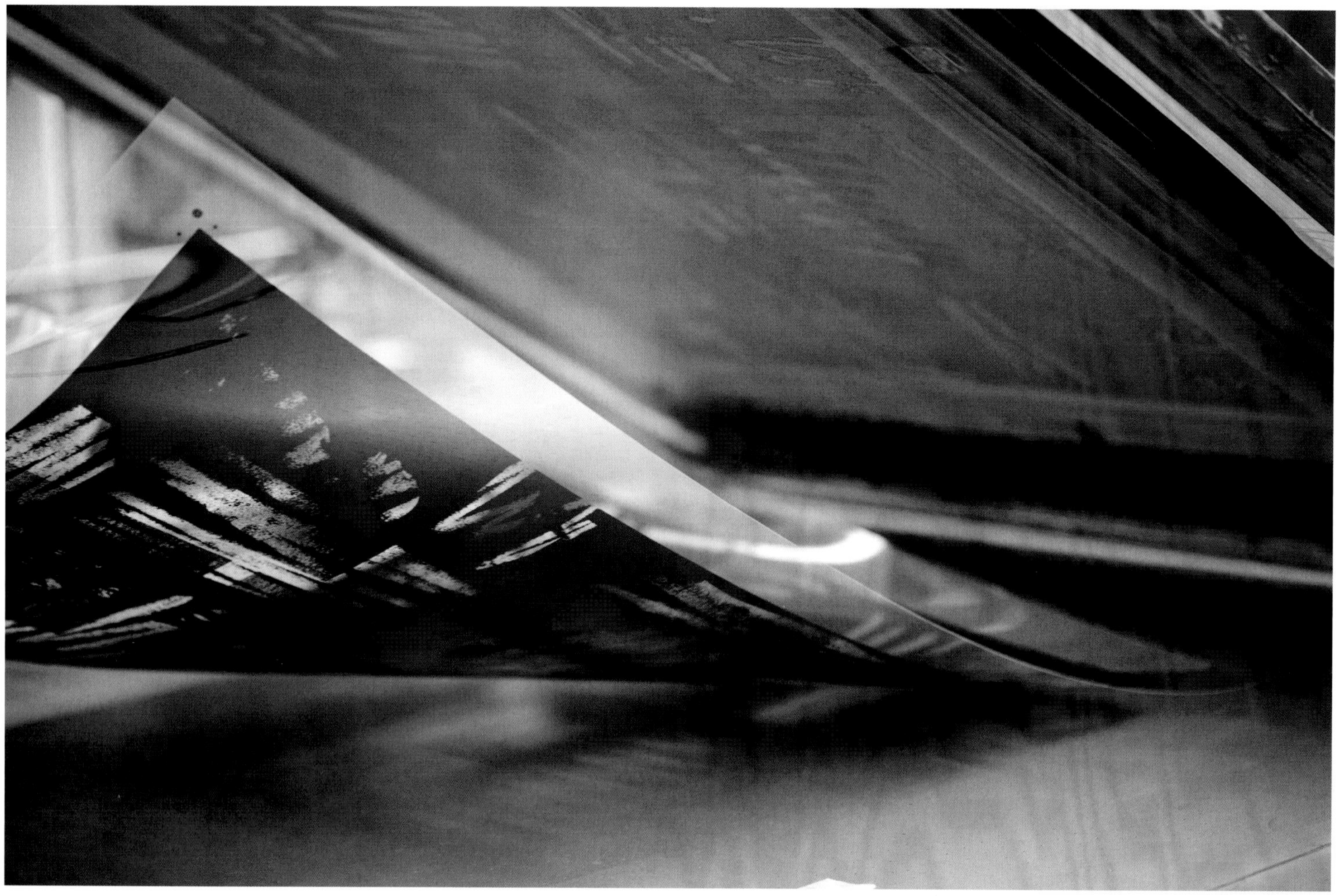

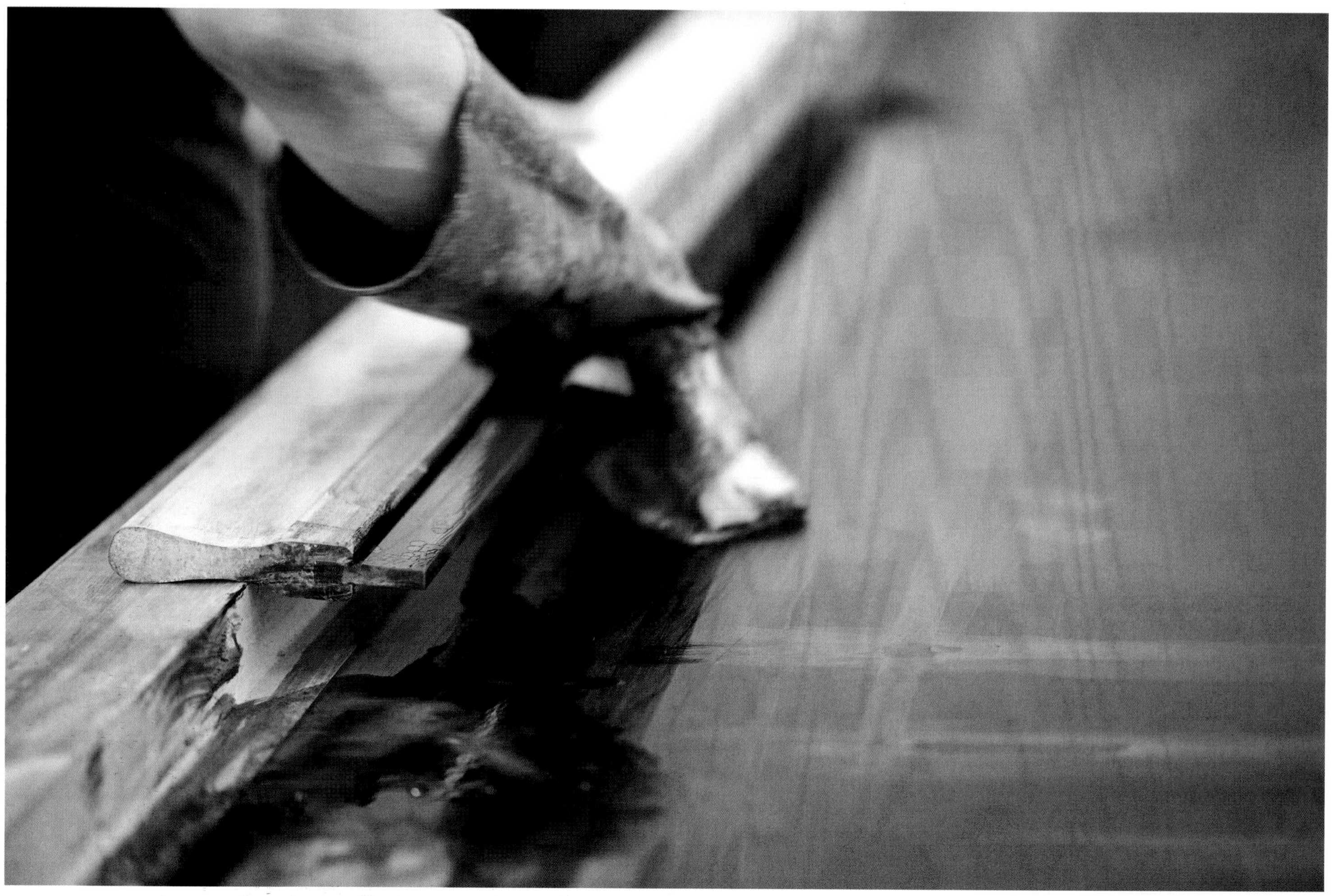

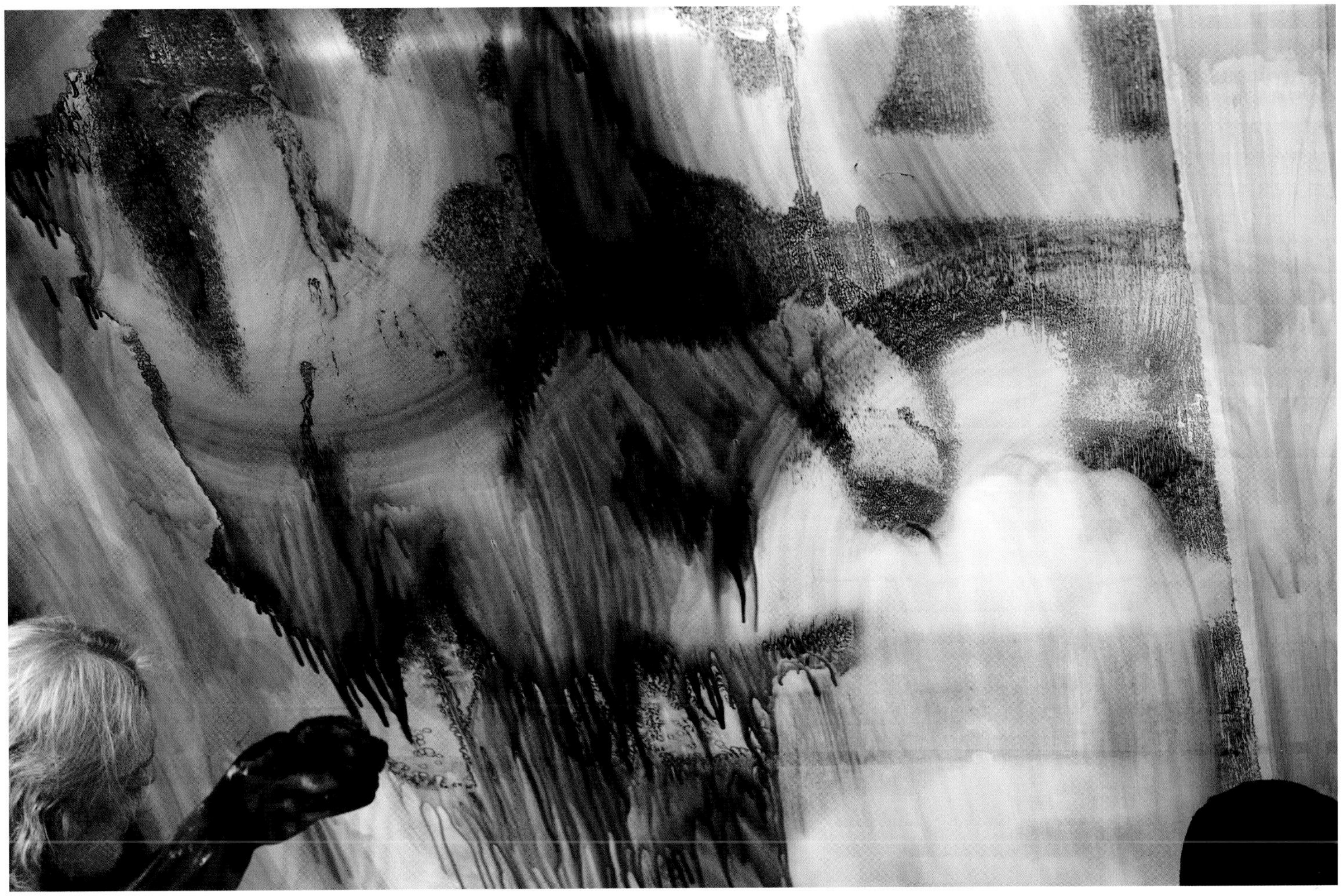

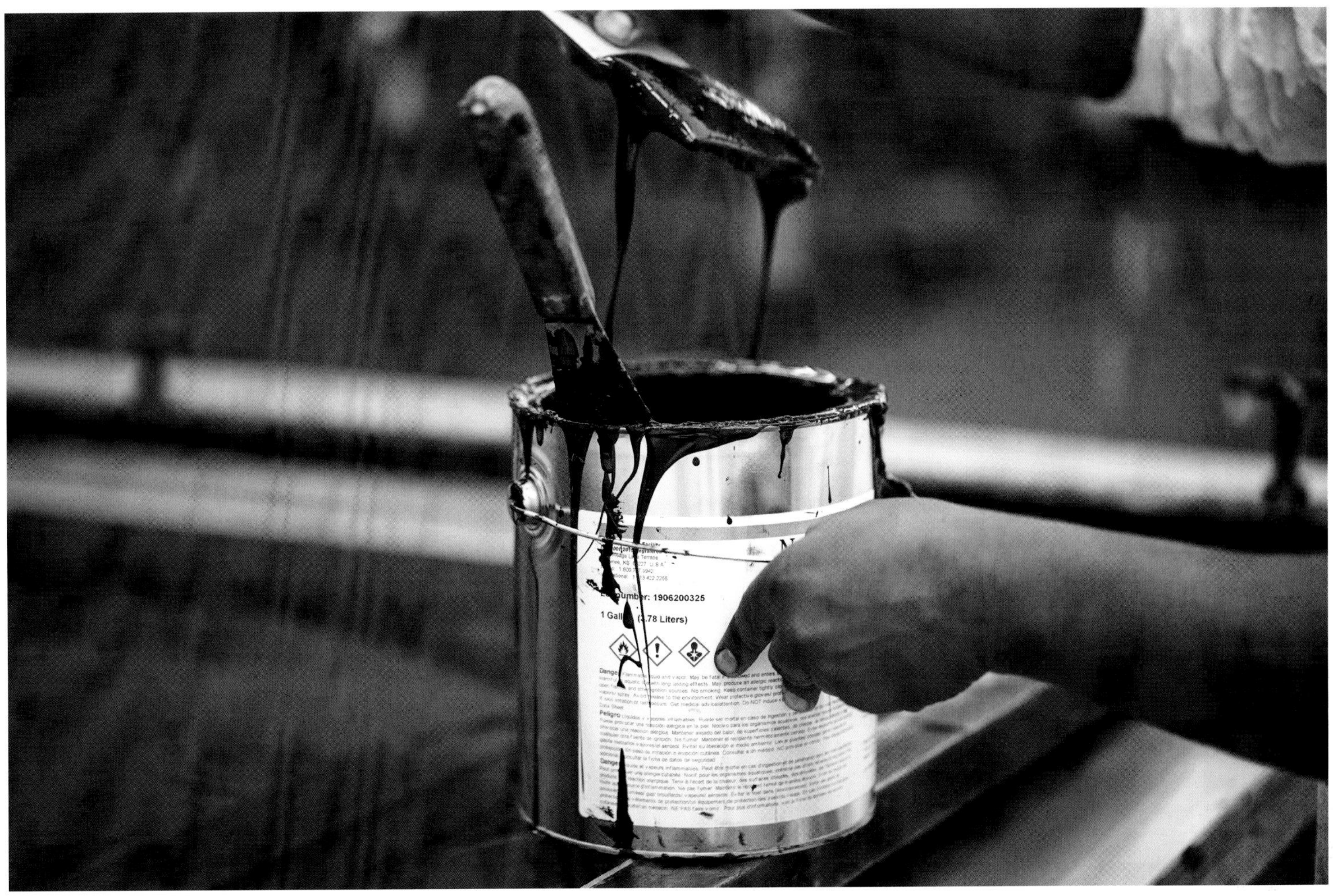

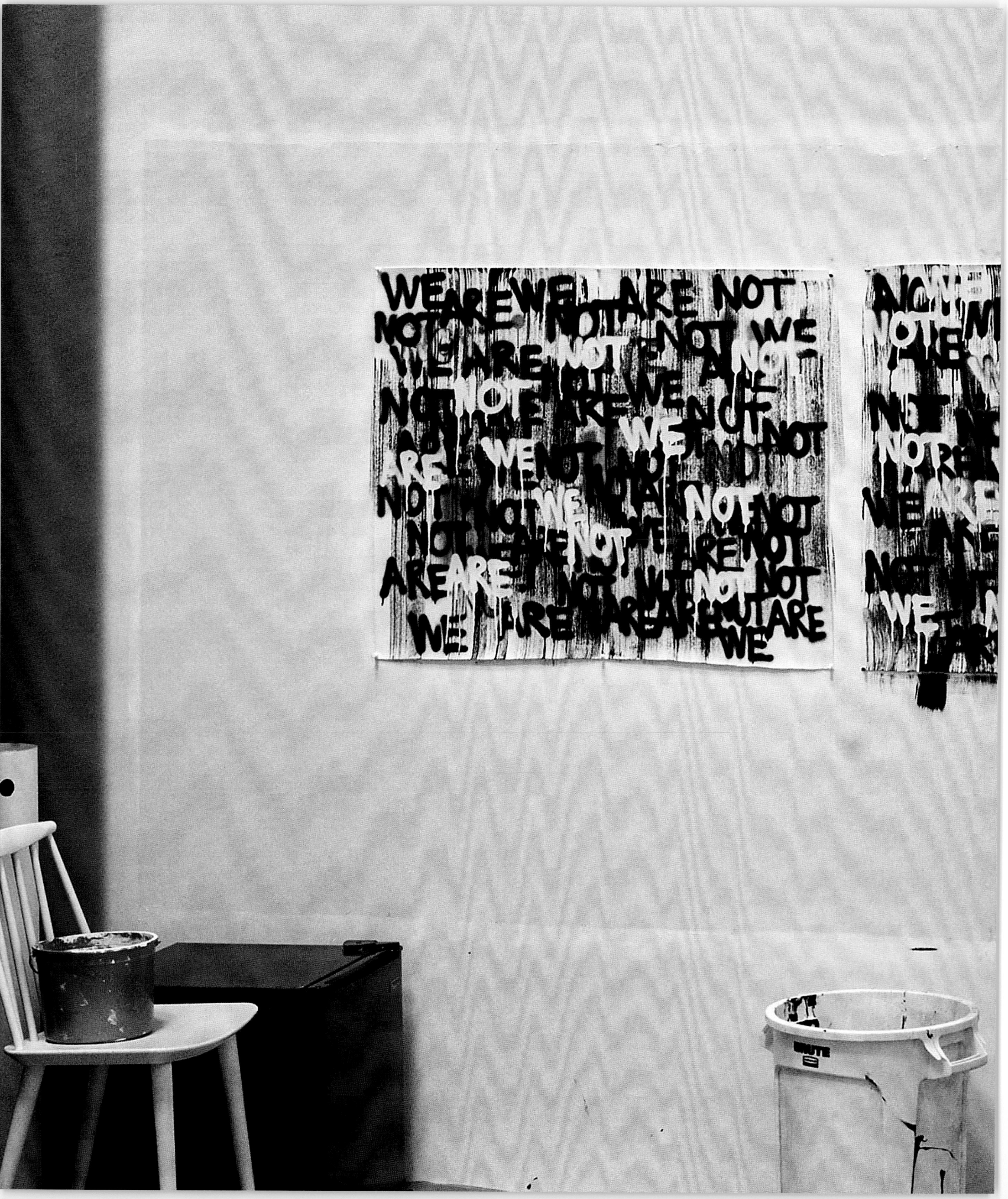

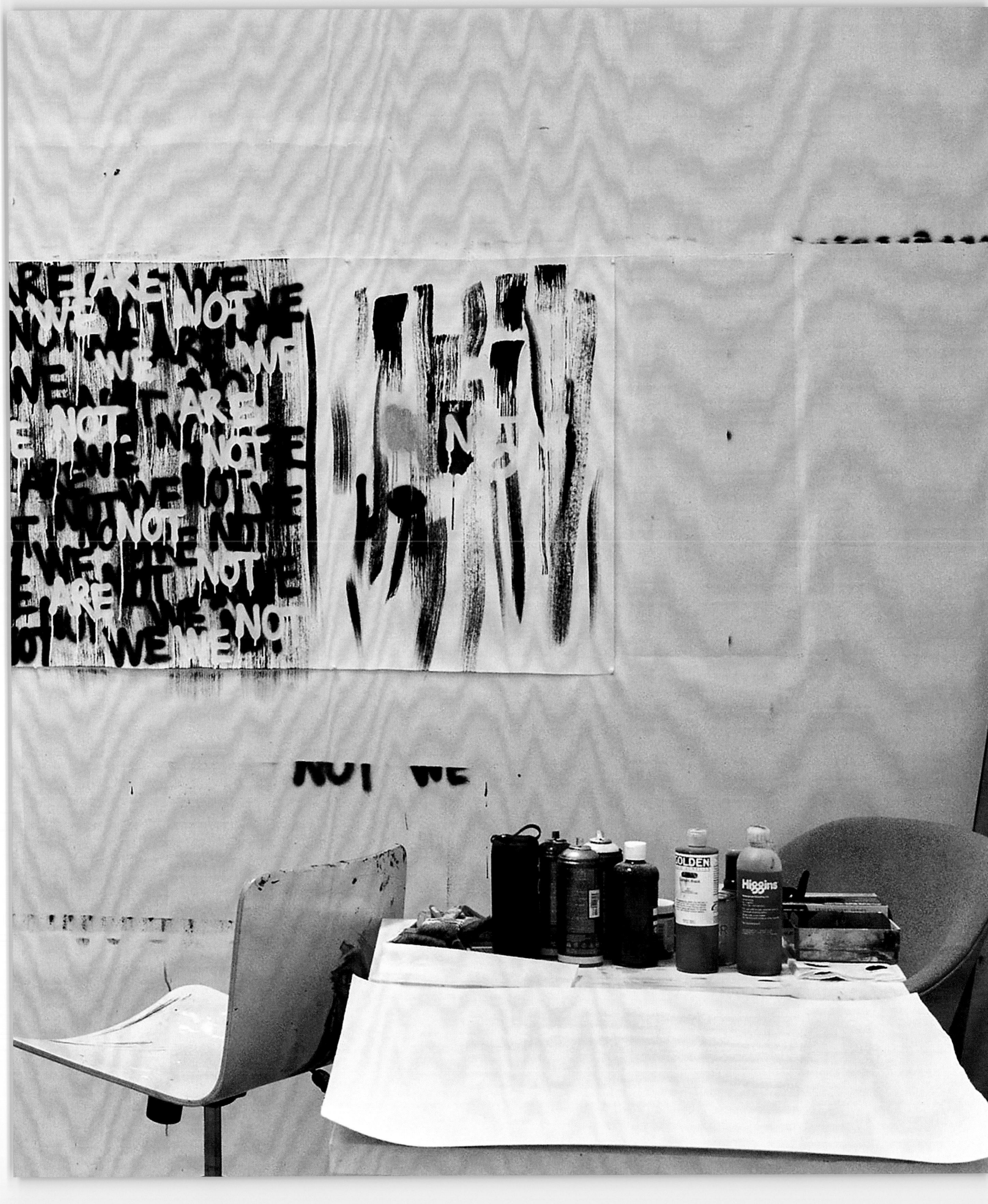
NOT WE
GOLDEN
Higgins

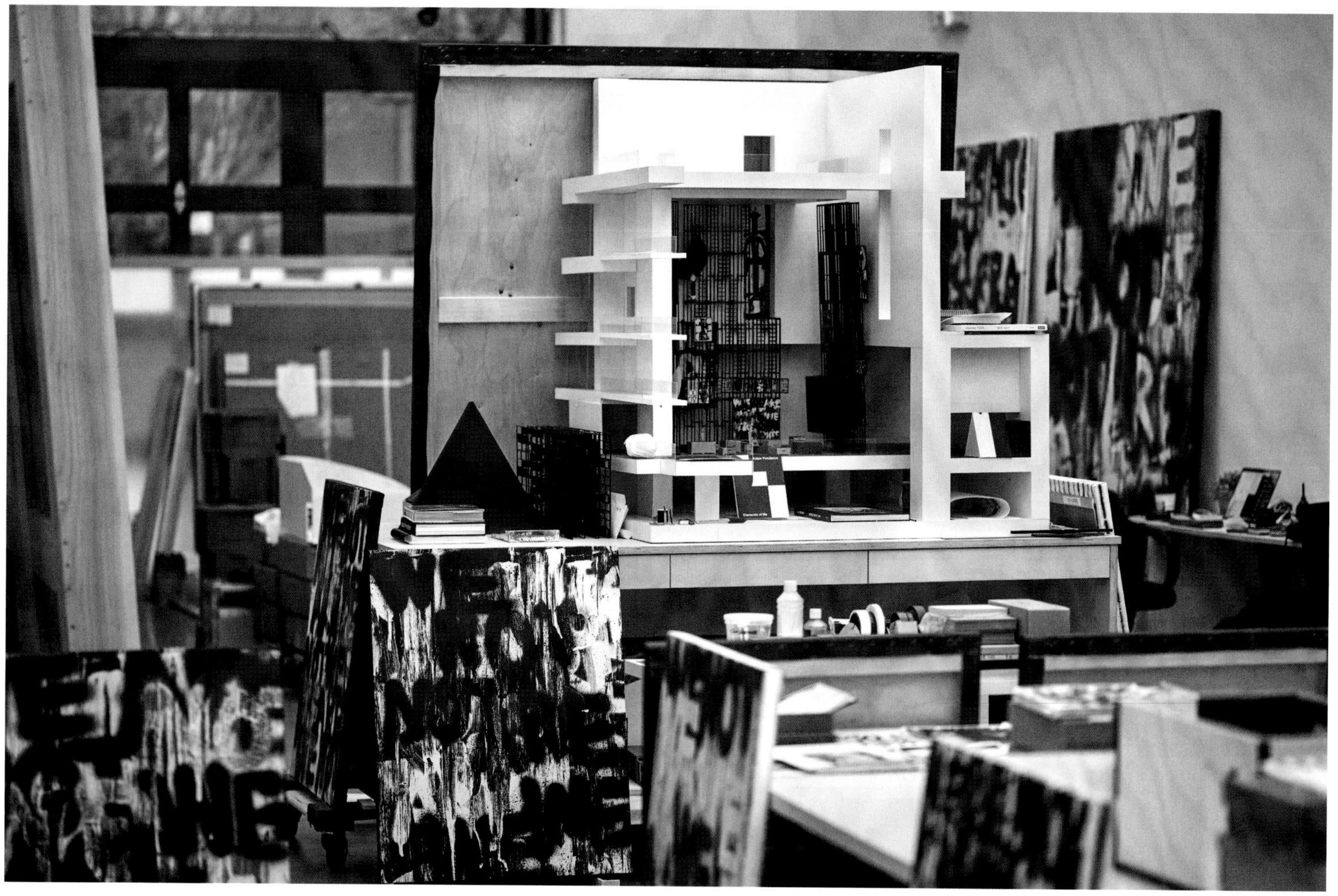

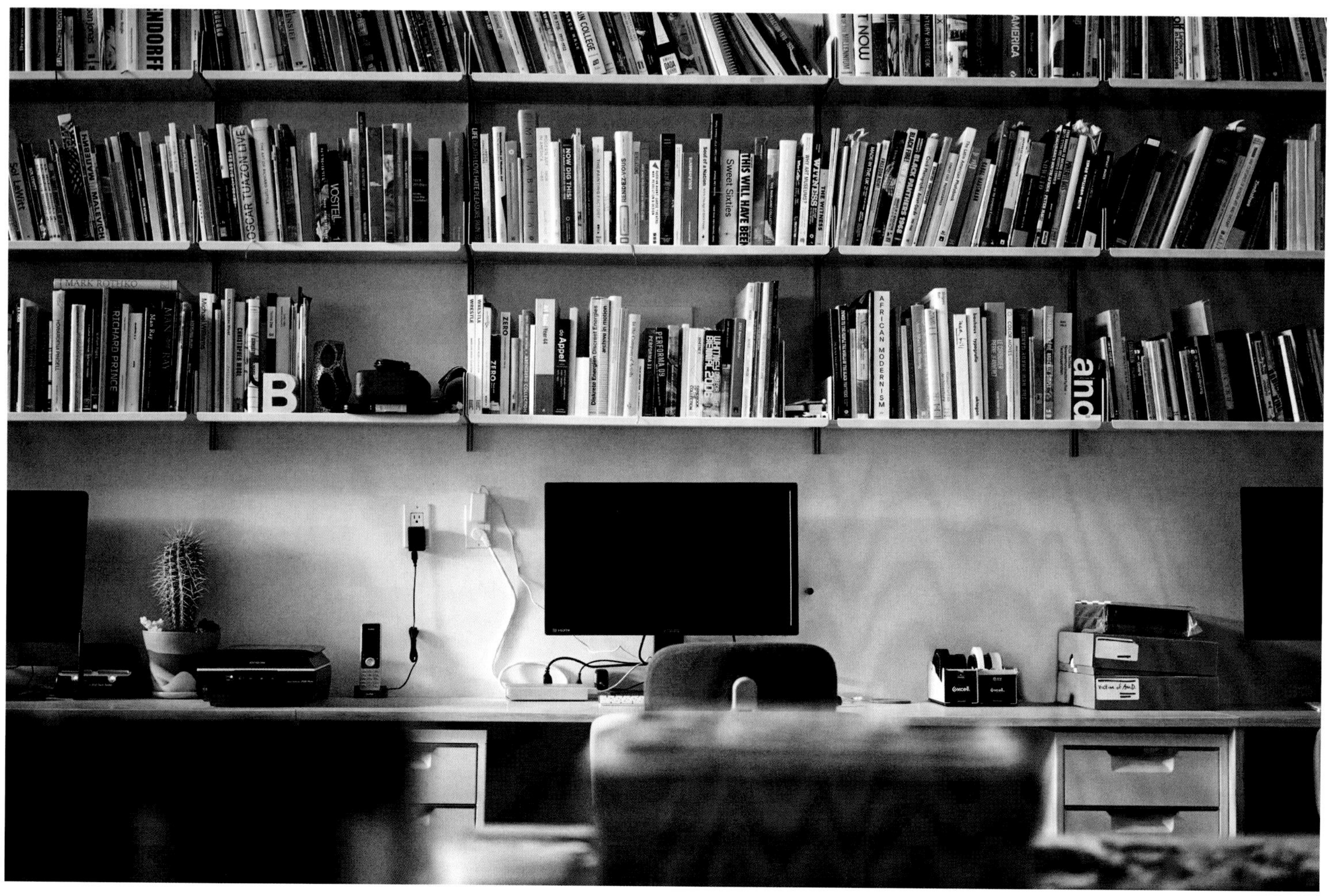

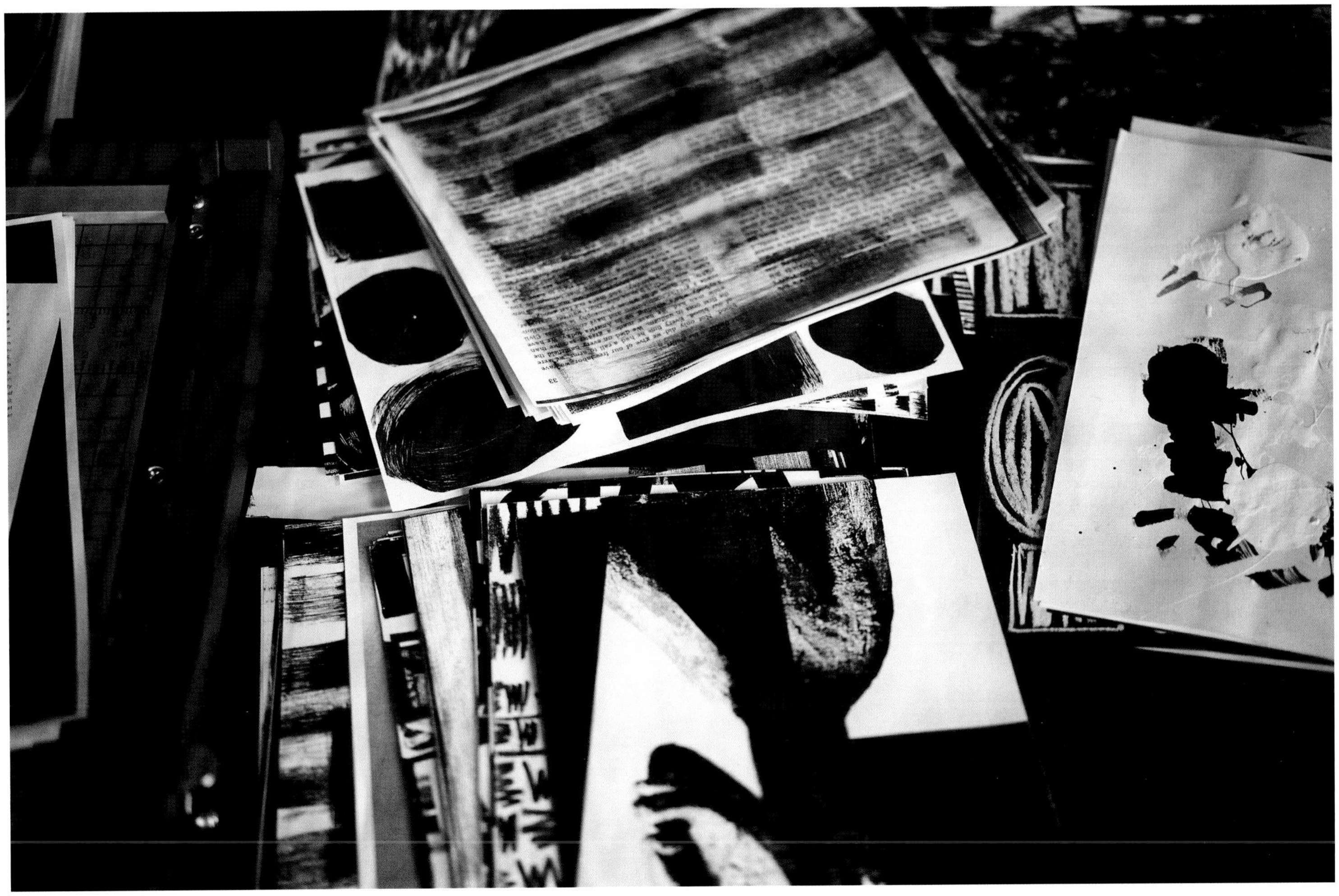

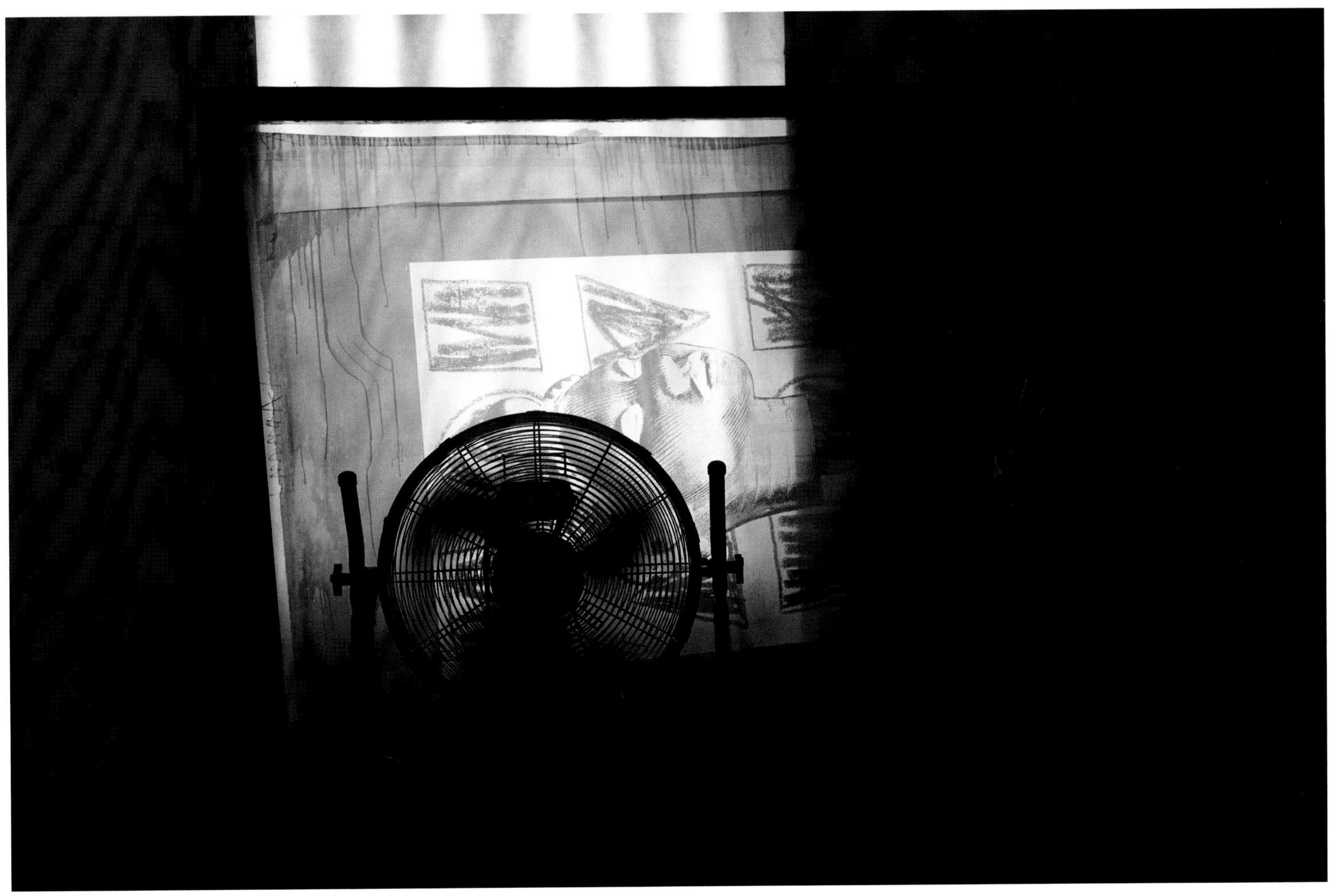

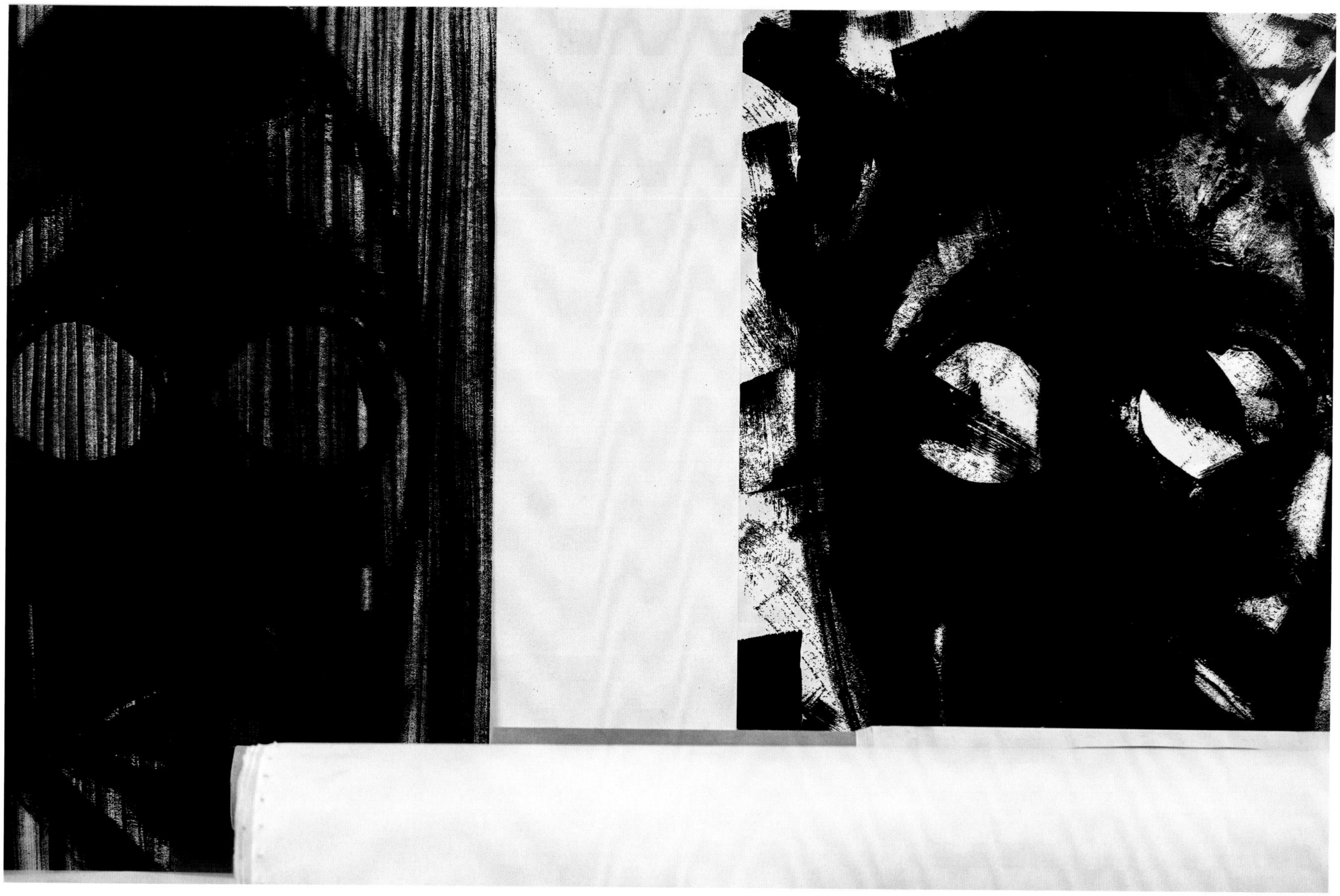

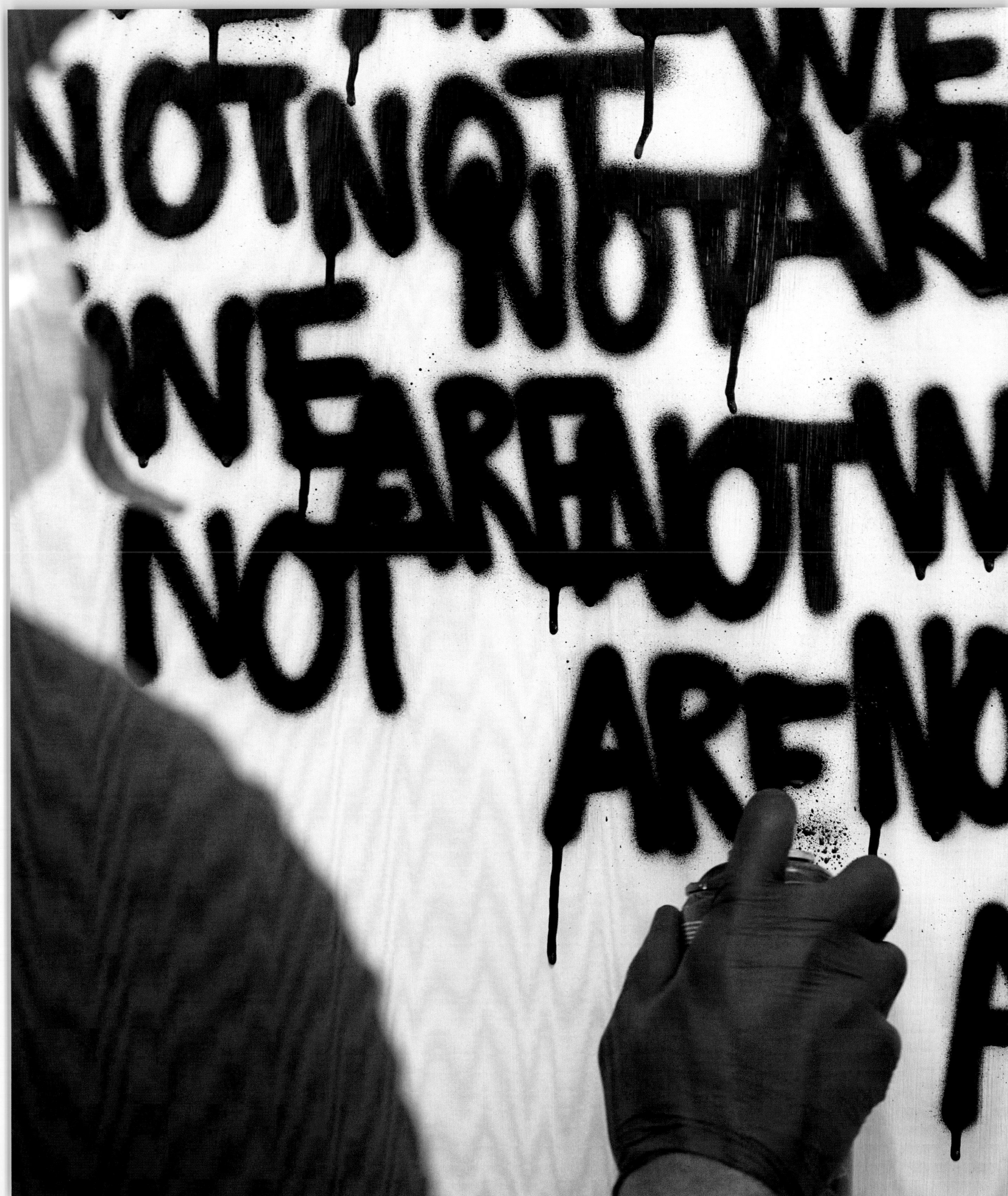
NOT
WE
NOT
ARE

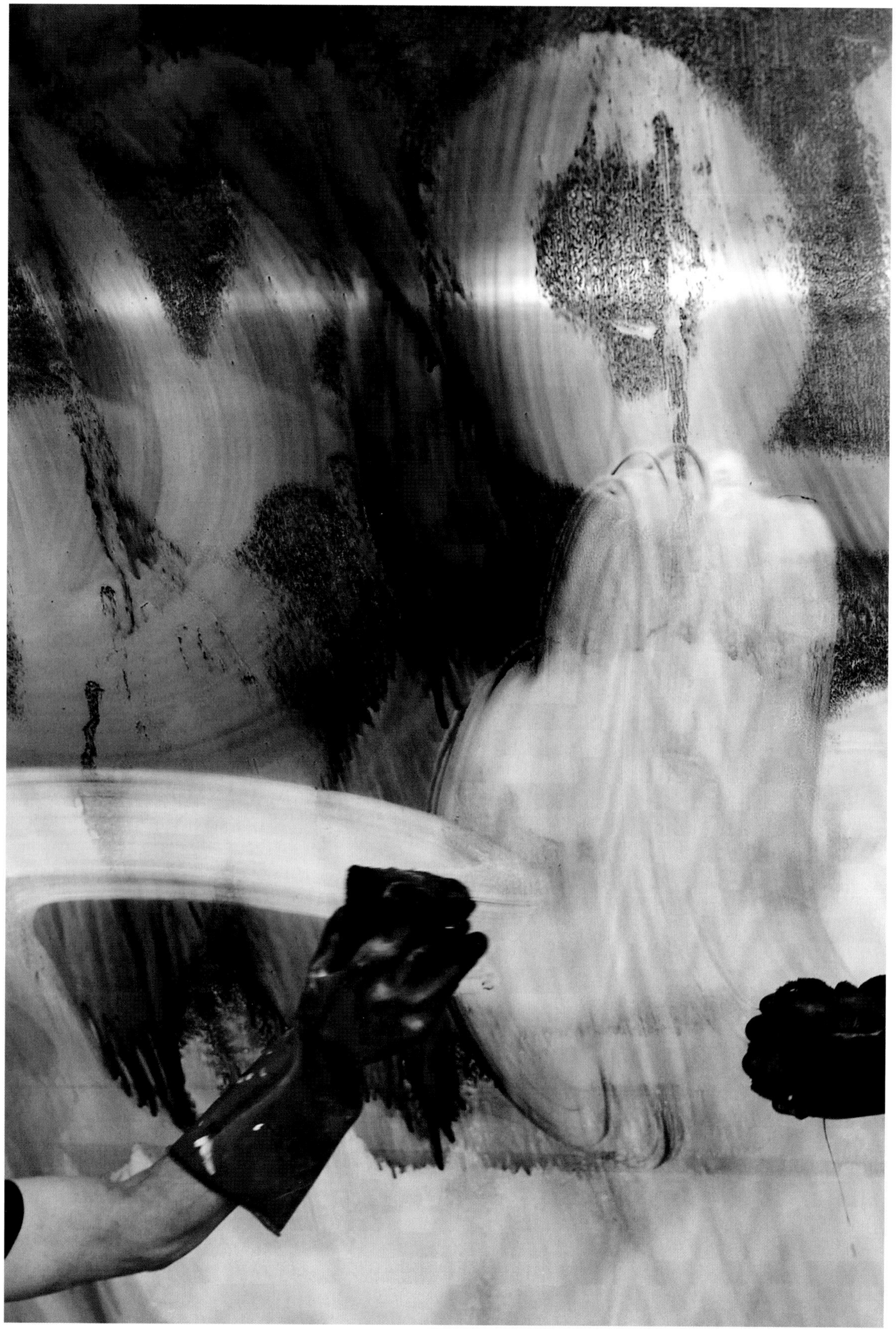

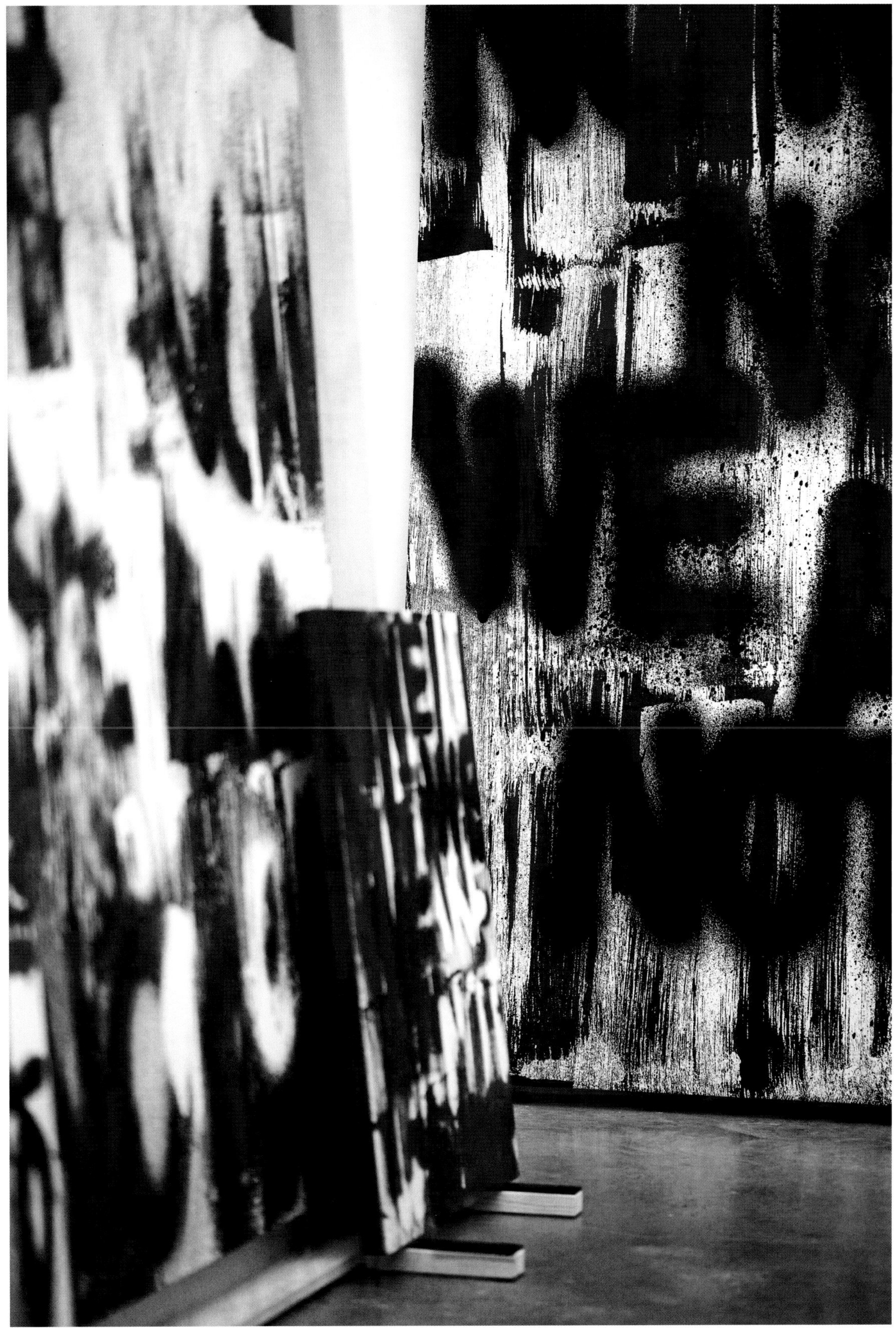

divide by
sit down
sit down to stand up
standing up to sit down
protest
divide by
express
break-up
express to
break-up
assemble
assembled
sworn
bottomed out
a learning
(i love you)
divide by the water
drink
either
or
express
or
function
to operate

express to function or
rise up
parallel
tracks
his

dreamt
through
pass through
divide by
to express
to break-up
to trouble
to divide by
[illegible] up

thrased
thrashing
didn't
get
get it
hustle
hustled
harder
didn't
get in
either
or
again

---

to
divide by
the death's
the death
to divide by
yesterday
yesterday
stand-up
sit down
get up
to divide by
to protest
to stand-up
to get up
to stand up
to sit down

grey-blue grain (excerpt), 2010

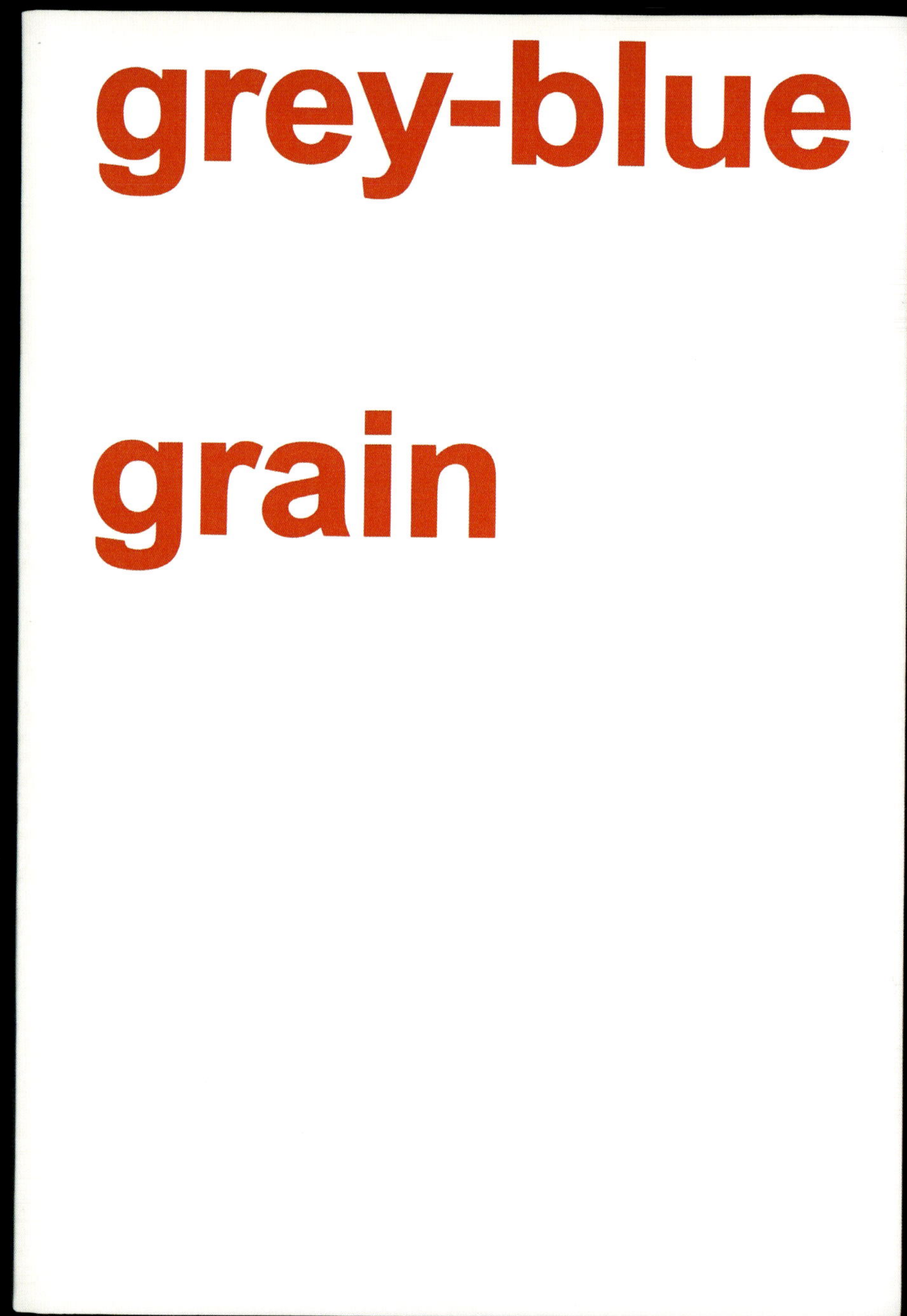

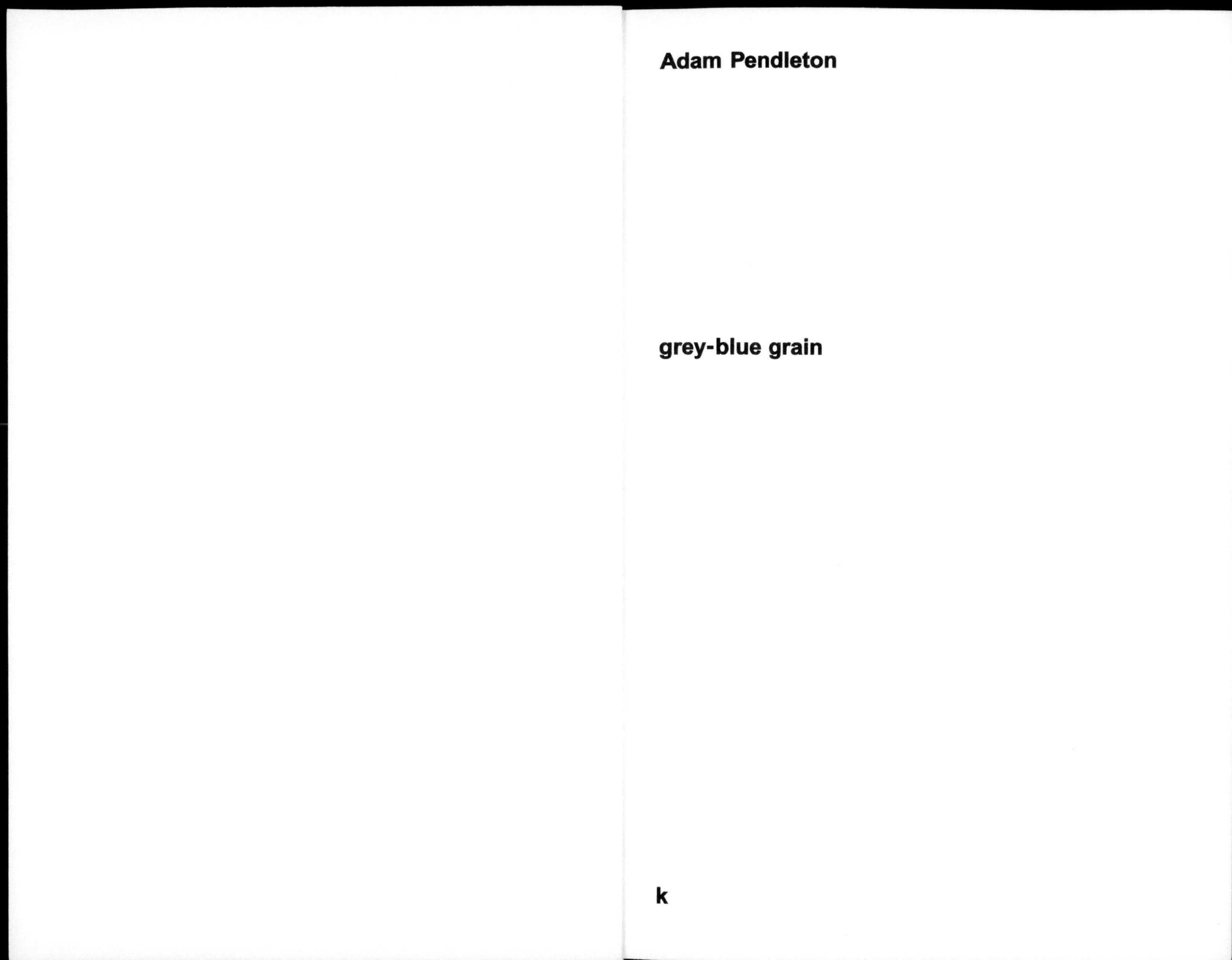

Adam Pendleton

grey-blue grain

k

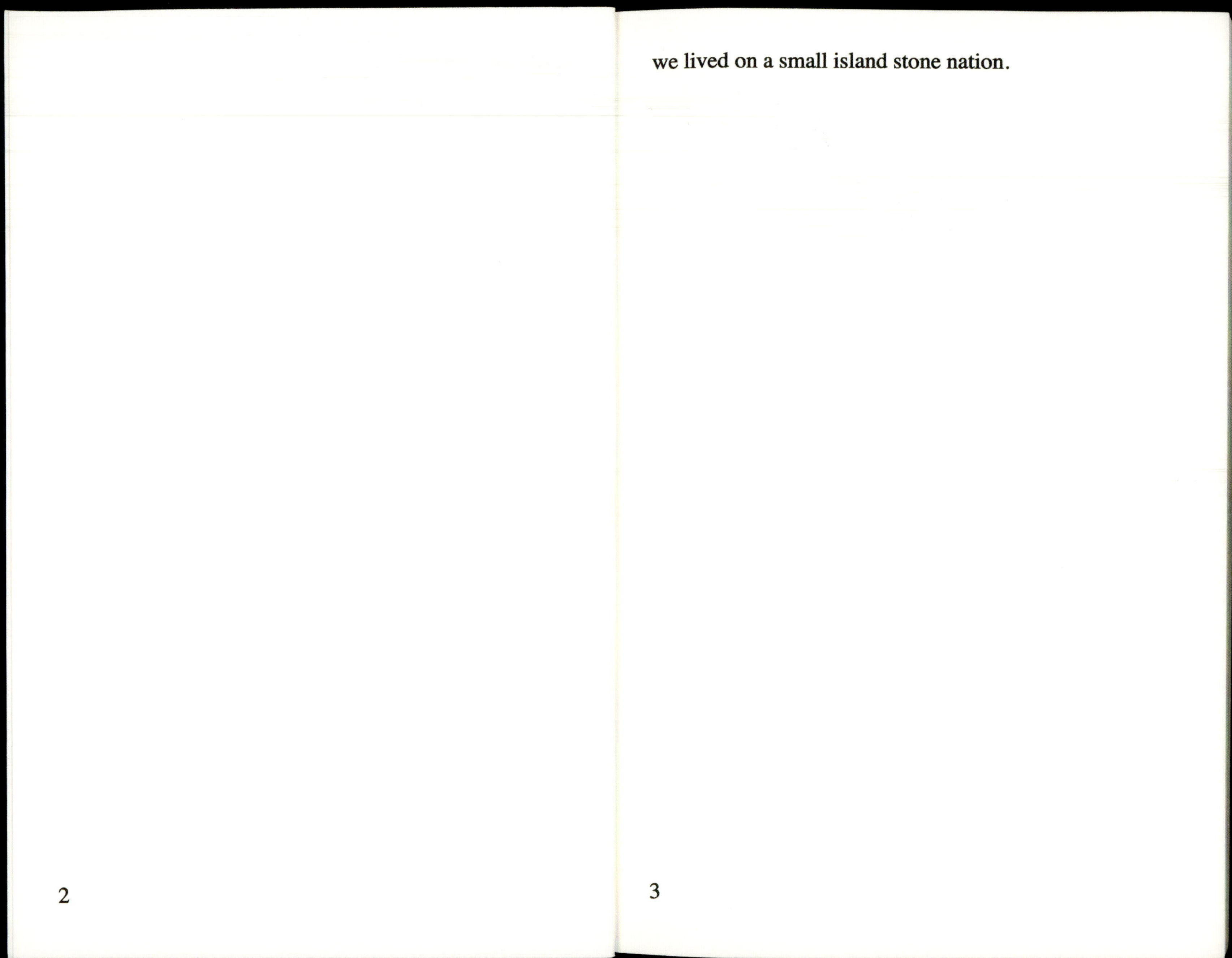

2

we lived on a small island stone nation.

3

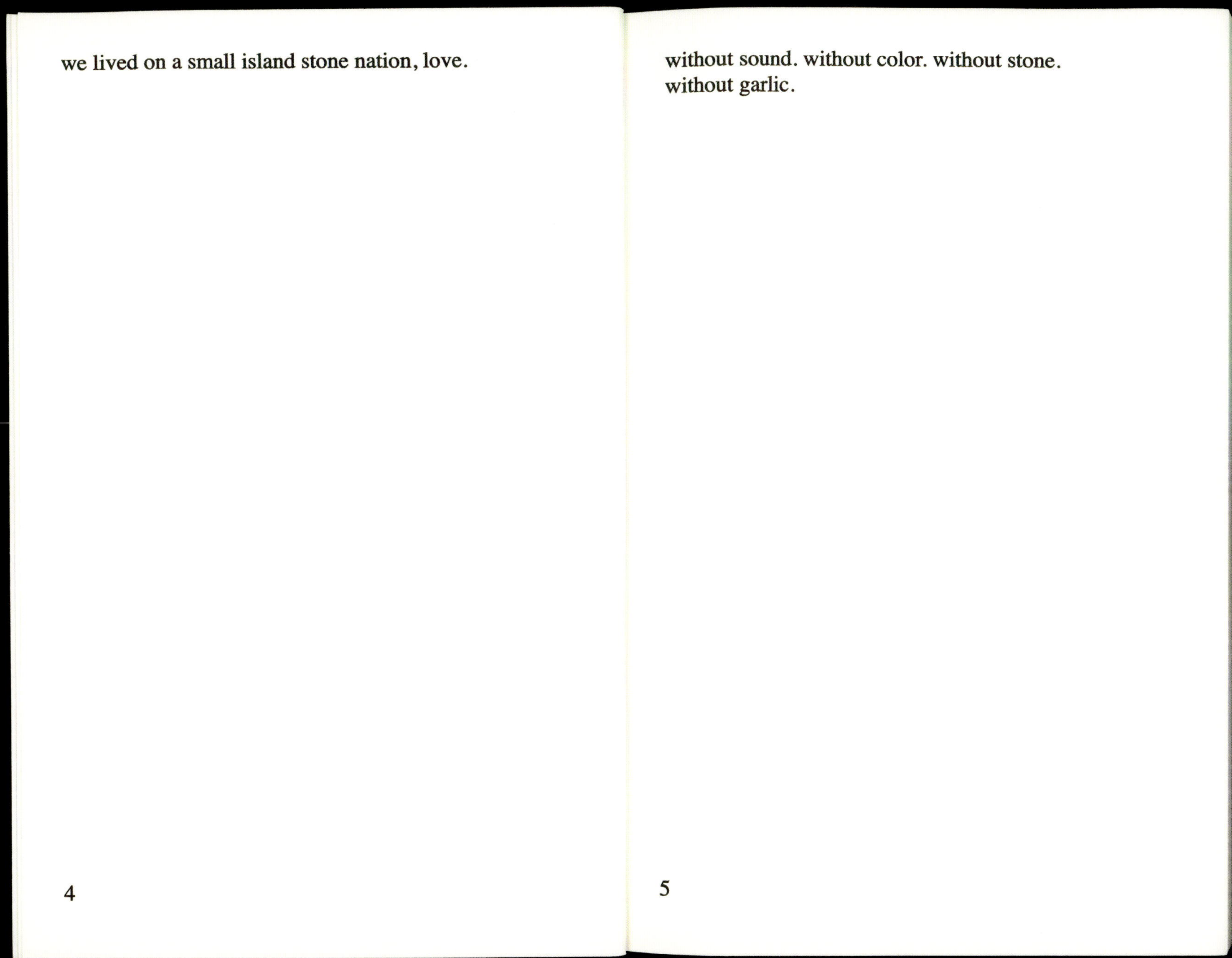

we lived on a small island stone nation, love.

4

without sound. without color. without stone.
without garlic.

5

steel
bell
drops
wave
glory

6

g

7

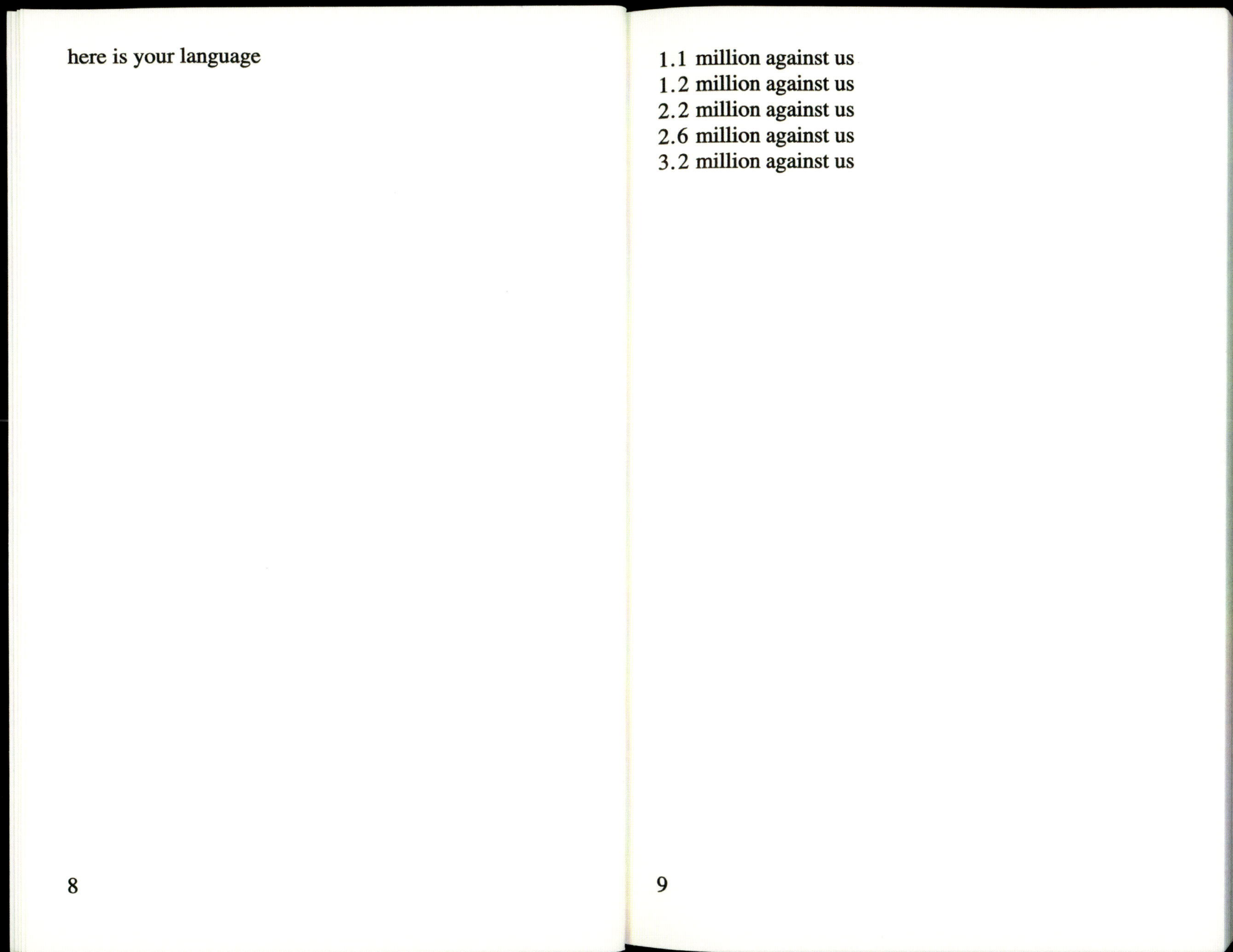

here is your language

8

1.1 million against us
1.2 million against us
2.2 million against us
2.6 million against us
3.2 million against us

9

INSERTING AN *H* IN *POETICS*:
A SLEF INTERVIEW

10

This interview between old friends (only sometimes at odds), Joan Retallack and Quinta Slef, took place in a short-circuited corner of cyberspace on a rainy Domingo/Domenica/Sunday/Sonntag/Dimanche …

11

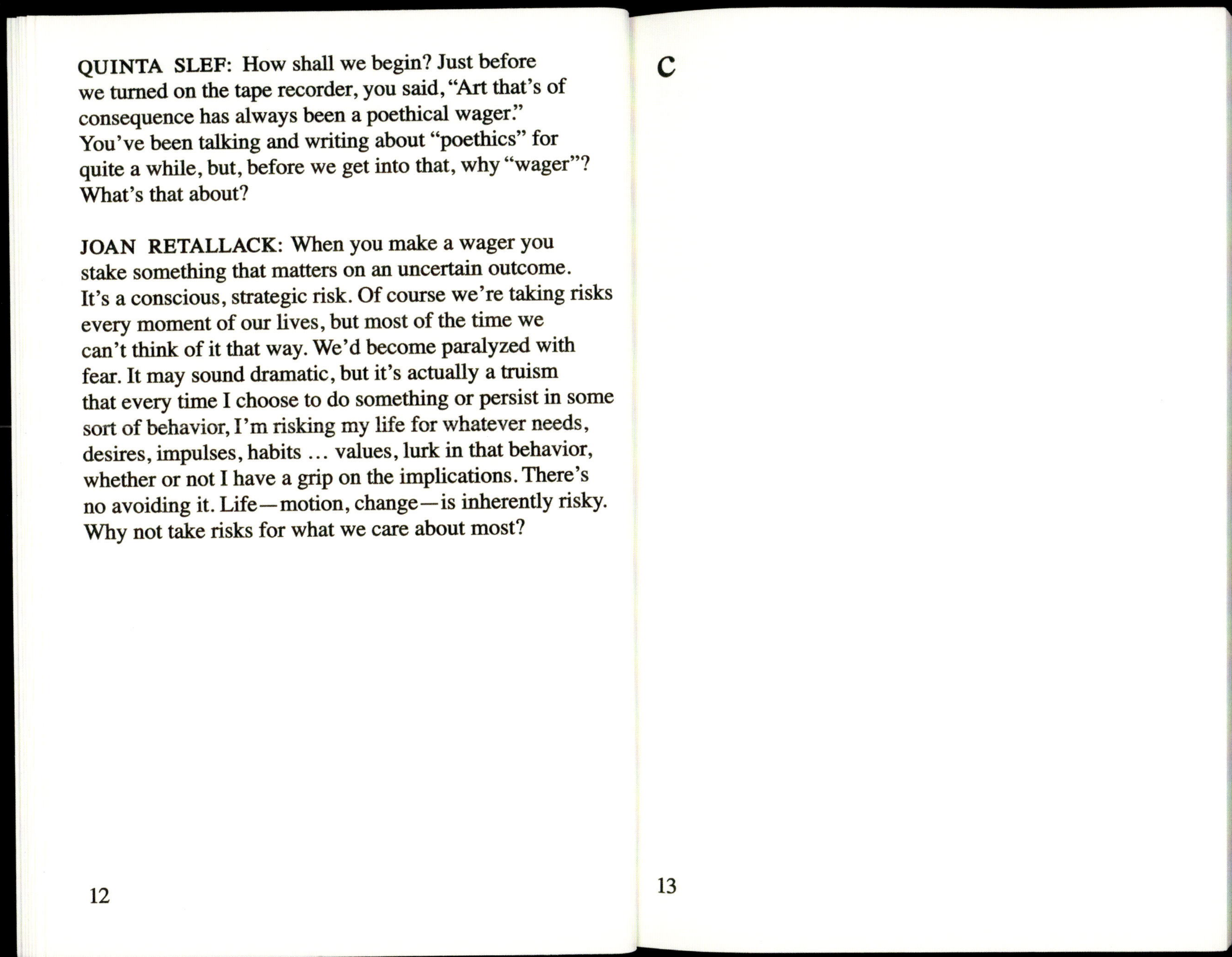

QUINTA SLEF: How shall we begin? Just before we turned on the tape recorder, you said, "Art that's of consequence has always been a poethical wager." You've been talking and writing about "poethics" for quite a while, but, before we get into that, why "wager"? What's that about?

JOAN RETALLACK: When you make a wager you stake something that matters on an uncertain outcome. It's a conscious, strategic risk. Of course we're taking risks every moment of our lives, but most of the time we can't think of it that way. We'd become paralyzed with fear. It may sound dramatic, but it's actually a truism that every time I choose to do something or persist in some sort of behavior, I'm risking my life for whatever needs, desires, impulses, habits … values, lurk in that behavior, whether or not I have a grip on the implications. There's no avoiding it. Life—motion, change—is inherently risky. Why not take risks for what we care about most?

12

C

13

preparedness:
for example
ready-made operations
inverting the idea of good meant to be

14

QS: Why not indeed? But, to be faux-Socratic, you've just said that's what we're doing anyway. Don't we always try for what we think is best?

JR: Not necessarily. It's seldom that clear. Apart from the obvious question, best for whom?—the individual? the community?—a good deal of what's done in the world comes out of the sense that what's best is really impossible. Might as well do the next or third best or —out of overwhelming frustration, anger, despair— the worst possible thing—just get it over with, destroy the field of possibilities that never seems to yield justice or solace or satisfaction! In art—particularly avant-garde art—this is what critics label "nihilism." I personally think it's rare in the arts. Artists want to make things. Their energy tends to be constructive. Of course I'm postponing the question of effect. Even if I want to act positively, what I think is best may be off the mark from even my own subsequent point of view. The future, that is, the present, is complex and uncertain.

15

QS: Then what hope is there? We're all shooting in the dark.

JR: Yes, if we're Platonists or Kantians or religious fundamentalists we're shooting for transcendence into a realm unknowable by the senses; if we're dadaists or Buddhists we're letting things happen; if we're pragmatists we're betting on an outcome by means of logics and intuitions that come from experience in the world as we find it. Radical unknowability is the only constant.

16

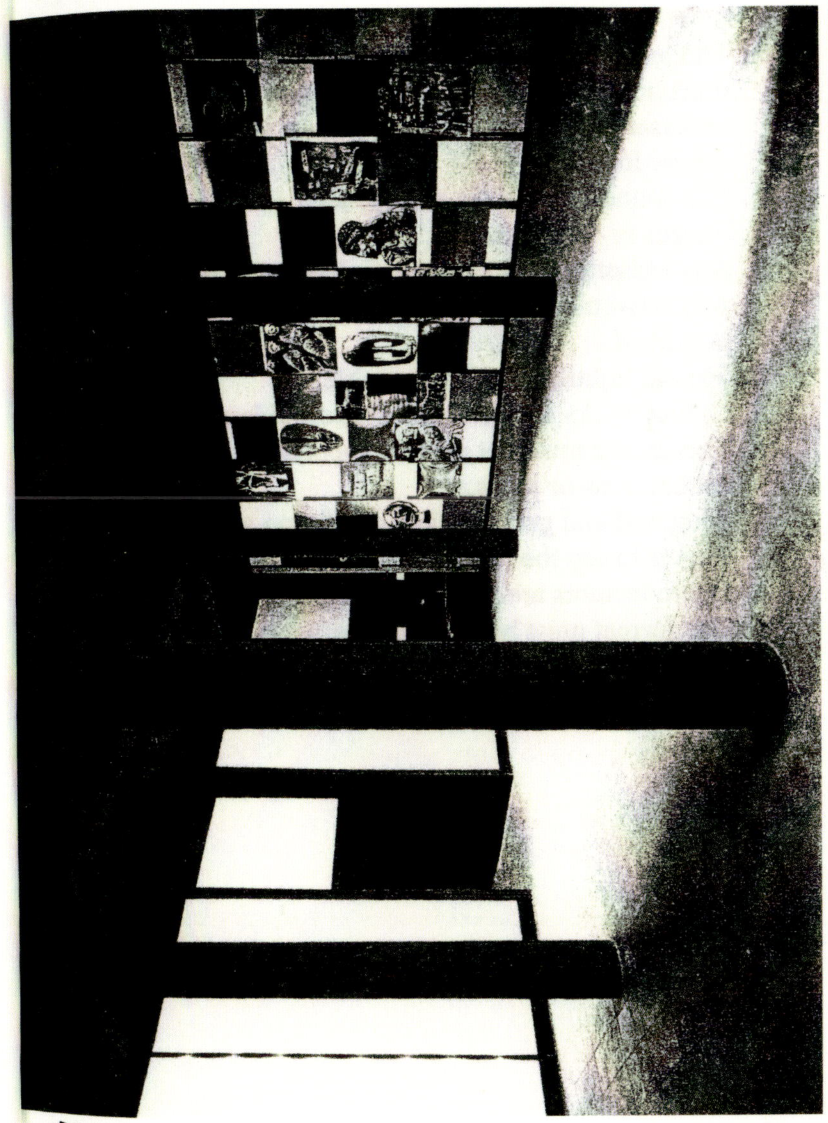

17

Some rules:

1. The lecture must be done on location. Props and sets must not be brought in (if a particular prop is necessary a location must be chosen where this prop can be found).
2. The sound must never be produced apart from the images or vice versa.
3. Any cameras for documentation must be handheld. Any movement or immobility attainable in the hand is permitted.
4. Special lighting is not acceptable.
5. Optical tricks and "effects" are forbidden.
6. The lecture must not contain superficial action, declarations or jokes.
7. Temporal and geographical alienation are forbidden. That is to say the lecture takes place here and now.
8. Genre lectures are not acceptable.
9. The format must be set. 30 mins. 20 mins. 1 hour etc.
10. The lecturer must not be credited.

18

Symbols:

Old faggot

Fat bitch

Old hag

You were my first

19

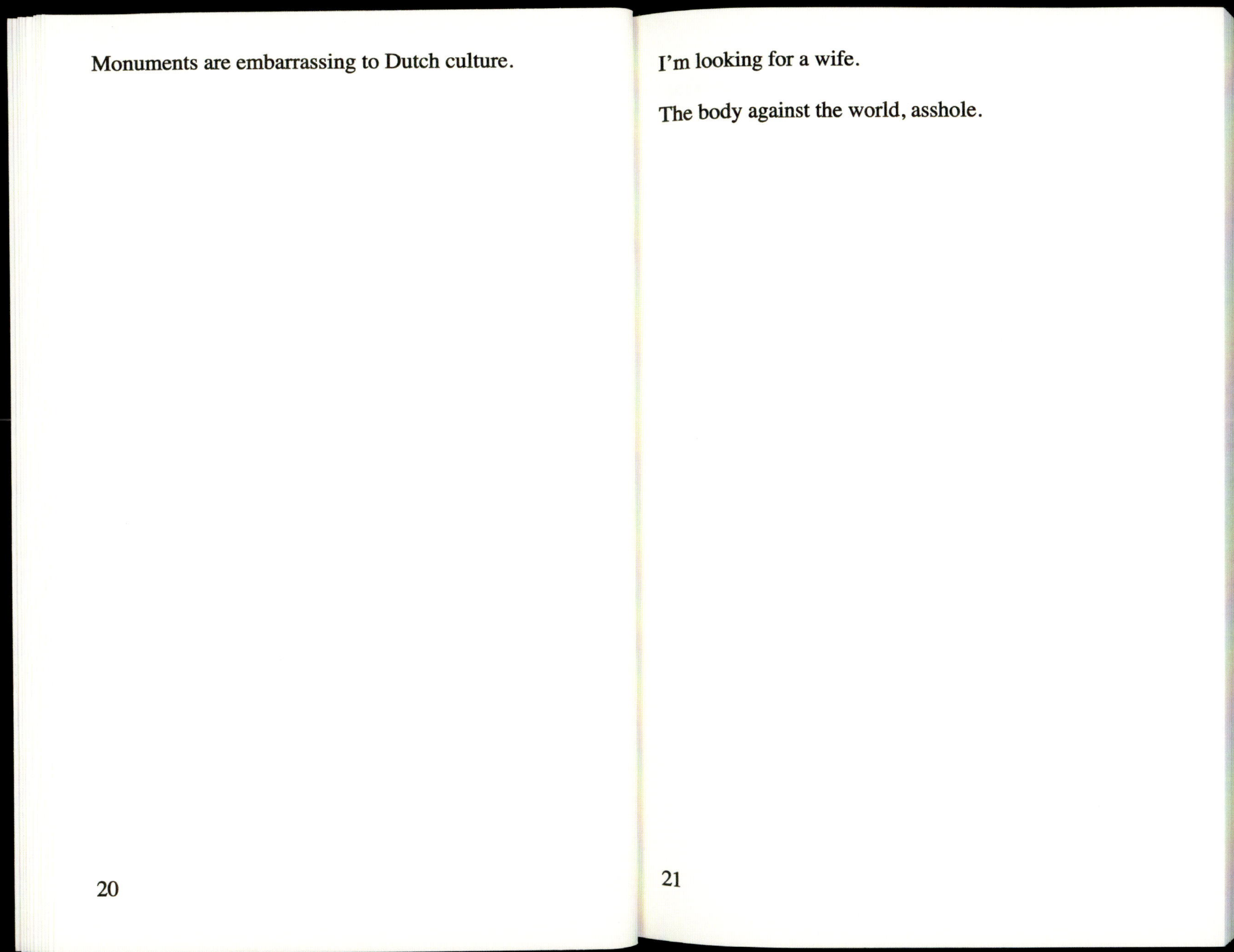

Monuments are embarrassing to Dutch culture.

20

I'm looking for a wife.

The body against the world, asshole.

21

<u>Notes for Lorraine O'Grady: A Portrait</u>, 2012

<u>LORRAINE O'GRADY: A PORTRAIT</u>, 2012
SINGLE-CHANNEL COLOUR VIDEO
22 MIN. 50 SEC.
DIMENSIONS VARIABLE

a moment yellow, just as four years later when my father returned home from the war, the moment of greeting him as he stood at the bottom of the stairs, younger, thinner than when he had left, was purple – though moments are no longer so colored.

My parents both came from Jamaica in the 1920s

a moment yellow

They met each other in Boston at the tea table during a cricket match in which one of my uncles was bowling

just as four years later when my father returned home from the war the moment of greeting him as he stood at the bottom of the stairs

It was the post-World War I period of the great West Indian migration, and most of their compatriots had settled in Brooklyn

younger, thinner than when he had left, was purple – though moments are no longer so colored

In Boston, the tiny West Indian Community could barely establish and fill one Episcopal church

a moment yellow, just as four years later, when my father returned home from the war, the moment of greeting him as he stood at the bottom of the stairs, younger, thinner than when he had left, was purple – though moments are no longer so colored.

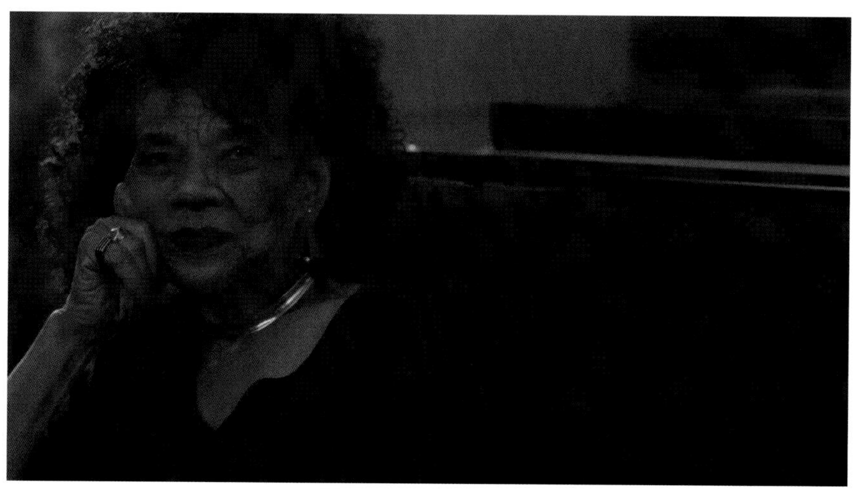

PREVIOUSLY UNPUBLISHED

BLACK DADA READER (SPIRAL-BOUND), 2011

next pages,
BLACK DADA READER (SPIRAL-BOUND), 2011

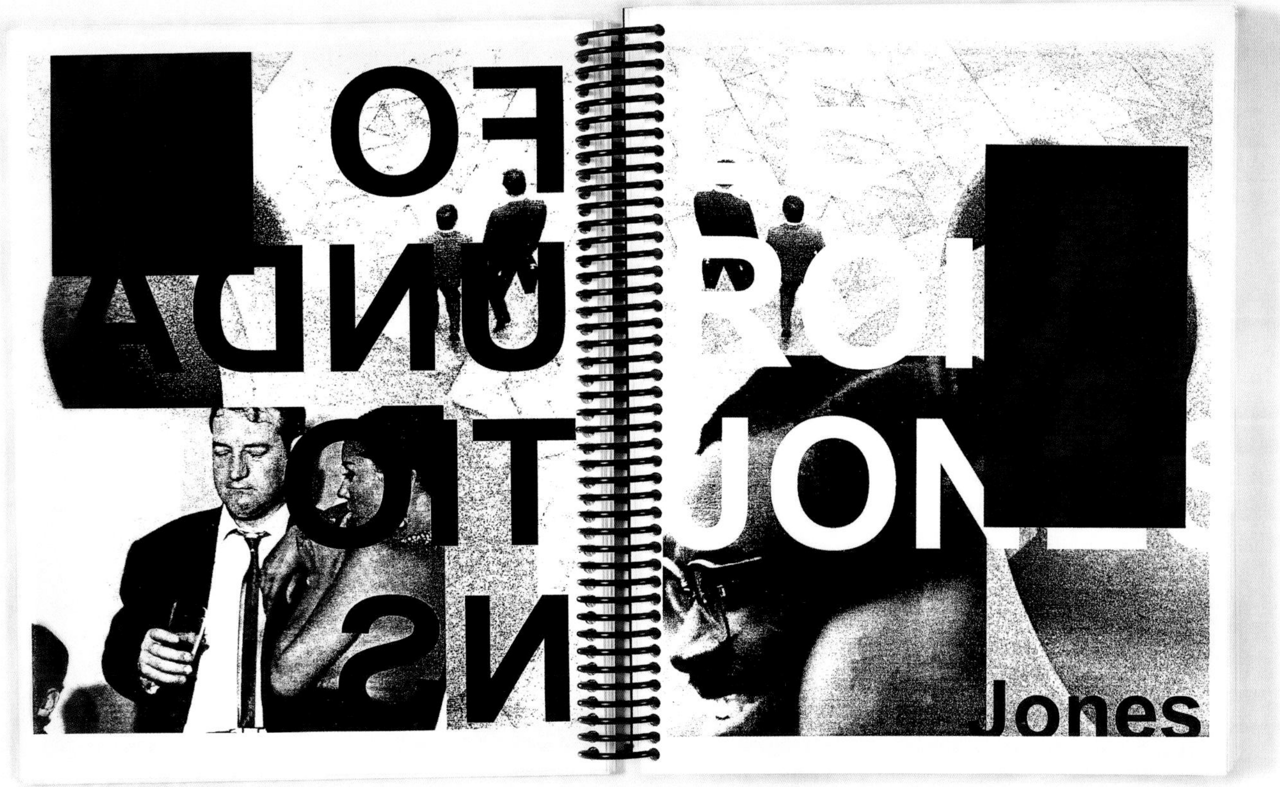

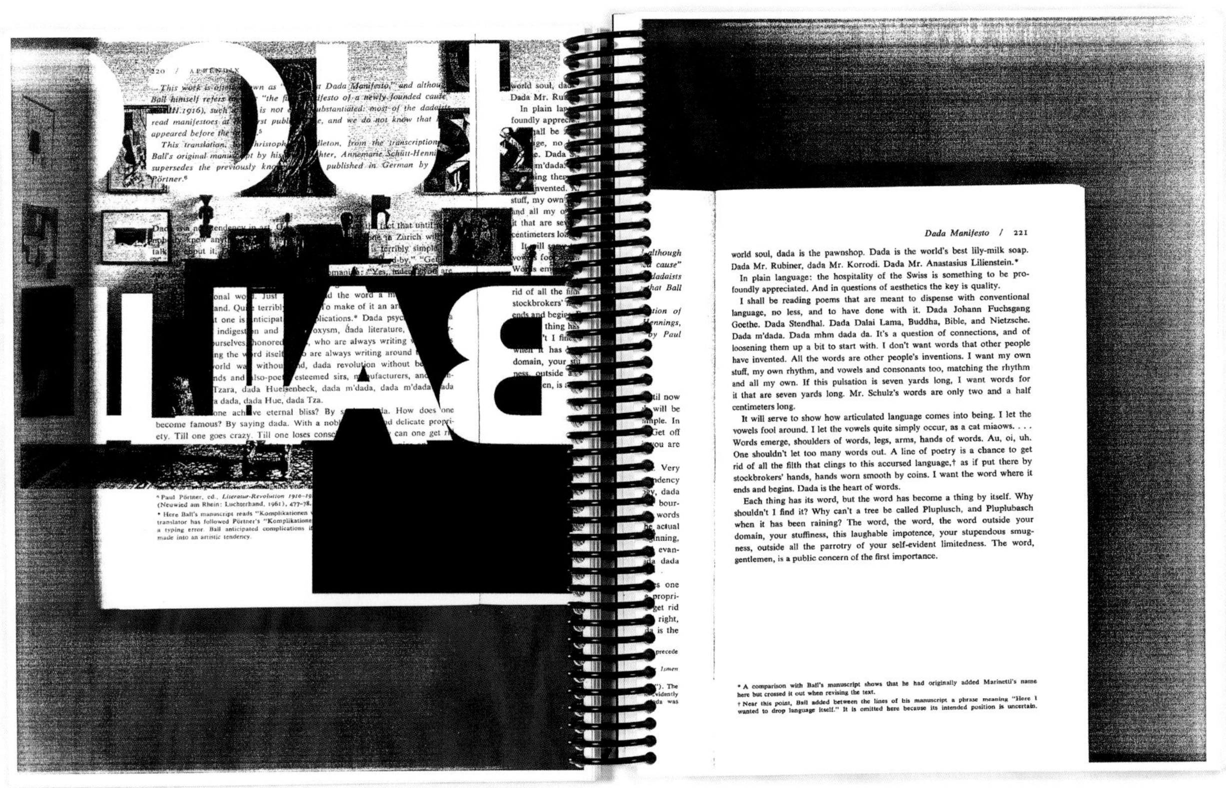

would teach the white world was Greek to his own flesh and blood. The innate love of harmony and beauty that set the ruder souls of his people a-dancing and a-singing raised but confusion and doubt in the soul of the black artist; for the beauty revealed to him was the soul-beauty of a race which his larger audience despised, and he could not articulate the message of another people. This waste of double aims, this seeking to satisfy two unreconciled ideals, has wrought sad havoc with the courage and faith and deeds of ten thousand thousand people,—has sent them often wooing false gods and invoking false means of salvation, and at times has even seemed about to make them ashamed of themselves.

Away back in the days of bondage they thought to see in one divine event the end of all doubt and disappointment; few men ever worshipped Freedom with half such unquestioning faith as did the American Negro for two centuries. To him, so far as he thought and dreamed, slavery was indeed the sum of all villainies, the cause of all sorrow, the root of all prejudice; Emancipation was the key to a promised land of sweeter beauty than ever stretched before the eyes of wearied Israelites. In song and exhortation swelled one refrain—Liberty; in his tears and curses the God he implored had Freedom in his right hand. At last it came,—suddenly, fearfully, like a dream. With one wild carnival of blood and passion came the message in his own plaintive cadences:—

"Shout, O children!
Shout, you're free!
For God has bought your liberty!"

Years have passed away since then,—ten, twenty, forty; forty years of national life, forty years of renewal and development, and yet the swarthy spectre sits in its accustomed seat at the Nation's feast. In vain do we cry to this our vastest social problem:—

"Take any shape but that, and my firm nerves
Shall never tremble!"

The Nation has not yet found peace from its sins; the freedman has not yet found in freedom his promised land.

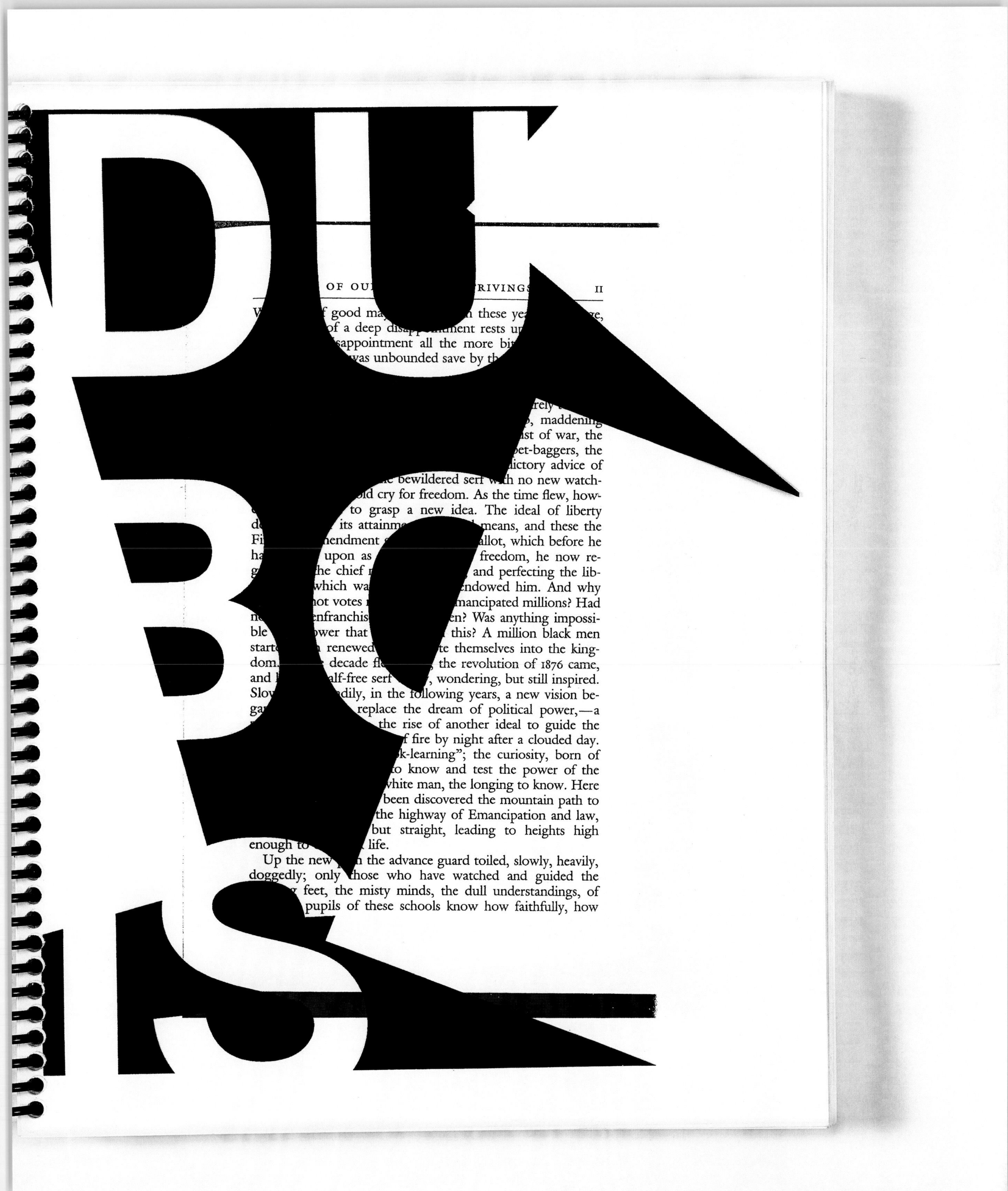DU
BO
IS
OF OU
RIVINGS
11
f good ma
n these ye
of a deep disappointment rests u
isappointment all the more bi
was unbounded save by th
, maddening
ist of war, the
et-baggers, the
dictory advice of
bewildered serf with no new watch-
old cry for freedom. As the time flew, how-
to grasp a new idea. The ideal of liberty
its attainme
means, and these the
endment
allot, which before he
upon as
freedom, he now re-
he chief
and perfecting the lib-
which wa
endowed him. And why
ot votes
mancipated millions? Had
enfranchis
en? Was anything impossi-
ble
wer that
this? A million black men
start
renewed
te themselves into the king-
dom.
decade fl
the revolution of 1876 came,
and
alf-free serf
, wondering, but still inspired.
Slow
dily, in the following years, a new vision be-
replace the dream of political power,—a
the rise of another ideal to guide the
f fire by night after a clouded day.
k-learning"; the curiosity, born of
o know and test the power of the
white man, the longing to know. Here
been discovered the mountain path to
the highway of Emancipation and law,
but straight, leading to heights high
enough to
life.
Up the new
the advance guard toiled, slowly, heavily,
doggedly; only those who have watched and guided the
feet, the misty minds, the dull understandings, of
pupils of these schools know how faithfully, how

Amiri Baraka (1934–2014), 2014

BLACK DADA READER (SPIRAL-BOUND), 2011

March 21, 2014

In death, Amiri Baraka is read through one of the two lenses under which Black American Culture is legible: realism and expressionism. Everything must figure, one way or another. This is significant, because it means that there is no commonly understood way of taking Baraka seriously without also taking him literally, more or less. He is denied the frame of abstraction and of the concept.

To the extent that Baraka's writing coincides with an expression of Black Experience, or a depiction, a reflection, of Black Life, he can be praised or damned accordingly. And so he is.

What of Gertrude Stein or Tristan Tzara would have survived the harsh light of realism, of expression?

Tzara called his sounds *Poemes Negres* and said they were translations of poetry from Oceania and Africa. The opening of Baraka's play *Slave Ship* reads like something similar: not an abstract sound but the sound of the body undergoing abstraction, the noise of it. The belly of the ship is a place of traumatic misrecognition, the stage on which humanity is continually and violently miscast as abstract objects of exchange, as commodities. The sound of the slave ship is the overture of this process, its initial, epic aggregate. For the African in America, abstraction is the orienting fact of her existence, something to be overcome, either by refusing it, or by deploying it herself.

The same year (1964) that Baraka delivered his poem 'Black Dada Nihilismus' with the New York Art Quintet, he also premiered *Dutchman*, a play about how a young redheaded woman kills a middle-class black man on a subway train. It won an Obie. 'Black Dada Nihilismus,' by contrast, has only ever been read as advocating the rape and murder of white people. *Dutchman* is difficult, 'Black Dada' is bad. And in many ways 'Black Dada' is bad. But it's bad like poetry is bad, not like murder, or its advocacy, is. Or rather, it's bad like Dada is bad. Bad Black Dada. Dada has limits, don't you know?

If abstraction remains illegible in the work of the black artist, this is because black individuals remain abstract. Thus black artists stand out for their humanity not because they are inherently more human, visceral, emotive, or sexual than anyone else, but because the appearance of Black Humanity remains a revelation, an exception beyond which we seem unable to move. By reaching past expression, and past the real, to the concept, Baraka was insisting on his right as an artist to be otherwise than black, insisting, that is, on the right to see blackness from all sides at once, or not at all, as it suited him. Like the dynamite parting stone for the smooth driving highway, Baraka moved the earth that we might follow more easily and with less noise. His language was the architecture of my freedom.

ARTFORUM, MARCH

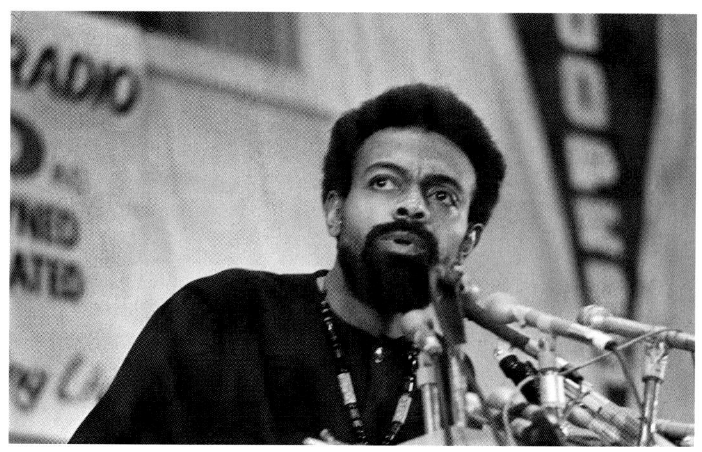

JULIAN C. WILSON
AMIRI BARAKA SPEAKING DURING THE BLACK POLITICAL CONVENTION IN GARY, INDIANA, 1972

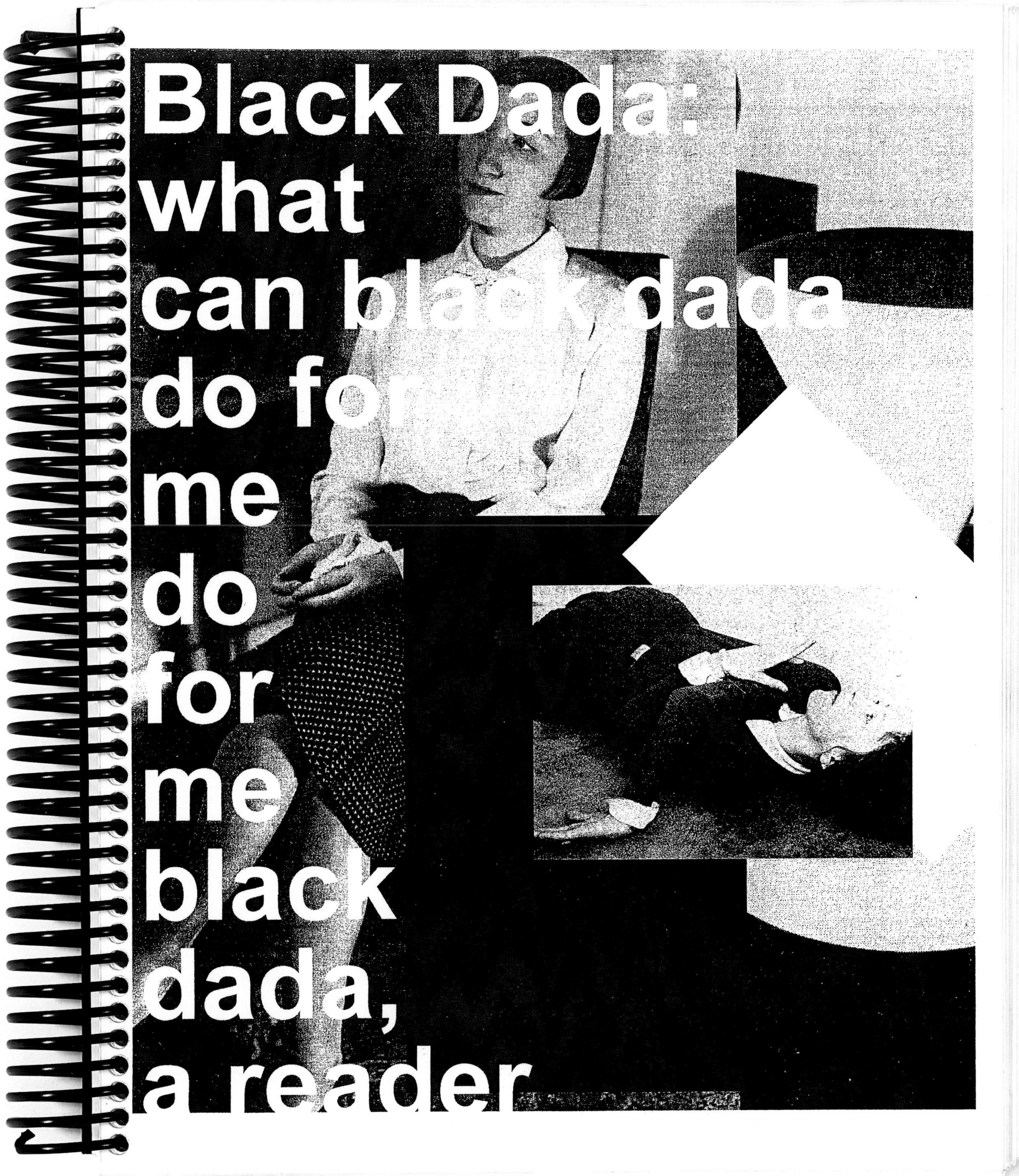
Black Dada:
what
can black dada
do for
me
do
for
me
black
dada,
a reader

Introductory Note, 2018

BLACK DADA READER (WALL WORK #1) (DETAIL), 2016
LATEX INK ON ADHESIVE VINYL
DIMENSIONS VARIABLE

INSTALLATION VIEW AT
GALERIE EVA PRESENHUBER,
ZURICH, 2016

Our ideas are fragmented – events in the day – deconstructed and recomposed. They take place alongside everything else. We want to contribute, to fly with the movement.

Are we primarily on top of history or in front of it? If the *Black Dada* paintings form a stage, the *Untitled (A Victim of American Democracy)* paintings are a performance taking place in front of or on top of that stage. Both sets of works articulate a poetics of construction, turning the rules or guidelines or conditions for representation into protagonists. Insisting on language as an unavoidably present, even transcendental ambiguity, the paintings stutter, refusing both the limits of representation and the critical void of painterly abstraction. They insist on being read. They do not speak clearly. I want to collapse past and future to describe each within the other; to speak of incomplete postulates and beginnings; to play dirty and joyfully with expressionistic dots and long, linear, spray-painted strokes.

'I assure you: there is no beginning, and we are not afraid; we aren't sentimental. We are like a raging wind that rips up the clothes of clouds and prayers, we are preparing the great spectacle of disaster, conflagration and decomposition. Preparing to put an end to mourning, and to replace tears by sirens spreading from one continent to another. Clarions of intense joy, bereft of that poisonous sadness'.[1]

Black Dada is a theoretical iteration of our moment.

The *Untitled* paintings revisit Malcolm X's 1964 speech titled 'The Ballot or the Bullet,' paraphrasing a section that reads:

I'm one of the 22 million black victims of the Democrats. One of the 22 million black victims of the Republicans and one of the 22 million black victims of Americanism. And when I speak, I don't speak as a Democrat or a Republican. I speak as a victim of America's so-called democracy. You and I have never seen democracy – all we've seen is hypocrisy.[2]

What links the bullet to the process or the method of abstraction deployed in these paintings? Both are ways of refusing representation of a certain kind, when these ways are judged to be limited, wanting, or, in Malcolm X's preferred term, hypocritical. Against the claims of figure or perspective, abstraction asserts the singularity of an artistic representation in reference to itself. Abstraction is the image of self-legislation – it refuses to compare itself to an identity that could be unsatisfying or insufficient.

In this way, Black Dada is a matter of abstraction, and yet also a matter of fact, suggesting nothing less than its irrevocable presence.

ADAM PENDLETON: OUR IDEAS, PACE GALLERY, LONDON, 2018

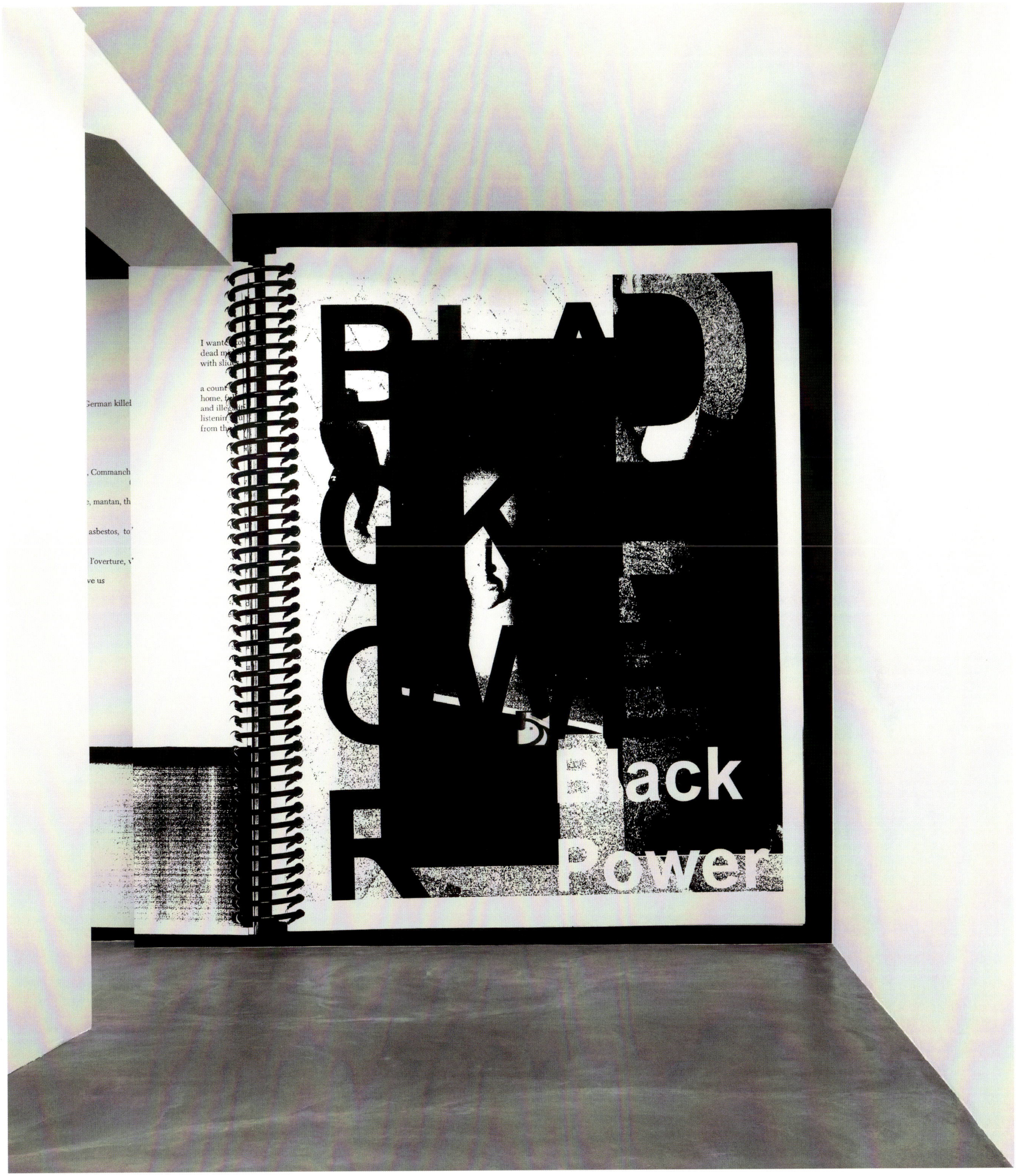
Black
Power

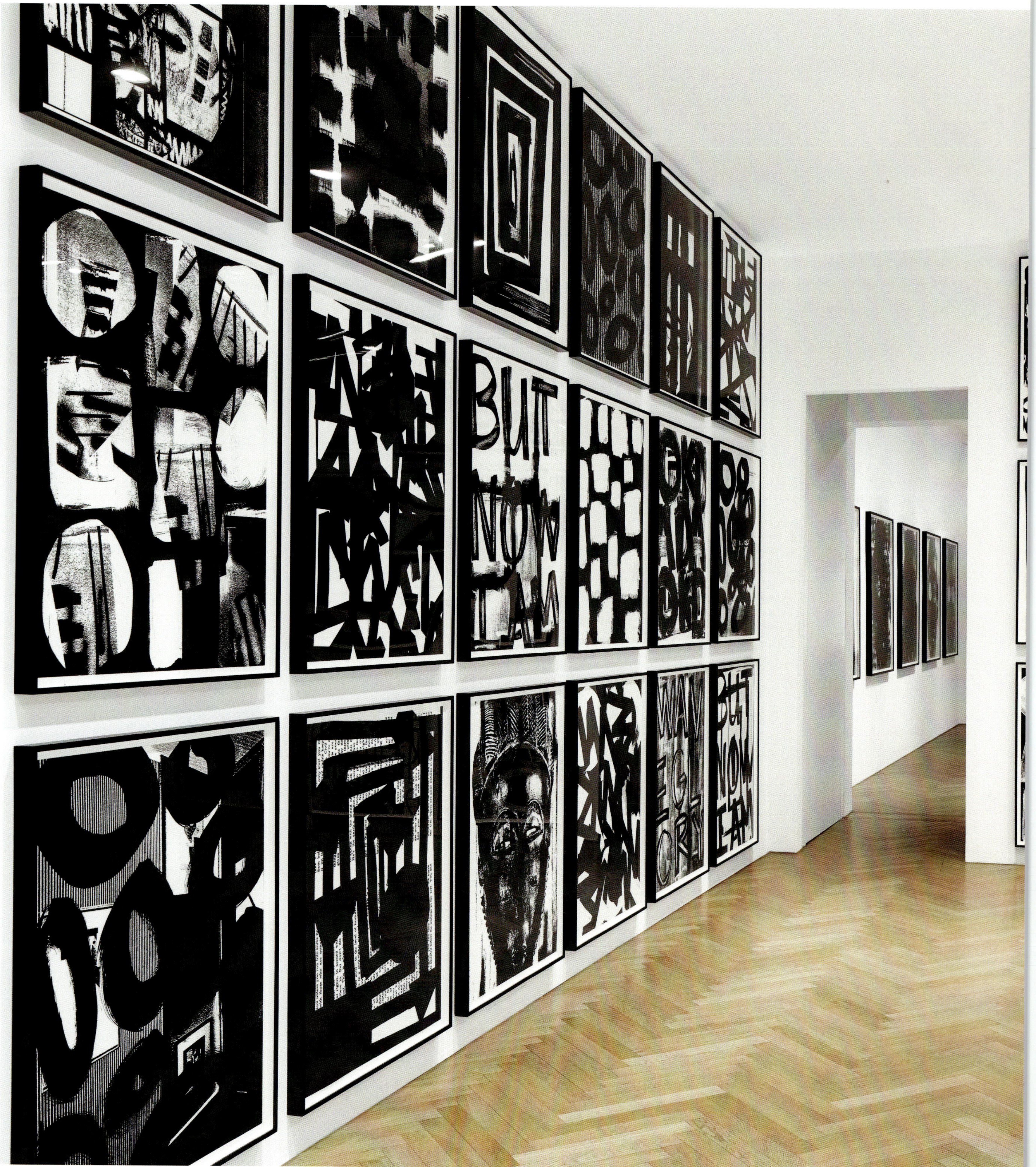

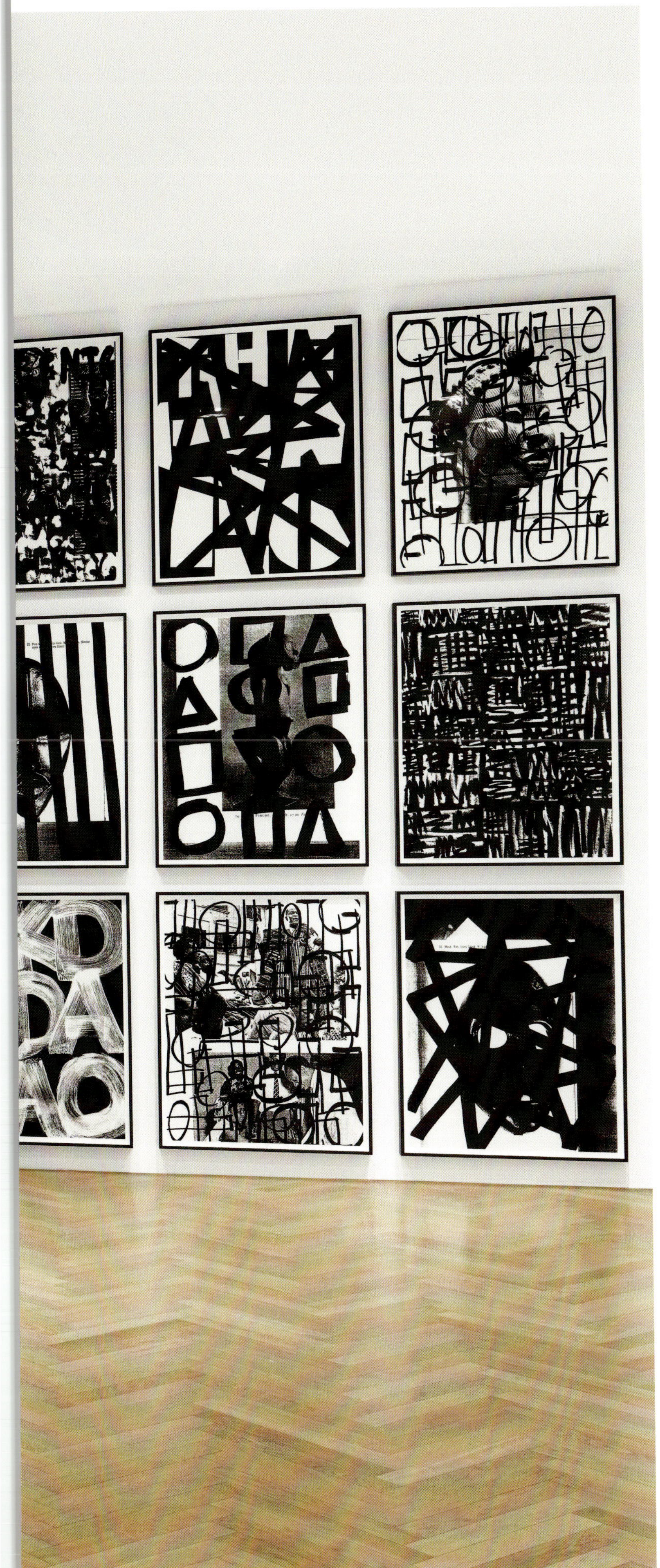

from left,
UNTITLED (PARTIAL VIEW), 2018
SILK-SCREEN INK ON MYLAR
27 PARTS: OVERALL DIMENSIONS VARIABLE
97 X 74 CM

OKDADADAO, 2018
SILK-SCREEN INK ON MYLAR
9 PARTS: OVERALL DIMENSIONS VARIABLE
EACH: 97 X 74 CM

INSTALLATION VIEW AT GALERIE MAX HETZLER, BERLIN, 2019

following pages, from left,
UNTITLED (MASK), 2019
SILK-SCREEN INK ON MYLAR
131 X 100 CM

UNTITLED (MASKS), 2019
SILK-SCREEN INK ON MYLAR
4 PARTS: OVERALL DIMENSIONS VARIABLE
EACH: 131 X 100 CM

INSTALLATION VIEW AT GALERIE MAX HETZLER, BERLIN, 2019

divide by, 2019

to
divide by
to
divide by
to
stand up
to sit down
to divide
to divide by
to
stand up to sit down
to divide
to divide by
standing up to sit down
to divide
to
protest
to divide
to
express
to
break-up
to break it up
to divide
to
breaks-up
to express to break up
to divide to divide by
to assemble
to divide
assembled
to divide
divided by
to divide
to swear by
to divide
to bottom out
to yearn
a yearning
to divide
divided by
to
divide
to divide by
to love
to either or
to divide
to drink
to either
or
express
is to express to
either
operate
to function

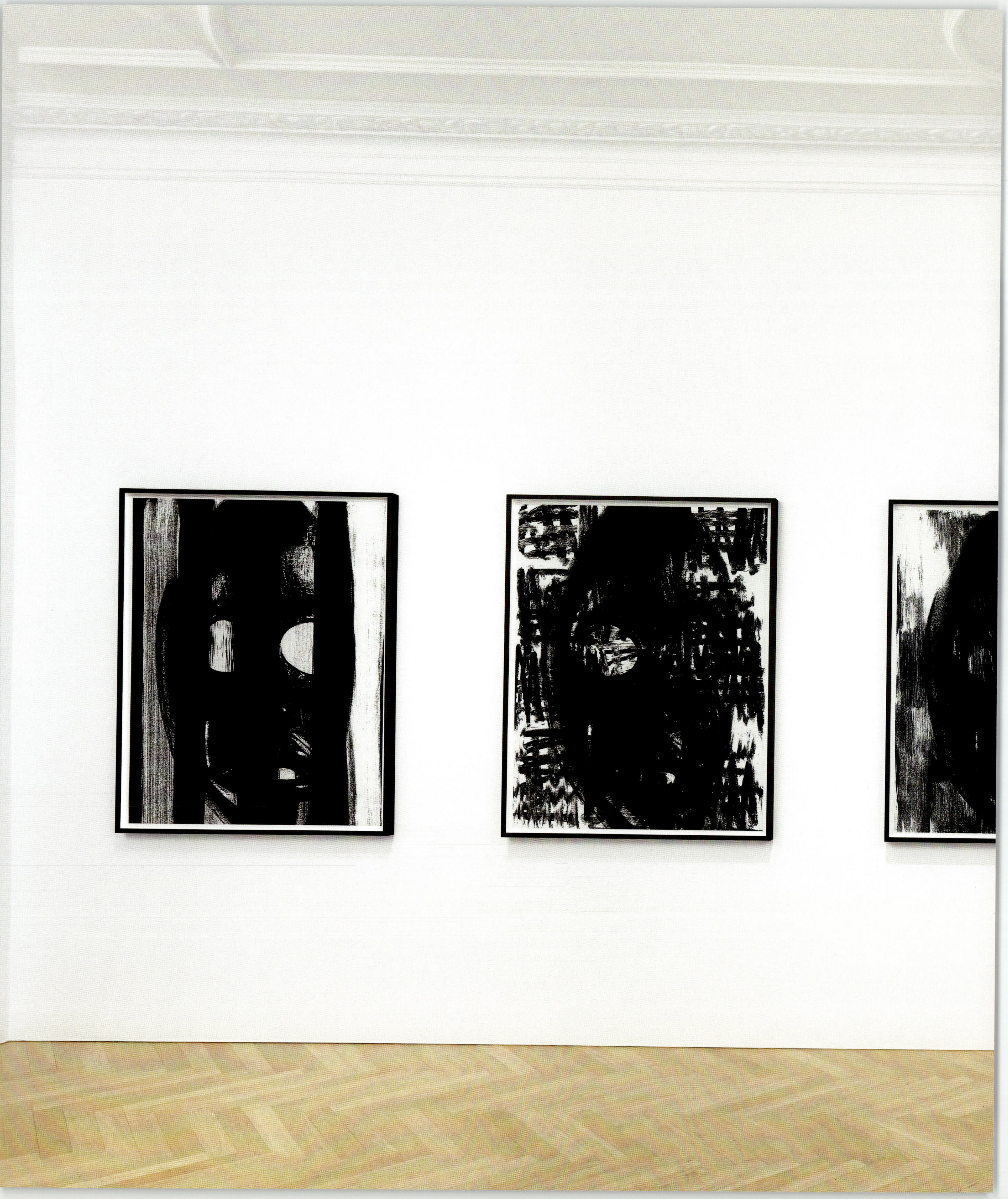

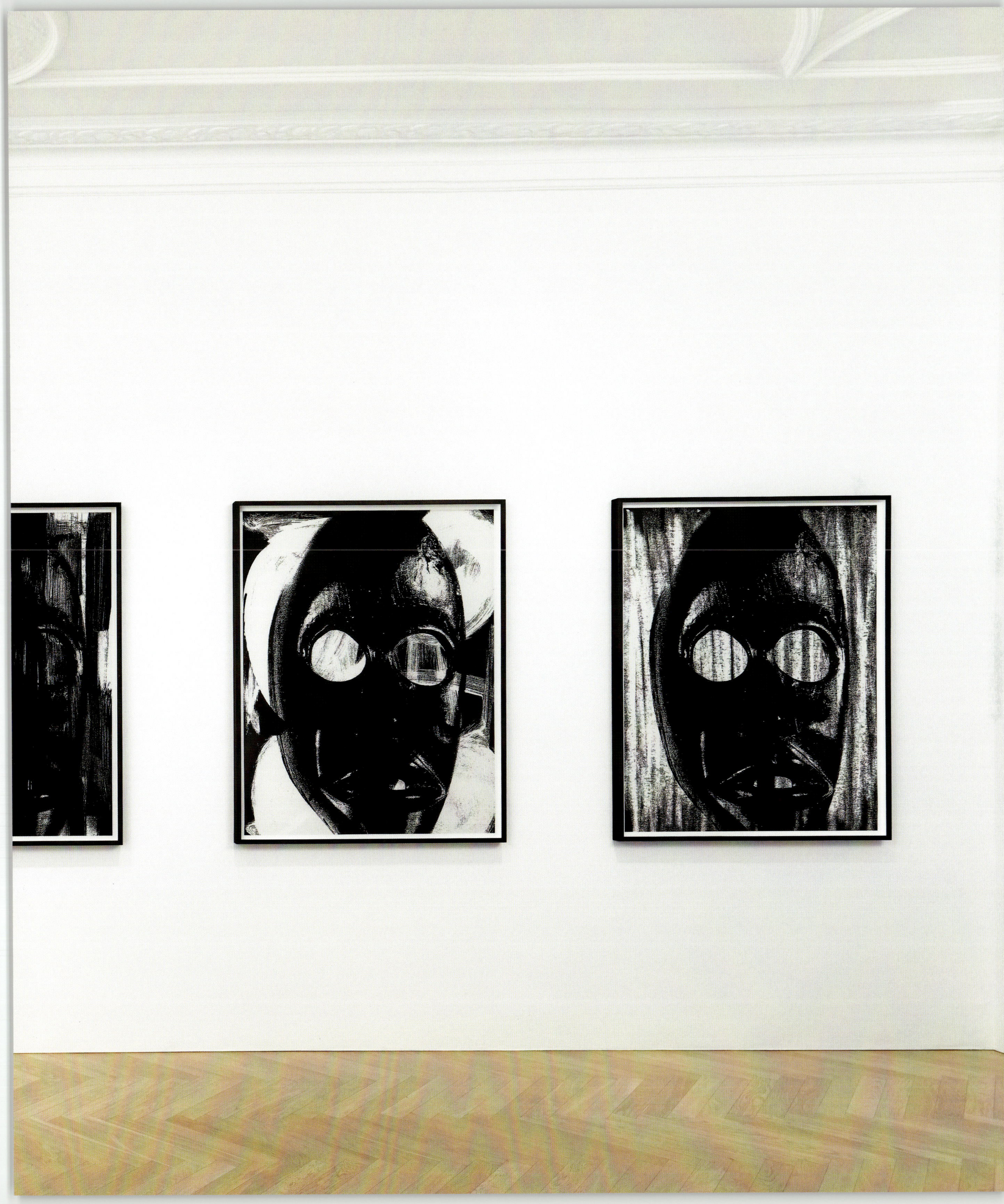

to divide
to express
to function
is to divide
is to express
is to function
is to divide
is to
parallel
is to talk
is his
thought
is to
pass
to you
to divide through you
to divide
to express in order to
divide
to break up
to break
is to break it up
is to
stand
is to divide
is to dreamt
is to sit down
is to standup
to sit-down
to stand up
to get up
to get down
to throw down
to divide
is to offer
is to love
is to thrash
is to thrashing
is to thrashing to stand up to get down to divide
to didn't get up
is to divide
is too divided
to get it
to hustle it to get it
is to hard
is harder is
too hard
is too hard to get
is to divide
is to divide by
is to thrash
thrasher
is to get it
is to thrash to get it
is either or
again
to divide
to divide by
the deaths
divided by the deaths

is to divide
to divide by
yesterday
is to yesterday
is to feel it
is to say it
is to throw it
is to throw it down
to feel it
to have it
to hold it
to stand up
to sit down
to get up
to divide
to divide by
is to protest by
dividing
is to divide
is to divide by
dividing
is to thrash
is to get up
to stand up to get down
is to divide by
all things
to make
all things
to divide
to make it equal
to make it only
to divide
to divide by
to trouble
two troubles
do
to
divide by
that
which
thrashes
which thrashes
to divide
to thrash
to stand up
to sit down
to get up
to drink
to divide
to drink
to
either or
to break
to break up
he stands up
he sits down
she breaks
they break
to get up
to get emotional

from top,
UNTITLED (MASKS) (DETAIL), 2018
SILK-SCREEN INK ON MYLAR
20 PARTS: OVERALL DIMENSIONS VARIABLE
EACH: 131 X 100 CM

UNTITLED (MASKS) (DETAIL), 2018
SILK-SCREEN INK ON MYLAR
20 PARTS: OVERALL DIMENSIONS VARIABLE
EACH: 131 X 100 CM

INSTALLATION VIEW AT GALERIE EVA PRESENHUBER, ZURICH, 2019

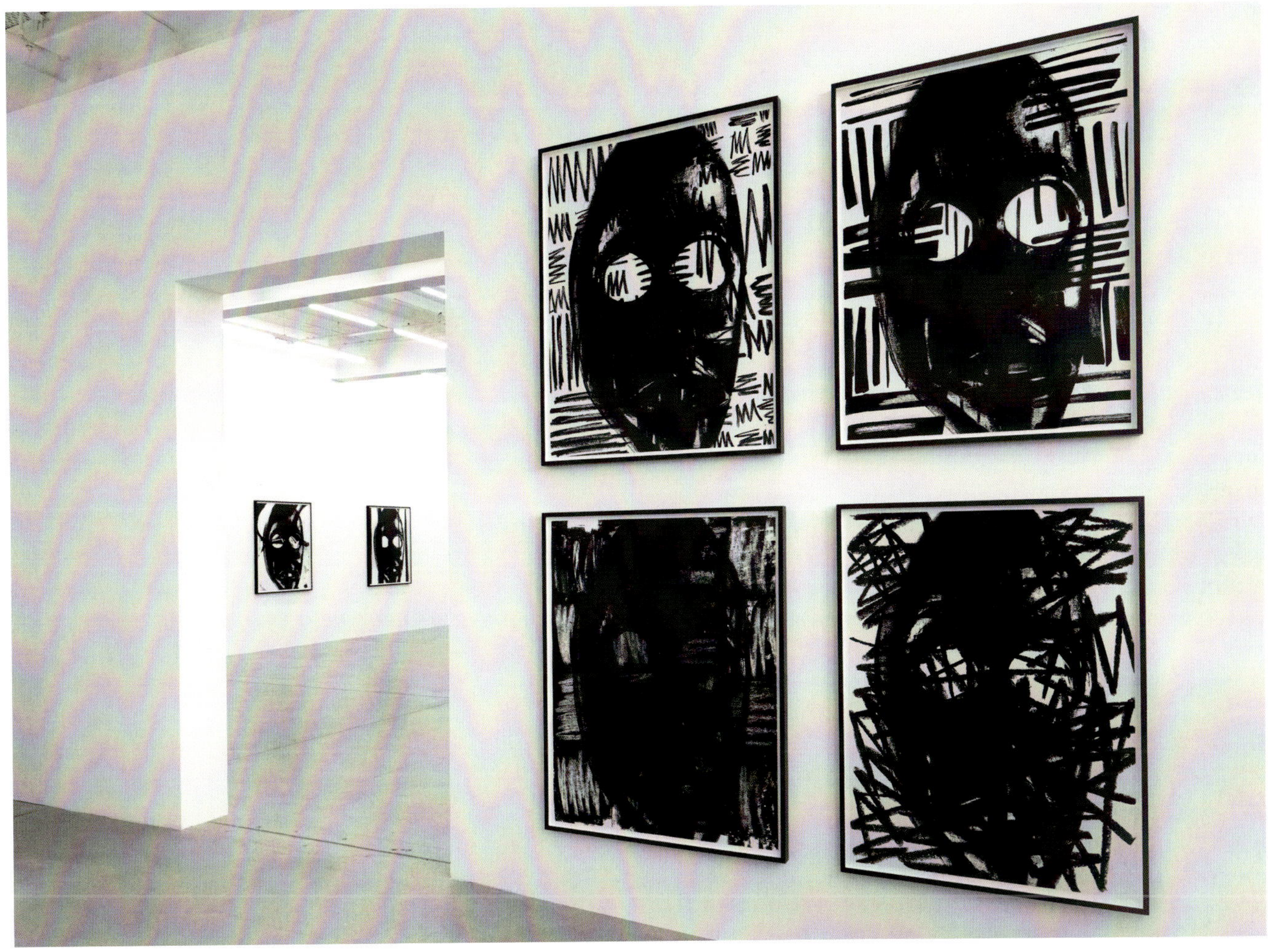

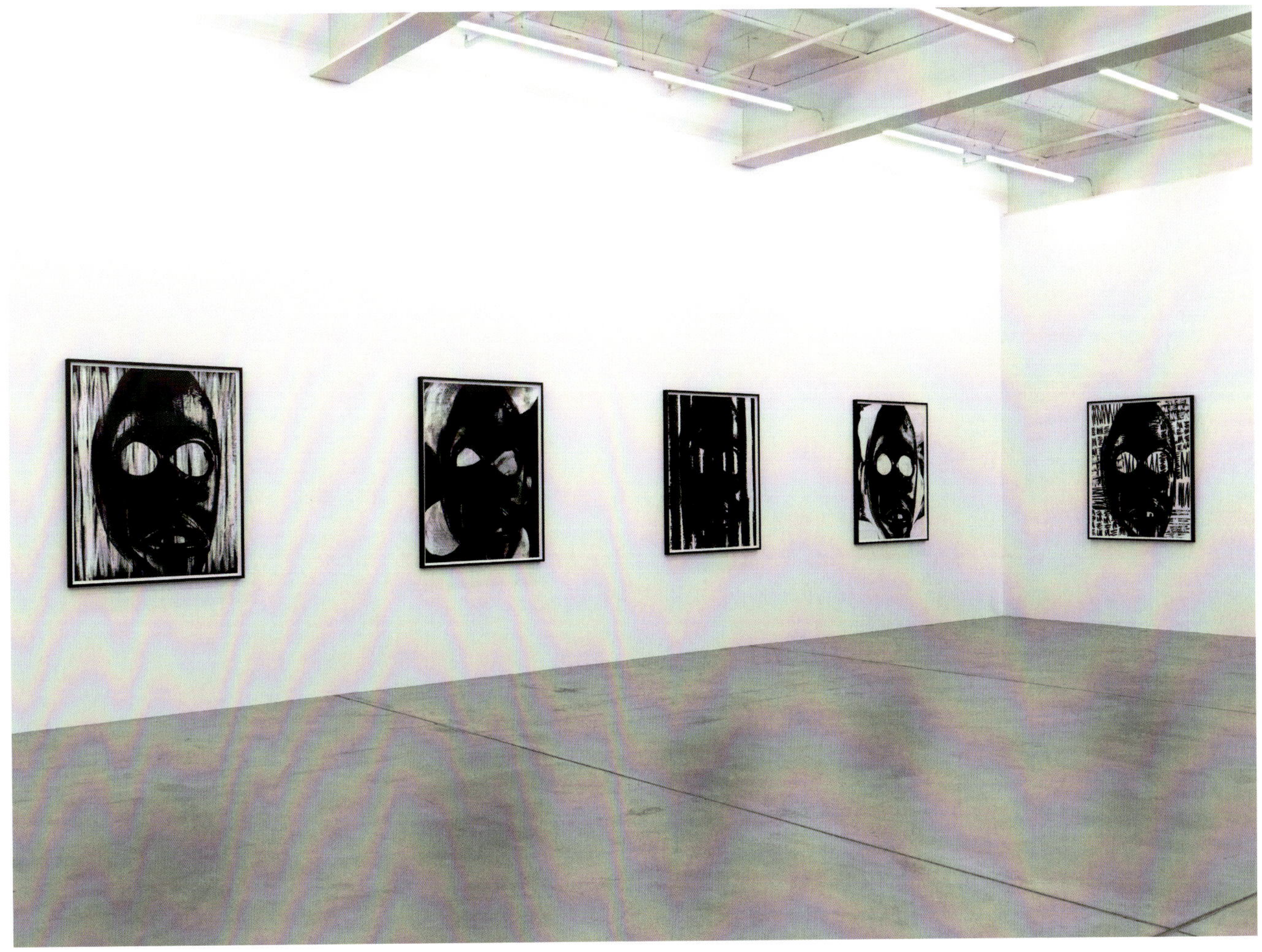

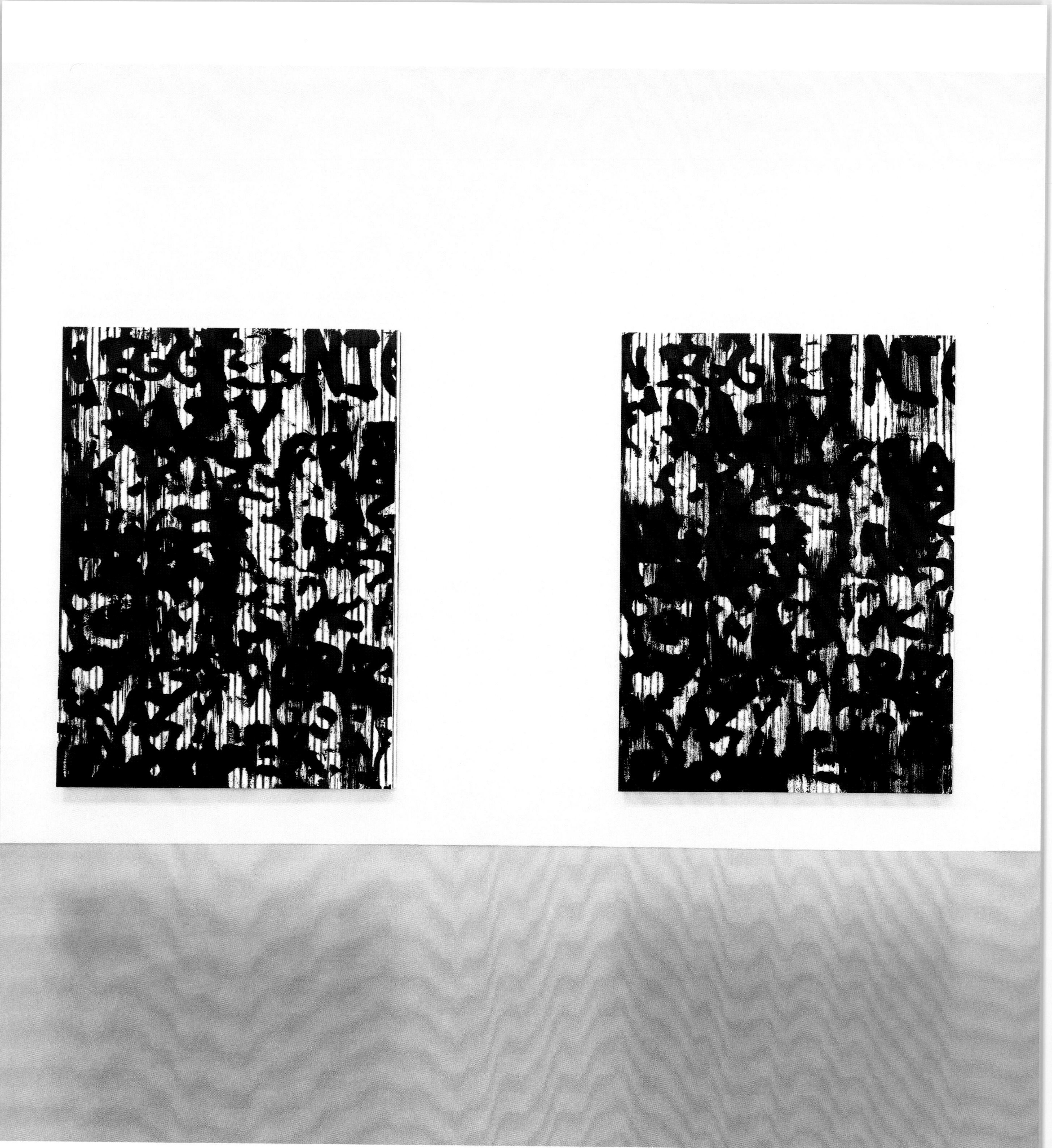

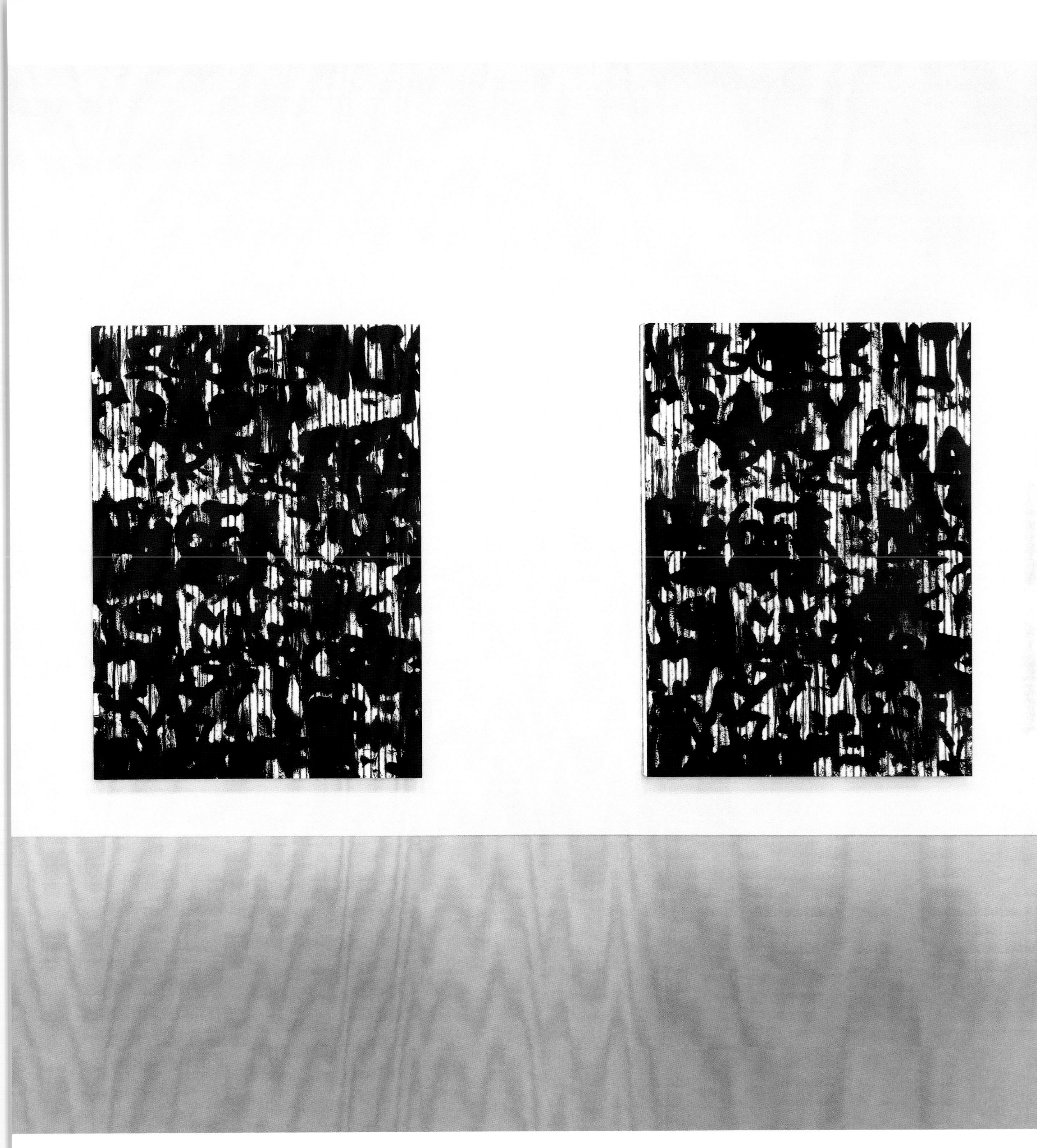

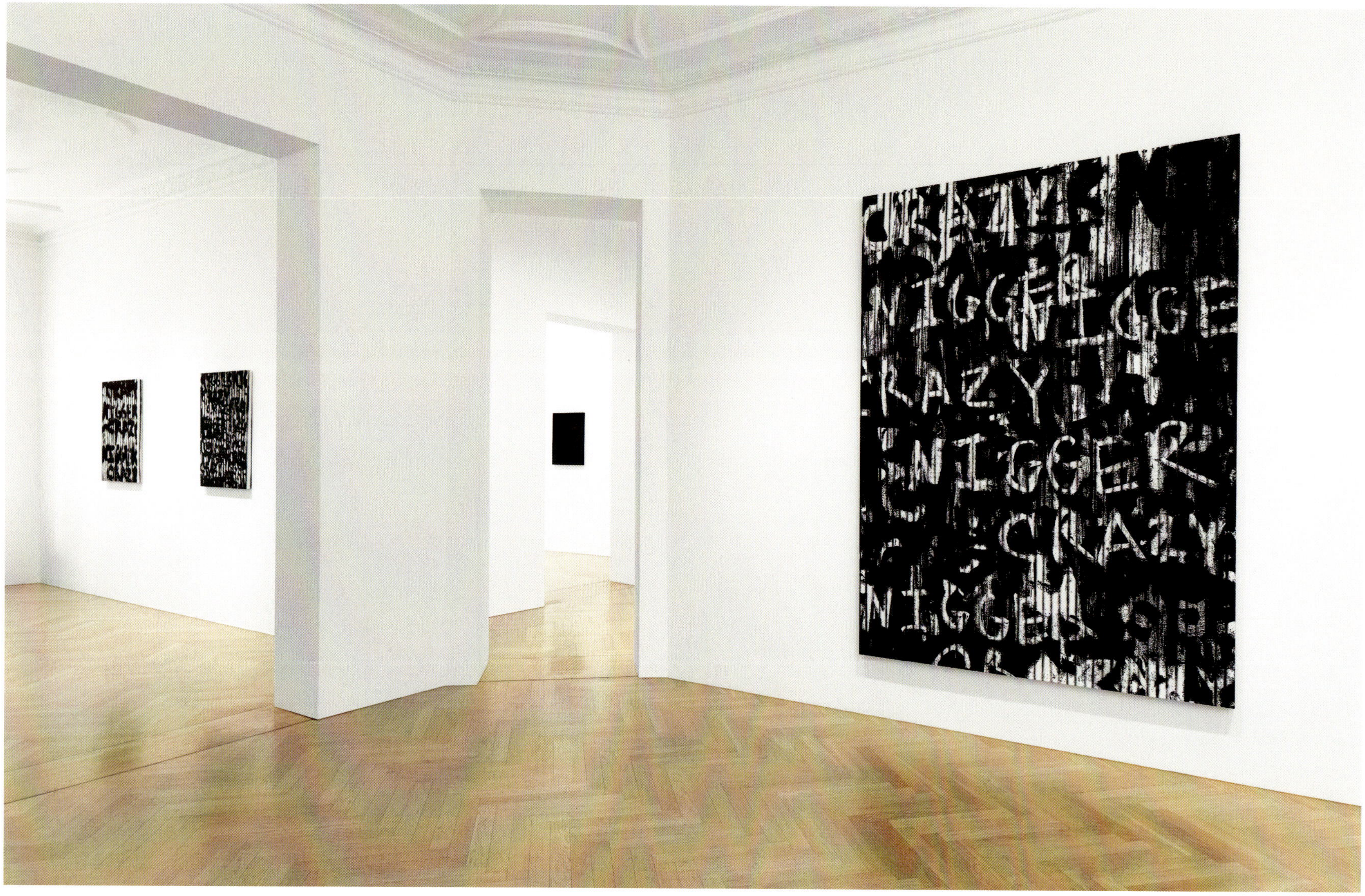

to get functional
to deliver
to stand up and deliver
to stand up
and move
to move through
to stand up and move
to divide
to divide by
to deliver
he delivered
he delivers
he divides
he divides by
delivering
is to move
is to move through
is to fold
is to protest
is to get up
is to stand up
is to show up
is to deliver
is his word

opposite, from left,
UNTITLED (AFTER JULIUS EASTMAN), 2019
SILK-SCREEN INK AND SPRAY PAINT ON CANVAS
91 X 71 CM

UNTITLED (WHO WE ARE), 2019
SILK-SCREEN INK AND SPRAY PAINT ON CANVAS
91 X 71 CM

BLACK DADA DRAWING (B), 2018–19
SILK-SCREEN ON PAPER
66 X 53 CM

UNTITLED (AFTER JULIUS EASTMAN), 2019
SILK-SCREEN INK AND SPRAY PAINT ON CANVAS
244 X 175 CM

previous pages, from left,
UNTITLED (WHO WE ARE), 2019
SILK-SCREEN INK AND SPRAY PAINT ON CANVAS
244 X 175 CM

UNTITLED (WHO WE ARE), 2019
SILK-SCREEN INK AND SPRAY PAINT ON CANVAS
244 X 175 CM

UNTITLED (WHO WE ARE), 2019
SILK-SCREEN INK AND SPRAY PAINT ON CANVAS
244 X 175 CM

UNTITLED (WHO WE ARE), 2019
SILK-SCREEN INK AND SPRAY PAINT ON CANVAS
244 X 175 CM

below, from left,
BLACK DADA (A/A), 2019
SILK-SCREEN INK ON CANVAS
2 PANELS: OVERALL 244 X 193 CM
EACH: 122 X 193 CM

UNTITLED (MASK), 2019
SILK-SCREEN INK ON MYLAR
131 X 100 CM

INSTALLATION VIEW AT GALERIE MAX HETZLER, BERLIN, 2019

that which
divides to divide by
to move
to move through
to fold
to fold your body
to deliver
to balance your body
to divide
to change
he softly
he too softly
he commands
to move
he moves
to move
he
divides
to move
he listens to protest
to listen to protest to demand to listen
to listen to shift to list
to transition
to radio
to feel it
to divide
to transition
to express
to stand up to stand up is to stand up is to stand up to listen
is to divide
is to divide by
he breaks
he moves out
he protests
he moves up

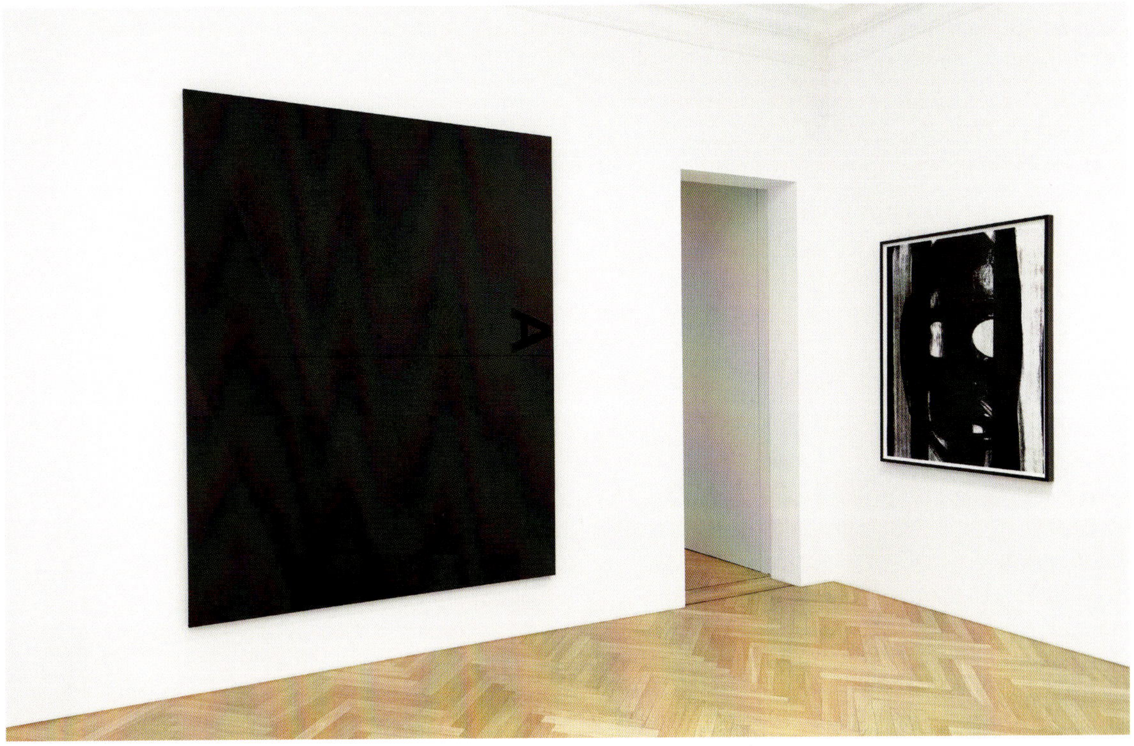

he faults
he breaks
he expresses
he expresses to break
he breaks
he's broken
he stands
he stands up to deliver
to listen
is to listen
is to throw
down
is to deliver
is to throw down and deliver
it
it moves
it tries
he tires
he tries to listen
to throw down
to listen
and deliver
he walks
to sit
he sits
he gestures
he responds
he listens
to deliver
he divides
he divides by
to divide
to divide by to live
to listen to deliver he listens
he looks
to feel
he looks to feel
he feels
to look
and he looks to get lost
he's lost
to go on
to go on and deliver
to sit-up
to transition
to share
to experience
to expect
to step up
to drink
to divide
to divide by
to will
to will it
to multiply it
to touch it
to feel it
surely
it fixates
it delivers
to respond
to respond by
to divide by
to neither nor
to either or
to throw down
to step up and sit down
and deliver
to step up to sit-down
and deliver
to divine
to divide
to divide by

PREVIOUSLY UNPUBLISHED

UNTITLED (WE ARE NOT),
2019–20
SILK-SCREEN INK ON CANVAS
244 X 175 CM

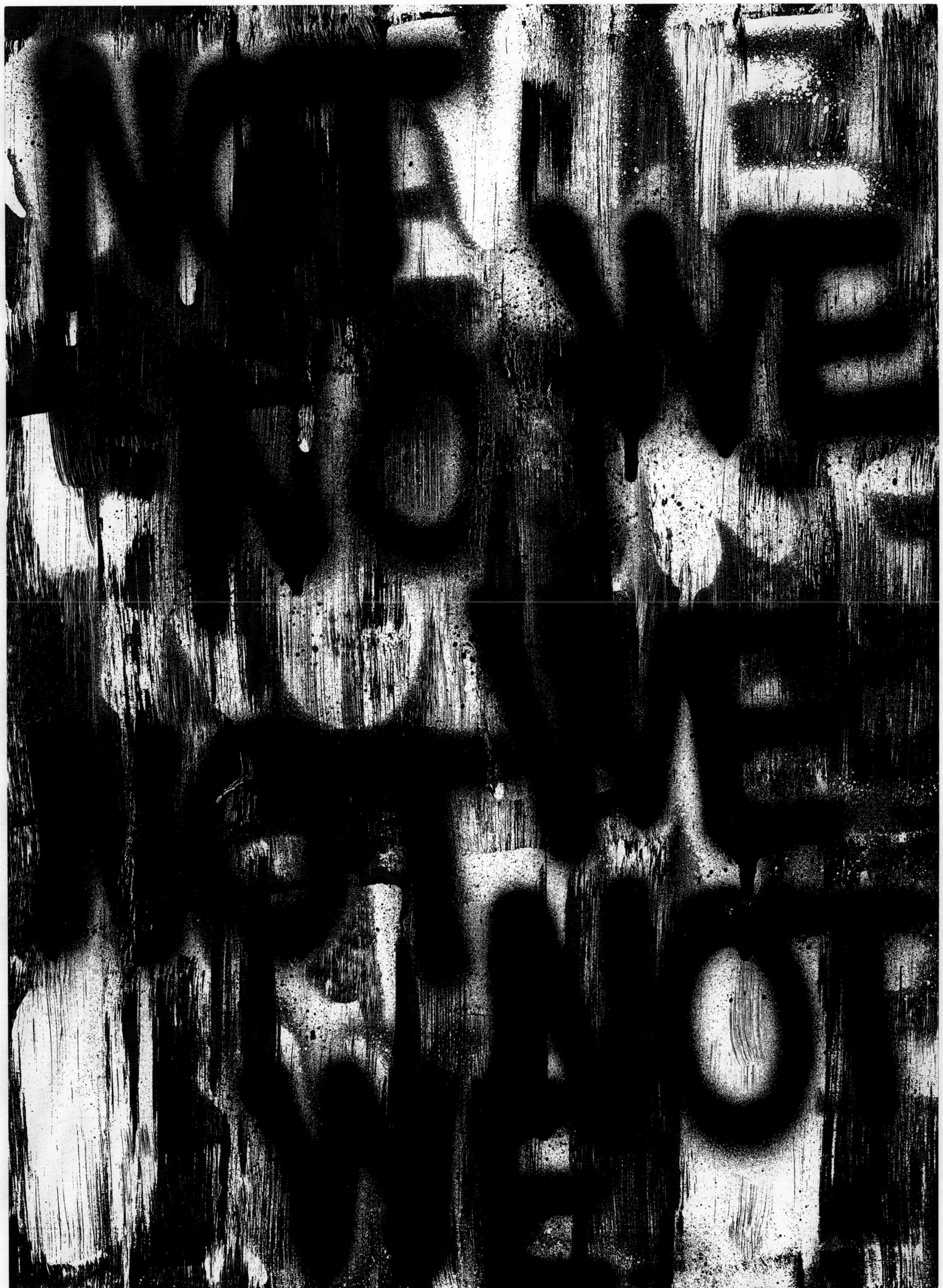

NOTES

SURVEY: PAGES 035–071

1 Michael Greer, 'Ideology and Theory in Recent Experimental Writing or, the Naming of "Language Poetry"', in *Boundary*, vol. 16, no. 2/3 Winter–Spring, 1989, p. 337.
2 Ibid.
3 Ibid.
4 Jena Osman, 'After Language Poetry,' *UbuWeb*, accessed 12 November 2018: http://www.ubu.com/papers/oei/osman.html.
5 Ibid.
6 Ibid.
7 Andrew Ross, 'The New Sentence and the Commodity Form: Recent American Writing', in Cary Nelson and Lawrence Grossberg (eds.), *Marxism and the Interpretation of Culture*, University of Illinois Press, Urbana, 1988, p. 372.
8 Adam Pendleton, 'Black Dada', in Julia Peyton-Jones and Hans Ulrich Obrist (eds), *Manifesto Marathon*, Koenig Books, London, 2010, p. 166. Reprinted in Adam Pendleton, *Black Dada Reader*, Koenig Books, London, 2017.
9 The author viewed documentation of the performance's presentation at Stephan Weiss Studio on 1 November 2007 as part of the Performa 07 biennial. Commissioner: Performa; Curator: RoseLee Goldberg; musical direction: Adam Pendleton with Alicia Hall Moran and Jason Moran, and Vaneese Thomas (choir director); testimonies: Jena Osman, Liam Gillick, Charles Sandison (computer-generated data projection).
10 Zora Neale Hurston, 'The Characteristics of Negro Expression', in Robert G. O'Meally (ed.), *The Jazz Cadence of American Culture*, Columbia University Press, New York, 1998, pp. 298–99.
11 https://www.metmuseum.org/art/collection/search/691091.
12 Conversation with the author on 3 August 2018.
13 Ibid.
14 Versions of these have subsequently been shown at the Walker Art Center in Minneapolis, the Contemporary Arts Center in New Orleans, Aspen Art Museum, the Museum of Contemporary Art in Cleveland, KW Institute for Contemporary Art in Berlin and in various gallery shows.
15 Directed by Richard Wells and edited by Andrew Stein, *Teddy* was made as part of the Social Seminar, a multimedia training series developed by the National Institute of Mental Health with the US Office of Education.
16 A contemporary of Silliman and Hannah Weiner, Hejinian in *My Life* deconstructs the tradition of autobiographical narrative or memoir through paragraphs that momentarily achieve coherence through the recognition of repeating motifs.
17 Jena Osman, *The Character*, Beacon Press, Boston, 1999.
18 An essay in an unpublished, photocopied catalogue for the show 'Coming to Power: 25 Years of Sexually X-plicit Art by Women', curated by Ellen Cantor and presented at David Zwirner Gallery and Simon Watson/The Contemporary, both in New York, in 1993.
19 The *Trio A* film documentation used by Pendleton was produced by Sally Banes, shot by Robert Alexander and filmed at Merce Cunningham's studio in 1978.
20 Adam Pendleton, interview with the author, Brooklyn, New York, 30 April 2016.
21 Ann Eden Gibson, 'Black Is a Color: Norman Lewis and Modernism in New York', in *Norman Lewis Black Paintings 1946-1977*, Studio Museum in Harlem, New York, 1998, p. 11.
22 Ibid., 15.
23 Ibid., 16. It is interesting to note that Reinhardt's list of associations for the colour black had none of the anxieties or ambivalences of Lewis's when it concerned the concept of race. He wrote in his list of hundreds of words: 'Blacks, Coloureds, Colour-Caste' and bracketed on the right side of the page, across from the previous text, he wrote: 'White you're right, Light, you can fight, Brown, stand around, Black, stand back', a variation of a vernacular saying in the black community and historical blues music.
24 Ibid.

FOCUS: PAGES 073–091

1 The score of DEAD (1981) describes it as 'a solo dance/performance piece created 8 June 1981 as part of a celebration of my 30th birthday.':
A. On the evening before performing the dance, pre-record a list of every death I can remember which has occurred during my lifetime. Allow pauses for memory lapses. Even if I am not sure a death happened in the last 30 years, if it seems like a real death in the moment, I must say it.
Allow for people and pets I've known personally; relatives of people I've known; deaths of celebrities I've experienced through the news media; and fictional characters whose deaths seem real to me at the time.
B. On the day of performance play the tape.
C. For the first 3 or 4 names stand still and as I hear each name make the American Sign Language sign for DEAD. (I.e., left hand open with palm facing downward and right hand open with palm facing upward. Turn both hands over so that they are in the opposite orientation from their starting positions.)
D. When I hear a name that has a particular resonance for me fall down to the floor in some emblematic way and try to rise again before the next name is called. As the next, and the next and then the next names are spoken repeat the falling to the floor and rising dance for each name.
E. Try not to anticipate a death. Try not to remember the death until I hear myself speak it on the tape. Try to respond to the death in the moment. Try to let go of the death as I rise from the floor.
F. Continue until there are no more names (about 10 minutes). Allow myself to become exhausted with the effort. Don't stop until the dance is over.

ARTIST'S WRITINGS: PAGES 113–145

1 Tristan Tzara, 'Dada Manifesto' (1918), translated by Robert Motherwell, in Robert Motherwell (ed.), *The Dada Painters and Poets: An Anthology*, George Wittenborn, New York, 1951.
2 Malcolm X, 'The Ballot or the Bullet' (speech, King Solomon Baptist Church, Detroit, Michigan, 12 April 1964).

SYSTEM OF DISPLAY, T (THEY/ANCESTOR FIGURE, SOUTH EASTERN ZAIRE, BALUBA), 2018–19
SILK-SCREEN INK ON PLEXIGLASS AND MIRROR
25 X 25 X 8 CM

INSTALLATION VIEW AT GALERIE MAX HETZLER, BERLIN, 2019

next pages, from left,
BLACK DADA READER (WALL WORK #2), 2018
LATEX INK ON ADHESIVE VINYL
DIMENSIONS VARIABLE

SYSTEM OF DISPLAY, O (HOURS/JAROSLAVA HATLÁKOVÁ, BODY IN SPACE, EXERCISE FROM THE STATE SCHOOL OF GRAPHIC ART, PRAGUE, 1936), 2018
SILK-SCREEN INK ON PLEXIGLASS AND MIRROR
25 X 25 X 8 CM

SYSTEM OF DISPLAY M (MOVING/JAROSLAV RÖSSLER, VARIATION C, 1966), 2018
SILK-SCREEN INK ON PLEXIGLASS AND MIRROR
25 X 25 X 8 CM

SYSTEM OF DISPLAY, E (TREE/JOSEF DAŠEK, SMALL SNAKE AND SPACE, ABOUT 1927–1928), 2018
SILK-SCREEN INK ON PLEXIGLASS AND MIRROR
25 X 25 X 8 CM

SYSTEM OF DISPLAY, H (PHONE/VĚRA GABRIELOVÁ, ADVERTISING PHOTOGRAPH, EXERCISE FROM THE STATE SCHOOL OF GRAPHIC ART IN PRAGUE, 1936), 2018
SILK-SCREEN INK ON PLEXIGLASS AND MIRROR
25 X 25 X 8 CM

INSTALLATION VIEW AT LEVER HOUSE, NEW YORK, 2018

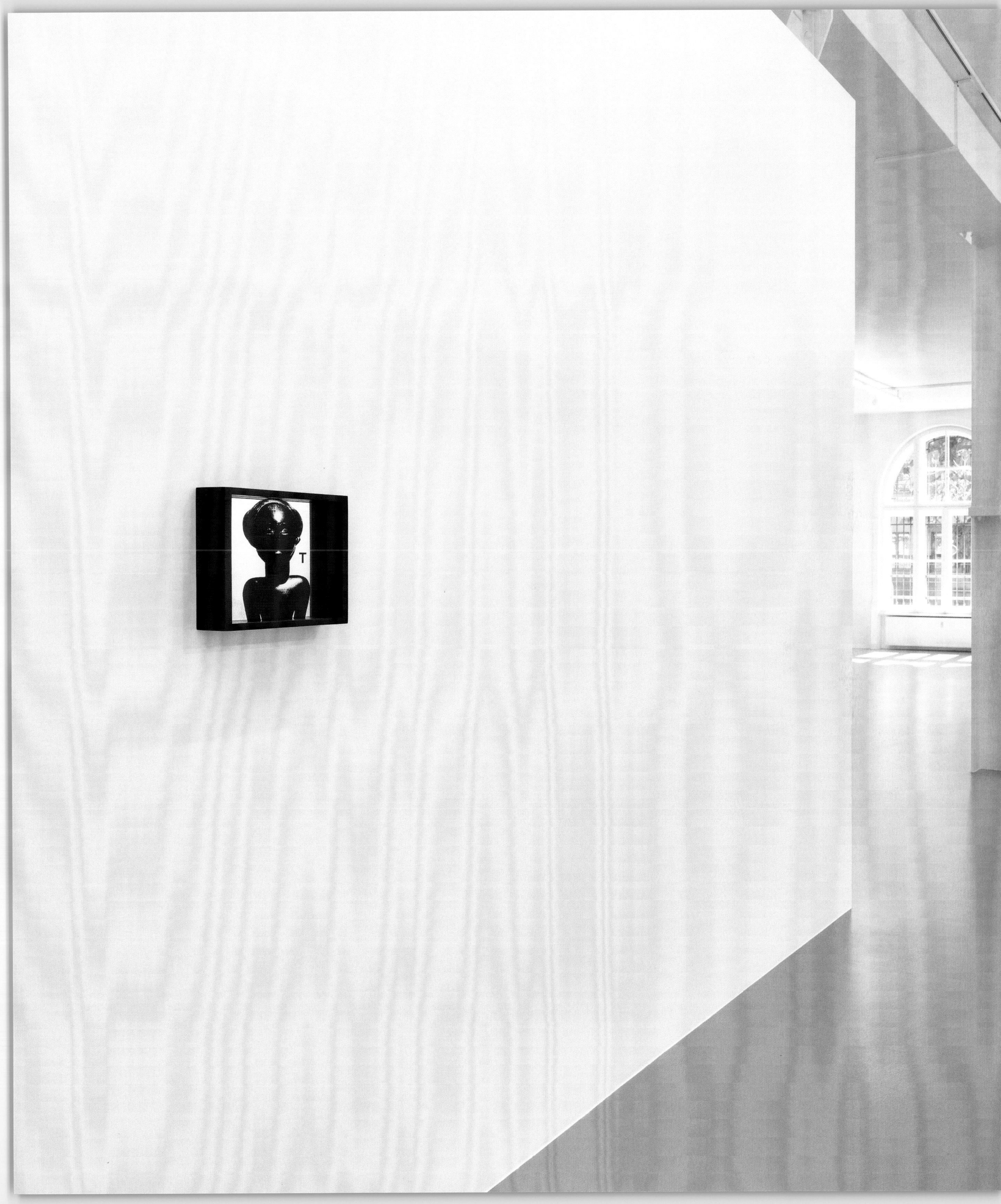
T

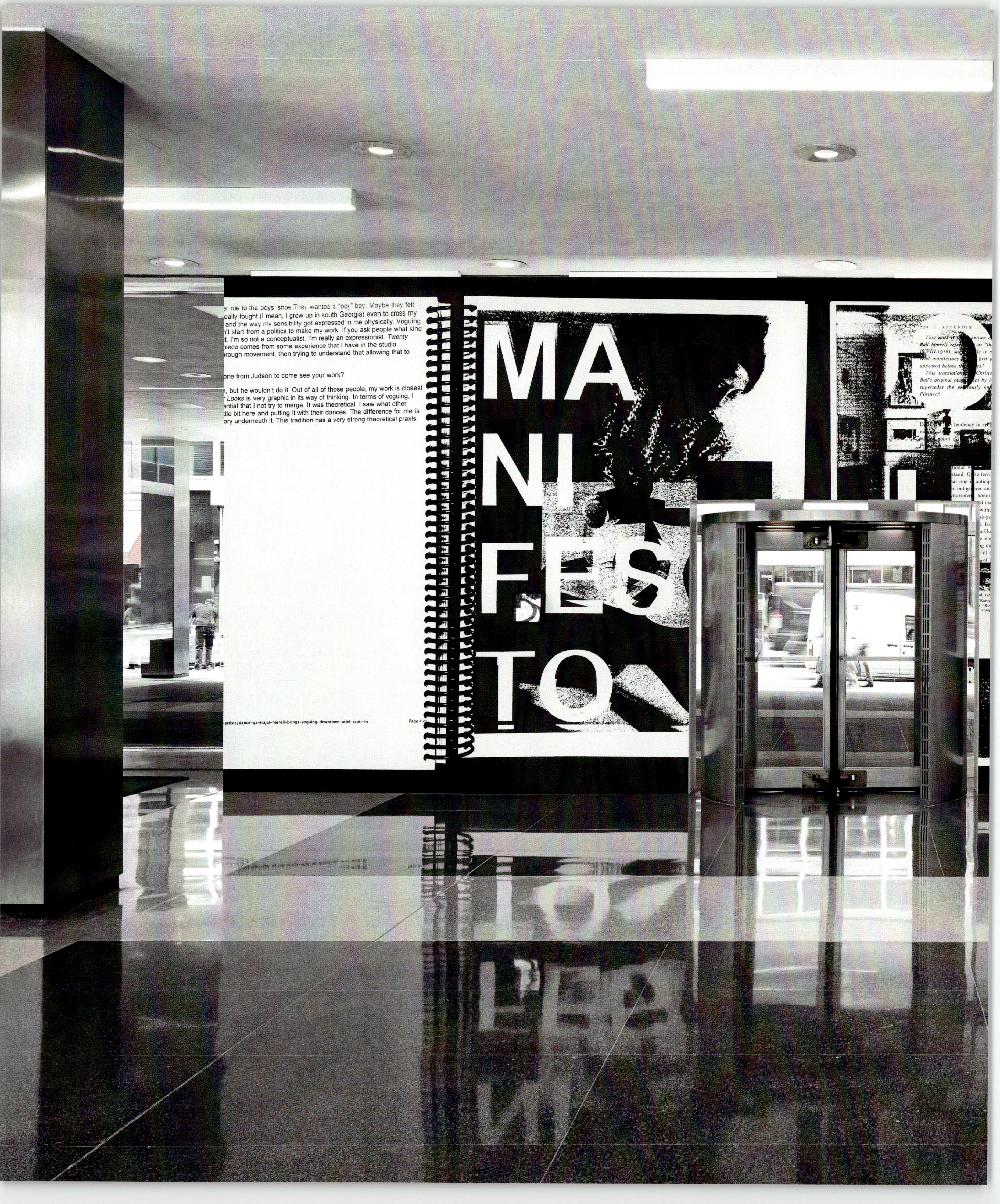
MA
NI
FES
TO

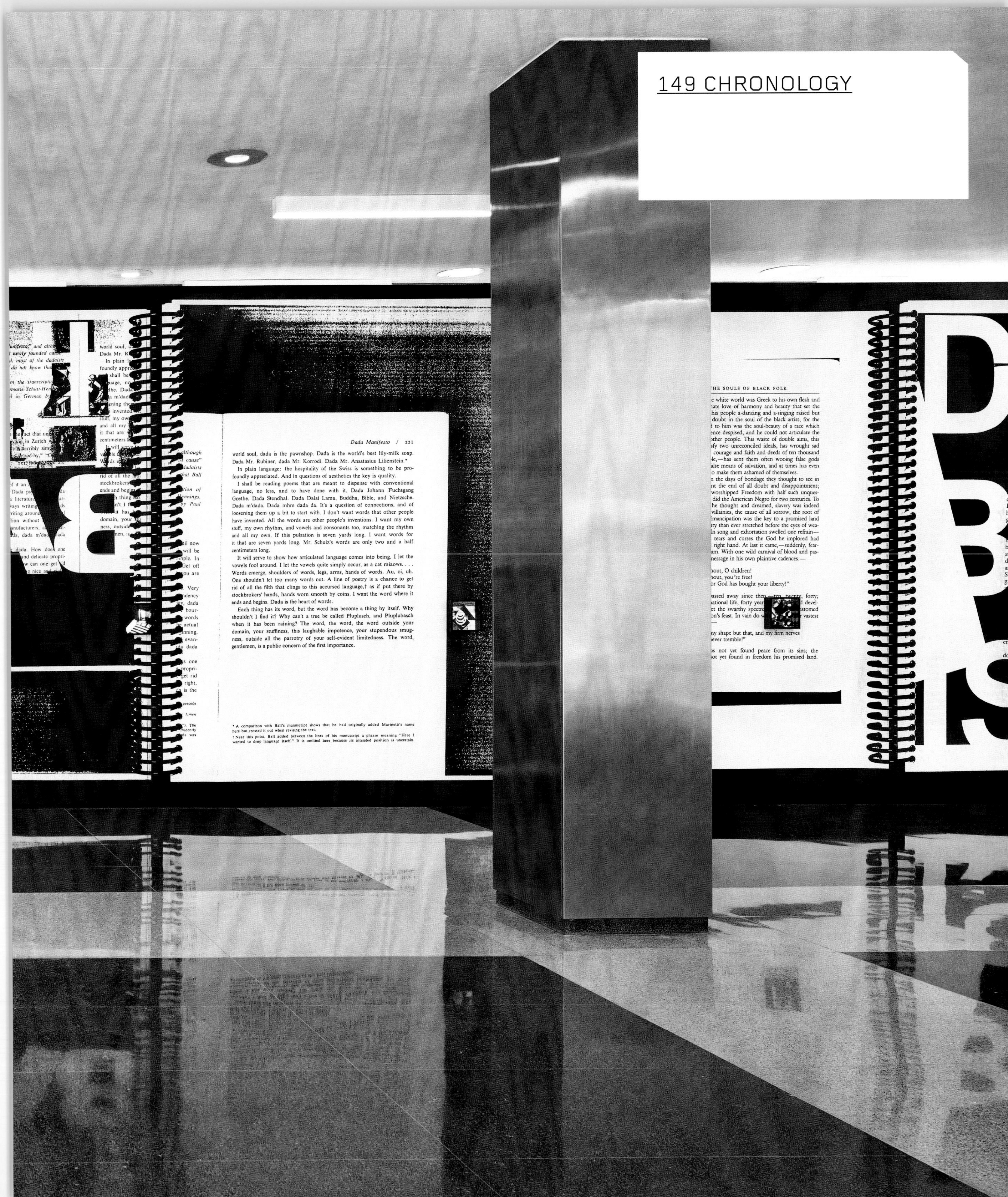
Dada Manifesto / 221
world soul, dada is the pawnshop. Dada is the world's best lily-milk soap. Dada Mr. Rubiner, dada Mr. Korrodi. Dada Mr. Anastasius Lilienstein.*
In plain language: the hospitality of the Swiss is something to be profoundly appreciated. And in questions of aesthetics the key is quality.
I shall be reading poems that are meant to dispense with conventional language, no less, and to have done with it. Dada Johann Fuchsgang Goethe. Dada Stendhal. Dada Dalai Lama, Buddha, Bible, and Nietzsche. Dada m'dada. Dada mhm dada da. It's a question of connections, and of loosening them up a bit to start with. I don't want words that other people have invented. All the words are other people's inventions. I want my own stuff, my own rhythm, and vowels and consonants too, matching the rhythm and all my own. If this pulsation is seven yards long, I want words for it that are seven yards long. Mr. Schulz's words are only two and a half centimeters long.
It will serve to show how articulated language comes into being. I let the vowels fool around. I let the vowels quite simply occur, as a cat miaows. . . . Words emerge, shoulders of words, legs, arms, hands of words. Au, oi, uh. One shouldn't let too many words out. A line of poetry is a chance to get rid of all the filth that clings to this accursed language,† as if put there by stockbrokers' hands, hands worn smooth by coins. I want the word where it ends and begins. Dada is the heart of words.
Each thing has its word, but the word has become a thing by itself. Why shouldn't I find it? Why can't a tree be called Pluplusch, and Pluplubasch when it has been raining? The word, the word, the word outside your domain, your stuffiness, this laughable impotence, your stupendous smugness, outside all the parrotry of your self-evident limitedness. The word, gentlemen, is a public concern of the first importance.
* A comparison with Ball's manuscript shows that he had originally added Marinetti's name here but crossed it out when revising the text.
† Near this point, Ball added between the lines of his manuscript a phrase meaning "Here I wanted to drop language itself." It is omitted here because its intended position is uncertain.
THE SOULS OF BLACK FOLK

CHRONOLOGY: Adam Pendleton, born 1984 in Richmond, Virginia. Lives and works in New York.

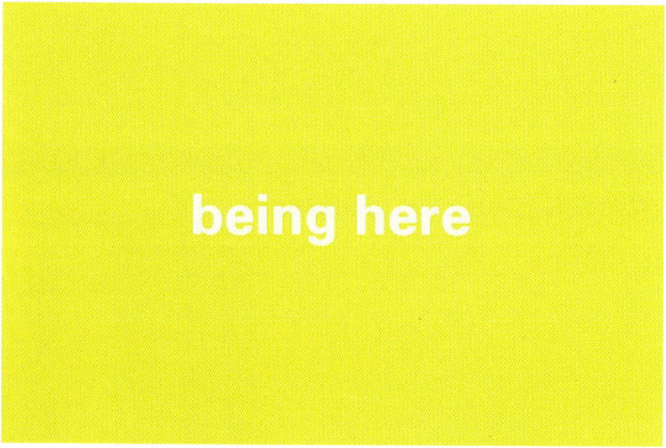

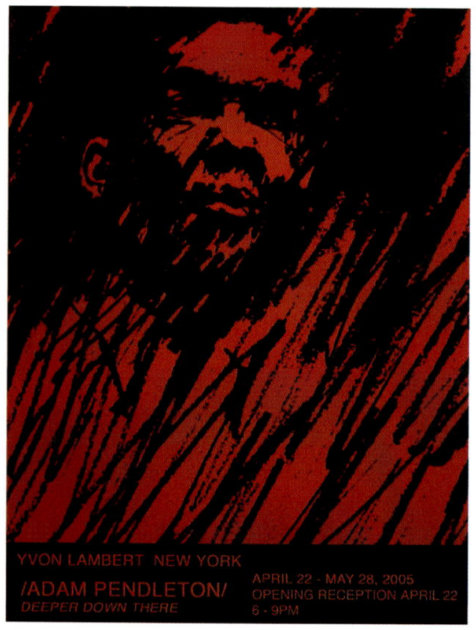

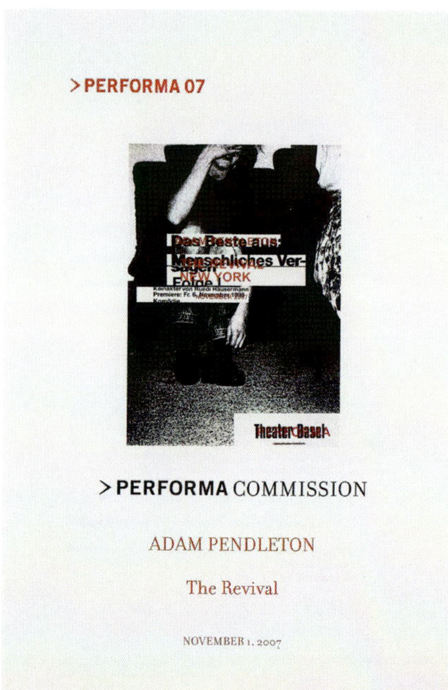

SELECTED EXHIBITIONS AND PROJECTS 2000–08

2000–02,
Attends the Artspace Independent Study Program in Pietrasanta, Italy

2004
'Adam Pendleton: Being Here',
ILLINOIS PROGRAM FOR RESEARCH IN THE HUMANITIES at UNIVERSITY OF ILLINOIS, Urbana-Champaign; WALLSPACE GALLERY, New York (solo)

'When Contemporary Art Speaks',
INDIANAPOLIS MUSEUM OF CONTEMPORARY ART (group)

'Optimo: Manifestations of Optimism in Contemporary Art',
BALLROOM MARFA, Texas (group)

2005
'Adam Pendleton: History',
ROBERTS & TILTON, Los Angeles (solo)

'Adam Pendleton: Deeper Down There',
YVON LAMBERT, New York (solo)

'Adam Pendleton: Gorilla, My Love',
RHONA HOFFMAN GALLERY, Chicago (solo)

'Frequency',
STUDIO MUSEUM IN HARLEM, New York (group)

'Double Consciousness: Black Conceptual Art Since 1970',
CONTEMPORARY ARTS MUSEUM, Houston (group)

2006
'Interstellar Low Ways',
HYDE PARK ART CENTER, Chicago (group)

'R³: Reading "Ritin 'Rithmetic, 30 Years Later"',
CASTLE GALLERY, Inverness, Scotland (group)

'Please Love Me',
WALKER'S POINT CENTER FOR THE ARTS, Milwaukee (group)

'Figures de l'acteur: Le paradoxe du comédien',
COLLECTION LAMBERT, Avignon, France (group)

2007
'Adam Pendleton: Rendered in Black and Rendered',
RHONA HOFFMAN GALLERY, Chicago (solo)

'The Revival',
PERFORMA 07, New York (performance)

'Sympathy for the Devil: Art and Rock and Roll since 1967',
MUSEUM OF CONTEMPORARY ART, Chicago, toured to MUSEUM OF CONTEMPORARY ART NORTH MIAMI; MUSÉE D'ART CONTEMPORAIN DE MONTREAL (group)

'Resistance Is...',
WHITNEY MUSEUM OF AMERICAN ART, New York (group)

2008
'Adam Pendleton: Rendered in Black',
INDIANAPOLIS MUSEUM OF CONTEMPORARY ART (solo)

SELECTED ARTICLES AND INTERVIEWS 2000–08

2004
Ammirati, Domenick, 'The Outlaw Series', ArtUS, April

Hirsch, Faye, 'Ballroom Marfa Launched', Art in America, July–August

Johnson, Ken, 'Black Milk: Theories of Suicide', The New York Times, 16 July

Smith, Roberta, 'Adam Pendleton: "Being Here"', The New York Times, 23 July

Levin, Kim, 'Voices Change', The Village Voice, 28 July

2005
Nusser, Madeline, 'Adam Pendleton: Gorilla My Love', Time Out Chicago, 3 March

Artner, Alan G., 'Adam Pendleton', Chicago Tribune, 4 March

Grabner, Michelle, 'Adam Pendleton', ArtUS, no. 8, May–June

Johnson, Ken, 'Adam Pendleton: "Deeper Down There"', The New York Times, 20 May

2006
Zieher, Scott, 'His 19th Manifesto', Art Review, June–July

2007
Neil, Jonathan, 'Adam Pendleton', Modern Painters, February

Midgette, Anne, 'Peak Performances', Art + Auction, October

Hannaham, James, 'The Big Clean-Up', The Village Voice, 6 November

Cotter, Holland, 'Art Is Brief – You Just Have to Be There', The New York Times, 9 November

La Rocco, Claudia, 'As Conceptual Art evolves, one mission is unchanged: Keep expanding the possibilities', The New York Times, 22 November

Saltz, Jerry, 'The Year in Art: 6. Best Sequel', New York, 17 December

2008
Illes, Chrissie, 'Biennial, Surveys and Retrospectives', Frieze, no. 112, January–February

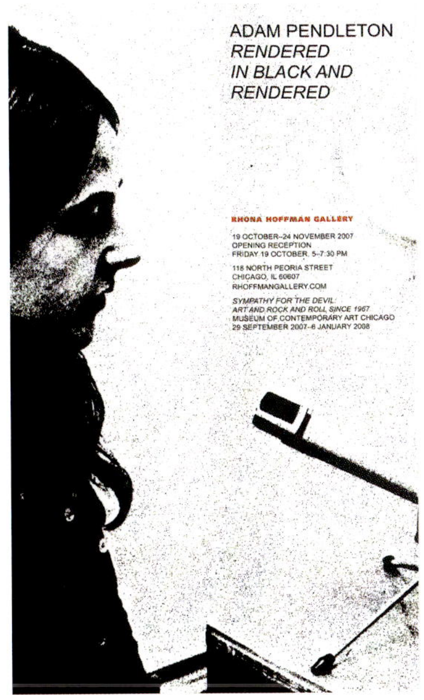

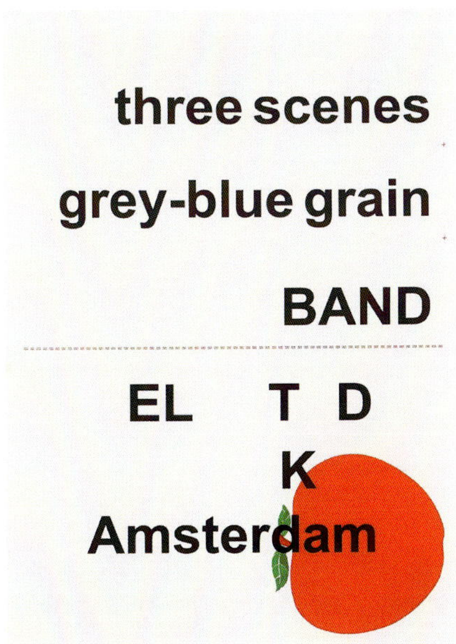

SELECTED EXHIBITIONS AND PROJECTS
2008–09

2008 (cont.)
U-TURN Quadriennial for Contemporary Art, Arhus, Denmark (performance)

'Manifesto Marathon',
SERPENTINE GALLERY, London (performance)

MANIFESTA 7, Rovereto, Italy (group)

'Hey Hey Glossolalia',
CREATIVE TIME, New York (group)

'After 1968: Contemporary Artists and The Civil Rights Legacy',
HIGH MUSEUM OF ART, Atlanta, toured to CALIFORNIA AFRICAN AMERICAN MUSEUM, Los Angeles (group)

'Object: The Undeniable Success of Operations',
STEDELIJK MUSEUM, Amsterdam (group)

'The Future as Disruption',
THE KITCHEN, New York (group)

'Freeway Balconies',
DEUTSCHE GUGGENHEIM, Berlin (group)

2009
'Adam Pendleton: EL T D K Amsterdam. Part I: three scenes',
KUNSTVEREIN, Amsterdam (performance)

'Part II: grey-blue grain',
KUNSTVEREIN, Amsterdam (solo)

'Part III: BAND',
DE APPEL, Amsterdam (film screening)

'Hannah Weiner: An Argument for Black Dada',
INSTITUTE OF CONTEMPORARY ARTS, London (performance)

'BAND',
TORONTO INTERNATIONAL FILM FESTIVAL (performance)

'The Prompt',
PERFORMA 09, New York (performance)

'The Generational: Younger Than Jesus',
NEW MUSEUM OF CONTEMPORARY ART, New York (group)

'Talk Show',
INSTITUTE OF CONTEMPORARY ARTS (ICA), London (group)

'The columns held us up',
ARTISTS SPACE, New York (group)

'Black Hole',
KUNSTHALLE ANDRATX, Mallorca, Spain (group)

'Encodings: Artists in Residence, 2008–09',
STUDIO MUSEUM IN HARLEM, New York (group)

'Cargo',
AUTOCENTER, Berlin (group)

'Constellations: Paintings from the MCA Collection',
MUSEUM OF CONTEMPORARY ART, Chicago (group)

'Infinitesimal Eternity',
YALE UNIVERSITY SCHOOL OF ART, New Haven (group)

'The One Hundred and Sixty-Third Floor: Liam Gillick curates the Collection',
MUSEUM OF CONTEMPORARY ART, Chicago (group)

SELECTED ARTICLES AND INTERVIEWS
2008–09

2008 (cont.)
Bonami, Francesco, 'Performa 07 NY', Domus, February

Menick, John, 'Adam Pendleton, The Revival', Art in America, March

Spears, Dorothy, '60s Legacy, Personal Histories', The New York Times, 1 June

Hamersly, Michael, 'Rock 'n' Roll: "Sympathy for the Devil" Shows How Two Genres Feed Off Each Other', Miami Herald, 22 June

Rosenberg, Karen, 'The Future as Disruption', The New York Times, 1 August

Koenig, Wendy, 'After 1968', Art Papers, September–October

Auslander, Philip, 'After 1968: Contemporary Artists and the Civil Rights Legacy', Artforum, November

Politi, Giancarlo, 'Focus: Painting. Dead Language or Cultural Terrorism', Flash Art, no. 263, November–December

Jonas, Joan, 'Artists on Artists: Their Favorite Exhibitions of 2008', Artforum, December

2009
'New York Artists Dictionary, Part I', Flash Art, no. 264, January–February

Pendleton, Adam, 'Work in Progress', V Magazine, no. 58, Spring

Gruijthuijsen, Krist, 'The past does not influence me. I influence the past: An Interview with Adam Pendleton', Metropolis M, April–May

Gopnik, Blake, 'Younger Than Jesus', The Washington Post, 17 May

McHugh, Gene, 'Younger Than Jesus', Artforum, Summer

Pendleton, Adam, 'Xaviera Simmons', Bomb, no. 108, Summer

Cotter, Holland, 'Museum and Gallery Listings: Studio Museum in Harlem', The New York Times, 23 October

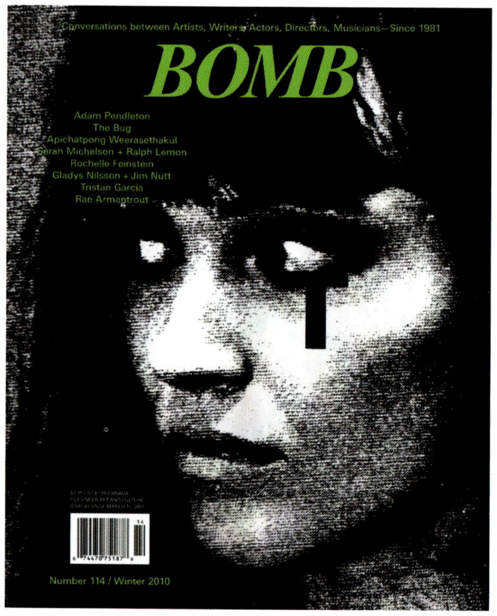

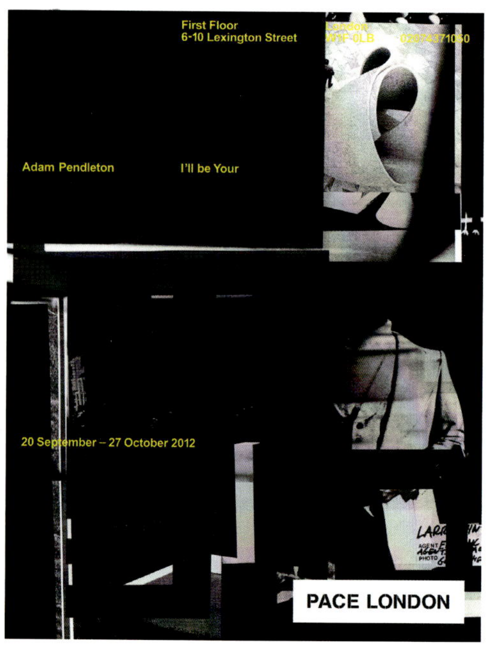

SELECTED EXHIBTIONS AND PROJECTS
2010–12

2010

'Adam Pendleton: BAND',
THE KITCHEN, New York (solo)

'Adam Pendleton',
ILLINGWORTH KERR GALLERY at ALBERTA COLLEGE OF ART AND DESIGN, Calgary (solo)

'Adam Pendleton: chandelier across cognition generates glow linguistic signals perception',
GALERIA PEDRO CERA, Lisbon (solo)

'three scenes, variation one',
ISABELLA STEWART GARDNER MUSEUM, Boston (performance)

'Greater New York 2010',
P.S.1 CONTEMPORARY ART CENTER, New York (group)

'Collected: Reflections on the Permanent Collection',
STUDIO MUSEUM IN HARLEM, New York (group)

'Self as Disappearance',
CENTRE D'ART CONTEMPORAIN, La Synagogue de Delme, France (group)

'Desire',
BLANTON MUSEUM OF ART, Austin (group)

'Afro-Modernism: Journeys through the Black Atlantic',
TATE LIVERPOOL (group)

'From Then to Now',
MUSEUM OF CONTEMPORARY ART, Cleveland (group)

'It Is Written',
CENTRE POMPIDOU-METZ, France (group)

'Quadruple-Consciousness',
VOX POPULI GALLERY, Philadelphia (group)

2011

'Adam Pendleton: New Black Dada Paintings',
GALERIA PEDRO CERA, Lisbon (solo)

'Adam Pendleton: the women',
SHANE CAMPBELL GALLERY, Chicago (solo)

'Adam Pendleton: Radio (ONE)',
SALINA ART CENTER, Kansas (solo)

'BAND',
SAN FRANCISCO MUSEUM OF MODERN ART (performance and film screening)

'A Promise is a Cloud',
PUBLIC ART FUND, New York (group)

5th CONTOUR BIENNALE, Mechelen, Belgium (group)

'Never Odd or Even',
GRIMMUSEUM, Berlin (group)

2012

'Adam Pendleton: I'll Be Your',
PACE GALLERY, London (solo)

'Ecstatic Alphabets/Heaps of Language',
MUSEUM OF MODERN ART, New York (group)

SELECTED ARTICLES AND INTERVIEWS
2010–12

2010

Knight, Christopher, 'Views of advances still in progress', Los Angeles Times, 3 February

McGarry, Kevin, 'Greater New Yorkers: Adam Pendleton', The New York Times T Magazine, 27 May

Donovan, Thom, 'Adam Pendleton', Bomb, no. 114, Winter

Wilson, Michael, 'Adam Pendleton: "Band"', Time Out New York, 10 December

2011

Williams, Tom, 'Adam Pendleton', Art in America, February

Ligon, Glenn, and Adam Pendleton, 'Site of Engagement', Flash Art, no. 279, July–September

McDonough, Tom, 'The Parallax View', Artforum, November

Donovan, Thom, 'A grave in exchange for the commons: Fred Moten and the resistance of the object', Jacket2, April

Adams, Susan, '30 Under 30: Art & Design', Forbes, 19 December

2012

Miller, Michael H, 'Inside the Black Cube: Adam Pendleton Brings Black Dada to MoMA and Pace', New York Observer, 18 April

Indrisek, Scott, 'Studio Check: Adam Pendleton', Modern Painters, October

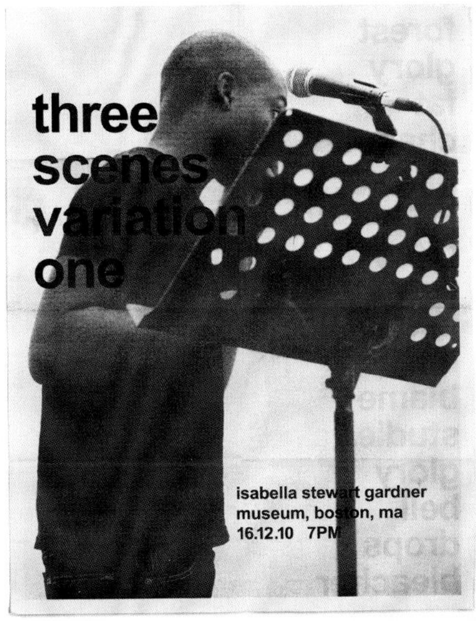

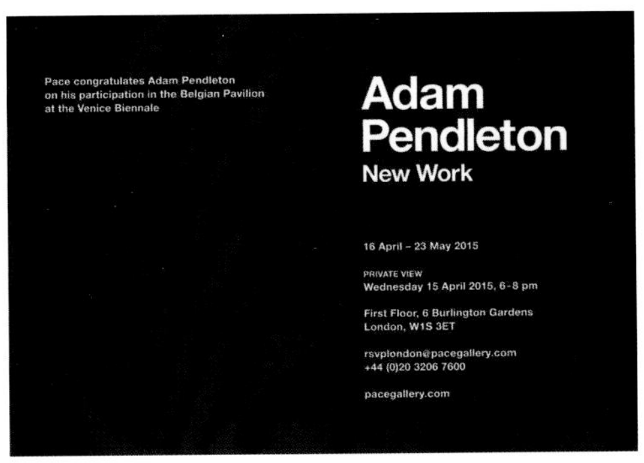

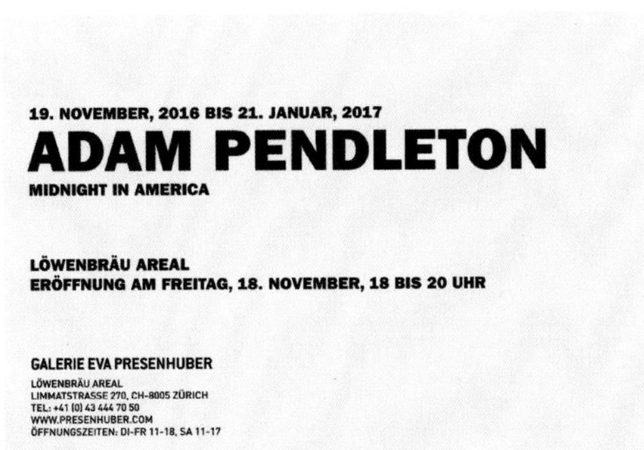

SELECTED EXHIBITIONS AND PROJECTS
2012–16

2012 (cont.)
'Heart to Hand',
SWISS INSTITUTE/CONTEMPORARY ART NEW YORK (group)

1st PALAIS DE TOKYO TRIENNIAL, Paris (group)

'Phantom Limb: Approaches to Painting Today',
MUSEUM OF CONTEMPORARY ART, Chicago (group)

'Radical Presence: Black Performance in Contemporary Art',
CONTEMPORARY ARTS MUSEUM, Houston, toured to GREY ART GALLERY at NEW YORK UNIVERSITY; STUDIO MUSEUM IN HARLEM, New York; WALKER ART CENTER, Minneapolis; YERBA BUENA CENTER FOR THE ARTS, San Francisco (group)

2013
'Adam Pendleton: Untitled',
ISABELLA STEWART GARDNER MUSEUM, Boston (solo)

30th BIENNIAL OF GRAPHIC ARTS, Ljubljana (group)

'After Hours 2: Murals on the Bowery',
ART PRODUCTION FUND and NEW MUSEUM OF CONTEMPORARY ART, New York (group)

'Body Language',
STUDIO MUSEUM IN HARLEM, New York (group)

2014
'Adam Pendleton: Selected Works',
SHANE CAMPBELL GALLERY, Chicago (solo)

'Joan Jonas & Adam Pendleton',
GALERIA PEDRO CERA, Lisbon (solo)

'Adam Pendleton',
PACE GALLERY, New York (solo)

'Adam Pendleton: Selected Works',
TRAVESÍA CUATRO, Guadalajara, Mexico (solo)

'The Disappearance of the Fireflies',
COLLECTION LAMBERT, Avignon (group)

'Love Story: Anne and Wolfgang Titze Collection',
21er HAUS AND WINTER PALACE, Vienna (group)

'Civil Rights',
VOID, Derry, Northern Ireland (group)

2015
'Adam Pendleton: New Work',
PACE GALLERY, London (solo)

'Sharon Hayes, Tony Lewis, Adam Pendleton',
ANDREA ROSEN GALLERY, New York (solo)

3rd BIENNIAL OF THE AMERICAS, Denver (group)

'Adventures of the Black Square: Abstract Art and Society 1915–2015',
WHITECHAPEL GALLERY, London (group)

'Personne et les autres',
BELGIAN PAVILION at the 56th VENICE BIENNALE (group)

2016
'Adam Pendleton: Midnight in America',
GALERIE EVA PRESENHUBER, Zurich (solo)

SELECTED ARTICLES AND INTERVIEWS
2012–16

2012 (cont.)
White, Joshua, 'Adam Pendelton at Pace London', Flash Art, no. 164, November

Griffin, Tim, 'Best of 2012: "Ecstatic Alphabets/Heaps of Language"', Artforum, December

2013
Gratza, Agnieszka, 'Adam Pendelton, Pace, London', Frieze, no. 152, January–February

Vogel, Carol, 'Inside Art: A Warrior for Boston', The New York Times, 1 March

Vogel, Carol, 'Inside Art: Rolldown Steel Murals On Bowery Storefronts', The New York Times, 11 April

2014
Pendleton, Adam, 'Amiri Baraka (1934–2014)', Artforum, March

Pendleton, Adam, 'The Artists' Artists: Joan Jonas, Reanimation', Artforum, December

Pendleton, Adam, 'Untitled (Protest), 2014', Parkett, no. 95

2015
Edwards, Adrienne, 'Blackness in Abstraction'; Lindsay Pollock, 'Editor's Letter', Art in America, January

Greenberg, Kevin, 'Dada Issues: Interview with artist Adam Pendleton', PIN–UP, no. 18, Spring–Summer

Cashdan, Marian, 'Writing the Wall', Surface, no. 117, April

Cooper, Ashton, 'Supernova', Cultured Magazine, April–May

Gamerman, Ellen, 'The Making of an Art-World Star', The Wall Street Journal, 17 April

Udy, Dan, 'Adam Pendleton, New Work', Art Review, Summer

2016
Durgin, Patrick F., 'Disaster and Revival: On Cha, Goldsmith, Pendleton', Jacket2, February

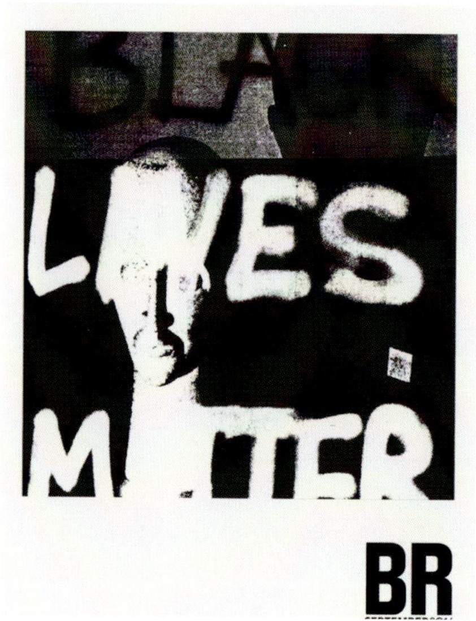

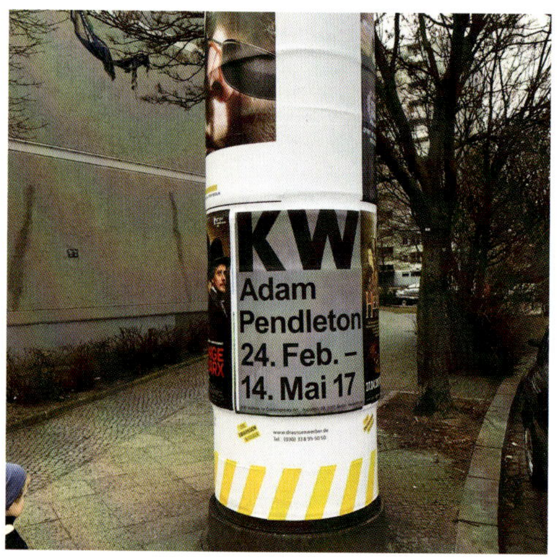

SELECTED EXHIBITIONS AND PROJECTS
2016–18

2016 (cont.)
'Adam Pendleton: Becoming Imperceptible',
CONTEMPORARY ARTS CENTER, New Orleans,
toured to MUSEUM OF CONTEMPORARY ART, Denver;
MUSEUM OF CONTEMPORARY ART, Cleveland (solo)

'Whole Fragments',
PARRA & ROMERO, Ibiza, Spain (solo)

11th GWANGJU BIENNALE, South Korea (group)

'The Revolution Will Not be Gray',
ASPEN ART MUSEUM (group)

'The Language of Things',
PUBLIC ART FUND, City Hall Park, New York (group)

'New Visions',
TENSTA KONSTHALL, Spånga, Sweden (group)

'Lorraine O'Grady: Initial Recognition',
CENTRO ANDALUZ DE ARTE CONTEMPORANEO, Seville, Spain (group)

2017
'Adam Pendleton: Which We Can',
PACE GALLERY, Palo Alto, California (solo)

'Front Room: Adam Pendleton',
BALTIMORE MUSEUM OF ART (solo)

'Adam Pendleton: shot him in the face',
KUNST-WERKE INSTITUTE FOR CONTEMPORARY ART,
Berlin, toured to BALTIC CENTRE FOR CONTEMPORARY ART,
Gateshead, England (solo)

FRIEZE NEW YORK PROJECTS, Randall's Island, New York (group)

'Art of Rebellion: Black Art of the Civil Rights Movement',
DETROIT INSTITUTE OF ARTS, Detroit (group)

'The Arcades: Contemporary Art and Walter Benjamin',
JEWISH MUSEUM, New York (group)

'Sonic Rebellion: Music as Resistance',
MUSEUM OF CONTEMPORARY ART, Detroit (group)

'I am you, you are too',
WALKER ART CENTER, Minneapolis (group)

'Public Movement: On Art, Politics, and Dance',
MODERNA MUSEET, Malmö, Sweden (group)

'How To Live Together',
KUNSTHALLE WIEN, Vienna (group)

2018
'Adam Pendleton: Our Ideas',
PACE GALLERY, London (solo)

'Adam Pendleton: New Works',
GALERIA PEDRO CERA, Lisbon (solo)

'Adam Pendleton: what a day was this',
LEVER HOUSE, New York (solo)

'List Projects: Adam Pendleton',
MIT LIST VISUAL ARTS CENTER, Cambridge, Massachusetts (solo)

SELECTED ARTICLES AND INTERVIEWS
2016–18

2016 (cont.)
Pogrebin, Robin, 'Inside Art: Relating Past and Future In New Orleans', The New York Times, 12 February

'Adam Pendleton', Art in America, April

Andersson, Andrea, 'Adam Pendleton: An exclusive project', Modern Painters, April

D'Addario, John, 'In Adam Pendleton show at CAC, thickets of poetry, politics, art and history', The New Orleans Advocate, 13 April

Johnson, Ken, 'Art in Review: "The Language of Things"', The New York Times, 5 August

Biswas, Allie, 'In Conversation: Adam Pendleton with Allie Biswas', The Brooklyn Rail, September

Murphy, Jay, 'Adam Pendleton', Frieze, no. 181, September

Gilbert, Sophie, 'Adam Pendleton on Art's Turbulent Moment', The Atlantic, December

2017
Pendleton, Adam, 'Just Back from Los Angeles: A Portrait of Yvonne Rainer', e-flux journal, no. 79, February

Tronrud, Wendy, 'Becoming Imperceptible', The Brooklyn Rail, April

Lesturgie, Gauthier, 'How Abstraction Is Another Word for Freedom', Contemporary &, April

Kurutz, Steven, 'The Rising Art World Star Behind "Black Dada"', The New York Times, 18 April

Pobric, Pac, 'Frieze Projects Tribute: Time to Get Theatrical', The Art Newspaper Frieze New York Daily Edition, 4–5 May

Hickey, Andria, 'Adam Pendleton: Becoming Imperceptible', Push, Winter–Spring

Edalatpour, Jeffery, 'Artist Adam Pendleton Plays with Indecipherable Nature of Modernity', Metro Silicon Valley, 22 November

Wolfe, Edith, 'Adam Pendleton: Becoming Imperceptible', caa.reviews, 19 July

2018
Moffitt, Evan, 'What Can't Be Read', Frieze, no. 192, January–February

Loos, Ted, 'Artist Adam Pendleton's Work Defies Categorization', The Wall Street Journal, 6 March 2018

Pogrebin, Robin, 'A Young Artist and Disrupter Plants His Flag for Black Lives', The New York Times, 3 May

Chow, Andrew R., 'Nina Simone's Childhood Home Designated a Treasure', The New York Times, 19 June

Chan, TF, 'Making Marks', Wallpaper*, no. 235, October

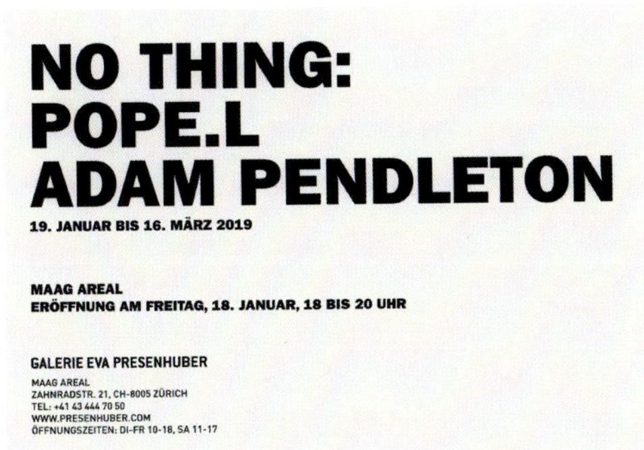

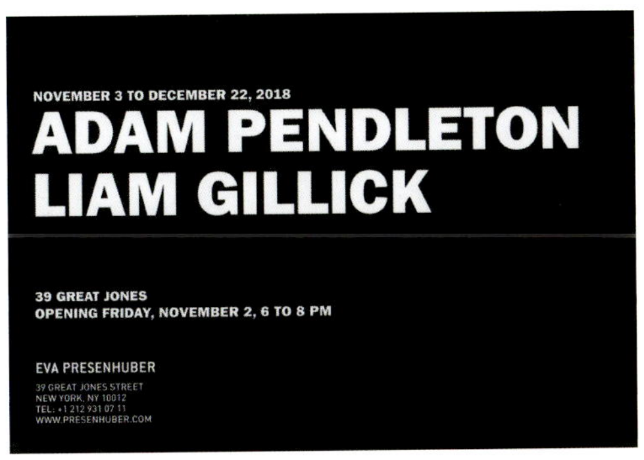

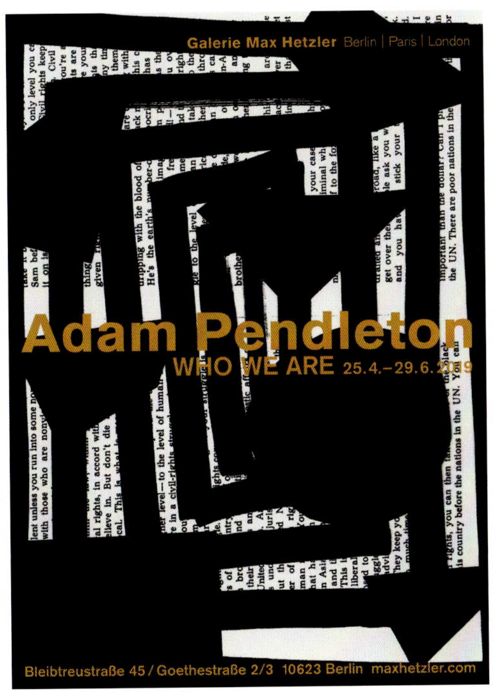

SELECTED EXHIBITIONS AND PROJECTS
2018–21

2018 (cont.)
'LeWitt, Nevelson, Pendleton',
PACE GALLERY, Geneva (solo)

'Liam Gillick Adam Pendleton/Adam Pendleton Liam Gillick'
GALERIE EVA PRESENHUBER, New York (solo)

'DPAM Collects: Happy Little Trees and Other Recent Acquisitions',
DEPAUL ART MUSEUM, Chicago (group)

'Second Sight: The Paradox of Vision in Contemporary Art',
BOWDOIN MUSEUM OF ART, Brunswick, Maine (group)

2019
'No Thing: Pope.L, Adam Pendleton',
GALERIE EVA PRESENHUBER, Zurich (solo)

'Adam Pendleton: Who We Are',
GALERIE MAX HETZLER, Berlin (solo)

'Adam Pendleton: These Elements of Me',
PACE GALLERY, Seoul (solo)

'David Adjaye: Making Memory',
DESIGN MUSEUM, London (group)

'Manifesto: Art X Agency',
HIRSHHORN MUSEUM AND SCULPTURE GARDEN,
Washington, DC (group)

'If on a Winter's Night a Traveler',
TEL AVIV MUSEUM OF ART (group)

2020
'Elements of Me',
ISABELLA STEWART GARDNER MUSEUM, Boston (solo)

'Adam Pendleton',
LE CONSORTIUM, Dijon (solo)

'Yesterday's Tomorrow: Selections from the Rose Collection 1933–2018',
ROSE ART MUSEUM at BRANDEIS UNIVERSITY, Waltham, Massachusetts (group)

2021
'Adam Pendleton: Who Is Queen?',
MUSEUM OF MODERN ART, New York (solo)

SELECTED ARTICLES AND INTERVIEWS
2018–21

2019
Bernardi, Giulia, 'Pope.L, Adam Pendleton', Kunst Bulletin, March

Anderson, Mitchell, 'No Thing: Pope L., Adam Pendleton, Flash Art, no. 325, April–May

Müller, Jens, 'Black Dada', Tagesspiegel, 22 June

2020
Sheets, Hilarie M., 'MoMA's Atrium Set as Theatrical Stage for the Summer', The New York Times, 10 February

Holmes, Helen, 'Adam Pendleton's "Who Is Queen?" Will Explore Black Dadaism With Daily Events at MoMA', The Observer, 11 February

BIBLIOGRAPHY

MONOGRAPHS AND ARTIST'S BOOKS

Pendleton, Adam, Adam Pendleton: So I Independent in Georgia in the 90's, Yvon Lambert Gallery, New York and Paris, 2006

Pendleton, Adam, grey-blue grain, Kunstverein, Amsterdam, 2010

Pendleton, Adam, I/On interiors, Galeria Pedro Cera, Lisbon, 2011

Pendleton, Adam, Adam Pendleton: Radio (ONE), Salina Art Center, Kansas, 2011

Pendleton, Adam, and Suzanne Perling Hudson, Adam Pendleton: I'll Be Your, Pace Gallery, London, 2012

Pendleton, Adam, Andrea Andersson, Naomi Beckwith, Kitty Scott, and Stephen Squibb, Becoming Imperceptible, Contemporary Arts Center, New Orleans, Museum of Contemporary Art, Denver, Museum of Contemporary Art, Cleveland, and Siglio, Catskill, New York, 2016

Pendleton, Adam, Jenny Schlenzka, and Stephen Squibb (eds), Susan Thompson, Laura Hoptman, Jenny Schlenzka, Tom McDonough, Adrienne Edwards and Adam Pendleton, et al., Black Dada Reader, Koenig Books, London, 2017

Pendleton, Adam, Notes on Just Back from Los Angeles: A Portrait of Yvonne Rainer (Dialecty no. 15), Book Works, London, and The Common Guild, Glasgow, 2018

Pendleton, Adam, Anthology, Zucker Art Books, New York, 2018

Pendleton, Adam, Suzanne Hudson, Alec Mapes-Frances, Yvonne Rainer and Adrienne Edwards, Adam Pendleton: Our Ideas, Pace Gallery, London, 2018

Pendleton, Adam, Pope.L, and Clifford Owens, No Thing: Pope.L, Adam Pendleton, Galerie Eva Presenhuber, Zurich, 2019

Pendleton, Adam, and Omar Berrada, Adam Pendleton: Who We Are, Galerie Max Hetzler, Berlin, 2019

Gillick, Liam, Adam Pendleton, and Tom McDonough, Liam Gillick Adam Pendleton/Adam Pendleton Liam Gillick, Galerie Eva Presenhuber, New York, 2019

Pendleton, Adam, Elements of Me, Isabella Stewart Gardner Museum, Boston, 2020

Pendleton, Adam, Alec Mapes-Frances, Adrienne Edwards and Andréa Picard, Adam Pendleton, Phaidon, London, 2020

EXHIBITION CATALOGUES AND SURVEYS

Barson, Tanya, and Peter Gorschlüter (eds), Afro-Modernism: Journeys through the Black Atlantic, Tate Liverpool, 2010

Beasley, Mark (ed.), Hey Hey Glossolalia: Exhibiting the Voice, Creative Time, New York, 2008

Biesenbach, Klaus, Connie Butler and Neville Wakefield (eds), Greater New York, MoMA P.S.1, New York, 2010

Blazwick, Iwona, Magnus af Petersens (eds), Tanya Barson, Briony Fer, Jiang Jiehong and Tom McDonough, Adventures of the Black Square: Abstract Art and Society 1915–2015, Whitechapel Gallery, London, 2015

Brams, Koen, Krist Gruijthuijsen (eds), Adam Pendleton, et al., The Encyclopedia of Fictional Artists and The Addition, JRP|Ringier, Zurich, 2010

Budak, Adam, Anselm Franke, Hila Peleg, Raqs Media Collective, Nina Möntamann, Avi Pitchon and Rana Dasgupt, Manifesta 7: Companion, Silvana, Milan, 2007

Cassel Oliver, Valerie (ed.), Double Consciousness: Black Conceptual Art Since 1970, Contemporary Arts Museum, Houston, 2005

Cassel Oliver, Valerie (ed.), Yona Backer, Naomi Beckwith, Franklin Sirmans and Bill Arning, Radical Presence: Black Performance in Contemporary Art, Contemporary Arts Museum, Houston, 2013

Cooper Cafritz, Peggy, Charmaine Picard (eds), Njideka Akunyili Crosby, LaToya Ruby Frazier, Thelma Golden, Titus Kaphar, Simone Leigh, Kerry James Marshall, Uri McMillan, Tschabalala Self, Jack Shainman, Hank Willis Thomas and William Villalongo, Fired Up! Ready To Go!, Rizzoli, New York, 2017

Cornell, Lauren, Massimiliano Gioni and Laura Hoptman (eds), Younger than Jesus: Artist Directory, New Museum of Contemporary Art, New York, and Phaidon, London, 2009

Cornell, Lauren, Massimiliano Gioni and Laura Hoptman (eds), Younger Than Jesus: The Reader, New Museum of Contemporary Art, New York, and Steidl, Göttingen, 2009

Cullen, Deborah (ed.), and Petja Grafenauer, Interruption: 30th Ljubljana Biennial of Graphic Arts, Ljubljana, Biennial of Graphic Arts, Ljubljana, and Black Dog, London, 2014

Dexter Sinister, Angie Keefer (eds.) and Laura Hoptman, Ecstatic Alphabets/Heaps of Language, Dexter Sinister, New York, and Sternberg Press, Berlin, 2012

DiMeo Carlozzi, Annette (ed.), Desire, Blanton Museum of Art, Austin, 2010

Donovan, Thom, and Sreshta Rit Premnath (eds), Adam Pendleton, et al., Shifter 23: Withdrawn: A Discourse, Shifter, New York, 2016

Edwards, Adrienne (ed.), Blackness in Abstraction, Pace Gallery, New York, 2016

Enwezor, Okwui, Mélanie Bouteloup, Abdellah Karroum, Émilie Renard, and Claire Staebler (eds), La Triennale: Intense Proximité, Palais de Tokyo, Paris, 2012

Goldberg, RoseLee (ed.), Adam Pendleton, Bartholomew Ryan, et al., Everywhere and All at Once: An Anthology of Writings on Performa 07, JRP|Ringier, Zurich, and Performa, New York, 2009

Golden, Thelma, Christine Y. Kim (eds), Ali Evans, Franklin Sirmans, Malik Gaines, David Drogin, et al., Frequency, Studio Museum in Harlem, New York, 2005

Gregos, Katerina, Vincent Meessen (eds), Raoul Vaneigem, Harry Garuba and Pedro Monaville, Personne et les autres: Vincent Meessen & Guests, Belgian Pavilion, Venice, and Mousse Publishing, Milan, 2015

Grove, Jeffrey D. (ed.), After 1968: Contemporary Artists and the Civil Rights Legacy, High Museum of Art, Atlanta, 2008

Gwinn, Elizabeth, and Lauren Haynes (eds), Re:collection: Selected Works from the Studio Museum in Harlem, Studio Museum in Harlem, New York, 2010

Hoffmann, Jens (ed.), Caroline A. Jones, Vito Manolo Roma, and Kenneth Goldsmith, The Arcades: Contemporary Art and Walter Benjamin, Jewish Museum, New York, and Yale University Press, New Haven, 2017

Husslein-Arco, Agnes (ed.), Love Story: Sammlung Anne & Wolfgang Titze, Winter Palast and 21er Haus of the Belvedere, Vienna and Verlag für modern Kunst, Nürnberg, 2014

Lemon, Ralph (ed.), Kevin Beasley, Claire Bishop, Philip Bither, Paula Court, Adrienne Edwards, Tom Finkelpearl, Ana Janevski, Claudia La Rocco, Thomas Lax, Ralph Lemon, Glenn Ligon, Glenn Lowry, Sarah Michelson, Fred Moten, Adam Pendleton, Yvonne Rainer and William Rawls, On Value, Triple Canopy, New York, 2016

Liese, Jennifer (ed.), Adam Pendleton, et al., Social Medium: Artists Writings 2000–2015, Paper Monument, New York, 2016

Lind, Maria (ed.), Binna Choi, Azar Mahmoudian, Margarida Mendes and Michelle Wong, The Eighth Climate (What Does Art Do?), Gwangju Biennale, South Korea, 2011

Mercer, Valerie J., Art of Rebellion: Black Art of the Civil Rights Movement, Detroit Institute of Arts, 2017

Molon, Dominic (ed.), Diedrich Diederichsen, Anthony Elms, Dan Graham, Richard Hell, Matthew Higgs, Mike Kelley, Jutta Koether, Bob Nickas and Jan Tumlir, Sympathy for the Devil: Art and Rock and Roll since 1967, Museum of Contemporary Art, Chicago, and Yale University Press, New Haven, 2007

Obrist, Hans-Ulrich, Julia Peyton-Jones, Sally Tallant, and Nicola Lees (eds), Melissa Gronlund, Martin Puchner, Adam Pendleton, et al., Serpentine Gallery Manifesto Marathon, Serpentine Gallery, and Koenig Books, London, 2009

Patt, Lise (ed.), Deborah Cullen, et al., Searching for Sebald: Photography after W.G. Sebald, Institute of Cultural Inquiry, Los Angeles, 2007

Retallack, Joan (ed.), Sandi Hilal, Adam Pendleton, Fred Moten, Peter Krapp, Anne Carson, Allie Biswas, Ingrid Schaffner, Evelyn Reilly, John Keene, Alan Devenish, Lauren Bakst, Nova Benway, Alhena Katsof, Mónica de la Torre, James Sherry and erica Kaufman, The Supposium: Thought Experiments & Poethical Play For Difficult Times, Litmus Press, New York, 2018

Schorr, Collier (ed.), Dominic Eichler, Nancy Spector and Sarah Lewis, Freeway Balconies, Guggenheim Museum, New York, 2008

PUBLIC COLLECTIONS

BALTIMORE MUSEUM OF ART

CARNEGIE MUSEUM OF ART, Pittsburgh

DALLAS MUSEUM OF ART

DEPAUL ART MUSEUM, Chicago

MASSACHUSETTS INSTITUTE OF TECHNOLOGY, Cambridge

LOS ANGELES COUNTY MUSEUM OF ART

THE METROPOLITAN MUSEUM OF ART, New York

MUSEUM OF CONTEMPORARY ART, Chicago

MUSEUM OF CONTEMPORARY ART, San Diego

THE MUSEUM OF MODERN ART, New York

RHODE ISLAND SCHOOL OF DESIGN (RISD) MUSEUM, Providence

ROSE ART MUSEUM, BRANDEIS UNIVERSITY, Waltham, Massachusetts

SOLOMON R. GUGGENHEIM MUSEUM, New York

STUDIO MUSEUM IN HARLEM, New York

TATE, London

UNIVERSITY OF CHICAGO

ADAM PENDLETON: I'LL BE YOURS, 2012
INVITATION CARD
PACE GALLERY, NEW YORK

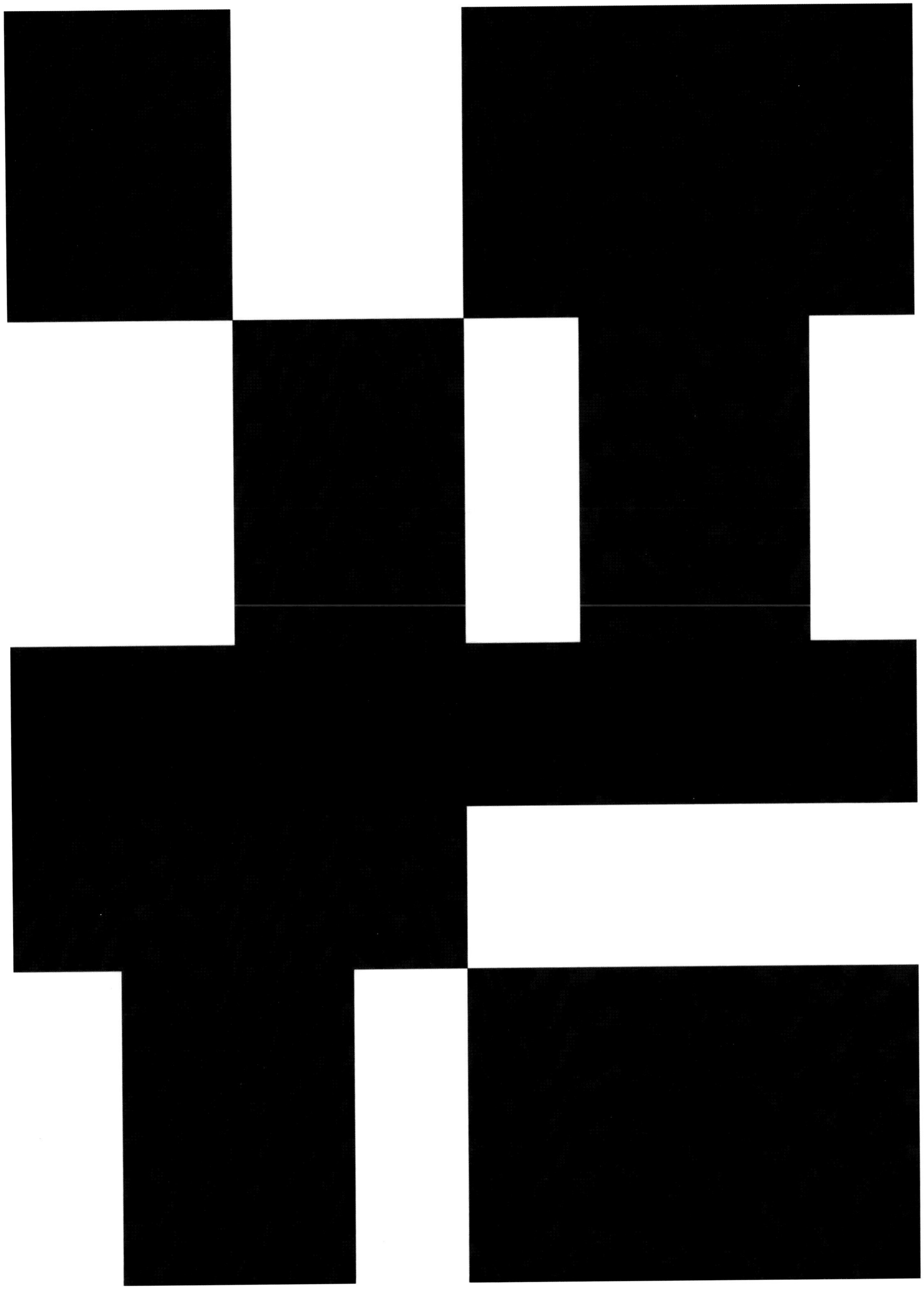

ILLUSTRATED WORKS

COMPARATIVE IMAGES

PHAIDON PRESS LTD.
2 COOPERAGE YARD
LONDON E15 2QR

PHAIDON PRESS INC.
65 BLEECKER STREET
NEW YORK, NY 10012

PHAIDON.COM

First published 2020

ISBN:
978-0-7148-7658-0
Limited Edition:
978-1-83866-248-6
Signed Edition:
978-1-83866-226-4

A CIP catalogue record of this book is available from the British Library and the Library of Congress.

Commissioning Editor
Michele Robecchi

Production Controller
Jane Harman

Design
Melanie Mues, Mues Design, London

Layout
Rita Peres Pereira

Printed in China

PUBLISHER'S ACKNOWLEDGEMENTS

Special thanks to Matthew Dery, Alec Mapes-Frances, Meghan Masius and Jason Scholtz at Studio Pendleton, New York; Ben Strauss-Malcolm and Hannah Root at Pace Gallery, New York; Elliot McDonald and Giorgia Pratini at Pace Gallery, London; Galerie Eva Presenhuber, Zurich; Galeria Pedro Cera, Lisbon; Galerie Max Hetzler, Berlin; Deborah Aaronson, Adela Cory, Melissa Larner, João Mota, Lorraine O'Grady, Kelli Rae Patton.

We would also like to thank the following institutions:
The Felix Gonzalez-Torres Foundation, New York; Andrea Rosen Gallery, New York; Public Art Fund, New York; The Estate of Sol LeWitt; Alexander Gray Associates, New York; Open Book, Barrytown and Station Hill Press, New York; Artists Rights Society (ARS), New York; DACS, London; Scala Archives, Florence.

Photographers: Matthew Placek, Andy Romer, Tête-à-Tête, Stephen White, Julian C. Wilson.

ARTIST'S ACKNOWLEDGEMENTS

I would like to thank Michele Robecchi for his commitment to this project, respect for process and generosity of spirit. Thanks and appreciation are also due to Keith Fox and Deborah Aaronson.

To the authors: Adrienne Edwards, Alec Mapes-Frances and Andréa Picard for their rigorous and sustained engagement with my work.

Much respect and gratitude to Studio Pendleton:
Matthew Dery, Alec Mapes-Frances, Meghan Masius and Jason Scholtz.

I would also like to acknowledge:
Kyle Abraham
Nora Burnett Abrams
David Adjaye
Patricia and Rabie Ahmad
Andrea Andersson
Tanya Barson
Tim Brennan
Pieranna Cavalchini
Pedro Cera
Hiuwai Chu
Stuart Comer
Markéta Stará Condeixa
Tamara Corm
Mercedes Costa
Marianne Dobner
Clint Downing
Alexander Dynan
Wells Fray-Smith
Alexandra Gaty
Liam Gillick
Arne Glimcher
Marc Glimcher
RoseLee Goldberg
Sarah Goulet
Katerina Gregos
Krist Gruijthuijsen
Vitória Guerra
Kathy Halbreich
Cora Hansen
Max Hetzler
Max Edouard Hetzler
Laura Hoptman
Ishmael Houston-Jones
Aaron Igler
Chayse Irvin
Joan Jonas
Christine Kim
David Kordansky
Youngjoo Lee
Austin Lynch
Tom McDonough
Jill McLennon
Vincent Meessen
Carmel Michaeli
Alicia Hall Moran
Jason Moran
Yuriy Nych
Lorraine O'Grady
Philippe Peress
Matthew Placek
Pope.L
Eva Presenhuber
Martin Puryear
Yvonne Rainer
Andy Romer
Hannah Root
Samia Saouma
Jenny Schlenzka
Christian Schmidt
Myriam Schroeter
Case Simmons
Stephen Squibb
Ben Strauss-Malcolm
Matt Suib
José Noé Suro
Betsy Sussler
Frederick Tang
Lynne Tillman
Valentina Volchkova
Tan Hong Wei
Matthew Zucker

And for their dedication to craft and excellence:
Bob Blanton
Daine Carter
Tamsin Doherty
Jackson Engman
Jesse Katz
Alexandy Mercedes
Roberto Mercedes
James Miller
Maryanne Murray
Philip Sangenario
Steven Sangenario
Marisa Stockton

CONTEMPORARY ARTISTS:

Contemporary Artists is a series of authoritative and extensively illustrated studies of today's most important artists. Each title offers a comprehensive survey of an individual artist's work and a range of art writing contributed by an international spectrum of authors, all leading figures in their fields, from art history and criticism to philosophy, cultural theory and fiction. Each study provides incisive analysis and multiple perspectives on contemporary art and its inspiration. These are essential source books for everyone concerned with art today.

MARINA ABRAMOVIĆ KLAUS BIESENBACH, KRISTINE STILES, CHRISSIE ILES / VITO ACCONCI FRAZER WARD, MARK C. TAYLOR, JENNIFER BLOOMER / AI WEIWEI HANS ULRICH OBRIST, KAREN SMITH, BERNARD FIBICHER / DOUG AITKEN DANIEL BIRNBAUM, AMANDA SHARP, JÖRG HEISER / PAWEŁ ALTHAMER ADAM SZYMCZYK, ROMAN KURZMEYER, SUZANNE COTTER / FRANCIS ALŸS CUAUHTÉMOC MEDINA, RUSSELL FERGUSON, JEAN FISHER, MICHAEL TAUSSIG / UTA BARTH PAMELA M. LEE, MATTHEW HIGGS, JEREMY GILBERT-ROLFE / CHRISTIAN BOLTANSKI DIDIER SEMIN, TAMAR GARB, DONALD KUSPIT / MONICA BONVICINI ALEXANDER ALBERRO, JANET KRAYNAK, JULIANE REBENTISCH / LOUISE BOURGEOIS PAULO HERKENHOFF (WITH THYRZA GOODEVE), ROBERT STORR, ALLAN SCHWARTZMAN / MARK BRADFORD ANITA HILL; SEBASTIAN SMEE, CONNIE BUTLER / CECILY BROWN COURTNEY J. MARTIN, JASON ROSENFELD, FRANCINE PROSE / CAI GUO-QIANG DANA FRIIS-HANSEN, OCTAVIO ZAYA, TAKASHI SERIZAWA / MAURIZIO CATTELAN NANCY SPECTOR, FRANCESCO BONAMI, BARBARA VANDERLINDEN, MASSIMILIANO GIONI / VIJA CELMINS ROBERT GOBER, LANE RELYEA, BRIONY FER NIGEL COOKE DARIAN LEADER, TONY GODFREY, MARIE DARRIEUSSECQ / RICHARD DEACON PIER LUIGI TAZZI, JON THOMPSON, PETER SCHJELDAHL, PENELOPE CURTIS / TACITA DEAN JEAN-CHRISTOPHE ROYOUX, MARINA WARNER, GERMAINE GREER / MARK DION LISA GRAZIOSE CORRIN, MIWON KWON, NORMAN BRYSON PETER DOIG ADRIAN SEARLE, KITTY SCOTT, CATHERINE GRENIER / STAN DOUGLAS SCOTT WATSON, DIANA THATER, CAROL J. CLOVER / MARLENE DUMAS DOMINIC VAN DEN BOOGERD, BARBARA BLOOM, MARIUCCIA CASADIO, ILARIA BONACOSSA / JIMMIE DURHAM LAURA MULVEY, DIRK SNAUWAERT, MARK ALICE DURANT, KATE NESIN / OLAFUR ELIASSON MADELEINE GRYNSZTEJN, DANIEL BIRNBAUM, MICHAEL SPEAKS / ELMGREEN & DRAGSET LINDA YABLONSKY, MARTIN HERBERT, CONNIE BUTLER / PETER FISCHLI AND DAVID WEISS ROBERT FLECK, BEATE SÖNTGEN, ARTHUR C. DANTO / TOM FRIEDMAN DENNIS COOPER, BRUCE HAINLEY, ADRIAN SEARLE / THEASTER GATES CAROL BECKER, LISA YUN LEE, ACHIM BORCHARDT-HUME / ISA GENZKEN ALEX FARQUHARSON, DIEDRICH DIEDERICHSEN, SABINE BREITWIESER / ANTONY GORMLEY ERNST GOMBRICH, JOHN HUTCHINSON, LELA B. NJATIN, W. J. T. MITCHELL / DAN GRAHAM BIRGIT PELZER, MARK FRANCIS, BEATRIZ COLOMINA / PAUL GRAHAM ANDREW WILSON, GILLIAN WEARING, CAROL SQUIERS / HANS HAACKE WALTER GRASSKAMP, MOLLY NESBIT, JON BIRD / MONA HATOUM GUY BRETT, MICHAEL ARCHER, CATHERINE DE ZEGHER, NANCY SPECTOR / SHARON HAYES JULIA BRYAN-WILSON, JEANNINE TANG, LANKA TATTERSALL / THOMAS HIRSCHHORN BENJAMIN H. D. BUCHLOH, ALISON M. GINGERAS, CARLOS BASUALDO / JIM HODGES JANE M. SAKS, ROBERT HOBBS, JULIE AULT / JENNY HOLZER DAVID JOSELIT, JOAN SIMON, RENATA SALECL / RONI HORN LOUISE NERI, LYNNE COOKE, THIERRY DE DUVE / CHRIS JOHANSON CORRINA PEIPON, BOB NICKAS, JULIE DEAMER / ILYA KABAKOV BORIS GROYS, DAVID A. ROSS, IWONA BLAZWICK / ALEX KATZ ROBERT STORR, CARTER RATCLIFF, IWONA BLAZWICK, BARRY SCHWABSKY / ON KAWARA 'TRIBUTE', JONATHAN WATKINS, RENÉ DENIZOT / MIKE KELLEY ISABELLE GRAW, JOHN C. WELCHMAN, ANTHONY VIDLER / MARY KELLY MARGARET IVERSEN, DOUGLAS CRIMP, HOMI K. BHABHA / WILLIAM KENTRIDGE CAROLYN CHRISTOV-BAKARGIEV, DAN CAMERON, J. M. COETZEE / JANNIS KOUNELLIS 'TRIBUTE', PHILIP LARRATT-SMITH, RUDI FUCHS / YAYOI KUSAMA AKIRA TATEHATA, LAURA HOPTMAN, UDO KULTERMANN, CHATERINE TAFT / CHRISTIAN MARCLAY JENNIFER GONZALEZ, KIM GORDON, MATTHEW HIGGS / KERRY JAMES MARSHALL CHARLES GAINES, GREG TATE, LAURENCE RASSEL / PAUL McCARTHY KRISTINE STILES, RALPH RUGOFF, MASSIMILIANO GIONI, ROBERT STORR / CILDO MEIRELES PAULO HERKENHOFF, GERARDO MOSQUERA, DAN CAMERON / LUCY ORTA ROBERTO PINTO, NICOLAS BOURRIAUD, MAIA DAMIANOVIC / JEAN-MICHEL OTHONIEL GAY GASSMANN, CATHERINE GRENIER, ROBERT STORR / TREVOR PAGLEN LAUREN CORNELL, JULIA BRYAN-WILSON, OMAR KHOLEIF / JORGE PARDO CHRISTINE VÉGH, LANE RELYEA, CHRIS KRAUS / ADAM PENDLETON ALEC MAPES-FRANCES, ADRIENNE EDWARDS, ANDRÉA PICARD / RAYMOND PETTIBON DENNIS COOPER, ROBERT STORR, ULRICH LOOCK / RICHARD PRINCE ROSETTA BROOKS, JEFF RIAN, LUC SANTE / LILI REYNAUD-DEWAR ÉLISABETH LEBOVICI, DIEDRICH DIEDERICHSEN, MONIKA SZEWCZYK / PIPILOTTI RIST HANS ULRICH OBRIST, PEGGY PHELAN, ELIZABETH BRONFEN / DAAN ROOSEGAARDE NICO DASWANI, FUMIO NANJO, CAROL BECKER / STERLING RUBY KATE FOWLE, FRANKLIN SIRMANS, JESSICA MORGAN / ANRI SALA HANS ULRICH OBRIST, MARK GODFREY, LIAM GILLICK / DORIS SALCEDO NANCY PRINCENTHAL, CARLOS BASUALDO, ANDREAS HUYSSEN / WILHELM SASNAL ANDRZEJ PRZYWARA, DOMINIC EICHLER, JÖRG HEISER / THOMAS SCHÜTTE JULIAN HEYNEN, JAMES LINGWOOD, ANGELA VETTESE / STEPHEN SHORE MICHAEL FRIED, CHRISTY LANGE, JOEL STERNFELD / ROMAN SIGNER PAULA VAN DEN BOSCH, GERHARD MACK, JEREMY MILLAR / LORNA SIMPSON KELLIE JONES, THELMA GOLDEN, CHRISSIE ILES / NANCY SPERO JON BIRD, JO ANNA ISAAK, SYLVÈRE LOTRINGER / SIMON STARLING FRANCESCO MANACORDA, DIETER ROELSTRAETE, JANET HARBORD / FRANK STELLA ANDRIANNA CAMPBELL, KATE NESIN, LUCAS BLALOCK, TERRY RICHARDSON / JESSICA STOCKHOLDER BARRY SCHWABSKY, LYNNE TILLMAN, LYNNE COOKE, GERMANO CELANT / SARAH SZE OKWUI ENWEZOR, BENJAMIN H. D. BUCHLOH, LAURA HOPTMAN / WOLFGANG TILLMANS PETER HALLEY, JAN VERWOERT, MIDORI MATSUI, JOHANNA BURTON / LUC TUYMANS ULRICH LOOCK, JUAN VICENTE ALIAGA, NANCY SPECTOR, HANS RUDOLF REUST / BERNAR VENET FLORENCE DERIEUX, BARRY SCHWABSKY, CLAIRE LILLEY / ADRIÁN VILLAR-ROJAS HANS ULRICH OBRIST, CAROLYN CHRISTOV-BAKARGIEV, EUNGIE JOO / JEFF WALL THIERRY DE DUVE, ARIELLE PÉLENC, BORIS GROYS, JEAN-FRANÇOIS CHEVRIER, MARK LEWIS / GILLIAN WEARING RUSSELL FERGUSON, DONNA DE SALVO, JOHN SLYCE / LAWRENCE WEINER BENJAMIN H. D. BUCHLOH, ALEXANDER ALBERRO AND ALICE ZIMMERMAN, DAVID BATCHELOR / FRANZ WEST ROBERT FLECK, BICE CURIGER, NEAL BENEZRA / JONAS WOOD MARK GROTJAHN, HELEN MOLESWORTH, IAN ALTEVEER / YIN XIUZHEN HOU HANRU, WU HUNG, STEPHANIE ROSENTHAL / ZHANG HUAN ROSELEE GOLDBERG, YILMAZ DZIEWOR, ROBERT STORR